After the Wall

After the Wall

Eastern Germany Since 1989

EDITED BY

Patricia J. Smith

Westview Press
A Member of Perseus Books, L.L.C.

Copyright © 1998 by Westview Press, A Member of Perseus Books, L.L.C.

Published in 1998 in the United States of America by Westview Press, 5500 Central Avenue, Boulder, Colorado 80301-2877, and in the United Kingdom by Westview Press, 12 Hid's Copse Road, Cumnor Hill, Oxford OX2 9JJ

A CIP catalog record for this book is available from the Library of Congress.
ISBN 0-8133-3209-5

The paper used in this publication meets the requirements of the American National Standard for Permanence of Paper for Printed Library Materials Z39.48-1984.

10   9   8   7   6   5   4   3   2   1

To Jenifer,
for her inspiration,
love, and support

Contents

PART TWO
Culture, Society, and Religion

PART THREE
Foreign Policy and Security

Tables

Tables

Preface

As part of the series on *Eastern Europe after Communism*, the objective of this book is to assess the political, economic, and social transitions that have occurred throughout the 1990s in the former German Democratic Republic (GDR), or East Germany. After the revolution of 1989 and the fall of the Berlin wall, the East German experience diverged dramatically from the transitions elsewhere in Eastern Europe. German unification, the historic merger of the GDR with the Federal Republic of Germany (FRG), or West Germany, resulted in an extremely rapid transition. Rather than gradually determining how to move from a centrally planned economy toward a market economy and from a communist to a democratic political system, East Germans opted for unification and ready-made economic and political systems. These monumental changes took place less than a year after the November 1989 revolution, with economic and monetary union occurring 1 July 1990 and political unification 3 October 1990. This book considers the impact of these changes on the former GDR and on East Germans.

Planning for the book began in late fall 1995 when experts on various aspects of Germany and/or Eastern Europe were invited to contribute chapters focusing specifically on the former German Democratic Republic. The volume brings together American and British scholars, most of whom have studied East Germany throughout their careers, and scholars from the former GDR with specialties in the fields of women's studies, religion, literature, and economics and politics. The varied backgrounds of the authors bring diverse perspectives to the volume; nevertheless, common themes emerge throughout the chapters. With its focus on East Germany rather than more broadly on all of Germany after unification, this book makes a unique contribution to the literature on post-communist transitions.

I am especially grateful to the chapter authors for their contributions and cooperation. The professionalism of all is evident in the high quality and insights of their manuscripts and in their adherence to timelines. Despite the difficulties posed by transatlantic communication and communication systems in transitioning states (I was in Romania during much of this two-year period), their diligence has enabled the book to go to press as scheduled. A special thanks to Sabrina Ramet, series editor, who read and commented on all chapters and provided invaluable guidance throughout the project. Thanks are also due to Rob Williams and Elizabeth Lawrence at Westview Press for their expert assistance. Others I would like to thank are my husband Bill for his patience and support; my mother Lovella Goering for proofreading the manuscript; Marty Charles for computer and formatting assistance; Kim Abson for useful discussions and reviews of portions of the book; and the Consulate General of the Federal Republic of Germany, Seattle, for financial assistance for translations of several chapters. Not to be forgotten are the hundreds of Germans from the former GDR who have shared their experiences and expertise, with particular thanks to Marianne and Peter Schulz, Maureen Kaufmann and Otto-Fritz Hayner, and Heide and Harry Sabelus for their friendship and support during my trips to Germany. Finally, a special thanks to Jenifer Smith for assistance in so many ways crucial to the accomplishment of this project--researching, discussing, editing, formatting, word-processing, mapmaking--and for inspiration.

In conclusion, I want to add a note on usage. The convention generally followed in this book is to capitalize East Germany and West Germany (and East Germans and West German) when referring to the period prior to German unification on 3 October 1990. After 1990, the terms eastern Germany and western German (and east Germans and west Germans) are used. In two chapters, McFalls's on cultural identity and Dölling's on women in eastern Germany, this convention is not always followed. In these cases, political realities and the division between East and West Germany are integral components of identity and continue to affect the thoughts and actions of women and men in eastern Germany in the 1990s. Consequently, "East Germans" is sometimes capitalized, even when referring to East Germans after unification, if the experience of being (or having been) an East German is important to the author's arguments.

Patricia J. Smith
Seattle, February 1998

About the Editor and Contributors

Patricia J. Smith is visiting lecturer in political science and international studies at the University of Washington, Seattle, and west coast director for Partnership Initiatives, a non-profit organization using video-conferences for international discussions. She taught political science and international relations in Romania from 1995-97 and spent 1991-92 in Berlin on an IREX fellowship. Smith received her Ph.D. in 1995 and is now revising her dissertation entitled "Democratizing East Germany" for publication. She previously worked in government as a legislative analyst, planner, and program administrator. Publications include *See How She Runs: Effective Political Techniques* and "German Economic and Monetary Union: Transition to a Market Economy."

Donald Abenheim received his Ph.D. in European history from Stanford University and is associate professor of national security affairs at the Naval Postgraduate School (NPS), Monterey, California; associate director, Center for Civil-Military Relations, NPS; and a visiting scholar at the Hoover Institution, Stanford University. He is author of *Reforging the Iron Cross, Bundeswehr und Tradition*, and various articles on German military professionalism, the Federal Republic, and the Atlantic Alliance.

Thomas A. Baylis is professor of political science at the University of Texas at San Antonio. His most recent book is *The West and Eastern Europe*. He is currently working on the relationship between elite and institutional change in eastern Germany and East Central Europe.

David Childs' sixteen books include ten on Germany. For his most recent, *The Stasi: The East German Intelligence and Security System* with Richard Popplewell, he interviewed Stasi officers and their victims. As his Stasi file revealed, he was regarded by the East German secret police as their most serious academic opponent in Britain. His *The GDR: Moscow's German Ally* is regarded as a classic. Professor emeritus of the University of Nottingham, Childs shocked many by taking a skeptical view of the GDR at the Fourth Pacific Workshop on German Affairs, Long Beach, California, in April 1989. Among his recent works are contributions on the far right in Germany since 1945.

Irene Dölling is professor of women's studies at Potsdam University. She studied philosophy at Humboldt University in Berlin and worked at the Institute for Cultural Studies as a professor for theory of culture. Dölling was a co-founder of the Interdisciplinary Center for Women's Studies at Humboldt University and until 1991 director of the Center. She has published numerous articles on gender issues and several books. The latest are *Der Mensch und sein Weib. Aktuelle Frauen- und Männerbilder, historische Ursprünge und Perspektiven* and, with Beate Krais (ed.), *Ein alltägliches Spiel. Geschlecter-konstruktion in der sozialen Praxis.*

Klaus Hammer is currently lecturer in literature and art history at the Technical University in Dresden. His publications include *Dramaturgische Schriften des 18 Jahrhunderts* and *des 19. Jahrhunderts* (vols. 1 and 2); works on Wilhelm Heinse, Christian Dietrich Grabbe, Paul Zech, Ludwig von Hoffman, George Rouault, Christoph Hein, and others; and anthologies of French, German, and Romanian fairy tales. Other works include *Literarische Träume*, theater lexicon; *Chronist ohne Botschaft*; and *Historische Friedhöfe und Grabmäler in Berlin.*

Molly C. Laster is currently a Masters degree candidate in international studies and public affairs at the University of Washington. She spent her childhood in Germany, returned to the land of her parents for college, and is now busy studying and enjoying the Pacific Northwest.

Laurence McFalls received his Ph.D. from Harvard in 1990. He is currently associate professor at the Univerité de Montreal, where he has taught since 1991. His publications concentrate on German and French political culture. His latest book is called *Communism's Collapse, Democracy's Demise? The Cultural Context and Consequences of the East German Revolution.* He is currently working on a follow-up study of ordinary East Germans' cultural adaptation to the enlarged Federal Republic.

Joseph E. Naftzinger, retired colonel, U.S. Army, is an assistant professor with Troy State University and has taught as an adjunct professor at the Joint Military Intelligence Center. He holds a Ph.D. from the University of Maryland and an M.A. from the University of Minnesota. Naftzinger's teaching and research focus on German and European politics as well as on national security issues, especially intelligence and arms control. He edited, with Catherine M. Kelleher, *Intelligence in the Arms Control Process: Lessons from INF.*

Detlef Pollack is currently professor of comparative sociology of culture in Frankfurt an der Oder and speaker of the section Sociology of Religion in the German Association of Sociology. He has been professor of sociology of religion and church at Leipzig University and a fellow at the Institute for Advanced Study in Berlin. Publications include *Religiöse Chiffrierung und soziologische Aufklärung: Die Religionstheorie Niklas Luhmanns; Kirche in der Organisationsgesellschaft: Zum Wandel der Gesellschaftlichen Lage der evangelischen Kirchen in der DDR;* and, edited with Dieter Rink, *Zwischen Verweigerung und Opposition: Politischer Protest in der DDR 1970-1989.*

Sabrina P. Ramet is a professor of international studies at the University of Washington. Born in London, she has lived for extended periods in England, Austria, Germany, Yugoslavia, and Japan, as well as in the United States. She is the author of seven books, among them *Balkan Babel: The Disintegration of Yugoslavia from the Death of Tito to Ethnic War; Whose Democracy? Nationalism, Religion, and the Doctrine of Collective Rights in Post-1989 Eastern Europe;* and *Nihil Obstat: Religion, Politics, and Social Change in East-Central Europe and Russia;* and editor or co-editor of eleven books. Her work has appeared in *Foreign Affairs, World Politics, Problems of Post-Communism, Orbis,* and other journals.

Jörg Roesler received doctorates in economics at Humboldt University and a professorship in economic history at the Academy of Sciences of the GDR. From 1992 until 1996 he was senior research fellow at the Institute for Contemporary Studies at Potsdam University and has been visiting professor at McGill University and the University of Toronto. Roesler has published several books and numerous articles about East German and East European economic and social history and political, social, and economic aspects of the recent transitions. Recent publications in English include "Privatisation in East Germany--Experience with the *Treuhand*" and "After the Collapse of Germany: Social Insecurity and Political Disillusion in the New *Länder.*"

Arthur Stahnke is a professor of political science at Southern Illinois University (Edwardsville). He earned his doctorate at the University of Iowa. From the late 1970s until 1989, Stahnke directed his scholarly interests toward GDR economic strategy and performance. Since 1990, he has focused on local level transformational processes in eastern Germany, the expected results of which will be a book. Stahnke was a frequent exchange scholar to the GDR in the 1980s, and more recently, he was a Fulbright research scholar at the Free University of Berlin.

Dirk Verheyen is associate professor of political science at Loyola Marymount University in Los Angeles. A native of the Netherlands, he pursued his studies at Macalester College and the University of California at Berkeley. He is the author of *The German Question: A Cultural, Historical, and Geographical Exploration* (second and revised edition forthcoming in 1998) and co-editor with Christian Søe of *The Germans and Their Neighbors*. He is currently completing a study entitled *Monumental Politics: Identity and Memory in Post-Cold War Berlin*.

Schleswig-
Holstein

Mecklenburg-
West Pomerania

Hamburg

Bremen

Lower Saxony

Berlin

Brandenburg

North Rhine-
Westphalia

Saxony-Anhalt

Thuringia

Saxony

Hesse

Rhineland
Palatinate

Saarland

Bavaria

Baden-
Württemberg

0   50 100

miles

Eastern Germany
(the former GDR)

The Federal Republic of Germany

Introduction

Patricia J. Smith

The Fall of the Wall

On the ninth of November 1989 the Berlin Wall fell, and East Germans streamed past the border controls to the West. Via television the world watched. We celebrated with Germans from both East and West as they climbed the Wall, joined hands, and toasted the end of the barrier that had artificially separated them. The building of the Berlin Wall in 1961 reinforced the division of Germany begun in 1945 a t the end of world war II as the allies carved up Berlin and Germany into occupation zones under Soviet, French, British, and U.S. control. In 1949 the barriers between the two parts of Germany grew. The three western sectors declared their independence as a sovereign state, the Federal Republic of Germany (FRG), and shortly afterwards joined the North Atlantic Treaty Alliance (NATO), while the eastern zone under Soviet control established itself as the German Democratic Republic (GDR) and allied itself with the Warsaw Treaty Organization (WTO). From then until the end of 1989 the two German states faced each other across the divide, standing as symbols of the cold war and the separation of Europe into two hostile blocs.

The fall of the regime and the opening of the Berlin Wall represented the culmination of months of oppositional activity in East Germany. The roots of this protest lay in environmental, peace, human rights, and other alternative groups that met and developed primarily under the protective roof of the Evangelical (Protestant) Church.[1] Since spring 1989, with a short summer recess, Leipzig groups had organized Monday night candlelight marches, winding through the ringed-city to draw attention to their demands for political change.

Beginning in September with about a thousand activists, the Leipzig marches grew in numbers and intensity throughout the fall. From late October through early November they attracted from 300,000 to 400,000 participants.[2] Supported by demonstrators from throughout the GDR, the protests spread to other cities and climaxed with a massive demonstration in Berlin on 4 November involving more than one million East Germans. Three days later the entire GDR government resigned, followed the next day by resignations of the communist party central committee and the politburo. The following day, 9 November 1989, the Berlin Wall opened, ending the forced separation of Germans and fore-shadowing the fall of communism throughout Eastern Europe and the end of the cold war.

A combination of factors made possible the historic events of 1989, including changes both in the GDR and in the international arena.[3] Mikhail Gorbachev's rise to power in the Soviet Union supported trends for political and civil rights which East German groups had pro-moted throughout the 1980s. Especially significant was Gorbachev's renunciation of the Brezhnev Doctrine and the use of force to keep communist governments in power throughout Eastern Europe. As Gorbachev noted in his speech to the United Nations on 7 December 1988, "It is obvious that the threat of force cannot be and should not be an instrument of foreign policy."[4] In other words, Soviet and Warsaw Pact troops would no longer quell domestic uprisings as they had in Hungary in 1956 and Czechoslovakia in 1968, and this provided a certain legitimacy for oppositional movements within Eastern Europe.

Two other factors in the international arena created an atmosphere which favored oppositional activity in the GDR. In May 1989 the Hungarian government decided to open its border with Austria--to the West. From 1961 on, the repressive GDR regime restricted travel and emigration opportunities, especially to the West but within Eastern Europe as well. However, many East Germans continued to attempt to go to the West by legal or illegal means. The opening of the Hungarian border with Austria set off a wave of attempted emigrations, as East Germans crossed over into neighboring Czechoslovakia, hoping to pro-gress on to Hungary and the West. The emigration of almost 50,000 GDR citizens (out of a population of 16.5 million) to West Germany during the first seven months of 1989 put an enormous pressure on the GDR regime and provided fuel for the demands of demonstrators.[5]

The Tiananmen Square massacres on 3 and 4 June 1989 and the response of GDR political and governmental leaders further under-mined the position of the East German government. Widely televised throughout the GDR, the crushing of the pro-democracy movement by Chinese authorities elicited negative responses from the vast majority of GDR citizens. The East German government's public support for the Chinese government's actions--stating that it was an appropriate use of governmental power to control domestic threats to public order--caused East Germans to fear similar brutality from their own authorities. As oppositional groups in the GDR regularly called attention to Tiananmen Square and to the East German government's response, they developed support for their criticisms of the government and for their demands for expanded rights.

Finally, a domestic issue--the GDR local elections in May 1989-- further undermined the legitimacy of the GDR regime. For the first time, GDR citizens could prove that government officials had falsified election returns, something that many had long suspected.[6] Unlike many issues promoted by groups, almost everyone in the GDR viewed the elections as applicable to her or his own situation. Thus, the election monitoring campaign was particularly significant for spreading support for oppositional groups more broadly through the population and for increasing the government's vulnerability to criticism.

With the legitimacy of the East German regime increasingly questioned, the dramatic growth of oppositional activity supported by much broader segments of the population resulted in the fall of the government and the regime in November 1989. East Germans had overthrown the dictatorial regime. They felt in control of the present and could design the future. But the heady times following the fall of the Wall disappeared, and the promises of the revolution, or the *Wende* (the change or turning point) as many prefer to call it, have not been fully realized. The rush to unification ended East German's primary roles in shaping their own future. Instead, they adopted the system and the trappings of the Federal Republic of Germany.

Unity and Marginality:
East German Participation in the New Germany

Although a large majority of citizens from the German Democratic Republic (GDR) favored rapid unification with the Federal Republic of Germany (FRG) by mid-1990, the process of unification created a Germany of unequal partners and marginalized East Germans. In the early months following the fall of the Berlin Wall, East German activists, other leaders, and ordinary citizens opened discussions about the future of the GDR. Possibilities included an independent and democratic German Democratic Republic as well as a German federation,[7] a new constitution, and a unified Germany created through the participation of Germans in both East and West. However, the landslide victory of the Conservative Alliance in the first free national elections in the GDR on 18 March 1990 provided the go-ahead for rapid unification. Consequently, any plans to join the two Germanies by dissolving both German governments and creating a new constitution, as provided for by Article 146 of the West German constitution, or Basic Law, were abandoned.[8] The decision to unify under Article 23[9] meant that East Germans essentially abdicated any significant role in the design and implementation of the unification process and accepted the Basic Law of the Federal Republic of Germany, along with the political, economic, and social systems and institutions of West Germany. In doing so, they implicitly accepted West German structures as superior and relinquished an active role in creating a new, united Germany.

Unification under Article 23

The decision to unify under Article 23 meant that East Germans entered the union as unequal partners. The reconstituted eastern *Länder*--Brandenburg, Mecklenburg-West Pomerania, Saxony, Saxony-Anhalt, and Thuringia, along with Berlin-East--were absorbed into the Federal Republic. (See map, p. xvii.) The German Democratic Republic lost its identity, but East Germans were not fully integrated into the new Germany. As one observer argues, for East Germans "the sense of civic competence and democratic consciousness" was "jeopardized by the rapid process of unification, the character of which will undoubtedly influence the East Germans' definition of their role as citizens in unified Germany. The nature of the unification process, characterized as 'corporate takeover' or *Anschluß*, lacks genuine democratic legitimation."[10]

The absorption of the East into the Federal Republic while the West maintained the *status quo* reflected the belief that western-style economic and political systems were superior to communist systems.[11] Westerners viewed Easterners as outsiders--and therefore as needing to be integrated. As "objects of deliberate campaigns of integration," they are "politically subordinate to West Germans" and "do not enjoy the full rights of political participation."[12] However, for East Germans "this mode of unification undoubtedly meant the loss of their political, and for many people also their personal identity."[13]

The Marginal Position of East Germans

The GDR's accession to the Federal Republic of Germany under Article 23 set the tone and the parameters for unification and for East Germany's integration into the political, economic, social, and cultural structures of Western Germany--as a marginal rather than a fully participating partner. The Merriam Webster dictionary defines marginal as "of, relating to, or situated at a margin or border;" "not of central importance," and "excluded from or existing outside the mainstream of society, a group, or a school of thought."[14] These definitions of "marginal" apply to most east Germans who find themselves excluded from the mainstream in terms of political, economic, and social life. Throughout the 1990s, from unification to the present, Germans from the East have played a subordinate role and have had little impact on decisions made in the united Germany. Rather, most east Germans have been "marginalized" and now stand at the edge or margins of what occurs in Germany. They view themselves as outsiders in their own country, as "colonized" by the West, and as "second-class citizens" (see David Child's *Epilogue*), while less than ten years ago they played central roles in their state, the German Democratic Republic.

In terms of employment, people from all sectors lost employment, responsibility, and status. And for many, few options presented themselves. The East German army general found no place in the newly united Germany's *Bundeswehr*, and, as his mother confided to me in an east Berlin restaurant, he was depressed since he saw no possibilities for finding other employment. When collective farms closed, the husband and wife in Mecklenburg-West Pomerania who had no money to buy land or equipment, and who did not really want to go into business for themselves anyway, were left without gainful employment. The professor who had taught economics at the university, but had trained in the East, found her education and experience discounted by West Germans who made the hiring decisions; so she was forced to leave academia. The chemical worker confronted with massive closures of chemical plants throughout the region could not find work. The high-level government employee was told her education and experience in the GDR did not qualify her for a responsible position under the new system; she was demoted and forced to work under a supervisor imported from western Germany who had much less education and experience and who earned many times the salary of Easterners in comparable positions. The young, single mother found that not only could she not find a well-paying job, but she also lost the benefit of low-cost childcare and other support services. Students, too, found themselves excluded from the full benefits of the new system; since their education was perceived by western decision-makers as less valuable than an education in the West, they faced the future with uncertainty.

A Recurring Theme

A theme running throughout this book concerns the marginality of Germans from the former GDR and their limited participation in many spheres in the new Germany. Thomas A. Baylis' chapter on "Institutional Destruction and Reconstruction" provides an overview of the difficulties of the unification process and how it tended to marginalize East Germans. The *way* unification was carried out--under Article 23 and by replacing almost all East German institutions with structures from the Federal Republic--made the political transition much more drastic than it would have been under Article 146, which would have involved the participation of both East and West Germans in developing a new constitution. As Baylis puts it, "the GDR lost its identity as a sovereign state and became part of a much larger and more powerful Federal Republic." "In what had been the GDR no single official entity remained--and none have since been created--that could speak for East German interests as a whole." The East German experiences stand in sharp contrast to those of most of her East European neighbors who benefited from the continuity provided by many older institutions kept in place during the transition process and from the participation of their citizens throughout the transition period. "[T]he price east Germans have paid for near-total institutional change in terms of individual careers, psychological shock, and the loss of control over their own affairs has greatly exceeded that paid by most of their neighbors."

Basing much of the chapter on his field research in eastern Germany since unification, Arthur Stahnke discusses the marginalization of east Germans in the political and governmental arena. Most of the new political leadership that had played a role in the old system--as members of the Party of Democratic Socialism (PDS, formerly the communist or Socialist Unity Party), of the Christian Democratic Party (CDU), or of the Free Democratic Party (FDP) in the GDR--were viewed as having little experience relevant for the new system. PDS members, especially, were ostracized and excluded from consideration for top positions and from cooperative ventures with other parties. In the initial period following unification, in order to cope with the magnitude of changes and the technical complexities involved in the transition to the West German system, experts were consulted and brought in from the West. Many of these Westerners assumed mid- to top-level administrative positions in the eastern *Länder*, receiving much more pay than the east German administrators, and more than administrators in comparable positions in the western *Länder*. The resolution of property claims also led to east Germans feeling marginalized; many Easterners who had lived in their housing for decades were threatened with evictions when others (particularly Germans from the West) filed claims, since the principle followed was "restoration before compensation."

In his chapter on the Party of Democratic Socialism Jörg Roesler analyzes the various faces of the PDS. In eastern Germany the PDS has strong appeal for those who feel disaffected from politics and not represented by the major political parties with power bases in western Germany. Highlighting the close relationship between the political behavior of east Germans and economic factors, Roesler predicts that a significant percentage of east Germans will continue to vote for the PDS as long as the economy in the East continues to stagnate or decline.

In their chapter on rightwing radicals and xenophobia, Molly C. Laster and Sabrina P. Ramet note that the radical right has tended to attract those who play marginal roles in society. This is not limited to eastern Germany but holds for rightwing groups in western Germany as well, and the phenomenon was also observed in East Germany before the revolution of 1989. Conditions today in eastern Germany and feelings of marginalization and alienation provide fertile grounds for the growth of rightwing movements. Recent newspaper accounts point to an upswing in far-right activity as Germany prepares for national elections in September 1998, with neo-Nazi groups "building on the spoiled hopes of Germany's unification."[15] An internet site helps co-ordinate radical right groups through a five-page manifesto which declares, "we help fellow citizens who are oppressed, marginalized, and persecuted."

As David Childs points out in his chapter on the East German state security services, a large proportion of East German citizens were on the Stasi payroll as full-time operatives or as informers. For a number of East Germans, collaboration with the Stasi has excluded them from participation in various positions, particularly at the middle to upper levels, e.g., in government, the military, etc., and has essentially ended their careers. The East German situation stands in contrast to the situation in several other East European countries where security police files have been sealed and have had no effect on employment oppor-tunities or where the presence of the security police was much less pervasive during the communist era. Not yet resolved, issues surround-ing Stasi collaboration continue to marginalize east Germans and split society, but perhaps to an even greater extent for west Germans collaborators, who have received even harsher treatment.

Focusing on the economic situation, I show how a number of political decisions have marginalized east Germans in the economic sphere. The early decision in favor of rapid privatization at the expense of restructuring meant that the majority of East German firms did not survive the transition, and West German firms stepped in to fill the vacuum, amid charges of "colonization." Moreover, the terms of economic and monetary union and the requirements for privatization developed by *Treuhand*, the German privatization agency, excluded most East Germans from entrepreneurial roles. As West Germans crossed over to fill mid- to upper-level positions in various economic spheres, East Germans played only marginal roles. Nor did workers or consumers fare much better. As firms died, unemployment skyrocketed, leaving almost one-third of eligible Easterners without jobs when including those taking early retirement and those in various short-term job creation schemes among the unemployed.

In his chapter on "Shock Therapy and Mental Walls," Laurence McFalls describes "The Wall in the head" that continues to affect east Germans today. For elites especially, unification has brought a loss of jobs, status, voice, and community. Consequently, in order to retain any standing in their fields, they have had to reject West German values and the "colonizing West" and to criticize the unification process. McFalls' interviews in eastern Germany since unification show that these mental walls affect the mass of ordinary east Germans differently from the way they do elites. Since ordinary citizens had little status in the GDR, they have had little or nothing to lose under unification. So while ordinary east Germans may wax nostalgic for the GDR, this does not prevent them from integrating into the new order.

Irene Dölling emphasizes the increasingly difficult economic position of East German women, often characterized as "the losers of unification." Despite efforts to have them conform to the model followed by West German women--career, a long pause for childrearing, and a return to career--East German women continue to resist the model. Relying on *Eigensinn*, their personal sources of strength developed in GDR times, the vast majority of women in eastern Germany continue to seek full-time employment, as they did in East Germany. Nevertheless, political, social, and economic conditions have made this quest increasingly difficult, and women in eastern Germany tend to be marginalized among the unemployed or in positions with few responsibilities and financial rewards.

In "Literature as Social Memory," Klaus Hammer cites Christoph Hein, a prominent writer from eastern Germany, in arguing that there will continue to be an East German literature as long as differences persist between the two parts of Germany. East German literature has been marginalized in the sense that German writers from the West consider their literature German rather than West German, while literature from the East is viewed as East German. Literary figures played major roles in the GDR as they articulated positions different from those of the state and helped lay the groundwork for the revolution of 1989. However, since unification, debates over literature in Germany have discounted the significance of GDR writers. As Laurence McFalls also points out, the critical debate begun in West Germany in 1990 over Christa Wolf, the GDR's poet laureate, forced Wolf and other East German authors "to abandon the all-German literary field" and withdraw to the margins of an East German literature.

Joseph Naftzinger finds relatively little evidence of the marginalization of east Germans in the electronic media. This is true, in part, because changes in the media in both East and West were well underway before 1989. Moreover, the provisions of the unification treaty covering the East German media called for decisions by eastern *Länder* governments and the creation of *Land* or regional broadcast networks throughout the East. In addition, east Germans continued to work at all levels of radio and television, and some programs and personalities, popular in the GDR, carried over into the programming after unification. Overall, the new media organizations in eastern Germany hired about 90 percent east German and only 10 percent west German employees. On the other hand, Germans from the West held the highest positions in the *Einrichtung*, the agency responsible for the media during the transition, and, as David Childs points out in the *Epilogue*, only a few of the top administrators in radio and television in the former GDR came from the East.

Donald Abenheim's chapter on the creation of a unified military through the incorporation of personnel from the GDR's *Nationale Volksarmee* (NVA) into the West German *Bundeswehr* especially illustrates the difficulties involved in unification and the resulting marginalization of East Germans. As Abenheim puts it, "The soldierly dimension of unity meant something very different from the merger of two German armies as intact institutions on equal terms; rather, one army ceased to exist, while its former opponent took over its personnel, equipment, and installations." Because of requirements imposed by the German government as well as by NATO and the conventional arms reduction talks, the total number and type of officers and non-commissioned personnel in the all-German army were severely constrained. Because much of the NVA training did not equip them with the types of broad knowledge and/or the specific technical skills needed within the Atlantic Alliance, many Easterners did not have the necessary qualifications to compete successfully for the limited slots. Others were eliminated in reference checks which revealed connections to the Stasi. In terms of both numbers and responsibilities, former NVA personnel entered the all-German army in marginal positions.

Nonetheless, that is not to denigrate the accomplishments of integrating the two former enemy armies into a unified German army that serves as a model for integrating military organizations throughout Europe in the post-cold war era.

In his study of religious patterns and beliefs, Detlef Pollack addresses a related theme--that Germans in the East are not so much marginal as different from their counterparts in the West in the religious sphere. As he compares and contrasts the attitudes of east and west Germans, Pollack provides evidence of quite different patterns of religiosity in the two sectors of the country. In general, a much lower percentage of Easterners than Westerners are church members and believe in God. Among church members, many differences in religious practices and attitudes can be explained by the predominance of Catholics in western and of Protestants in eastern Germany, but when comparing only Lutherans, the patterns show much greater similarity, as they do for non-traditional beliefs.

Dirk Verheyen's chapter on German foreign policy diverges from the focus of most chapters on eastern Germany because foreign policy is a central government function affecting all of Germany. He focuses instead on how the joining of East and West affects the foreign policy of the united Germany and how Germany's geographical position in the center of Europe influences her foreign policy. Prior to unification, the foreign policy of both the GDR and the FRG can be described as politics at the margins--with East Germany at the edge of the east bloc and West Germany at the edge of the western alliance. However, since unification and the end of the cold war, Germany now stands at the center rather than at the margins of Europe--at the edge of the divide. Her current foreign policy, characterized as *Scharnierpolitik* or "hinge policy," returns Germany to a key position in central Europe (*Mitteleuropa*), where she plays the critical function of linking East and West.

Despite the enormous difficulties faced in integrating east Germans and notwithstanding the gigantic financial costs borne by west Germans, the unification of Germany in 1990 stands as a preeminent event of the twentieth century. Germans seized the moment to press for unification and received the blessings of the critical players in the international arena. If Germans had waited and attempted to delay unification, the window of opportunity might have disappeared. Nevertheless, if different political and policy choices had been made concerning how to join the two states, unification might have been accomplished more easily. So, although unification has not gone smoothly and problems persist, few Germans would prefer to return to the old order. German unification stands as a defining moment for the new era.

Notes

1. See Patricia J. Smith, "Democratizing East Germany: Ideas, Emerging Political Groups, and the Dynamics of Change," Ph.D. dissertation, Seattle, University of Washington, 1995. Research was supported in part by a grant from the International Research and Exchanges Board (IREX) with funds provided by the National Endowment for the Humanities and the United States Information Agency. The Deutscher Akademischer Austauschdienst (DAAD) and Humboldt University also provided support. See also Dirk Philipsen, *We Were the People: Voices from East Germany's Revolutionary Autumn of 1989* (Durham and London: Duke University Press, 1993).

2. Smith, "Democratizing East Germany," pp. 173-85.

3. *Ibid.*, pp. 75-76.

4. *Current Digest of the Soviet Press*, Vol. 40, No. 49 (January 4, 1989), p. 3.

5. Smith, *Democratizing East Germany*, pp. 298-301.

6. *Ibid.*, pp. 206-16.

7. See "Modrow's Plan for a German Federation, 1 February 1990," in Konrad H. Jarausch and Volker Gransow, trans. by Allison Brown and Belinda Cooper, *Uniting Germany: Documents and Debates, 1944-1993* (Providence, RI and Oxford, UK: Berghahn Books, 1994), pp. 105-106.

8. As stated in Article 146, the "Basic Law becomes invalid on the day on which a constitution comes into being which has been created by the German people in a free decision. . . ," "Basic Law of the Federal Republic of Germany, 23 May 1949," in Jarausch and Gransow, *Uniting Germany*, p. 8. See also, Donald P. Kommers, "The Basic Law and Reunification," in Peter H. Merkl (ed.), *The Federal Republic of Germany at Forty-Five* (Boulder, CO: Westview Press, 1995), pp. 187-90.

9. Article 23 states, "For the time being, this basic law applies in the territory of the Länder of Baden, Bavaria, Bremen, Greater Berlin, Hamburg, Hesse, Lower Saxony, North-Rhine Westfalia, Rhineland-Palatinate, Schleswig-Holstein, Württemberg-Baden, and Württemberg-Hohenzollern. In other parts of Germany, it shall be put into force on their accession. . . ." *Ibid.*, p. 7.

10. Michael Minkenberg, "The Wall after the Wall: On the Continuing Division of Germany and the Remaking of Political Culture," in *Comparative Politics*, Vol. 26, No. 1 (October 1993), pp. 63-64.

11. Petra Bauer-Kaase and Max Kaase, "Five Years of Unification: The Germans on the Path to Inner Unity?", *German Politics*, Vol. 5, No 1 (April 1996), p. 5.

12. Peter O'Brien, "Germany's Newest Aliens: The East Germans," in *East European Quarterly*, Vol. 30, No. 4 (January 1997), p. 456.

13. Bauer-Kaase and Kaase, "Five Years of Unification," p. 5.

14. Merriam Webster, *WWWebster Dictionary* (http://www.m-w.com/cgi-bin/dictionary), 1997.

15. *New York Times*, 8 February 1997, p. 3.

PART ONE

Politics and Economics

1

Institutional Destruction and Reconstruction in Eastern Germany

Thomas A. Baylis

The central tenet of the "new institutionalism" in political science is the rather straightforward assertion that institutions have con-sequences--for the conduct of political life and, more broadly, for the life of individuals living under a particular political system.[1] It follows that a profound and sudden change in institutions is likely to be particularly far-reaching in its impact on elites and ordinary citizens alike. One of the ways in which the experience of the former German Democratic Republic (GDR) differs from those of its East European neighbors is in the thoroughness and speed with which the political, economic, and social institutions of the old order were discarded and replaced by ones imported from the old Federal Republic. While institutional changes were extensive nearly everywhere in the former Soviet bloc, especially in the political sphere, many structures from the communist era survived, albeit often in modified form. While much of the institutional environment facing Poles, Czechs, Hungarians, Russians, and so on thus remains familiar to them, east Germans have been required to adapt to a radically unfamiliar set of institutions, ones to which their west German compatriots have long become accustomed.

Richard Rose and Christian Haerpfer have cheerfully touted the advantages east Germans enjoyed in being provided a "ready-made state" in 1990.[2] But it is easier to believe that a good deal of the *malaise* that continues to afflict east Germans and impedes their easy integration with the west can be explained by this drastic alteration of institutional orientation points. As in all societies, individuals' careers, friendships, family lives, and even their attitudes and opinions were tied in one way or another to the GDR's institutions, however unloved some of them were. While for certain individuals, new institutions can be liberating as a source of fresh opportunities, it seems plausible that for others--perhaps most--a sudden change in nearly all relevant social institutions would prove profoundly disorienting.

In this chapter I attempt to account for the thoroughness of east German institutional restructuring, survey its major dimensions, examine several of its consequences, and identify some of the relatively few islands of institutional continuity and the meaning they have acquired since unification. The very fact that the GDR lost its identity as a sovereign state and became part of the much larger and more powerful Federal Republic of course makes the extent of political and constitutional/legal transformation understandable. But I want to suggest that the *way* in which German unification was realized made the political transformation even more drastic than it would otherwise have been and contributed to almost equally thoroughgoing changes in the economic and social spheres.

Institutional Changes and the "Rush to Unity"

The dissidents who emerged at the head of the protests and demonstrations that ultimately brought down the communist regime did not envision the rapid absorption of eastern Germany into the Federal Republic but favored rather a democratized, still independent, and in some sense still "socialist" GDR. Such a GDR would without doubt have retained much of the institutional configuration of the old regime while seeking to reform it from within. Indeed, in the few months following the opening of the Wall, most of the GDR's existing institutions--governmental bodies, parties, economic enterprises, universities, the former "mass organizations"--experienced serious efforts at reform from within, while a wide variety of new voluntary associations, inspired in part by the citizens' movements, emerged.[3] But by the time of the *Volkskammer* election of March 1990 the program of the dissidents had long since become anachronistic; the election's outcome set an irresistible course for rapid political and economic unification, even though popular support for it was perhaps less unanimous than has often been assumed. A mounting economic crisis, the continued stream of emigrants to the West, and the allure of western consumer goods made it difficult for east Germans to advocate retention of any elements of the old order.

The negotiation process over the terms of union was dominated by West Germans; Wolfgang Schäuble, who led the West German negotiating team on political union, was brutally candid in informing the East Germans that "this is not the unification of two equal states."[4] The decision to unite the country on the basis of Article 23 of the Basic Law (which provided for "accession" of other territories to the existing Federal Republic), rather than via Article 146 (which would have required the calling of a new constitutional convention and the *replacement* of the Basic Law) made the substitution of western institutions for eastern ones all but inevitable. As Gerhard Lehmbruch has remarked, the authorities in Bonn had quickly decided that "the institutional framework (*Mantel*) of the GDR was to be entirely liquidated. There was to be as little organizational continuity as possible."[5]

The East German negotiators, led by the Christian Democratic Union's (CDU's) Günther Krause, a technical college teacher, were inexperienced and in any case little inclined to challenge western priorities.[6] After all, the electoral victory of the "east" CDU and its allies did not reflect the popularity of this former satellite party but rather the campaigning (and campaign promises) of Chancellor Kohl and other western politicians.[7] Communist reformers and non-party intellectuals, who had played a significant role in the negotiated settlements in Poland, Hungary, and Czechoslovakia, had been stripped of any influence over the process in the GDR by the election results. In other words, those who had reason to be especially conscious of having a vested interest in existing institutions were left virtually without any voice in shaping the terms of German union. Overall, unification took place through a "bureaucratic process" that allowed little room for popular involvement and whose specifics were based in considerable measure on the drafts of experts in Bonn.[8]

It is also useful to recall the atmosphere of the time. Unification euphoria was in the air; sober voices warning of the pitfalls of an over-hasty push towards German union were not absent, but were hardly listened to. With the implementation of the currency union on 1 July East German goods virtually disappeared from eastern store shelves; everything western was simply assumed to be superior to everything eastern.[9] The harsh West German judgment that the GDR could bring nothing of value to a united Germany except *Land und Leute* (territory and population) was for the moment shared by many East Germans. In these circumstances, the wholesale abandonment of East German institutions in the wake of the treaties of economic and political union was not surprising.

Political and Legal Institutions

Unification meant the abrupt end of the authority of the GDR Constitution, as modified in the months following the opening of the Berlin Wall, and the liquidation of the institutions of the GDR's national and regional governments and administrations. Elsewhere in Eastern Europe, the former communist-era constitutions[10] were initially amended rather than abolished; indeed, as late as early 1997 Poland and Hungary were still governed under the provisions of their old, drastically amended, constitutions. Like its neighbors, east Germans acquired competitive elections and pluralistic, democratic parliamentary systems in place of single party rule, rubber-stamp parliaments, and prime ministers and cabinets that had been *de facto* responsible to the ruling party rather than to the parliament and public. Most other countries, however, did not lose their central governments altogether; Czechoslovakia and Yugoslavia, of course, are the other notable East European exceptions, but even in those cases there was some institutional continuity between the old governments and the new Czech and "rump Yugoslav" regimes. In what had been the GDR no single official entity remained--and none have since been created--that could speak for East German interests as a whole.[11]

Moreover, the introduction into the former GDR of West German-style federalism also meant the abolition of the former *Bezirk* (regional) governments and their replacement by new *Land* authorities.[12] Subsequently, the number of East German *Kreise* (districts) was reduced by nearly two-thirds. Thus only on the communal level was there continuity even in the identity of governing units.[13] Perhaps the most significant element of this governmental restructuring was the elimination of the GDR's old national and regional administrative structures.[14] In other East European states, such structures display considerable continuity, and that continuity is reflected in the greater persistence, at least below the top levels, of much of the old bureaucratic personnel.

Of at least equal importance was the substitution of West German law and the West German legal and judicial system for those of the GDR. "It is largely overlooked," writes Hettlage, "that in the negotiations over the Unification Treaty the fundamental decision was made consciously to employ the law of the old Federal Republic as the instrument *(Träger)* of social change."[15] The East German legal system was seen as basically incompatible with the--in the West highly revered--principles of the *Rechtsstaat,* asserting as it did throughout the years of communist rule the subordination of law to the leading role of the ruling party. Although the unification treaty provided that GDR law was to remain in effect when it did not conflict with the Basic Law, in general East Germans found themselves confronted by a new, complex, and highly formalized legal framework taken over from the West--one that, as Hans Misselwitz has noted, was "blind to the specifics of GDR socialization."[16] Moreover, the East German judicial system was restructured to correspond to that of the Federal Republic, and the judiciary underwent an extensive purge, with fewer than half the GDR's judges and state prosecutors retained. Legal education was also reorganized in order to conform to western models.

East German political parties, as we shall see, display a greater degree of continuity with the communist past than those in several other formerly communist countries. But the political party and electoral *systems* are entirely different. Instead of facing a hegemonic party joined by loyal satellites presenting a single slate of candidates in elections in which no competition was permitted, east Germans now have a genuine choice among rival parties and differing coalition possibilities. Voting is no longer compulsory, and turnout has been below both earlier GDR and present west German levels.[17] Party membership is no longer a ticket to career advancement, and is far smaller than before. All this is also true in Poland, Hungary, the Czech Republic, and elsewhere, but the east German party system can fairly be characterized as somewhat more stable than it is in most other East European states. In most but not all ways it was shaped by and resembles the West German system.

An institution which has survived with relatively little change in some other former communist states is the military. In Poland, for example, it has continued to win high approval ratings, just as it did before the fall of the old regime. The East German *Volksarmee,* however, has been dissolved, although some of its personnel have been incorporated into the Federal Republic's *Bundeswehr.*

Economic Institutions

The treaty of economic, monetary, and social union, providing (among other things) for the replacement of the GDR's currency by the West German Mark, had the effect of imposing a level of "shock therapy" whose immediate impact far exceeded that of the measures taken in Poland, Czechoslovakia, or elsewhere. Major East German enterprises lost any chance at remaining economically viable in their existing form; most were either closed down or sold off (often in segments) to West German companies by the *Treuhandanstalt*. In other formerly communist East European states, reform proceeded much more slowly. Not all major firms were privatized, and among those that were, many continued to operate much as they did before, since formal privatization did not necessarily bring with it any basic restructuring or changes in management. Thus while the East Germans' Interflug airline, Trabant autos, and Robotron electronics firm disappeared, the Hungarians' Malev airline, the Czechs' Skoda automobiles, and Poland's Ursus tractor factory continue to exist and in some cases flourish. While Western investment in Polish, Czech, and Hungarian firms has been extensive, the emerging economic landscape in eastern Germany is dominated by west German companies. The structure of the labor force has changed drastically: apart from high unemployment, it is characterized by a sharp decline in manufacturing jobs and a relative increase in those in construction and services, and a substantial drop in the proportion of female workers. It is fair to say that in almost every respect the world of work faced by east Germans has been radically altered since 1989. While job insecurity, economic inequality, and manifestations of "wild-west" capitalism have greatly increased throughout Eastern Europe, nowhere has the change been more massive than in the former GDR.

Trade unions belonging to the west's *Deutsche Gewerkschaftsbund* (DGB), seeing the opportunity to expand their membership and to protect their western members against low-wage competition, moved into the GDR and soon supplanted the East German unions in spite of the latter's own efforts at reform. The DGB unions refused to consider a formal merger with the former communist unions, but did accept their members and some officials on an individual basis.[18] The one economic area in which economic transformation was more limited was in agriculture, where some 60 percent of agricultural land is still owned by the successors to the GDR's collective farms.[19]

Research, Education, and Social Services

The GDR's research and educational establishment, a source of substantial pride to the regime during the years of communist rule, was subjected to the process of *Abwicklung*, a term that can be translated as "winding up" and came to carry rather sinister overtones in the period immediately after unification. The GDR's Academy of Sciences, organized on the Soviet model and including some 25,000 researchers housed in institutes in virtually all scientific fields, was dismantled. While it was intended to integrate some of the academy's more respected and less politicized components into the university system, financial constraints appear to have prevented this plan from being carried out in most cases.

Most East German universities survived *Abwicklung*, but all but a few faculty members in "suspect" fields (apart from Marxism-Leninism, the social sciences, law, and in part the humanities) were dismissed, and certain faculties were closed down entirely. Overall, some 70 percent of the staff of universities and technical schools are said to have lost their jobs.[20] Nearly all newly-hired faculty members came from the West. The Economics Academy in Berlin-Karlshorst, where many top GDR economic officials and managers had been trained, was closed, unlike its counterparts in Prague, Bratislava, and Budapest, which continue to have significant links to their countries' new political elites. The rationale for the dismissals, carried out on the basis of recommendations of commissions dominated by western scholars, was economic as well as political, since east German universities were greatly overstaffed by comparison with their west German counterparts, and since east German *Land* governments had little money. Nevertheless, in some cases new universities were established, notably in Brandenburg.

The contrast with other East European countries is considerable.[21] In spite of financial constraints even more severe than those burdening the east German *Länder*, relatively few faculty members have been dismissed from their university positions, and the Academies of Sciences continue to be pivotal research institutions. Neither they nor the universities were subject to the same sort of review that their east German counterparts were: commissions made up primarily of outsiders who evaluated programs and faculty both for political suitability and professional competence. It is thus perhaps not surprising that academic reforms elsewhere in eastern Europe were less sweeping.

Primary and secondary education in eastern Germany were also restructured along west German lines. In practice, this meant the replacement of the GDR's comprehensive polytechnical schools with a more differentiated, selective system, capped by western-style *Gymnasien*. To be sure, Brandenburg, under Social Democratic rule, continued to emphasize comprehensive schools, while the other four *Länder*, led initially by conservative governments, instituted a two- or three-way partition of students into academic and general or vocational schools after their completion of primary school. These changes were carried out under the influence of administrators from west German "partner states," some of whom remained in senior positions in the East.[22] Most teachers, however, are carryovers from the previous system.

East Germans also experienced radical alterations in their systems of social services, health care, and housing. While some of these changes brought undoubted advantages to them--a sharp improvement in the standard of living of pensioners, for example--others meant the loss of institutions that were highly valued. The closure or rationalization of enterprises meant the end of a variety of services provided through them; as Regine Hildebrandt, the popular Social Democratic minister for labor, social affairs, health, and women in Brandenburg has pointed out, the enterprises were the "focal point and supporter of a whole infrastructure," including day care for young children, vacation camps, cultural and sports facilities, and much more.[23] The virtually universal availability of day care in the GDR, for example, had been possible due to its provision through the workplace. As has often been noted, the closing of day-care facilities and the replacement of the GDR's *Baby-Jahr* by the Federal Republic's less generous system of parental leave has placed an especially heavy burden on east German women and may well have contributed to the dramatic fall in the region's birth-rate.[24] Housing arrangements were also affected. Sharply increased rents, privatization, and claims for the restitution of property by former owners brought with them heightened insecurity among east Germans if not actual displacement from their homes.

The GDR's popular "polyclinics" fell victim to the restructuring and privatization of health care along west German lines.[25] Minister Hildebrandt describes the changes in medical treatment in an area from her own experience--care for the chronically ill. A dramatic improvement in the availability of needed medicines and medical equipment was accompanied by the dismantling of carefully developed systems of treatment--in her case, for diabetics. As she laments, "our . . . system did not fit into the structure of the Federal Republic's approach to health care."[26]

Islands of Continuity

Given the degree of institutional devastation that unification has left in its wake, it would not be surprising to see at least some east Germans cling nostalgically to the small number of familiar institutions that remain. In some cases, but not all, this supposition can be confirmed. The two institutions that maintained some measure of autonomy under communist rule and thus might be expected to have profited from its demise have not fared especially well. The Evangelical Church, now reunited with its western counterpart, has not enjoyed a resurgence of support among the population at large, although former pastors and individuals associated in one degree or another with the church still play an unusually large role in east German politics. The eastern part of Germany continues to be characterized by one of the lowest rates of religious adherence in the world--about 30 percent.[27]

Major cultural institutions played an ambivalent role in east German communism. East German literature, certain journals, theater, film, and musical institutions were sources of considerable pride for many east Germans and lent a degree of (largely undeserved) prestige to the regime. At the same time they offered an opportunity and were sometimes utilized for social criticism not otherwise available in the society. With some regularity the regime found itself at odds with its artists, removing editors, occasionally closing down publications entirely, banning, censoring or delaying works on sensitive subjects, reprimanding signers of petitions, and forcing a remarkable number of prominent intellectuals into exile. A surprising number of such cultural institutions have survived, at least in comparison to the institutional carnage in other sectors, and retain a good deal of their prestige; Leipzig's Gewandhaus Orchestra and Berlin's Deutsches Theater are examples. Most suffer from severe financial pressures, however, because of the loss of subsidies and the uncertainties of the new market environment, and others have been the object of debilitating power struggles, as in the case of the Berliner Ensemble, the institutional inheritor of the Bertolt Brecht legacy.

The continuing popularity of east German regional newspapers and the failure of major west German publications to attract a substantial readership in the new states has attracted considerable comment. It is reported that in 1992 seven of the ten German regional daily newspapers with the largest circulation were former GDR *Bezirks-zeitungen*.[28] Now owned by west German firms, they continue to employ many of their former journalists; while they do not follow their former ideological agenda, they appear to benefit from familiarity and the ability to cater to the feelings and voice the discontents of their readers.

East German radio and television have been replaced by new services following the west German model and led by west German personnel. Some programming, however, survives from GDR times, apparently in response to popular demand, and 95 percent of the services' personnel are said to be east Germans, many of them holdovers from the communist era.[29] Conservative critics have gone so far as to call the new Brandenburg service, ORB, "Red radio" (*Rotfunk*).[30]

Whatever the justice of this charge, the fact that most east Germans favored western programming long before Fall 1989 suggests that the impact of the changes in radio and television has been smaller than in other sectors.

Perhaps the most striking example of institutional continuity is found among political parties. They are not, of course, precisely the same parties they were, and they function in a radically changed political environment. But it is noteworthy that in east Germany, in contrast to other East European states, no notably successful new parties emerged from the political opposition to communist rule. *Bündnis 90*, founded by members of *Neues Forum* and other opposition groups and subsequently merged with the largely west German Greens, has fared poorly in east German elections. The east German Christian Democrats and Free Democrats are the successors of GDR satellite parties, now tied to their bigger west German brothers. Many of their elected officials and remaining members, however, are carryovers from GDR times.[31] The east German Social Democrats come the closest to being a "new" east German party (it was founded in the heady days of Fall 1989 and subsequently merged with the west German SPD), but its heritage goes back to the long history of German Social Democracy.

The most interesting case is that of the PDS.[32] Some of the party's opponents have charged that it is nothing more than the continuation of the "totalitarian" SED and therefore ought to be outlawed. But if the PDS were simply a renamed but otherwise unreconstructed version of the SED, it would not have attracted the popular support that it has. Much of its aging membership (over 80 percent belonged to the SED) doubtless values its links to the old ruling party, and remains nostalgic for the days of communist power. But for many of its (much younger) voters the continuity it represents is not literally that with the SED; what they appear to value is its willingness to defend elements of the GDR past that they recall with some fondness, or at least what they see as part of their own identity and that they see as coming under indiscriminate and uninformed attack from the West.

The PDS is no longer a monolithic ruling party commanding enormous resources, but rather an outsider party under unrelenting political and legal attack from its rivals, the federal government, and former dissidents. Riven by internal conflict and division, the party relies heavily on the popular appeal of its leaders and of its attacks on the German status quo; unlike its predecessor, the SED, it cannot attract members because of its intimate association with state power. In fact, only a small proportion of those who once belonged to the SED remain in the PDS, and virtually none of its leaders, with the exception of Hans Modrow, the party's honorary chairman, occupied significant leadership posts under the former regime. In considerable measure the PDS's electoral success has been based on its reputation for serving as the clearest and possibly the only "voice" speaking on behalf of the interests of ordinary east Germans--arguably just the opposite of the role played by the SED.[33]

Consequences

There can be little doubt that the "GDR nostalgia" that by all accounts has grown markedly in the years since unification is tied in large measure to the loss of familiar institutions and their replacement by unfamiliar ones. An EMNID study published in *Der Spiegel* in 1995 revealed that in seven of nine policy areas in which east Germans were asked to compare the performance of the GDR and that of the Federal Republic, the GDR's was given preference. Many of these reflect the institutional changes I have described: apart from protection from crime and equal treatment of the sexes, those interviewed cited social security, education, vocational training, health care, and the provision of housing as areas of GDR superiority.[34] Surveys comparing the trust of west and east Germans in governmental institutions and political parties reveal a continuing gap between the two, with east Germans scoring them on average one point lower on a scale of -5 to +5.[35]

Studies of individual policy areas produce similar responses. In 1993 only 11.5 percent of east Germans surveyed expressed trust in the new (Western) legal system, while 42.3 percent said they had no confidence in it.[36] One-quarter of those surveyed in 1995 felt *nothing* should have been changed in the GDR's former school system, while another 55 percent preferred the structure of the GDR's system (i.e., comprehensive, "polytechnic" schools with an additional two-year course for those going on to higher education) without its ideological bias.[37] Another study shows a drop in support for the market economy from 77 percent in 1990 to 34 percent in 1995.[38] The loss of a sense of security that many east Germans feel to have been the price of unification appears to be at the heart of GDR nostalgia; it can easily be associated with the disappearance of those institutions that, looked upon in retrospect, seemed to provide or at least symbolize that security.

A direct consequence of the replacement of East German institutions by western ones was to make irrelevant the training and skills of many east Germans. "The new state and legal, scientific and economic institutions that are now emerging on western models massively devalue [East German] cultural capital," Sigrid Meuschel has remarked. "Only a few are able to utilize what they have learned."[39]

The "delegitimation of the biographies" of east Germans (Hans Misselwitz) goes back in part to the abolition or discrediting of GDR institutions in which individuals were educated and pursued their careers as well as to charges of complicity in the sins of the former regime.[40] Conversely, the need to fill critical positions in the "new states" in government, the legal sector, the economy, education, and elsewhere with west Germans reflects the demands of institutions transferred from the West which could be readily manned only by those with western training and experience.[41] To function in this brave new world at all, east Germans have had to learn new rules and coping strategies. As one writer has put it, they have had to acquire a new "language" which most will never be able to use with quite the fluency of west German "native speakers."[42]

The difficulty that many east Germans have had in adapting to their new institutions has not always elicited much sympathy from western commentators. Instead it is sometimes attributed to a fundamental "deformation" in the character of east Germans imposed by years of socialization under communism. In some interpretations, these "pathological" disabilities may take generations to overcome. The expression of such views itself, one might think, does not contribute greatly to the furtherance of east-west integration.[43]

The retention elsewhere in Eastern Europe of many institutions from the communist era, even in greatly modified form, is by no means an unambiguous advantage. Some continue to provide shelter for individuals who were seriously compromised politically under the old regimes and for others of questionable competence. When institutions survive, the authoritarian and bureaucratic habits associated with them may well survive, too. In many cases tested western institutions are undoubtedly superior in terms of efficiency and sometimes equity to former communist-created or dominated institutions that have undergone only superficial democratic face-lifting.

Insofar as other post-communist systems have changed their institutions, surveys indicate that the new institutions are objects of at least as much distrust as they are in eastern Germany. Voting turnout has similarly fallen. Even in the Czech Republic, one-quarter of those surveyed in 1997 believed they were better off prior to the Velvet Revolution, and the birth rate fell by nearly one-third between 1990 and 1996.[44]

Nevertheless, the price east Germans have paid for near-total institutional change in terms of individual careers, psychological shock, and the loss of control over their own affairs has greatly exceeded that paid by most of their eastern neighbors. To claim, as Glaessner has, that this process of rapid and comprehensive institutional transfer is a "success story" since east Germany did not "have to waste time and energy by arguing about how to shape demo-cratic institutions" seems to me to overlook these costs.[45] To have spent "time and energy" arguing about the proper form of democratic institutions might well have been a prudent investment, requiring a degree of participation in and commitment to the shaping of the new political system that could have made east Germans more comfortable with it.[46] The burden the imposition of institutional changes and the reactions to them have placed on the task of achieving "inner unity" in the Federal Republic can hardly be minimized.

The institutional transformation of east Germany is symbolized in some ways by its architectural transformation. *The Palast der Republik* in Berlin, for example, is seen by many (especially in the West) as a symbol of totalitarian rule; it was, after all, the place where the SED's quinquennial Congresses were held, and the meeting place of the GDR's rubber-stamp parliament, the *Volkskammer*. But it also contained theaters and restaurants and served as a gathering-place for ordinary east German citizens. In the prolonged dispute over the fate of the *Palast,* east Berliners favored keeping it, while west Berliners wanted it torn down--perhaps to be replaced by a new incarnation of the Hohenzollern palace whose remains were pulled down by the communists after the war. It now appears that the *Palast* will indeed be demolished, just as the nearby GDR Foreign Ministry already has been. On the other hand, rising everywhere on one side or the other of the former Wall are new government and commercial buildings, designed for the most part by western architects and built to satisfy west German standards of comfort and design. To be sure, visible reminders of the GDR era will remain in Berlin for decades to come-- the television tower, the countless *Plattenbau* housing silos. But it is not surprising that the effort to eradicate nearly all institutional as well as many architectural remnants of the GDR past is regretted even by many of those east Germans--the great majority--who would not want the GDR itself to return. As one east German told *Der Spiegel:* "*Niemand will die DDR wieder haben. Aber keiner will sie sich nehmen lassen.*"[47]

Notes

An earlier version of this article was delivered at the 1997 Annual Meeting of the American Political Science Association, Washington, D.C., August 28-31, 1997. My thanks to Helga A. Welsh for her comments on it.

1. See Kathleen Thelen and Sven Steinmo, "Historical Institutionalism in Comparative Politics," in Sven Steinmo, Kathleen Thelen, and Frank Longstreth, eds., *Structuring Politics: Historical Institutionalism in Comparative Analysis* (Cambridge: Cambridge University Press, 1992), pp. 2-3.

2. Richard Rose and Christian Haerpfer, "The Impact of a Ready-Made State: East Germans in Comparative Perspective," *German Politics*, Vol. 6, No. 1 (April 1997), 100-21. Rose's and Haerpfer's optimism is based in large measure on a 1993 survey whose findings do not correspond well with those of other, later studies.

3. See Jan Wielgohs, "Strategies of West German Corporate Actors in the Creation of Interest Associations in East Germany," *German Politics*, Vol. 5, No. 2 (August 1996), pp. 202-03.

4. Konrad Jarausch, *The Rush to German Unity* (New York: Oxford University Press, 1994), p. 170.

5. Gerhard Lehmbruch, "Die deutsche Vereinigung: Strukturen und Strategien," *Politische Vierteljahresschrift*, Vol. 32, No. 4 (December, 1991), p. 596.

6. "Unlike de Maizière, Krause never gave the impression that he intended to save much from the old GDR to pull over into the new state. . . . [F]or Schäuble, Krause was indispensable." Manfred Görtemaker, *Unifying Germany, 1989-1990* (New York: St. Martin's, 1994), pp. 206-07.

7. See Ute Schmidt, "Von der Blockpartei zur Volkspartei? Die Ost-CDU im Umbruch 1989-1994," *German Studies Review*, Vol. 20, No. 1 (February 1997), pp. 105-37.

8. See Jarausch, *The Rush to German Unity*, p. 176.

9. "Tempted by glossy ads, East Germans indiscriminately preferred western goods to their own familiar wares. FRG chains also systematically displaced eastern products via exclusive contracts with their new affiliates. While local cherries rotted outside Potsdam, Berlin stores offered fruit flown in from Washington state," Jarausch, *The Rush to German Unity*, p. 149.

10. "In the institutional dimension, despite fundamental changes in the domestic and international political and economic environments, the structure of the Polish government is almost exactly the same as the one inherited from the old regime," Grzegorz Ekiert and Jan Kubik, "Collective Protest and the Structure of the Polity in Post-Communist Poland, 1989-1992," paper delivered at the Ninth International Conference of Europeanists, Chicago, March 31-April 2, 1994, p. 14. The Polish electorate approved a new constitution in May 1997.

11. Michael Brie, "Die Ostdeutschen auf dem Wege vom 'armen Bruder' zur organisierten Minderheit," Working Paper of the Arbeitsgruppe Transformationsprozesse in den neuen Bundesländern, Max-Planck-Gesellschaft, May 1994, p. 20.

12. The five east German *Länder* were essentially re-established versions of states abolished by the communists in 1952.

13. Robert Hettlage, "Integrationsleistungen des Rechts im Prozess der deutschen Einheit," in Hettlage and Karl Lenz (eds.), *Deutschland nach der Wende: Eine Zwischenbilanz* (München: Verlag C. H. Beck, 1995), p. 43.

14. See Gert-Joachim Glaessner, "Regime Change and Public Administration in East Germany—Some Findings from a Research Project in Brandenburg and Saxony," *German Politics* Vol. 5, No. 2 (August 1996), pp. 191-92. Glaessner notes that in Saxony, intermediate level *Regierungsbezirke* have been created whose boundaries are nearly identical to those of the former GDR *Bezirke;* reportedly this has permitted a somewhat greater continuity of "old structures."

15. Hettlage, "Integrationsleistungen," p. 25.

16. Hans-J. Misselwitz, *Nicht länger mit dem Gesicht nach Westen* (Bonn: J. H. W. Dietz, 1996), p. 56. See also Inga Markovits' account of the abrupt and some-times brutal transition from the GDR's "socialist" legal system to that of the Federal Republic: *Imperfect Justice: An East-West German Diary* (Oxford: Claren-don Press, 1995).

17. Ilse Spittmann, "Vertrauensverlust," *Deutschland Archiv,* Vol. 29, No. 6 (November-December 1996), p. 841.

18. See Michael Fichter, "From Transmission Belt to Social Partnership? The Case of Organized Labor in Eastern Germany," *German Politics and Society,* No. 23 (Summer 1991), pp. 21-39; M. Donald Hancock, "Reinventing Trade Unionism in Unified Germany," in Peter H. Merkl, ed., *The Federal Republic of Germany at Forty-Five* (New York: New York University Press, 1995), pp. 321-24. The east German FDGB was formally dissolved in September 1990.

19. Wielgohs, "Strategies," p. 209; Hans Luft, "Entwicklung der Ostdeutschen Landwirtschaft," *Deutschland Archiv,* Vol. 29, No. 3 (May-June 1996), pp. 422-28.

20. Wolfgang Dümcke and Fritz Vilmar, "Was heißt hier Kolonisierung?" in Dümcke and Vilmar (eds.), *Kolonisierung der DDR: Kritische Analysen und Alternativen des Einigungsprozesses* (Münster: agenda Verlag, 1996), p. 17. See also Peer Pasternak, "Wandel durch Abwarten: Ost und West an den ostdeutschen Hochschulen," *Deutschland Archiv,* Vol. 29, No. 3 (May-June 1996), pp. 371-80.

21. See the informative series of articles on "Intellectual Trends, Institutional Changes and Scholarly Needs in Eastern Europe," emphasizing the social sciences, in *East European Politics and Societies,* Vol. 6, No. 3 (Fall 1992) and Vol. 7, No. 1 (Winter 1993).

22. See Edward Neather, "Education in the New Germany," in Derek Lewis and John R. P. McKenzie, (eds.), *The New Germany: Social, Political and Cultural Challenges of Unification* (Exeter: University of Exeter Press, 1995), pp. 148-72.

23. Regine Hildebrandt, *Was ich denke* (Munich: Wilhelm Goldmann Verlag, 1994), p. 79.

24. The birth rate is said to have dropped 65 percent between 1988 and the end of 1992. Sarina Keiser, "Die Familien in den neuen Bundesländer zwischen Individualisierung und 'Notgemeinschaft,'" in Hettlage and Lenz, p. 175.

25. On the role of west German doctors' associations in the liquidations of polyclinics, see Wielgohs, "Strategies," pp. 204-05.

26. Hildebrandt, *Was ich denke,* pp. 49-50.

27. Helmut Frank, "Kreuz des Ostens," *Die Zeit*, June 27, 1997, p. 7. Of the 30 percent, about half report "never" going to church.

28. John Sanford, "The Press in the New *Länder*,"in Margy Gerber and Roger Woods, eds., *Studies in GDR Culture and Society*, Nos. 14-15 (Lanham, MD.: University Press of America, 1996), p. 220.

29. Irene Charlotte Streul, "Von der Abwicklung des SED-Rundfunks zum öffentlich-rechtlichen Rundfunk in geeinten Deutschland," *Deutschland Archiv*, Vol. 29, No. 1 (January-February 1996), p. 109.

30. Johannes Dieckmann, "Was heißt im Osten Opposition?" *Die Zeit* (German ed.), 12 April 1996, p. 3.

31. See Thomas A. Baylis, "Elite Change After Communism," *East European Politics and Societies*, forthcoming.

32. There is already a sizeable literature surrounding the PDS. One comprehensive study is Gero Neugebauer and Richard Stöss, *Die PDS: Geschichte. Organisation. Wähler. Konkurrenten* (Opladen: Leske + Budrich, 1996).

33. At the end of 1996 the figure was 83.3 percent. *Frankfurter Allgemeine Zeitung*, 26 May 1997, p. 5.

34. See Thomas A. Baylis, "East German Leadership after Unification: The Search for Voice," paper delivered at the Fifth Conference of the East German Studies Group, Stanford University, 16-19 November 1995.

35. "Stoltz aufs eigene Leben," *Der Spiegel*, 3 July 1995, p. 43.

36. Dieter Walz, "Vertrauen in politischen Institutionen in vereinten Deutschland," *Deutschland Archiv*, Vol. 29, No. 2 (March-April 1996), p. 244.

37. Misselwitz, *Nicht länger*, p. 57.

38. Willhelm Schrader, "Der Blick auf die alte Schule verklärt sich," *Frankfurter Rundschau*, 9 May 1996, p. 6.

39. Spittmann, "Vertrauensverlust," p. 842.

40. Sigrid Meuschel, *Legitimation und Parteiherrschaft in der DDR* (Frankfurt am Main: Suhrkamp Verlag, 1992), p. 335. "It is less the lack of competence of east Germans in itself but rather the devaluation of context-related competence that produces the superior capacity for action of many west German actors," Brie, "Die Ostdeutsche," p. 7.

41. Misselwitz, *Nicht länger*, p. 35.

42. Thomas A. Baylis, "Leadership Change in Eastern Germany: From Colonisation to Integration?" in Merkl, *The Federal Republic*, pp. 243-62.

43. Bertolt Fessen, "Ressentiment und Fehlwahrnehmung: Deutsche Mühen mit der Vereinigung," *Berliner Debatte INITIAL*, No. 4-5, (1995), p. 138.

44. See Lothar Fritz, "Gestörte Kommunikation zwischen Ost und West," *Deutschland Archiv*, Vol. 29, No. 6 (November-December 1996), pp. 921-28.

45. Radio Prague E-News, 24 June 1997; Radio Free Europe/Radio Liberty Newsline, 6 August 1997.

46. Glaessner, "Regime Change," pp. 186-88.

47. On this point, see Dümke and Vilmar, "Kolonisierung," pp. 19-20.

48. "No one wants to have the GDR again. But no one wants it taken from them." "'Wir lieben die Heimat,'" *Der Spiegel*, 3 July 1995, p. 64.

2

Local Government and Politics Since the *Wende*[1]

Arthur A. Stahnke

Before the breakup of the old East German political order, the place of local government and politics there was firmly set. It was one of unequivocal and nearly total subordination to central direction. Town mayors and councils and their *Kreis* (county) counterparts all had a minimum of autonomy, and the extent to which they had discretionary authority over the resources for which they were officially responsible was also very small.[2] To call them all puppets would be a bit extreme, perhaps, but their essentially reactive character nevertheless calls the comparison to mind.

Today, the place of local government and politics in the "new German states" is also firmly set if not yet fully in place. The new model was developed and tested in West Germany over the past several decades; following unification, it was carried over into the eastern part of the country. In substance, the new system greatly enhances the authority and the responsibilities of grass-roots level political institutions.

The move to the new, empowering system of local government in the East has not been easy, despite the existence of a proven constitutional framework and many examples of its successful operationalization in the West. That this is true has rested more with the objective if unforeseen problems involved, than with avoidable error. These problems have included: the limited qualifications of the new political and administrative elites and the uniqueness of the situations they have faced; the organizational vacuum that existed while comprehensive changes were being carried out; the presence of extended agendas that have included both transition-specific and normal or recurring issues; and, the limiting consequences of unresolved national political matters. Each of these problems will be taken up here as it played out during the first legislative period under the post-SED (Socialist Unity Party) system, and then the chapter will conclude with an assessment of how things stand as of the most recent past.

The New Local Political and Administrative Elites

The formal installation of grassroots political leadership in the GDR came only after the 5 May 1990 local elections. Well before that, however, during the last months of 1989, individual reformers and local groupings that were extensions of the 1989 Citizens' Movement *(Bürgerbewegung)* began to speak out and to press their local governments to democratize their processes. By January 1990 local equivalents of the Round Table in East Berlin were being organized across the country, to oversee town[3] and county governmental actions, to investigate for past and ongoing local wrongdoing, and to prepare and supervise the upcoming elections.

These local Round Tables[4] were open to all, and individuals with quite varied political views and orientations joined them for the common purpose of bringing serious reform. At the same time, however, most of these early activists had close ties to the alternative groups that had sprung up in late 1989 and they shared a commitment to participatory democracy and the need for a clean and thorough break with the past.

These activists, not surprisingly, were one important source of the new local political leadership that emerged in May 1990. Generally, they were motivated more by the worthiness of a cause than by self-interest and this standpoint sometimes translated into righteous indignation toward others more prone to expedient compromise. Their comparatively early involvement in the new politics also led them to feel superior to those who had entered the arena only later when such a step was more fashionable than dangerous.

Whether because of their experiences in 1989 or "natural inclination," these leaders, once in local parliaments, tended to be more comfortable in opposition than in sharing responsibility for governance. As outsiders, they were often very effective with their criticism.

However, their influence over general program development and implementation was also limited by their stance.

A second wave of new local political leaders became active only in early 1990, when the March and May elections were scheduled. In their approach to politics, these individuals were typically quite different from the first group in that they were more interested in specific policy outcomes and personal considerations, and less likely to be motivated by moral outrage. They also tended to see the West German political order as an appropriate model for their own emulation, including the place it gave to political parties. Usually, as a result, they formed or joined a local Socialist Democratic Party (SPD) or Christian Democratic Party (CDU) group, or some other local extension of a western-based party. They also accepted the acquisition and use of public power as a normal and desirable political objective.

A final segment of the new political leadership was composed of individuals who had had some degree of direct involvement in the old political order. These "holdovers" comprised almost all who joined local Party of Democratic Socialism (PDS) bodies, as well as a significant minority within CDU and Free Democratic Party (FDP) ranks.[5] Mostly, these individuals were no more than past and continuing members of their respective parties. Only a minority of them had been party or government functionaries before 1989. Hence, their "experience" was most often of little possible utility in the new system.

Whether or not such experience might have been useful was seldom seriously considered, for these holdovers were usually marginalized in the new governments. PDS groups were everywhere categorically ostracized when it came to inter-party cooperation and treated as unwanted step-children in most parliamentary activity. Holdovers from the CDU (and FDP) were not so unconditionally isolated, but some of their leaders were excluded from consideration for the top positions of mayor or county executive[6] explicitly because of their old political ties. On the other hand, past experience in the *Rathaus* or county seat at lower levels was sometimes considered useful, even essential, when certain technical/administrative positions were filled, provided the individual involved was not personally culpable in any way.

The general intent to remove old public officials was greatly tempered when it came to clerical personnel. Here, the need for continuity in procedures, the relatively mundane character of the jobs involved, and the legal rights protecting such job-holders all mitigated against wholesale dismissals. Aside from those with specifically unacceptable personal records, most were retained in the public employ.

This mix of local public officials was organized in each local council[7] by party fraction. With substantial variation from one instance to the next, the CDU (with its "Alliance" partners) and the SPD together won about 55-60 percent of all local parliamentary seats in 1990. Often they entered into governing coalitions or informal working majorities, an obvious consequence of the election results, the isolation of the PDS, and the oppositionist orientation of the Citizens' Movement fractions.

In the first weeks and months after the election, when knowledge and skill levels among eastern leaders were lowest and the legal and constitutional framework was most fluid, most new governments actively sought expert advice and assistance from the West. Often, this help was requested from "sister cities," where such ties had already been forged, or from national level western party organizations. For eastern towns without such previous connections, partnerships were pursued by the new governments after the election.[8]

This assistance was generously supplied, and it was no doubt important if not crucial for such successes in the reorganization of eastern local governments as subsequently occurred, especially during 1990 and 1991. Western experts were sent to work with and train eastern counterparts, sometimes for periods up to six months; eastern administrators and executives went west to observe local government in action there; instructional booklets and pamphlets were prepared in the West for general distribution to local officials throughout the new German states; east-west telephone contact developed and flourished between parallel specialists. Almost every local political entity in the East was aided in this fashion, and the result was at least the avoidance of complete system breakdown.

With the passage of time, eastern German towns and counties also hired administrators who had been trained in the West to head such bodies as their budget offices, their legal sections, and/or their departments for public order. Usually, these individuals were chosen for tasks no locals could perform adequately, and the government in Bonn encouraged Westerners to leave the relative comfort of Frankfurt am Main or Munich for the more Spartan environs of Magdeburg or Rostock by providing them special wage and retirement incentives.

The experience of hiring and bringing in western specialists was not entirely positive. Many such imports, to be sure, were able, expert and sensitive in their work and relationships with their new colleagues. Others, however, proved to be near disasters. Some came because they were otherwise unemployed or because their careers in the West were going nowhere. Some acted diplomatically, but others seemed to think they were colonial officials responsible for keeping "the Natives" in line. Overall, the problem stemmed from the simple fact that the more successful the western administrator was at home, the less likely he or she would be willing to move to the East.

Hiring western specialists also brought another problem, that of preserving morale between them and their eastern co-workers. The transplants were paid substantially more, even than their superiors, and the price of inducing them to move sometimes entailed the provision of housing or other fringe benefits. Such discrepancies in reward were not always a cause of tension, but they hardly facilitated work-place harmony.

In the end, the performance abilities and skills of the new east German local political and administrative leaders improved only over time. All benefited from on-the-job training, whether they were members of legislative bodies or the administration, and most who were publicly employed, from administrative leaders to clerical help, enrolled in correspondence courses or night schools. With time as well, those who could not or would not perform effectively were weeded out so that by the time the second legislative session began in 1994, the experience and training levels were no longer a major problem in most eastern towns and counties.

Structural Reorganization

When the 1990 local elections were held, East Germany still formally existed, and its laws still determined local competence and responsibility. Below the central structure in East Berlin, the intermediate governmental level was composed of 14 *Bezirke* (districts) that had been created in 1952. It was from them that local governments received direction.

All of this was soon to change. The GDR itself was set for swift incorporation into the Federal Republic, at which time West German law would take effect. In addition, there was to be a reorganization of the intermediate governmental level, where the *Bezirke* were slated for prompt replacement by the five *Länder* they had superseded in 1952.

All of this could only result in confusion for the new county and town governments. It was only after several years that the new federalist structure could be made fully operational, with functioning entities from the national to the grassroots level, and with an adequate body of federal and *Länder* level law pertaining to local matters. The new *Land* parliaments were particularly slow in enacting the laws and directives under which the local governments were to operate and be regulated.

Even this was not the end of reorganization at the local level, for the new German states also undertook *Gebiet Reform* designed to consolidate and/or amalgamate counties, towns and villages into larger entities that would be more efficient and professionalized. Counties were collapsed into larger units.[9] Small communities were encouraged to combine into administrative unions with neighboring villages while keeping their own mayors and councils, or to seek incorporation into larger towns where appropriate.

These reforms were completed only in 1994. In the process, many serious and time-consuming political controversies arose, over the location of county boundaries, the selection of the towns that would serve as county seats, the staffing of the new administrative entities, and the location of the new amalgamated administrative offices. Even after the reforms were completed, time was required to routinize procedures and to gain public acceptance of the changes.

Implementing Conversion Programs

As these structural and organizational changes were being effected, a number of one-time, substantive programs also had to be initiated to bring eastern localities up to western standards. This involved such things as converting energy usage from coal to natural gas; modernizing the telephone system; privatizing certain types of communal property and/or reorganizing other kinds into autonomous, quasi-public corporations; reorganizing kindergartens and schools; renovating and/or reconstructing historic buildings and town centers; upgrading water supply and sewage treatment systems; and, repairing most town and county streets and roads. There obviously was much to be done.

In some cases these improvements were made with relative ease and speed. But in most instances, this was anything but true, and for several reasons. For one thing, these matters often had a non-technical dimension where values and/or interests determined the decision-makers' policy preferences. Most communities, for example, held title to properties that had commercial possibilities. Some local officials favored their sale at prices favorable to the buyer, while others preferred to lease such assets to would-be developers, thus to preserve a public influence over their use. Similarly, disagreement was common over the appropriate strategy for developing town centers. Some favored the demolition of old structures and the reconstruction of new, commercially profitable buildings in their place. Others wanted to preserve "tradition," even at an economic cost. Settling these disagreements by expert assessment was simply not possible, for at issue was the balancing of high priority but conflicting values. And while such conflict might be an ever present element of politics, this was a new experience for eastern German local officials, many of whom were greatly troubled when they could not reach consensus about the correct and "true" way to resolve a problem.

Second, in many instances these issues also involved great technical complexity that required time-consuming professional analysis. Towns, for example, were required to prepare comprehensive land use plans before they could apply for special funds for renovation or re-construction, and in fact, such applications themselves required detailed explanations of the ways the requested money would be expended. Where such complexity was involved, many local leaders were unable to master the relevant materials. Nevertheless, govern-mental action was required, if progress were to occur, and the result was often uninformed debate in both the legislative body and within the administration, with excessive claims and/or misplaced criticisms dominating the discourse. It also was a circumstance ideal for the interested to cloak their politically-based preferences in technical or "scientific" garb. In this context, critics or opponents of any given plan generally had the advantage: they could raise countless objections, with or without merit, to which their opponents had difficulty responding. When that happened, the easy and usual consequence was to delay until the "experts" could be called in.

A third consideration that sometimes thwarted prompt local decision making was the finality and/or irreversibility of many of the pending issues once resolved. Commercial property when sold is gone; streets once laid assume permanence; and a long-term contract once signed with an energy supplier sets conditions and obligations for its duration. Local politicians, whose inexperience and lack of expertise had already made them cautious, were often pushed even further toward indecision and procrastination by this consideration. They were also most uncomfortable when choosing a merely acceptable alternative today when something superior (if illusive) might be identified and implemented at some indefinite time in the future.

Finally, and paradoxically, the massive transformational programs east German local governments were mandated to undertake often had adverse effects for at least some segments of the citizenry. Repairing roads or building new ones brought major inconvenience and individual costs to those whose homes fronted on them. The laying of phone and gas lines was also accompanied by disruptions for affected families. Closing kindergartens and schools meant the dismissal of some teachers and possible inconvenience for affected parents and students. Privatizing housing resulted in higher rent and lengthy intrusions in the home during the accompanying massive renovation. The outsider is apt to see these inconveniences as a small price to pay for the benefits involved. For the people on the spot, however, the dislocations during the transition assumed significant proportions, magnified perhaps by their general disillusionment with the course of post-unification development. In that context, local political leaders showed great sensitivity to public complaints, and they often delayed action while they tried to mollify all critics.

By 1994, despite the spate of problems here outlined, the accomplishments in this "catch-up" category of public policy implementation were not insignificant. A modern telephone system was in place, and tens of thousands of housing units were modernized or in the last stages of renovation. Considerable progress with the restoration of town centers was also recorded, though here much still remained to be done. The privatization of communal property and the promotion of economic and commercial activity also proceeded, if sometimes at an uneven pace. All in all, there was visible and tangible achievement, though the question remains whether more might have been done.

Routinizing Procedures

As these immediate, one-time issues were being confronted by local governmental leaders, there was also a need to normalize, even routinize the normal and recurring processes of government, at both the political and the administrative levels. In local councils, simply mastering procedures was often difficult for many deputies, particularly in the first sessions. They spoke without waiting for recognition and then carried on side discussions as others held the floor. Debates, were also needlessly long, especially on simple issues about which each member felt competent to voice an opinion, and many a local legislative body spent endless hours writing resolutions while in plenary session.

A related but less obvious problem in parliamentary practice was the misuse or nonuse of committees. On paper, these mini-parliaments (on which all fractions were represented) were to consider and make recommendations on non-emergency bills within their jurisdiction, all prior to plenary action. In practice, however, they were often circumvented, and when they did report out a bill, subsequent parliamentary debate still often proceeded entirely without regard to committee findings or recommendations.

These might seem to be trivial and certainly correctable problems. Taken together, however, they had serious consequences, for they considerably reduced parliamentary effectiveness, which in turn contributed to the diminution of their public reputation. They also resulted in wasting time, a particularly scarce commodity.

The task of normalizing the executive side of town and county government was especially difficult and complex. Even setting up a sound and workable organizational scheme and then heading departments and bureaus with able leaders was no easy matter; coordinating and leading them all in some coherent fashion and according to law and regulation was a test few mayors and county executives were able to pass. Thus, as might have been expected, deadlines were often missed, procedures were not correctly followed, budgets were overspent, and/or local legislative directives were not followed.

Often, there were serious and direct negative consequences when such lapses occurred. Special funding from *Land* or federal level governments might be denied, and/or local ordinance might be nullified by higher authority. Politically, public exposure of serious ineptitude might bring discredit upon the offending official or office, or even on the entire government from the mayor or county executive on down.

In the extreme case until the law was changed by *Länder* governments in 1992 and 1993, councils held the authority to vote their top executives out of office by passing "no confidence" motions, though passage of such bills required a two-thirds vote. Initiating such motions was a very common occurrence, and with surprising frequency, they passed.[10] By so acting, local council members showed themselves to be extremely active watchdogs over administrative actions, usually with salutary effect.

Of all recurring local governmental activity, budgeting and finance was and is clearly the most crucial, if only because of its role as prerequisite for virtually all other public actions. It is also among the most complex and arcane of subjects for the uninitiated and untrained, comprising as it does a special vocabulary, endless detail, and a multiplicity of rules for its calculation and integration.

Even this fails to show the full measure of difficulties faced by the new officials in the first months of their terms in office, for their situations were further complicated by the currency reform that brought the *Deutsche Mark* and by the organizational changes discussed earlier that complicated the timely flow of revenue from higher levels. Local officials also found the new, money-driven system of resource allocation to be fundamentally different from all their experience in the old days, when the plan determined who got what, when and how.

In those first days, stop-gap budgetary measures were the norm. Funds came in short-term infusions from superior level bodies. Western advisors were especially utilized in the finance area, though the situations they now faced were often unlike anything they had previously experienced. Only in rare cases did individual leaders show a special awareness and competence regarding public finance, and even then, they could make little difference. Local governments everywhere barely survived the first year, as far as funding was concerned.[11]

Thereafter, the process of normalizing the administrative side of planning the budget and then over-seeing its implementation made real if uneven headway. Many local governmental units hired western specialists as their chief accountants; holdover administrators with such responsibility completed crash training courses. Moreover, guidelines and direction from above also improved and were better understood, so that by 1993 or 1994 at the latest, the administrative processes for local public finance were essentially in place and functioning, at least in most localities.

The more difficult problem with public finance was political. Partly, this was so because the demands for absolutely necessary public services and programs were extraordinary. Had the resources made available been even greater, local government officials would still have faced financial scarcity, and given this exceptional need, local legislators found it difficult, even unconscionable, to curtail the outflow of funds.

Another problem, at least for the longer term, was the initial availability of special or targeted funds that were provided by *Land* or federal level sources. "Aufschwung Ost," a program that provided a one-time infusion of general purpose funds, is probably the best known, but targeted funding was also provided for such things as museums, theaters, and special social service facilities like hospitals. Local governments were also able to tap into the ABM[12] program that provided salaries for additional teachers, librarians and the like.

Initially, the infusion of these moneys was a great benefit. For the longer term, however, the practice also brought adverse consequences. In some cases, grants provided for start-up support but not for long-term, ongoing costs. In addition, the generous flow of initial funding also led many a local leader to hope or even to expect that Bonn or the *Land* level government would continue to provide "bail outs" as needed. In any case, not many public officials developed a "pay as you go" mentality in those early years.

A final factor contributing to financial woes for eastern local governments had different and partly external roots, but still should be noted here. That was the nature and limits of revenue generation under the formulae set under the new western-developed system. These rules, for example, said that towns were to receive 15 percent of the federally collected income tax. The problem here for the eastern recipient

entities was that the funds thus collected were allocated on the basis of
the income taxes paid by their own residents. Since easterners earned
lower salaries and wages than their western counterparts, town funding
was also comparatively low. The tax base in the east was also reduced
by the comparatively large number of locally unemployed.

Other funds were allocated on a per capita basis. Since most eastern
towns and counties experienced population outflows during these years,
their funds diminished over time, however great their needs. Finally,
towns received some of their funding from counties, which had
significant discretionary authority in setting the amounts. This
procedure would tend to set county against town in any case. But given
the special need for funds felt by all local governments during the
transition period, conflict between town and county over money
distribution was made even more serious.

It should be noted that both the federal and *Länder* governments
redistributed funds downward to compensate "revenue disadvantaged"
local entities. These equalization payments made up at least part of
any disparity. Even so, the net result for the East was a still substantial difference between their funding and that received by towns and
counties of comparable size in the West. Eastern towns also had only
quite limited opportunities to generate funds from local taxes. They
could charge license fees for pets or collect fines of various sorts, but such
sources were hardly serious revenue producers. Only by taxing
commercial activity could substantial sums be raised, and that source
was curtailed by the dismal state of the local economy.

Altogether, the financial condition of eastern local governments was
usually quite precarious by the end of the first legislative period in
1994. The result was that many towns and counties were forced to cut
back on investment and/or to draw on credit to cover programs beyond
the absolutely necessary. At the same time, the substantial progress
achieved by local governments in normalizing their budgeting processes
meant that their leaders had a much clearer understanding of the need
for austerity, and a better idea as to how that need might be met.

The Impact of External Factors

Despite their relative empowerment under the new system of
Selbstverwaltung or self-administration, local governments in eastern
Germany remained quite limited in authority and available resources.
In fact, they sometimes were confronted with problems for which they
were held accountable by their constituents, but about which they could
do little or nothing. Two of these problems were especially serious in

the first years, one in good part the result of national policy, and the other a dilemma apparently beyond solution by leaders at any governmental level.

The latter problem was the swift collapse of the East German economy in 1989-1990, and its continued depressed condition since then. One might dispute the causes involved and the inevitability of its coming, but what is relevant here is the indisputable fact of its occurrence. Its impact on the local governments of eastern Germany has been pervasive.

Often, the sorry state of the local job market was the only real obstacle to legislative action on a needed reduction of administrative personnel. In other cases, preferential treatment of local businesses and merchants was mandated by councils when contracts were given or supplies were purchased. In some towns, open air markets were shut down or severely restricted in the hopes of keeping outside sellers away. While no one thought that such actions could have much overall positive impact, at least sympathy was being shown for those in need.

The most serious attempts to promote job creation and economic stimulation centered on the efforts of many towns to develop commercial districts on previously undeveloped lands. Towns that had suitable available space moved to gain title to it, to lay down the needed infrastructure, and then to lease space to firms that agreed to make jobs-producing investment. For this undertaking, local governments were given access to special credits, and they also received favorable consideration by *Treuhand*,[13] the privatization agency, in the resolution of some types of outstanding property claims. The long-term benefits of such commercial districts, once fully in place, might well prove to be very significant. Their economic impact after several years, however, was slight. Acquiring properties was a difficult problem in itself; laying power and water lines and building roads took time, and could begin only after all property in the planned development had been acquired; most important of all, finding investors, who would open job-rich production plants proved particularly difficult in this age of high productivity and robotics. About the best result local leaders were able to obtain by the end of their first legislative term was the creation of some new jobs, but surely not enough to much change the continuing high unemployment rate.

The other external factor that bedeviled local governments was the explosion of claims on properties that had been improperly seized or taken over during the SED era. Almost no one disputed the legitimacy of most of the several million such claims that were filed, nor was there any disagreement about providing the victims compensation of some sort. But there was nearly universal objection in the East to Bonn's decision to apply the principle of *Rückgabe vor Entschädigung* or "restoration before compensation" in the settlement of these many claims, for it seemed to ignore eastern interests entirely. Residents in reclaimed housing, even if they had lived there for decades and had played no part in the original confiscation, were faced with the likelihood of expulsion. Often they had no idea where they might resettle. From this perspective, it is clear why most Easterners thought that some other form of compensation would have been more just. The fact that Bonn had decided otherwise was generally taken as evidence of their own second-class status.

Local governments in the East were not directly involved in all this, except in specific cases where contested property was in communal hands, or when a public use of such lands was planned. Yet many individual cases were tragic, and the sheer number of people facing uncertainty or worse made it a major community problem. When local leaders did respond, with individual protests or parliamentary protest resolutions, their impact was nil, which in turn could only diminish their public standing.[14]

Summary and Conclusion

Between December 1993 and June 1994 each of the new German states held local elections. By so doing, they forced incumbent town and county officials to explain and defend their records, and they gave an opportunity to alternative groups and individuals to criticize the officeholders and to offer their own visions and programs to the people. The public was then given a chance to register its own collective evaluation of accomplishment and failure. Finally, elections provided a convenient occasion to compare eastern German local government and politics as of 1994 with that of four years earlier.

The victors in the 1993-1994 local elections were a mix of old and new faces. In the typical local council, 50-50 percent of the deputies were newly installed. But while that was true, the key positions within the parliamentary fractions were nearly always taken by re-turnees or others who had been politically active during the first legislative period. Successful candidates for mayor or county executive (both of whom were now elected directly) were also either incumbents or individuals with substantial and well-known public records.

Within the executive branch of local governments, the personnel turnover rate was somewhat lower than for elective bodies. A new mayor might bring associates to the new team, but there were always others on it with experience and connections as well. At lower levels, public office-holders were hardly affected by election outcomes. By this time as well, most of them had completed special courses and had a good bit of on-the-job training.

Altogether then, the full range of local officialdom from top executives and legislators down to the lowliest of clerks was more qualified and better trained to conduct the public business of towns and counties than ever before. Even the differences between locals and western transplants diminished with the passage of time. This is not to say that personnel problems ceased to exist, or that elected officials were never ineffectual, narrow-minded, or self-serving. Rather, the point is that, generally, the mix of public officials in the East had become quite like that found in the West, in skill, training and perspective.

By 1994 as well, the restructuring of the system from the federal level down to local entities was mostly accomplished--or at least clearly mapped out. More than that, laws from above ordering relationships were in place, and the new vertical communication flows and resource allocation systems were functioning. The near vacuum of four years earlier had essentially been filled, and with the now experienced personnel, procedures were mostly normalized and set.

A somewhat positive assessment also seems warranted as to the implementation of special programs and efforts to overcome the East's relative backwardness. Telephone service was now reliable and the air no longer reeked of burning *Braunkohle*; homes were outfitted with new baths, kitchens, and individual thermostats. Though much remained to be done, it was difficult to deny that real and substantial progress had been made.

This is a rather favorable appraisal of the advances local eastern German governments had realized in a short period of time, and it stands in fairly sharp contrast to the collective judgment of the voters there, as of 1993-1994. Rather consistently throughout the new German states, voters turned unmistakably away from the parties of the center, i.e., the CDU and the SPD, to the PDS[15] and to so-called Free Voter Associations.[16] This is not to say that the CDU and SPD were annihilated in the 1993-1994 votes, and in fact, their combined vote often remained above 50 percent of all ballots cast. Rather, they were put on guard collectively, and in specific cases they were clearly rejected. Moreover, when the new local councils were constituted and the SPD now looked for coalition or cooperation partners, they sometimes found the now larger PDS fractions to be the most promising alternative, while the CDU now sometimes worked quite easily with the new Voter Associations. Voter turnout in 1993-1994 was well below that of 1990, another indication of voter dissatisfaction. In the earlier election 74 percent of the eligible electorate had turned out,[17] as against roughly 60 percent in the second.[18]

The question that suggests itself here is why did the voters show only limited satisfaction with the achievements of their local governments when here, in the above analysis, their collective records were rated rather more positively. The answer lies in the fact that here the emphasis has been given to organizational and procedural development, while the voters were primarily interested in substantive results. Beyond that, popular assessment seems to have been more diffuse than specific, not on the basis of how many streets had been paved or buildings renovated, but rather, whether one's general situation in 1994 was an improvement over that of 1990. Given the continued economic plight in the East and the continuing absence of a predicted upturn for the near future, easterners often saw things in a pessimistic light.

It therefore seems quite appropriate to conclude that local governments in the new German states are in a position to be effective participants in a viable democratic political order. To be so, however, requires that Germany achieve a level of integration and economic performance that still lies disturbingly well in the future. Even then, the question will remain whether effective local governments will translate that capacity into policies that are supported by their people. Until then, fairly or not, town and county officials and bodies will be accorded a generous share of the blame for the frustrations eastern Germans continue to have.

Notes

1. This chapter is based in part on field research conducted in 1991-92 and 1994. Funding was received from the *Fulbright Kommission* and the *Deutsche Akademischer Austausch Dienst*.

2. For an authoritative explanation of the role of local government in East Germany before 1989, see Klaus Sorgenicht, *Unser Staat in den achtziger Jahren* (Berlin: Dietz Verlag, 1982), especially pp. 63-65, 90-108, 167-70, and 221-25.

3. Germans make a clear distinction between *Gemeinde* (villages or very small towns) and *Städte* (towns and cities). The word "town" is used for both in this chapter. It should also be noted that the focus here will be on towns and cities smaller than the major metropolitan centers like Berlin or Leipzig.

4. The names given these groups varied, but *Bürgerkomitee* and *Runde Tisch* were most common.

5. The PDS (Party of Democratic Socialism) was the successor party of the SED or Socialist Unity Party that had ruled during the old era. The post-1989 CDU (Christian Democratic Union) was a reformed version of a "bloc" party of the same name, and the FDP (Free Democratic Party) had its roots in another bloc party, the LDPD (Liberal Democratic Party of Germany).

6. The German term for this position is *Landrat* or "district magistrate." The term "county executive," however, is more suggestive of the nature of the position.

7. The term council is used here to include all local legislative bodies in eastern Germany, past and present. Under earlier usage, a village had a *Gemeinde Rat*, while a town had a *Stadtverordneterversammlung*. Since 1994, the corresponding terms have been *Gemeinde-* and *Stadt-Rat*.

8. For an interesting report on the problems faced by the local political leaders in the first months after they assumed office, see Martin Osterland and Roderich Wahsner, "Der Schwierige Weg zur Demokratie," *Arbeitspapier* No. 6 of the Zentrale wissenschaftliche Einrichtung "Arbeit und Region," Universität Bremen, Dec. 1992. See also Oliver Scheytt, "Städte, Kreise und Gemeinden im Umbruch: Der Aufbau der Kommunalverwaltungen in den neuen Bundesländern," *Deutschland Archiv*, Vol. 25, No. 1 (Jan. 1992), pp. 12-21.

9. The *Land* Thuringia, for example, combined its previous 35 *Bezirke* into 17 new such units.

10. Apparently to help local legislators proceed with no confidence motions, Willi Buechner-Uhder published a brief article explaining the legal requirements for such action. See "Rechtliche Voraussetzungen zur Abberufung eines Bürgermeisters" in *Verwaltungsorgan*, Vol. 25 (1991), No. 11, p. 25.

11. See Gert-Joachim Glaessner, *Der Schwierige Weg zur Demokratie* (Opladen: Westdeutscher Verlag, 1992), p. 99.

12. This acronym stands for *Arbeitsbeschaffungmassnahmen* or "job creation measures."

13. The *Treuhandanstalt* (trust institution) was the agency created especially to privatize the public commercial assets in eastern Germany.

14. In early 1992, in the *Gemeinde* of Zepernick near Berlin, a deputy from the town council wrote a protest letter to Chancellor Kohl and then took his own life to underscore the seriousness of the problem. Zepernick was especially hard hit by claims; over 2,300 of them were filed in a village of about 8,000.

15. Calculating the PDS' share of votes for the entire area of the new German states is not easily done, since the elections were held at the *Land* level. Two comparisons, however, at least show the trend. In Zepernick (Brandenburg), the PDS received 14.1 percent of the vote in 1990, and 27.3 percent in 1993; in Arnstadt (Thuringia), the corresponding figures are 10.4 percent in 1990, and 15.4 percent in 1994. Data was provided the author by the *Hauptamt Leiter* of each town administration.

16. A "Free Voter Association" is a group set up under the law for the sole purpose of placing a slate of candidates on the election ballot. Such organizations have at times been successful in both eastern and western Germany when the

established parties have stood low in public esteem. Their typical appeal has been that they are above politics and for the welfare of all.

17. See Statistisches Amt der DDR, *Kommunalwahlen der DDR am 6. Mai 1990,* (Berlin: Datenverarbeitungszentrum, no date).

18. While the 1990 local election was conducted GDR-wide and was reported with GDR-wide results, the local elections of 1993-1994 were held individually at various times by each eastern German state. As a result, no single official source gives an exact overall turnout figure. The 60 percent approximation used here is based on the fact that Brandenburg reported a turnout of 59.73 percent, and in the *German Information Center* reported that turnouts in the June 12 local elections in Saxony, Mecklenburg-Vorpommern, Saxony-Anhalt, and Thuringia were right at 60 percent. For Brandenburg, see Landesamt für Datenverarbeitung und Statistik, *Kommunalwahlen 1993* (Potsdam: März, 1994). See also The German Information Center, "Local Elections: CDU Gains in West, Remains Strong in East; PDS becomes Third Strongest Eastern Party," *The Week in Germany*, (New York: June 17, 1994).

3

The Party of Democratic Socialism in the German Unification Process, 1989-1997

Jörg Roesler

The Party of Democratic Socialism is the youngest and the most controversial political party in Germany. Most of the literature about it has been written by either followers[1] or outspoken opponents[2] of the party. Only in 1996 was a book published about the PDS that was widely accepted as the successful attempt at an impartial and sober analysis.[3] In this chapter the focus will be on the development of the PDS as a part of the integration of the former communist society and structures into the Federal Republic of Germany. The first section gives an overview of the development of the PDS and asks how it was influenced by the processes of unification. The second section presents the different "faces" of the PDS and tries to explain why the party became able to attract quite different social strata of voters. A third section is dedicated to the demands of the integration processes on the PDS in the middle of the 1990s. It describes how these demands were discussed within the party and which strategies were proposed to keep pace with the changes in society and structures. The last section considers the controversial question of whether or to what degree the PDS by its existence supports or tries to prevent the integration of the East into the larger Germany. This section ends up with a tentative look at the insecure future of both--the integration processes and the PDS.

An Overview of PDS History 1989-1997

The Origins of the PDS

The PDS came into being in an attempt to modernize the old communist state party, the Socialist Unity Party SED (*Sozialistische Einheitspartei Deutschlands*). The party had to be made competent to campaign in the first free elections which were to decide the future of the German Democratic Republic. This process lasted from December 1989 to March 1990. A number of main events occurred during these months. First, the election of Gregor Gysi in December 1989 and the change of the party name from Socialist Unity Party (SED) into SED-PDS (Party of Democratic Socialism) underlined the new commitment to a pluralistic socialist society. Secondly, the SED-PDS congress in February 1990 defined the role of the party in the discussion of German unification as "pro-GDR." The congress also made decisions about the decentralization and democratization of party structures, nominated the reformer Hans Modrow, prime minister of the GDR from November 1989, as its top candidate, and changed the party name to Party of Democratic Socialism. In the March 1990 elections the PDS won a notable sixteen percent of the votes. It became the main opposition party to the GDR governing coalition of Christian Democrats and Social Democrats, both of which favored immediate economic and political unification.[4]

The Expected Downturn of the PDS, 1990 -1991

During summer 1990 the PDS was involved in creating a party organization in the west of Germany as well. The PDS leadership hoped to convince supporters of the left in the electorate of the old *Länder* that the PDS as a socialist party could fill the gap in the political spectrum there.[5] However, in the federal elections in December 1990 the postcommunists got only between 0.5 and 1.0 percent of the votes in the old states. In the new states the PDS share of the votes decreased from 16 (March 1990) to 11 percent. On average the PDS received 2.4 percent of all votes in Germany.[6] Under normal conditions the PDS would not have gained access to parliament, but the entrance hurdles had been removed for the first all-German election.[7]

At the end of 1990 problems were obvious: the PDS had failed to establish itself in the West as a socialist party left of the Social Democratic Party (SPD). It had also notably lost votes in the East.[8] According to opinion polls, the PDS lost ground during the entire year 1991. In December 1991 only five percent of east Germans were ready to vote for the postcommunists in the next elections. The PDS downturn was also reflected in a rapid decrease in party membership, a process which had begun in the autumn revolution in 1989. Membership fell from 2.3 million in September to 1.5 million in December 1989. By March this number had halved again. Membership continued to decrease in 1990 and 1991: it fell from 400,000 in May 1990 to 284,000 in December 1990 and to 150,000 in September 1991.[9] Some German political scientists were convinced at that time that the PDS would not survive the next years. With the end of GDR, the PDS had lost one of its main issues of the spring elections. The party seemed to have electoral support now only from the former party and administrative elite, and the party was torn by inner divisions and plagued by financial difficulties. Forced to dismantle the once powerful party apparatus it had taken over from the SED, the PDS would become insignificant during the next years, unable to play a role in the 1994 elections.[10]

The Unexpected Rise of the PDS After 1991

In the Berlin elections of June 1992 the PDS became the strongest party in the eastern districts of Berlin. There it gained from 20 to 40 percent of all votes.[11] The state elections in Berlin not only stopped the down turn of the PDS in elections; it also showed that the party was now on an upswing. Since then the PDS has continually increased its share of the votes in the new states. In the 1994 federal elections it was able to double its percentage (4.4 percent compared with 2.4 percent in 1990). Though the PDS remained below the five percent mark, it was able to enter parliament for the second time by winning four districts in east Berlin--compared with only one in 1990. Its number of seats in parliament increased from 17 to 30.[12] However, the party's growing success in elections was not accompanied by a general improvement of the situation of the PDS. Membership continued to decrease. It fell from 173,000 at the end of 1991 to 147,000 in 1992, 131,000 in 1993, 124,000 in 1994, and 115,000 in 1995.[13] The party's financial situation also remained unfavorable compared with that of the established parties.[14]

The number of paid party officials had to be reduced to less than two hundred compared with the 44,000 party bureaucrats of SED times,[15] and the strife within the leadership of the PDS between marxists and pragmatists did not end. It became more intense again in 1995 and 1996.[16] Thus, the upswing of the PDS resulted probably more from developments outside than inside the party.

If we look at the annual opinion polls for the new states we find a very important explanation. Among the population in the East, skepticism grew about the ability of the market economy to avoid high unemployment and to create a self-sustained "upswing East"[17] as did the discontent with the political and party systems of west Germany, introduced in 1990.[18] Positively astonished by the results it had obtained in the Berlin state elections of June 1992, the PDS leadership began to rethink its basic strategies, a process, which up to now has continued. The party began to change from what was mainly a reservoir of opponents to unification into a party increasingly representing eastern interests in the united Germany.[19]

The Faces of the PDS

Party Structure and PDS Pluralism

The predecessor of the PDS, the SED was a typical eastern bloc communist party with a streamlined ideological argumentation for the public and tight party discipline for the membership. Many of the former SED members who remained in the party (in winter 1989-90) acknowledged that unanimity of voice and strict party discipline were two of the reasons why the old SED had been unable to reform itself and the GDR. The first factions appeared spontaneously in January 1990.[20] At the party congress in February 1990 the former SED reformers, now in the lead, decided that the PDS should no longer be a party with a unified world view (*Weltanschauungspartei*). There should be room for different and also contradictory political views within the PDS.[21] The new party structure made room for the creation of groups within the party on the basis of common political ideas, which classified them as "left of center" or "far left" (*Plattform, Forum*); common social backgrounds (*Arbeitsgemeinschaften*); common interest on certain topics (*Interessengemeinschaften*); as well as for the realization of short-term political goals (*Initiativgruppen*).[22] As a result of this decentralization and liberalization, the PDS has many faces and the party attracts different groups of the electorate. In the following section four "faces" are discussed.

The Party of "Real Opposition": Left of the Social Democratic Party

During the 1970s and 1980s the differences between the programs of the established parties of the Federal Republic diminished. They focused increasingly on the middle class *(Mittelstand)* and the political center. In the 1980s the Greens, a new party founded at the beginning of the 1980s, also began to represent middle class interests.[23] For those dissatisfied with the increasingly centrist orientation of the SPD and the Greens, the PDS represented an alternative. Most such dissatisfied voters lived in the old *Länder*, but their number was limited. In 1994 between 0.6 percent of the electorate (Bavaria) and 2.7 percent (Bremen) voted for the PDS. In 1990 half of them had voted for the Greens or the SPD. In the new states supporters of the "left of the SPD" strategy had their strongholds among activists in Berlin; however, as part of the whole electorate of the PDS, their number should not be underestimated--it probably constituted one-fifth.[24]

The Party of Fundamental Opposition to Capitalism

When the socialist GDR vanished in 1990, some of the communist hard-liners stayed in the PDS. Others vigorously rejected the general accusations of the western parties and media that the GDR had been an unlawful state. They also saw the PDS as their stronghold against the flood of west-German-style political, social, and economic "mod-ernization" measures. Members with these opinions organized them-selves as early as January 1990 in the "communist platform."[25] The GDR institutions had been demolished by the West; thus, the members of the communist platform concentrated their attention on the GDR past. They defended it indiscriminately against all accusations from the 1989 revolutionaries and the West German media and politicians. The minority--among the party members it may be perhaps even a majority--was silent during the party's debates after 1990. Only in the last few years did they begin to express their views more vigorously. They became bolder in their demands, when the disadvantages of the West German political system and of the market economy became more obvious for former GDR citizens during the middle of the 1990s. In 1995 through 1996 economic growth in east Germany began to falter.[26] The eventual catching up with the West in living standard was postponed to the first decade of next century,[27] and unemployment remained stable at a high level.[28] GDR nostalgia, in the West often seen as a mark of the whole of the PDS, was highly represented in this group.

The People's Party of Eastern Solidarity

Supporters of this view of the PDS derive their critique of the West less from the socialist past of East Germany than from the present problems of transition. They are pragmatists, who pledge to stick together against west German dominance[29] in political and economic life. West Germans have taken over most of the former state-owned property in east Germany: they own most of the enterprises and rental accommodations.[30] A large-scale exchange of elites was organized. The west German sociologist Klaus v. Beyme described the reason for it in the following way: "shortly after unification, the great 'witch hunt' started in the former GDR; a negative cadre policy and an anti-nomenklatura policy[31] were developed and implemented in reunified Germany."[32]

In early 1990, the governing Christian Democratic Union (CDU) appeared to have no interest in investigating the past in East Germany. By 1992, however, even a liberal minister of education was under increasing pressure to dismiss a number of former East German administrators, teachers, and professors. Since the "elite transfer,"[33] west Germans hold leading positions in the administrations of the eastern state governments and at the universities.[34] Thus, in the eyes of east Germans, westerners are responsible for enterprise closure because of mismanagement, insecurity of the property of easterners, rent increases, unfriendly behavior of the bureaucracies, etc.[35] To protect the population against the adverse social consequences of the market economy and west German dominance, many PDS members work at local levels in the administration, or play leading roles in organizations for the protection of tenants and small entrepreneurs of east German origin. They are engaged in the defense of those who are threatened by property claims of west Germans. These party members think more of the East-West axis, concentrating on the difference between *Ossis* and *Wessis*, than on the old Marxist division of the vertical axis of "above and below," or between expropriators and expropriated.[36] A typical example is the PDS-influenced east German small entrepreneurs' associations. [37]

In the first years after unification the small capitalists of the new states hoped for advice and support from the three employer organizations of the Federal Republic. The west German employer's organizations supported a variety of tax breaks and investment incentives to stimulate economic growth in the new states. But as its critics have charged, they are "more interested in securing lucrative opportunities for large west German firms than in helping create an indigenous entrepreneurial class in east Germany."[38] In autumn 1994 the east German entrepreneurs therefore created an employers' organization of their own, OWUS *(Offener Wirtschaftsverband der klein- und mittelständischen Unternehmer, Freiberufler und Selbständigen)* for the *Länder* Berlin and Brandenburg. Other new states followed suit. The new employers' organizations were promoted by the PDS and Christa Luft, former economics minister in the Modrow government (1989-90), and Christine Ostrowski, a leading figure of the PDS in Dresden, who played decisive roles in initiating the first OWUS organizations in Berlin-Brandenburg and Saxony.[39]

East German entrepreneurs see their main enemy in the large (west German) banks and corporations.[40] There are also demands for restrictions on wages and social subsidies in their enterprises, publicly pronounced at a PDS entrepreneurs conference in Saxony in June 1996. This has notably embarrassed the marxists in the PDS.[41]

The Party of Calculated Protest

Protest voters are usually those who vote for a party with political goals they do not particularly share. Nevertheless, they vote for it because they are dissatisfied with the actual policy of the party of their choice. These voters may return to their original party at a later election.

When the PDS had it first successes beginning with the Berlin state elections in June 1992, its upswing was seen by some political scientists as a result of protest votes and therefore certain to be short-lived. But an analysis of PDS electors after the 1994 federal elections presented another explanation. Nearly seventy percent of the PDS-electorate had been adherents of the party four years earlier. Compared with the 1990 federal elections in the East only 15 percent of PDS voters had changed from the SPD to the postcommunists and only 9 percent from the CDU.[42] However, protest votes did play a role in the election gains of the PDS in the new states for the people who disagreed with most of the PDS's theses but nevertheless voted for the postcommunists. This can be demonstrated by the fact that 50 percent of the PDS voters in 1994 believed that the former GDR "had fewer good sides than bad ones." Some forty percent were even against a take-over of large parts of the economy by the state. One-third of the PDS voters had doubts about or rejected completely the thesis that "socialism was a good idea, only badly managed in the GDR."[43]

For protest voters the main reason to vote PDS was to register their disappointment with not one or another of the other parties, but with all of them, because even their east German deputies of mainstream parties have not been able to represent and fight for the interests of east Germans. The established parties of the Federal Republic, especially the CDU, successfully imposed parliamentary party discipline on the east German deputies to the Bundestag. That means the east German deputies had to submit to the aims of the west German dominated parties, and in parliamentary debates east German deputies speak with the same voice as their west German counterparts--if they speak at all. The PDS, sometimes together with eastern deputies of the Greens, is the only exception.[44] As one east German politician put it: "The PDS derives its strength from the weakness of the eastern wings of the other parties."[45]

Is There a Dominant "Face" of the PDS?

The electorate which votes for the PDS, 19.8 percent of the population in east Germany in the 1994 election, stems from all social strata of the population in the new states. It is an unexpected mixture if we have in mind the background of its predecessor the SED as "a workers party." The present party includes more entrepreneurs and other self-employed (16.9 percent) than workers (14.7 percent), more privileged civil servants *(Beamte)* (34.6 percent) than "average" employees *(Angestellte)* (26.3 percent), fewer pensioners (16.5 percent) than people in vocational training and university (28.4 percent), and slightly more unemployed (23.7 percent) than employed (20.4 percent). While the PDS membership is aging and newcomers represent only five percent of the membership, the PDS share of juvenile voters (18-24 years old) and young adults (25-34 years old) is notably higher (22.6 and 23.0 percent respectively) than that of pensioners (16.9 percent). The PDS voters are fairly evenly split by gender (20.3 percent of all male and 19.7 percent of all female voters).[46]

Given the heterogeneous social background of the PDS voters, it is not difficult to understand the different "faces" of the PDS. But which of the "faces" is the dominant one? Gero Neugebauer and Richard Stöss, who in 1996 published the most serious analysis of the PDS so far, refrained from assessing the "ideology structure" of the party.[47] Patrick Moreau and Jürgen Lang, who provide another analysis of the PDS, reduce the faces more or less to one: the party of fundamental opposition to market economy and western-style democracy. While they think that the whole PDS is leftist and dangerous for the Federal Republic, the FRG ministry of the interior assesses only some groups inside the PDS as belonging to the left extremists.[48] It seems that it is too early to analyze the strength of the adherents of the different "faces" of the PDS. But one way to give an answer to the question is to analyze which face of the PDS has impressed the other parties in east Germany in their policies towards the PDS.

In the first years after unification the established parties described the PDS mainly as the party of fundamental opposition to market economy and western democracy and treated the Party of Democratic Socialism as non-existent. Later on, influential members of the federal leadership of the SPD and the Greens became aware of the democratic potential of the PDS as a party "left of the SPD." Arguments in favor of cooperation with the PDS on local and state but not central levels were published. After the 1994 state elections in Saxony-Anhalt, a minority government of the SPD and Greens was created, which depended on the support of the PDS deputies in the state parliament in order to surpass the blocking votes of the CDU opposition.[49] Meanwhile, in Mecklenburg-West Pomerania and Thuringia the SPD is thinking about cooperation with the PDS in case the shaky "grand coalitions" with the CDU in both states cannot be renewed after the next elections.[50]

Most impressed by and at the same time worried about the image of the PDS as "the peoples party of Eastern solidarity" were the established parties. In this connection two arguments play primary roles. The first argument concerns the day-to-day party work of the PDS in towns and villages. PDS members, as mayors or representatives of organizations protecting the population against rent increases, property losses, bureaucratic administrators, etc. are "able and hard-working" with sympathy and understanding for the grievances of youth, the unemployed, pensioners, and other groups. This could be heard repeatedly from independent, CDU and SPD speakers from the new states at a conference about the PDS at Tutzing in March 1996.[51] The second argument concerns the representation of eastern interests in the federal parliament, on the central boards of the established parties, etc. At the Tutzing conference on the PDS one SPD member from the state of Brandenburg said bluntly, "If former GDR citizens are ousted from the supra-regional committees (of the SPD, CDU etc.), or are only tolerated as *Alibi-Ossis* (token east Germans), its not surprising that the PDS is seen as the only legitimate representative of the East."[52] The feeling that they must do more for the interests of the east German population is widespread among the eastern deputies of the established parties in the new *Länder*. In the first half of 1996 some "rebellions" of CDU, SPD, and Green deputies were predicted. But they were quelled by the federal leadership.[53] Thus it seems that at least since 1996 the PDS face of the "peoples party of eastern solidarity" has been the most influential of the different PDS factions in the political landscape of the new *Länder*.

Debates Inside the PDS in the Middle of the 1990s

The decentralized PDS party structure, created in 1990, favored debates and "struggle" among party members and factions from the beginning. The following section presents some of these debates which took place predominantly in 1996. Most of these debates reflect new developments in the process of integration of the new states and represent challenges for the PDS.

The Debate on Participation in Government

During the first years after unification when the PDS was boycotted by the established parties, it developed a self-understanding as a party of "real opposition." For the 1994 elections the PDS presented the slogan, "Change begins with opposition," thus indicating that opposition should not be its permanent role in the future. In 1994 the PDS got into a role of "tacit partnership" with the Social Democratic Party of Saxony-Anhalt and in a certain sense also in Mecklenburg-West Pomerania. The debates among the postcommunists concentrate on the question of whether the PDS can remain a party of "real opposition" and the party of solidarity with the common people, if it has to make political compromises as an official or tacit member of a (minority) government. The most outspoken supporters of future government participation are André Brie, the PDS leader responsible for organizing elections, and Gregor Gysi, leader of the parliamentary party of the PDS and its former chairman.[54] The most vigorous opposition comes from the fundamentalists of the communist platform. This group fears that the PDS as a governing party would develop into a "second social democratic party" and would thus make itself superfluous.[55] In addition, the more moderate "Marxist Forum" is concerned about the readiness of the PDS leadership to take over government responsibility.[56]

The Debate on "Coping with the GDR Past"

Those groups in the SPD and the Greens which favor cooperation with the PDS demand that the PDS separate itself from its leftist groups, especially from the "communist platform."[57] In addition to the pressure of the established parties the ministry of interior also demands that the PDS leadership expel all "left extremism" in the party. In May 1995 a group headed by the deputy of the federal parliament Uwe-Jens Heuer, which later formed the *Marxistisches Forum*, warned the party leadership against giving in to outside pressure.

At the same time the indiscriminate defenders of the GDR past began to raise their voices more publicly. That has provoked a new heated debate about Stalinism in the SED and GDR and especially about the role of the GDR secret service, the Stasi.[58] The most outspoken condemnation of the undemocratic GDR past came from those members of the PDS leadership who also favor cooperation with the established parties and government participation in the future: Gregor Gysi and André Brie.[59]

The Debate About the PDS
as an Entrepreneur-Friendly People's Party

This debate was initiated by a "letter from Saxony," written by Christine Ostrowski and other leading PDS members from the Dresden region.[60] The letter puts the small east German entrepreneurs in the center of "left economic policy," maintaining that "without an indigenous *Mittelstand* there will be no self-sustained economic development." The authors renounce any "class struggle," but argue that a stronger *Mittelstand* will create more working places and thus increase social security and the standard of living of everyone. They demand that the PDS concentrate exclusively on eastern Germany and dissolve its party bureaus in the old *Länder*. The PDS should become a "socialist people's party" which is honored for the practical fight for justice and freedom, e.g. undertaking actions in the parliaments and on the streets against rent increases and cuts in the local traffic network. The authors dismiss a policy "left of the SPD" and demand that the party give up its "fruitless attempts" to get roots in the West.

The "letter from Saxony" initiated a fierce debate inside the PDS. Opponents characterized the theses of the letter as giving up the social interests of the PDS for "national" (east German) interests. They attacked the authors' support of the private sector and the fact that they have given up the "all German commitment" of the PDS.[61]

From Party Congress to Election Program:
The PDS Between January and December 1997

The debates discussed above preceded the PDS congress in January 1997, and all who participated in the debates had in mind and often referred to the upcoming congress. The official topic of the congress was "the social question." However attention inside and outside the PDS focused on which of the above-mentioned currents within the PDS would dominate the congress, and a decision about joining or supporting governments in the 1998-99 federal and *Länder* elections was also expected.

At the congress a clear majority favored taking part in future governments formed by the SPD and the Greens. This was a victory for the leadership of the PDS, which supported the PDS as a left-wing "all-German" party. The vote represented a defeat for the other groups within in the party, which looked more to the new *Länder*, but especially for the communist platform. However, this platform was not ousted as some PDS leaders originally wanted. The heated debate about "Stalinism," which had taken place in 1996, did not continue at the 1997 Congress. PDS leader Lothar Bisky was re-elected with a comfortable majority (88 percent), and the candidates for the party board *(Vorstand)* favored by Bisky were also elected.[62]

The draft of the election program published in December 1997 gave unresolved social questions (low economic growth, mass unemployment, social injustice) a high priority, thus continuing the main topic of the party congress from January. Declaring that "many problems in east Germany are the difficulties of the whole country, only sharpened to a point," and demanding a social and ecological reshuffling of German politics and society, the program underlines the PDS claim to be the party of real opposition for the left electorate in the whole of Germany and a possible partner for the SPD and the Greens. But the program also includes the demand for a special economic program for the new states and it especially promises support for small- and medium-sized enterprises in eastern Germany. This pleases those parts of the electorate that will vote for the PDS as an entrepreneur-friendly people's party of eastern solidarity. The program rebukes the demands of the communist platform and makes the task of "coping with the GDR past," a marginal topic.[63]

The PDS and the Integration of the New States
into Germany: An Assessment

Political Integration

The political integration of east Germany into the Federal Republic has been often defined as adoption of the west German political systems and especially the political party system. In this narrower sense, political integration began even before economic and administrative integration really took place. It began as early as spring 1990, when the main parties of West Germany took patronage over old or newly-founded parties in the GDR, influencing their structures and programs. In the March 1990 elections nearly three-quarters of all votes went to those parties already existing in the West, or to their new eastern allies.[64] The parties of the revolutionaries of autumn 1989 received less than ten percent of the vote and did not continue to play a role in the political landscape of east Germany. The only stumbling block which remained for a complete unification of the party system was the PDS with 16 percent of the vote. The 1990 *Länder* elections as well as the federal election in the second half of 1990 confirmed the change in the political party landscape in conformance with west German patterns. The PDS was reduced to 11 percent of the vote in the East.

However, the tendency to create the typical party landscape of the old *Länder* in the new *Länder*--a party system with four parties: CDU, FDP, SPD and Greens--ended in 1992-1993 at the state level and in 1994 at the federal level. Since autumn 1994 two distinct party landscapes have existed in Germany--a western one with Christian Democrats, Social Democrats, Free Democrats, and Greens, and an eastern three-party system with the CDU, SPD, and PDS.[65]

If one reduces the problem of political integration to the party structure, then the PDS was and is the main cause for a delayed completion of the political integration of the East. But such a conclusion would be short-sighted for it involves, in my opinion, three errors from independent, CDU, and SPD speakers from the new states.

The first error: reducing integration into the West to imitation of the West. Imitation means the renunciation of any distinct political development in the East. This is a very narrow definition of integration, and it contradicts even West German historical experience. The party landscape of Bavaria differs from that of the other old states. It has a Christian and democratic party of its own, the Christian Social Union, CSU, which favors a special "Bavarian identity" inside the Federal Republic. CSU deputies in the federal parliament (and CSU ministers in the government) are eager and successful in fighting for Bavarian interests in Bonn. The special role of the CSU has been often described by political scientists, but nobody has characterized the CSU as a disintegrative power.[66] It would be only fair to assess the (predominantly) regional party of eastern Germany, the PDS, from the same point of view as the CSU. But in contrast to the CSU in Bavaria with its centralized party structures, the PDS is characterized by decentralization. Therefore, it is necessary to look to the different "faces" of the PDS in order to discover its attitude toward integration into Germany in the wider sense.

Those members and sympathizers of the PDS who think of it as a party of "real opposition left of the SPD" intentionally pursue a course of *political* integration, with special emphasis on the federal and state level. For supporters of the entrepreneur-friendly "people's party of eastern solidarity," *economic* integration into the market economy is the obvious feature. Political integration is pursued notably on the local and state level in order to get into better administrative positions to protect the *Ossis* from western dominance. Only the adherents of the PDS as a "party of fundamental opposition to capitalism" reject political as well as social and economic integration into the capitalist state. Advocates of this thinking, who mainly belong to the communist platform within the party, represent only a minority within the PDS with estimates ranging from 500 to 6,000 members[67] or approximately one to five percent of the PDS membership. To identify this face of the PDS with the whole party, would simply be wrong.

Up to now I have excluded those PDS voters for whom the PDS is predominantly a party of calculated protest. I turn to them now when speaking about the second mistake in the assessment of the PDS attitude toward integration: reducing the electorate to those who vote. This assessment forgets the non-voters, but they should not be overlooked, not least because of their magnitude. They appeared for the first time as a "mass movement" in the Berlin state elections of 1992, when non-voters represented the strongest "party" in Berlin with 39 percent of the whole electorate.[68] In the federal elections of 1994, their number exceeded the three million mark in the new states, with more than a quarter of the eligible population not voting, compared with less than 20 percent in the old states. In three of the state elections in the new *Länder* (Saxony, Saxony-Anhalt, and Brandenburg) the number of non-voters was even higher--between forty and forty-five percent.[69] Compared with 1990 voting patterns, the general trend in the East was an increase in non-voters. The structure of east German non-voters in the new *Länder* was somewhat unusual for Germany as revealed in an analysis by Ursula Feist. The share of youth and of young men and women was extraordinarily high. Feist wrote about a "dramatic aggravation" of abstentions and described the majority of non-voters as protesters against the repercussions of the new political and societal system, introduced by the West in the former GDR.[70]

That characterization of the majority of non-voters as protesters is also supported by other analysts.[71] Dissatisfaction continued to exist in 1996, as shown by an opinion poll of the news magazine *Die Zeit*, which stated that 63 percent of east Germans were dissatisfied with the economic system, 57 percent with the social security system, and 54 percent with the state of democracy in Germany.[72] The opinion poll also reveals that only a minority of those who were dissatisfied with the political system and with the process and direction of economic and social changes that have taken place since 1990 in eastern Germany voted for the "protest party" PDS. There is a notable difference between the two types of protest. Those who voted for the PDS also voted against the established party system of the Federal Republic, but for the political system of parliamentary democracy.[73] It seems therefore doubtful to add the 10 to 15 percent of the adults who voted for PDS to the 25 to 45 percent of non-voters.

The disparity between the two groups should be underlined. The PDS voters signal their disagreement with the methods and results of political, social, economic, and cultural integration, but also their willingness to take part in the transformation. At the same time, by taking part in the elections, they hope to influence the transformation concerning how to tackle problems and eliminate failures. In this sense Neugebauer and Stöss characterize the PDS as a necessary and useful part of the political system of the Federal Republic.[74]

The third error: viewing political developments as independent developments. Rather, political developments are influenced by social and economic changes. The interdependence of these factors should be taken into consideration to explain the role of the PDS in the process of German integration.

The history of the PDS is the best example of the close interaction between political, social, and economic developments. The renewed upswing of the PDS since 1992 was not caused by an attractive new strategy of the PDS, and the party was astonished by the positive response of a large part of the electorate toward the postcommunists. This has been confirmed repeatedly by the PDS leadership.[75] Not the virtues of the PDS leadership, but the disappointment of large part of the east German population with the politics of the CDU-led government,[76] has been the main cause for the election successes of the PDS in the years since 1992. If the PDS had not existed in 1992, it would have had to be invented. Indeed there had been several attempts between December 1991 and May 1992 to found a special east German party.[77] These attempts became superfluous because the PDS, after months of aimlessness, was able to take over this function.

The completion of the social and economic integration of the new *Länder* has been postponed further, eventually into the first decades of the new century. Self-sustaining economic growth of the east German economy had not been reached by 1997. The often proposed "second economic miracle" did not take place in the new *Länder*.[78] The East remains a distinct area of Germany in social and economic terms, as a comparison of several economic and social criteria for the old and new *Länder* demonstrate. Compared with the West (100) in 1995, real GDP per employee was 44 percent in the East, nominal income per head 52 percent, private consumption 69 percent, and wage-based costs of production *(Lohnstückkosten)*, 135 percent.[79] The initial change in the political landscape of east Germany in 1990-1991 according to west German patterns was not lasting. East Germany turned back to a political landscape of its own, because the predicted rapid economic and social equalization of the new *Länder* to the west German level did not take place.

The Future of the Integration of the Länder and the Future of the PDS

Political scientists have given different answers to questions about the future of the PDS, some cautiously optimistic and others predominantly pessimist, but mainly relying on the (other) mentality of the east Germans.[80] Another way of answering this question is to rely on the connection between political, economic, and social development. Data about the economic and social development of the new *Länder* are available. Can they be used for a more reliable prognosis about the future of the PDS?

Beginning the analysis of the future prospects of the PDS not with data about the mentality of the population, but instead with data about economic development in the new *Länder* is an advantage only superficially. On the one hand, it makes the prognosis easier because economists have a well-developed apparatus for forecasts of short-, medium-, and long-range. On the other hand, it aggravates the forecast because most economists hesitate to give a prognosis about the eventual economic integration of the East into the (West) German economy.[81] Wegener refers to the large number of miscalculations by economists since 1990 concerning economic development in the new *Länder*.[82] For instance, it was calculated that the "upswing East" would begin immediately after currency union in summer 1990, but an upswing occurred only in 1992.[83] When the growth began, some leading economists expected an annual increase of ten percent, in some years predicting even 15 to 20 percent.[84] The highest growth in GNP reached by 1996 was 8.5 percent in 1994. But even the growth at the lower than expected level of 8 percent (the average of the years 1992-1994) could not be achieved during the following two years, when only 70 percent (1995) or 38 percent (prognosis for 1996) of the 1992-94 average was reached.[85] The downturn in the growth rates of the new *Länder* was as embarrassing for most economists as was the late start of "upswing East" some years before.

What makes any economic prognosis for eastern Germany extremely difficult is the fact that its economic growth depends not simply on the development of the region itself but also on outside factors. Such factors include the amount of money that will be transferred to the new *Länder* from the old. Therefore eastern growth depends on economic development in west Germany and on the readiness of the west German population to share their income with east Germans. Though the peak of transfers (1993) has passed, the payments involved have been large up through 1996, when 34.7 percent of the east German GDP was derived from transfers. These transfers correspond to 4.3 percent of west German GNP.[86] How large the amount of western transfers to the East will be in the future is an economic *and* a political question.

Another outside influence is an economic one: since 1990 east Germany has been turned into a branch plant economy of west Germany. The large and medium-sized enterprises in the new *Länder* are "nearly exclusively" subsidiaries of west German and foreign corporations. The headquarters of nearly all larger enterprises in the East are situated outside the new *Länder*.[87] This means decisions about investments or closures of enterprises in the East are based predominantly on the needs of the corporation and not necessarily on east German economic conditions and interests.

These factors explain why economists hesitate to make prognoses about the "upswing East" in the future.[88] Since these forecasts are not available, it will be difficult to describe the future of the PDS. But is an economic prognosis really not possible? The majority of economists agree on certain points: the economy of east Germany will not be in line with that of west Germany before the first or second decade of the next century. The income of easterners will not catch up with that of westerners in this century. And mass unemployment will remain permanently high, higher than in the old *Länder*.[89]

Accepting this common understanding of economists as a reliable prognosis, some political predictions can be made. Without full integration, special social and economic interests will remain dominant in eastern Germany and will find their political expression. As long as the established parties of the Federal Republic of Germany are structurally unable to express the interests of large parts of the east German population, and as long as the PDS remains dominantly the "people's party of eastern solidarity," it best corresponds to the political situation of the new *Länder*. Under these two preconditions, the PDS has in the long-term a future in the east of Germany.

Notes

1. Lothar Bisky, Jochen Czerny, Helmut Mayer, and Michael Schumann (eds.), *Die PDS-Herkunft und Selbstverständnis. Eine politisch-historische Debatte* (Berlin: Dietz, 1996).

2. Manfred Gerner, *Partei ohne Zukunft? Von der SED zur PDS* (München: Tilsner Verlag, 1994); Patrick Moreau, Jürgen Lang, and Viola Neu, *Was will die PDS?* (Frankfurt am Main/Berlin: Ullstein Verlag, 1994); Patrick Moreau and Jürgen Lang, *Linksextremismus. Eine unterschätzte Gefahr* (Bonn: Bouvier, 1996).

3. Gero Neugebauer and Richard Stöss, *Die PDS: Geschichte - Organisation - Wähler - Konkurrenten* (Opladen: Leske + Budrich, 1996). See references in *Der Tagesspiegel*, 15 July 1996; Gerd-Rüdiger Stephan, "Ein differenziertes Bild" in *Das Parlament*, Vol. 46, No. 26 (1996), p. 23.

4. Neugebauer and Stöss, *Die PDS*, pp. 35-43.

5. Hasko Hüning, "PDS-Systemopposition oder Reformpolitik? Eine Zwischenbilanz" in *Deutschland Archiv*, Vol. 22, No. 11 (1990), pp. 1676-78.

6. Wolfgang G. Gibowski and Max Kaase, "Auf dem Weg zum politischen Alltag. Eine Analyse der ersten gesamtdeutschen Bundestagswahl vom 2. Dezember 1990," in *Aus Politik und Zeitgeschichte: Beilage zur Wochenzeitung Das Parlament*, Vol. 41, No. 11-12 (1991), pp. 3-5.

7. Since the second federal election in 1952 there has been a so-called five percent hurdle. Parties with less than a five percent share of votes were barred from parliament as "splinter parties." Only one exception was allowed. If at least three mandates were gained directly by the party (*Direktmandate*), it could enter the parliament at full strength according to the results of proportional voting. David P. Conradt, *The German Polity* (New York and London: Longman, 1993), pp. 113-15.

8. Siegfried Suckut and Dietrich Staritz, "Alte Heimat oder neue Linke? Das SED-Erbe und die PDS-Erben" in *Deutschland Archiv*, Vol. 24, No. 10 (1991), pp. 1045-47.

9. Rainer Linnemann, *Die Parteien in den neuen Bundesländern: Konstituierung, Mitgliederentwicklung, Organisationsstrukturen* (New York/Münster: Waxmann, 1994), p. 100.

10. Patrick Moreau, "Die PDS: eine postkommunistische Partei" in *Aus Politik und Zeitgeschichte*, Vol. 42, No. 5 (1992) pp. 35-44.

11. Neugebauer and Stöss, *Die PDS*, p. 200; Heinrich Bortfeld, *Von der SED zur PDS. Wandlung zur Demokratie?* (Bonn: Bouvier, 1992), p. 295; Patrick Moreau, *PDS. Anatomie einer postkommunistischen Partei* (Bonn: Bouvier, 1992), p. 459.

12. Conradt, *The German Polity*, p. 114; *The October 16, 1994 Election and Three State Elections in the Federal Republic of Germany* (New York: German Information Center, 1990), pp. 1-2.

13. Gunnar Winkler (ed.), *Sozialreport. Daten und Fakten zur sozialen Lage in den neuen Bundesländern* (Berlin: Gesellschaft für sozialwissenschaftliche Forschung und Publizistik, 1996), p. 358.

14. For more details see Neugebauer and Stöss, *Die PDS*, p. 119-20.

15. Linnemann, *Die Parteien*, p. 103.

16. See section two of this chapter, "*The Faces of the PDS.*"

17. With great skepticism, partly with protest, large parts of the east German population reacted to the Treuhand privatizations, which were accompanied by high unemployment hitherto unknown in east Germany. See Jörg Roesler, "Mass Unemployment in Eastern Germany: Recent Trends and Responses by Workers and Policy Makers" in *Journal of European Social Policy*, Vol. 1, No. 2 (1991), pp. 129-36 and "Privatisation in Eastern Germany: Experience with the Treuhand" in *Europe-Asia Studies*, Vol. 46, No. 3 (1994), pp. 505-17.

18. Between 1990 and 1992 the number of people who thought it was "important" or "very important" "to live in a pluralistic society" halved (90 percent in 1990, 46 percent 1992). At the same time the importance of "social security" had even grown (97 percent in 1990, 99 percent in 1992). See Gunnar Winkler (ed.), *Sozialreport 1992. Daten und Fakten zur sozialen Lage in den neuen Bundesländern* (Berlin: Morgenbuchverlag, 1993), p. 277.

19. Neugebauer and Stöss, *Die PDS*, p. 302.

20. *Ibid*, p. 134.

21. The basic decision of February 1990 has remained valid up to now, Neugebauer and Stöss, *Die PDS*, p. 13. This was underlined again in two inter-views in 1996 by the party chairman of the PDS, Lothar Bisky, the successor to Gregor Gysi since January 1993, *Der Tagesspiegel* (Berlin), 12 August 1996 and 10 November 1996.

22. Linnemann, *Die Parteien*, p. 105.

23. Conradt, *The German Polity*, pp. 126-32.

24. The PDS west German electorate numbered 090,000 in the 1994 federal elections, or 18.2 percent of the total number of PDS voters, and the east German electorate 1,742,000, Jürgen W. Falter and Markus Klein, "Die Wähler der PDS bei der Bundestagswahl 1994. Zwischen Ideologie, Nostalgie und Protest" in *Aus Politik und Zeitgeschichte*, Vol. 44, No. 51-52 (1994), pp. 22-25.

25. There are different descriptions concerning circumstances of the foundation of the communist platform. See Gregor Gysi in *Neues Deutschland* (Berlin), 22 August 1996; Eberhard Czichon, "Gregor Gysis Nostalgie" in *Mitteilungen der Komunistischen Plattform der PDS*, Vol. 7, No. 9 (1996), p. 2.

26. Gross Domestic Product (GDP) increases in 1995 were the equivalent of two-thirds of 1994 growth and in 1996 were projected at only one-third of the

1994 figures, with a projected decrease in 1997, Manfred Wegener," Die deutsche Einigung oder das Ausbleiben des Wunders. Sechs Jahre danach: eine Zwischen-bilanz" in *Aus Politik und Zeitgeschichte*, Vol. 46, No. 40 (1996), p. 15.

27. Consumption per head in the new states has increased only slowly since 1992 compared with the level of the old states, from 59 percent to 69 percent, Wegener, "Die deutsche Einigung," p. 16.

28. The number of registered unemployed was 1,170,000 in 1992 and 1,175,000 in 1996, Wegener, "Die deutsche Einigung," p. 21.

29. A detailed description of west German dominance has been given by a group of social scientists from the Free University of Berlin. See Wolfang Dümcke and Fritz Vilmar (eds.), *Kolonisierung der DDR. Kritische Analysen und Alternativen des Einigungsprozesses* (Münster: Agenda Verlag, 1995).

30. In real terms this means that a share greater than 90 percent of east Ger-many's productive assets fell into the hands of west German corporations and entrepreneurs. In addition to the transfer of stocks of productive assets, 40 percent of the land surface of the former GDR fell to *Treuhandanstalt's* portfolio. See John Hall and Udo Ludwig, "East Germany's Transitional Economy," in *Challenge*, Vol. 37, No. 5 (1994), p. 30. Compared with households in the old *Länder*, the fortunes in the new states remained low and even declined. On the day of currency union (1 July 1990) the eastern level of net income per household was 20.8 percent of the income of an average west German household, and in 1994 it was 14.6 percent. See Ulrich Busch, "Vermögensdifferenzierung und Disparität der Lebensverhältnisse im vereinigten Deutschland" in *Berliner Debatte INITIAL*, Vol. 6 , No. 6 (1996), p. 115.

31. In 1990 all state officials were dismissed. They were allowed to reenter office only after an evaluation of their former positions and activities. Persons in higher positions (*Nomenklaturkader*) or those who had done wrong (according the findings of the evaluation commissions) were not allowed to continue to work as officials in administrations, teachers in schools, or professors at universities.

32. Klaus v. Beyme, "Regime Transition and Recruitment of Elites in Eastern Europe," in *Governance*, Vol. 6, No. 3 (1993), p. 411.

33. Klaus König, "Bureaucratic Integration by Elite Transfer: The Case of the Former GDR" in *Governance*, Vol. 6, No. 3, (1993), pp. 389-95.

34. Wolfgang Schluchter, "Die Hochschulen in Ostdeutschland vor und nach der Einigung" in *Aus Politik und Zeitgeschichte*, Vol. 44, No. 25 (1994) pp. 20-21. Figures are difficult to get. In one of the newly founded universities, in Frankfurt am Oder, in Autumn 1996 only five of 45 full professors were from the former GDR, *Neues Deutschland*, 12-13 October 1996.

35. "All disadvantages and risks which are connected with the transition," the political scientist Helmut Wiesenthal wrote,". . . are blamed on one cause, the methods and conditions of German unity," Helmut Wiesenthal, "Die neuen Bundesländer als Sonderfall der Transformation in den Ländern Ostmittel-europas" in *Aus Politik und Zeitgeschichte*, Vol. 46, No. 40 (1996), p. 50.

36. Michael Brie, "Das politische Projekt PDS - eine unmögliche Möglichkeit. Die ambivalenten Früchte eines Erfolges," in Michael Brie, Martin Herzig, and

Thomas Koch (eds.), *Empirische Befunde und kontroverse Analysen* (Köln: Papyrossa, 1995), p. 13.

37. East Germany's *Mittelstand* is characterized by small firms with less than twenty employees. As a result these firms are not in the mainstream of the east German economy, with respect to earnings, assets, or number of employees. Their main problems from the start have been a low equity share, liquidity problems and restricted access to loans from (west German) banks and to markets (controlled mainly by west German trade chains). The number of bankruptcies is generally higher in the new than in the old *Länder*. In the eastern *Land* of Saxony-Anhalt it is four times higher than in prosperous Bavaria and in the best-off eastern *Land* Thuringia 1.5 times higher than in the worst-off western *Land* of Lower Saxony. Data about bankruptcies for the first two quarters of 1996 reported in *Neues Deutschland*, 4 July 1996, and interview with Christa Luft, economist and former economics minister in the Modrow government in *Neues Deutschland*, 2 July 1996. The average equity share for enterprises in west Germany is about 50 percent. In the East the figures for the better-off one-third of enterprises is 16.5 percent and for the bottom half only 11.6 percent, *Neues Deutschland*, 7 July 1996.

38. Conradt, *The German Polity*, p. 102.

39. Günther Licht, "Linke Kapitalisten. Unternehmer in Ostdeutschland gründeten eine PDS-nahe Mittelstandsvereinigung" in *Die Zeit*, Vol. 49, No. 41 (1994), p. 10; *Neues Deutschland*, 11 January 1995.

40. Because many former representatives of the GDR elite have taken over small enterprises, the PDS on the local level has often turned into an "economic party," the SPD mayor of a large suburb of Berlin told a confernce on the "PDS in the party landscape of the united Germany" in Tutzing, Bavaria in March 1996, Erich Scheck, "Die PDS in der Parteienlandschaft" in *Deutschland Archiv*, Vol. 29, No. 3 (1996), p. 472.

41. See interview with the chairman of the Saxony OWUS, Barbara Lässig and related commentaries, *Neues Deutschland*, 12 June 1996.

42. The situation in the old states, with 18 percent of the PDS electorate, was a different one: twenty-seven percent of PDS voters there had voted for the SPD and the same percentage for the Greens in the 1990 federal election. For those 76 percent of voters in the old states who voted for the PDS for the first time in 1994, protest votes probably played a big role, Falter and Klein, "Die Wähler der PDS," pp. 24-25.

43. *Ibid.*

44. The east German deputies of the CDU and the SPD and the ministers of the CDU-led Bonn government are sometimes named *Alibi-Ossis*, e.g., token east Germans, Scheck, "Die PDS," p. 472.

45. Hans-J. Misselwitz, *Nicht länger mit dem Gesicht nach Westen. Das neue Selbstbewußtsein der ostdeutschen Parteien* (Bonn: Verlag J. H. W. Dietz, 1996), p.105.

46. *Dokumentation zum "exit poll" bei der Bundeswahl* (Mannheim: Forschungsgruppe Wahlen e.V., 1994), pp. 78-79. See also Misselwitz, *Nicht länger*, pp. 103-106.

47. Neugebauer and Stöss, *Die PDS*, pp. 12-13.

48. Moreau and Lang, *Linksextremismus;* the 1995 report of the interior secret service of the FRG *"Verfassungsschutzbericht"* especially referred to the "communist platform," the study group *(Arbeitsgemeinschaft)* of young party members *(Arbeitsgemeinschaft junger GenossInnen),* the autonomous groups *(Autonomen Gruppen),* the Marxist discussion group *(Marxistisches Forum)* and the Liberal discussion group *(Libertäres Forum),* quoted in *Neues Deutschland,* 25-26 May 1996.

49. See interview with Reinhard Höppner (SPD), prime minister of Saxony-Anhalt, and interview with Christoph Bergner, leader of the CDU opposition in the parliament, the PDS party in the parliament of Saxony-Anhalt (ed.), *Magdeburg: Modell oder Experiment?* (Magdeburg: Landtagsreport, 1996), pp. 3- 27.

50. Der Tagesspiegel, 3 August 1996.

51. Scheck, "Die PDS," p. 471; see also Neugebauer and Stöss, *Die PDS,* p. 98.

52. *Ibid,* p. 472.

53. The strategic paper "CDU 2000," published by the CDU party of the Mecklenburg-West Pomeranian parliament in February 1996, urged party members to learn from the success of the PDS on the local level and demanded support for eastern interests, *Neues Deutschland,* 10-11 February 1996. The SPD created an "east German discussion group" *(Ostdeutsches Forum)* inside the party in order to give east German SPD members greater public participation. See interview with Manfred Stolpe, SPD member and Prime Minister of Brandenburg, *Neues Deutschland,* 8-9 June, 1996.

54. Interview with André Brie in *Stern,* Vol. 51, No. 32, p. 104; Heinz Kallabis, "Positionen, die geeignet sind, der PDS ihre Rolle als reale sozialistische Oppositionskraft zu nehmen" in *Weißenseer Blätter,* Vol. 15, No. 3 (1996), pp. 24-26; Patrick Moreau and Jürgen Lang, "Aufbruch zu neuen Ufern? Zustand und Perspektiven der PDS" in *Aus Politik und Zeitgeschichte,* Vol. 46, No. 6 (1995), pp. 57-58; *Neues Deutschland,* 3 June 1996; *Der Tagesspiegel,* 3 August 1996; *Neues Deutschland,* 9 August 1996; *Neues Deutschland,* 19 August 1996; *Der Tagesspiegel,* 24 August 1996; *Neues Deutschland,* 30 September 1996.

55. See the arguments of the leading members of this group: Ellen Brombacher, Sahra Wagenkecht, Michael Benjamin, Thomas Hecker, Heinz Marohn, Fredrich Rabe, *Zur Debatte in der PDS,* leaflet, Berlin, 11 September 1996, pp. 1-5. See also the "strategic discussion" about the future of the PDS, Sahra Wagenknecht and André Brie, "Wie macht die PDS sich nicht überflüssig?" in *Neues Deutschland,* 12 November 1996.

56. Uwe-Jens Heuer, "Linke und Regierungsbeteiligung heute" in *Geschichts Korrespondens,* Vol. 2, No. 4 (1995), pp. 22-28.

57. Joschka Fischer (interview): "Die Lust am Verändern" in *Der Spiegel,* Vol. 50, No. 34 (1996), p. 55; Scheck, "PDS", p. 472.

58. The communist platform rejects the charges that it is "stalinist" and the reproach of being against the federal constitution. This has been underlined repeatedly by its intellectual leaders, Michael Benjamin "Gedanken zum Thema: Was wollen die Kommunisten heute" in *Was wollen Kommunisten heute,* leaflet, Berlin, June 1996, pp. 1-5.

59. Moreau and Lang, "Aufbruch," p. 59; *Neues Deutschland*, 18-19 May 1996; *Neues Deutschland*, 16 August 1996.

60. It was published in *Neues Deutschland*, 8 May 1996.

61. Rosemarie Müller-Streisand, "Bodenständige ostdeutsche Volkspartei der 'Mitte'? Zu Christine Ostrowskis und Ronald Weckesser 'Brief aus Sachsen'" in *Weißenseer Blätter*, Vol. 15, No. 3 (1996), p. 26-31; *Neues Deutschland*, 8 May 1996; *Neues Deutschland*, 10 May 1996.

62. Heinrich Bortfeldt, "Die PDS auf dem Weg aus der Isolation?" in *Das Parlament*, Vol. 47, No. 5 (1997), p. 10; *Neues Deutschland*, 18-19 January 1997 and 20 January 1997.

63. *Neues Deutschland*, 18 December 1997, p. 13. The draft of the party board *(Vorstand)* has to be officially confirmed by the party congress, which will take place April 1998 in Rostock.

64. Konrad H. Jarausch and Volker Gransow, *Uniting Germany: Documents and Debates 1944-1993*, translated from German by Allison Brown and Belinda Cooper (Providence and Oxford: Berghahnbooks, 1994), pp. 118-124, 126.

65. Matthias Jung and Dieter Roth, "Kohls knappster Sieg. Eine Analyse der Bundestagswahl 1994," in *Aus Politik und Zeitgeschichte*, Vol. 44, No. 51-52 (1994), p. 15.

66. Hans-Jürgen Leersch, "Die CSU: eine neue Form der Bayernpartei?" *in Aus Politik und Zeitgeschichte*, Vol. 42. No. 5 (1992), pp. 21-23; Eckhard Jesse. "Die CSU im vereinigten Deutschland" in *Aus Politik und Zeitgeschichte*, Vol. 46, No. 6 (1996), pp. 31-34.

67. The lowest assessment was made by André Brie, interview, *Stern*, Vol. 51, No. 32 (1996), p.104; the highest by the west German PDS deputy Gerhard Zwerenz in *Disput*, Vol. 7, No. 8 (1996), p. 4. About the development of the membership see Neugebauer *et al., Die PDS*, p. 134.

68. *Ibid.*, p. 199.

69. Ursula Feist, "Nichtwähler 1994. Eine Analyse der Bundestagswahl 1994" in *Aus Politik und Zeitgeschichte*, Vol. 44, No. 51-52 (1994), pp. 36, 39.

70. *Ibid.*, pp. 42-43.

71. Misselwitz, *Nicht länger*, pp. 103-104.

72. "Eine Umfrage zur Zeit-Serie" in *Die Zeit*, Vol. 51, No. 41 (1995), pp. 24-25.

73. As mentioned earlier, only the members of the communist platform within the PDS renounced the political system of the Federal Republic, Moreau and Lang, "Aufbruch," p. 58.

74. Neugebauer and Stöss, *Die PDS*, p. 286.

75. This was underlined by party chairman Bisky in an interview, *Der Tagesspiegel*, 10 November 1996.

76. In the election of March 1990 Chancellor Helmut Kohl promised the GDR population that with the introduction of currency union "we are enabling the people of the GDR to participate directly in what the people of the Federal Republic developed and attained through decades of hard work. This will create the conditions necessary for rapid improvements in the East German standard of living," quoted in Jarausch and Gransow, *Uniting Germany*, p. 123.

77. Peter Bender, "Zwei, drei, viele Ostparteien. Plädoyer für eine Rebellion der Ostdeutschen" in *Wochenpost*, Vol. 33, No. 25 (1991), p. 4; *Neues Deutschland*, 31 December 1990-1 January 1991.

78. Wegener, "Die deutsche Einigung," p. 23.

79. *Ibid.*, p. 16.

80. Neugebauer and Stöss, *Die PDS*, p. 306; Moreau and Lang, "Aufbruch," pp. 55-56. In November 1996, sociologists on the commission for research on social and political change in the East referred to the fact that a remarkable part of the population in the new states would mentally not become a part of the Federal Republic. They warned against the illusion "that the PDS could be marginalized within two or three years." Quoted in *Neues Deutschland*, 17 November 1996.

81. Wiesenthal, "Die neuen Bundesländer," p. 54.

82. Wegener, "Die deutsche Einigung," p. 22.

83. Hans Willgerodt, Barbara Dluhosch, and Malte Krüger (Institute of Economic Policy, University of Cologne), *Vorteile der wirtschaftlichen Einheit Deutschlands* (Bonn: Presse- und Informationsamt der Bundesregierung (1990), p. 44.

84. Wegener, "Die deutsche Einigung," p. 22.

85. *Ibid*, p. 15.

86. *Ibid.*, p. 20.

87. *Ibid.*, p. 19.

88. One of the typical characterizations of the situation in the East as shaky and unpredictable was given by economic experts of the employers associations, *Der Tagesspiegel*, 18 September 1996.

89. *Neues Deutschland*, 30 May 1996 and 15 September 1996. Wegener thinks that the catching up process in the new states "will last another 15 to 20 years," Wegener, "Die deutsche Einigung," p. 22.

4

Xenophobia and Rightwing Extremism in Germany: The New *Bundesländer*

Molly C. Laster and Sabrina P. Ramet

After the implosion of the German Democratic Republic (GDR), Germany has witnessed a surge in xenophobic violence in both eastern and western halves. Why has this occurred? What does this surge portend for the future? How significant are these incidents?

Although the subject of rightwing extremism has become more topical since 1989, neo-Nazi groups have been active in both parts of Germany all along. So the phenomenon is not new. Nor is the presence of foreign workers, both Germanys having permitted the influx of non-Germans already in the 1960s (primarily Turks, Italians, Greeks, and Yugoslavs to West Germany, Vietnamese, Slavs, and sundry Africans to East Germany).

Some observers have attributed the explosion of far right violence in eastern Germany since 1990 to the stress provoked by reunification. As Thomas Schmid points out, the population of the GDR was, at the time of reunification, unaccustomed to the principles and procedures of liberal democracy, and not yet comfortable with thinking within a liberal democratic framework.[1] Add to this the economic hardship that many eastern Germans have experienced since reunification, and it is easy to understand the temptation that some have experienced to scapegoat foreign workers.

Regula Heusser has described the adaptive difficulties in the new *Länder*. Not only are the models of life that were promulgated in the GDR no longer acceptable, but there is the discouragement associated with the overnight relegation of many east Germans to a kind of second-class status within Germany. West Germans have come to eastern Germany to serve as enterprise directors, professors, judges, administrators--bosses--leaving locals feeling estranged from the process of political and social transformation engulfing their society. Even in 1991, some 11 percent of east Germans looked back to the old GDR with nostalgia; as of 1996, the figure was 22 percent. While both west and east Germans have had to cope with the costs of reintegration, the costs have been higher in the East. East Germans, for example, were earning about 25 percent less than their west German counterparts as of 1995, while, in a poll conducted in early 1996, some 52 percent of east Germans expressed concern about high unemployment.[2] Unemployment has remained higher in the east than in the west[3]--a differential reinforced by the smaller size of eastern German enterprises.[4] In addition, the number of homeless in eastern Germany has continued to climb, reaching 7,800 by late 1996, in Saxony-Anhalt alone.[5] Not surprisingly, discontent with the system is widespread in the new *Bundesländer*.[6] Add to that the fact that some 15 percent of Germans are thought to share extreme-right views (as of June 1997), with 31.8 percent of young people of Brandenburg expressing the conviction that Germany needed a "new *Führer*," and the fact that there are some 50 far-right groups active in Germany (as of March 1997), and you have the makings of trouble.[7]

But the aforementioned theories, although accounting perhaps for the increase in xenophobic violence during reunification, do not explain violent trends before 1989; nor do they completely explain why the traditional guest workers, the contract workers, were often targeted by rightwing extremists even before 1989.

Trends in the 1980s

Rightwing extremism is nothing new to eastern Germany. Radical right groupings existed in the GDR for many years, particularly among the young.[8] Already in the early 1960s, the GDR experienced unprovoked attacks on foreigners; in the 1970s, there were reports that the swastika had been painted on house walls.[9] By 1981, informal groups of young people assumed definition at football games and heavy metal concerts. Beginning in 1983, a more formal radical-right scene started to take shape in the GDR. Although GDR authorities tried to deal with the problem by packing off the leading figures to the West, there they were able to establish ties with rightwing extremists already operating in the Federal Republic of Germany (FRG).[10] As of 1988, for example, police reported that skinheads and "faschos" in the GDR had developed contacts with neo-fascist (or neo-Nazi) organizations in West Germany and in Hungary.[11] Returning in many cases with the removal of the Berlin Wall, they joined skinheads and rightwing militants who had been released from prison under amnesty.

Skinhead groups in the GDR became especially active in the years 1984-87; some of them created the so-called Lichtenberg Front in 1986.[12] By 1986, East German skinheads were terrorizing punks, whom they considered "left-wing."[13] In 1987 alone, the State Security Service had to deal with some 38 functioning rightwing extremist groups.[14]

A 1988 study conducted by the Ministry for Youth and Sport in the GDR among some 3,000 14-25 year-olds found that among those surveyed, 4 percent sympathized with skinheads, more than 10 percent expressed "great sympathy" for fascism, and 30 percent expressed "understanding" for skinhead activities. A study conducted the same year by the Center Institute for Youth Research found that 13.4 percent of young people would not object to a takeover by a revived Nazi party, and that 5.8 percent would actively welcome and support such a takeover.[15]

As resentment toward foreigners increased through the 1980s, there was an increase in the number of underground skinhead and neo-Nazi movements. From 1983 to 1988, the frequency of criminal acts perpetrated by rightwing extremists quintupled.[16] Hate slogans--some of which were directed at foreigners--were commonly heard in the GDR, for example at soccer games.[17]

In the best-known case of violence in the GDR, an opposition concert taking place in a church was stormed by neo-Nazis in October 1987. Following a soccer game in Berlin, attended by 400-500 rightwing extremists, about 50 of them had gone to a party at the Sputnik Tavern before converging on the church. The group included members of the *Lichtenberg Front*, a rightwing group that had been established the previous year and that included Ingo Hasselbach and Andre Reichert-- later to play key roles in the *Nationale Alternative*, a major radical-right political organization.[18] About one thousand environmentalists, Christian activists, pacifists, and political dissidents had gathered at the *Zionskirche* for a punk concert. Following the party at the Sputnik, about 20-25 skinheads stormed the church, wielding bottles and bicycle chains. The skinheads were eventually beaten back by the punks and moved from there to attack suspected homosexuals.

Twelve of the skinheads involved in this attack were later

identified, thanks to police photographs, and were brought to trial. Initially sentenced in a show trial to terms of one to two years in prison, for rowdiness and the public expression of fascist, racist, and militaristic ideas, they were later subjected to stiffer terms ranging from one-and-a-half to four years in prison. This trial was the first radical right incident in the GDR to be reported in the East German press. Like events that would later occur in unified Germany, these acts were treated as criminal fare, not as political opposition. The signs and slogans were attributed to the influence of Western ideology.

The radical right in the GDR first focused its wrath on punks and "Goths" (also known as *Grufti*)--a group known for having celebrated the melancholy of life with all-black clothing and powdered pale faces--later expanding its hostility to foreigners and homosexuals. After the incident at the *Zionskirche*, the skinheads became more political and violence soared. Young people in Halle and Dresden were put on trial for having assaulted African guest-workers. From November 1987 to February 1988, the East Berlin Jewish cemetery was vandalized five times. During roughly the same period, nine skinhead cases were prosecuted, involving 49 people aged 16 to 25.[19] Estimates are that by 1988, there were already 1,000 to 1,800 hard-core skinheads and neo-fascists in East Germany, of which 450 to 600 lived in East Berlin. The first xenophobic attacks were predominantly directed at contract workers from Vietnam, Mozambique, Angola, and Cuba.[20]

Contract Workers in the GDR

Prior to its collapse in 1989, there were 191,190 foreigners living in the GDR, according to the statistical office of the GDR, representing 1.2 percent of the total population of 17 million. Some 80 percent of these came from Vietnam, Poland, Mozambique, the USSR, and Hungary. Most of these were "contract workers," i.e., guest workers who came to the GDR under work contracts with "socialist fraternal countries."[21] While approximately 40,000 foreigners had permanent residence status in the GDR as the spouses of East German citizens or as refugees, with about the same number residing in the GDR temporarily for study or vocational training, 95,000 out of the 191,190 foreigners in the GDR were contract workers brought in to make up for the shortage of labor.[22] Coming to the GDR predominantly in the early 1980s, the contract workers were usually invited for a period of four to five years. Among their number were 60,067 Vietnamese, working mostly in textiles, 15,483 Mozambicans, working mainly in heavy industry, and about 1,300 Angolans.[23]

Officially there had been no foreigners in the GDR. The contract workers remained isolated, placed in separate housing at a distance from East German citizens. Permission was required for any close contact between East Germans and foreign contract workers.[24] Their contracts specified what they could and could not do, who could visit their dormitories and when, how many bicycles they could buy, and so forth.

Seventy percent of the contract workers were male. Women coming from Mozambique and Vietnam were forbidden to have children during their stay, while Cuban women were shipped back to Cuba if they were found to be pregnant. Parents were only given two months in five years to visit children remaining in their home countries. Contract workers usually held the lowest-paying jobs. In the case of the Cubans, 60 percent of their pay was automatically sent to bank accounts in Cuba.

In spite of all of these restrictions, and in spite of the generally poor working and living conditions, East Germans were given to suspicions that the contract workers enjoyed "special privileges" and that they were able to buy goods that were not available to East Germans themselves. As Klaus Bade notes, these rumors tended to magnify negative emotional states, such as resentment, envy, hatred, and even fear of foreigners.[25]

In summer 1990, the governments of Vietnam, Angola, and Mozambique signed new agreements with the lameduck government of the GDR. These agreements stopped the entry of additional guestworkers, but allowed those already in the country to remain after the end of the period stipulated in their contracts. By then, many of the contract workers were unemployed and had already decided on their own part to return to their home countries.[26]

With the collapse of the GDR, many contract workers left, returning to their homelands or seeking asylum in West Germany. Those whose contracts had not yet expired and those who were gainfully employed were allowed to remain. Cuban contract workers were ordered home by Castro, in order to minimize their contact with the West. Many of these workers had lived in the GDR for more than 10 years. The Berlin Minister for Non-citizens, Barbara John (CDU), estimated that there were probably a few hundred Cubans left in 1994, seeking asylum in Germany.[27]

Soon after the reunification of the two Germanys, 70,000 contract workers were ordered to leave eastern Germany by early October 1990. This number included 54,000 Vietnamese, 13,900 Mozambicans, and 950 Angolans. These workers were to receive 70 percent of their salary for three months and a plane ticket to their home country. Their employers were required to pay DM 3,000 to assist them in their reintegration at home. Those staying to finish out their contracts were to receive temporary work permits, but could only remain in their workers' hostels for three months, at which time they would be responsible for their own housing.[28] In December 1990, the GDR residence title for contract workers was converted into a residence title for specific purposes, meaning that guest workers could remain only as long as they could support themselves financially through legal means.

In April 1991, there were approximately 120,000 foreigners in the new *Länder* and East Berlin, down from the 191,190 in 1989. This included 71,000 gainfully employed workers. By the end of 1992, because of the new distribution system for asylum seekers, the number of foreigners had increased to 182,541 in the new *Länder*, to which 35,000 more must be added from East Berlin. This accounted for about one percent of the population, a lower proportion than in 1989. The number of foreigners who were employed in 1992 can be estimated from the 59,600 work permits that were issued in that year.[29]

In 1993, the Standing Conference of the Ministers of the Interior resolved that guest workers could qualify for a residence title for exceptional purposes. The 15,000 to 20,000 contract workers that were assumed to be still in Germany at this time could remain in Germany only as long as they were able to secure their livelihood through legal, gainful employment. Under this resolution, the entire German labor market was open to the remaining foreign workers from the GDR. Workers were permitted to go to the western portion of Germany to seek employment, if they were unable to find employment in the new *Länder*. At this time, Vietnamese still made up the largest part of the remaining contract workers. With numbers estimated at 10,000-15,000, they accounted for more than half of the remaining workers.

The German government set 17 April 1994 as a final deadline for the return of all remaining foreigners from the former GDR to their native homelands. Those wishing to stay in Germany would have to secure a residence permit either on the basis of employment or as asylum seekers. By the end of March 1994, 2,897 former contract workers had applied for residence permits. Of these, 1,324 applications were accepted and 220 were rejected. The deadline did not apply to contract workers whose contracts would not expire until 1995. The Ministry of the Interior of Saxony stated that in order to qualify for a residence permit, contract workers would have to verify that they would not live on the dole.[30]

In spite of the intention of the FRG government to return all unemployed contract workers in 1990, the process was held up by delays in negotiations with the government of Vietnam. In some cases, returning Vietnamese workers had not been allowed into Vietnam--a circumstance that had provoked criticism on the part of German government spokespersons. After a year of negotiations, the German and Vietnamese governments announced that they had reached an agreement for the return of Vietnamese citizens. The agreement established that by the year 2000, the 40,000 Vietnamese in Germany without residence permits would be returned to their homeland. This included illegal immigrants, rejected asylum seekers, and criminal guest workers of the GDR.[31] In July 1995, about 97,000 Vietnamese still lived in the FRG.[32] A quota system for the initial returns was set up: 2,500 in 1995, 5,000 in 1996, 6,000 in 1997, and 6,500 in 1998. For the remaining 20,000 Vietnamese to be deported, no specific timetable was established. Among the initial deportees would be those Vietnamese who had been convicted of crimes in Germany or who had entered Germany illegally.[33]

Germany smoothed the agreement by restoring DM 75 million in development aid that had been frozen in September 1994, promising another DM 25 million in aid, and pledging economic cooperation.[34] Officially, however, it was maintained that the aid did not have any connection with the return of the Vietnamese.

Asylum Seekers

The German *Grundgesetz*, or Basic Law, provides that all politically persecuted persons will enjoy the right of asylum.[35] With the rise of the "foreigner problem," following German unification, there have been numerous calls to limit this right.

The reunification of eastern and western Germany turned out to be more expensive and more difficult, both economically and socially, than had been expected. In spite of the stress faced by the new *Länder*, the federal government ignored warnings about assigning asylum-seekers to the east. Instead, the Unification Treaty established that 20 percent of asylum-seekers would be assigned to the new *Länder*, based on the population in each *Land* (ranging from 2.76 percent in Mecklenburg-West Pomerania to 6.44 percent in Saxony).[36] The foreigners were assigned to areas that lacked the infrastructure to accommodate them. Local police in the east were unable, or indisposed,[37] to extend proper protection to the foreigners, and complaints multiplied. In Rostock in August 1992, when skinheads beat local non-Germans, police arrived late and then withdrew without having resolved the problem. In Magdeburg, police had advance warning of rightwing extremist violence in May 1994, but took no prophylactic measures. Shortly thereafter, in Halle, police, although arriving soon enough on the scene of a beating of an asylum-seeker from

Chad, made no effort to apprehend the assailants. Similar reports have come from other eastern German towns.[38] There were also reports of widespread racism among Berlin's police force, and in July 1994, there were 26 criminal investigations underway against Berlin police officials on charges of having abused Vietnamese cigarette dealers.[39] The problem is not unique to the eastern *Länder*, but appears to have been more frequent there.

But complaints on the part of asylum-seekers have not been limited to police abuse and unresponsiveness. There have also been repeated complaints about primitive housing conditions, discrimination, and other forms of abuse.

Bernd Mesovic of the Workers Benevolent Society in Frankfurt said that the placement of refugees in the east had been executed without proper forethought. Indeed, the officials misunderstood the issue at first, worrying only about possible threats to local German populations; as they later learned, it was the foreigners who were at risk, not local Germans. In many areas of eastern Germany, the number of foreigners actually fell initially in the wake of the collapse of the GDR. Many contract workers went home, and, in spite of some assumptions to the contrary, the influx of asylum-seekers tapered off. In Magdeburg, for example, the number of foreigners actually declined from 1990 to 1992 (from 9,200 in 1990, to just 1,400 two years later), while in Saxony-Anhalt as a whole, the number of foreigners declined from 30,000 in 1990 to 12,000-14,000 in 1991.[40] The declining trend reversed itself in 1992, however, as more asylum-seekers were sent to Saxony-Anhalt.[41] Throughout the new *Länder*, the increases in the number of foreigners from 1991-92 to 1993 were tangible, as shown in Table 4.1. (See next page.) But the bulk of non-Germans were to be found in the western provinces, as a comparison of the figures in Tables 4.1 and 4.2 suggests.

Rather than addressing the problems of xenophobic violence, debate shifted to the asylum law. A report by Helsinki Watch states that "government officials . . . failed to address the underlying economic and social problems that . . . contributed to the dramatic rise in anti-foreigner violence, and instead . . . used the violence to further the political goal of a restricted right to asylum."[42] This trend was clearly apparent after the Rostock riots, when attention shifted to the asylum debate. Minister-President Bernd Seite announced that the rioters were in no way anti-foreign, but merely unprepared to accept the abuse of the right to asylum. Interior Minister Lothar Kupfer added that the police should be thanked for having prevented injury to the asylum workers, completely ignoring the trapped Vietnamese. Commentators in the German press criticized these statements by government officials, however.

In September 1992, the Minister of the Interior announced the signing of a treaty with Romania which would speed the deportation from Germany of Romanians rejected for asylum--60 percent of whom were Romany (Gypsies). Confirming the growing tendency on the part of FRG government officials to shift the blame for rightwing extremism onto the foreigners themselves, Chancellor Kohl presented the plan as an important step in the direction of ending violence against foreigners.

TABLE 4.1 Foreigners in the New German *Länder*

	1991	1992	1993	% Increase
Brandenburg	19,567	54,976	61,915	216.4
Mecklenburg	10,227	22,544	28,702	108.6
Saxony	47,906	50,780	61,169	27.7
Saxony-Anhalt	19,675	33,929	38,027	93.3
Thuringia	13,141	20,312	22,563	71.7

Source: Daten und Fakten zur Ausländersituation (Bonn: Beauftragte der Bundesregierung für die Belange der Ausländer, 1994).

TABLE 4.2 Number of Foreigners Living in Germany as of 31 December 1995

Country of Origin	Number
Turkey	2,014,311
F.R. Yugoslavia	797,754
Italy	586,089
Greece	359,556
Herzegovina Bosnia	316,024
Poland	276,753
Croatia	185,122
Austria	184,470
Spain	N/A
Portugal	125,131
United Kingdom	115,826
Netherlands	113,063
Romania	109,256
United States	108,539

Source: Focus (Munich), 27 October 1997, pp. 20-21.

The motivation for this shift in focus may be that the debate on the asylum law stirred anti-foreigner emotions, thereby diverting attention away from the costs of reunification. Condemnations of rightwing violence directed at foreigners by the federal government occurred in the context of calls for restricting the number of asylum-seekers in Germany.[43] Politicians from most of the major German political parties, including the CDU and the SDP, have attributed the increase in violence to the great number of asylum-seekers and to the allegedly lax asylum law.

But Christopher Husbands challenges this explanation. Husbands studied data on anti-foreigner violence in Germany between 1991 and 1993, controlling for region. He found, although raw figures showed a larger number of anti-foreigner incidents occurring in the western provinces, adjusting the data on a modified per capita basis (per 1,000,000 non-foreign inhabitants and per 100,000 foreigners), that ". . . the new regions are perhaps between five and ten times more likely to be the location for any extreme right xenophobic action,"[44] even though there were more non-Germans, on a per capita basis, settled in the western provinces.

Be that as it may, in summer 1993, the CDU/CSU, SPD, and FDP reached an agreement on a new federal law governing the right of asylum. Under this law, asylum-seekers crossing a safe country in order to seek asylum in Germany would be referred to the safe country through which they arrived. This reformed law withstood a constitutional challenge in May 1996, when the Constitutional Court declared it compatible with the basic law of the land.[45]

Hoyerswerda

East German police estimated that there were about 500-1,500 members of the hard-core neo-Nazi scene in the GDR as of 1989--compared with 30,000-40,000 rightwing extremists said to have been active in the FRG about the same time (to which figure one might add the 10,000--15,000 *Republikaner*).[46] As of July 1990, official statistics indicated that there were about 1,500 rightwing extremists in the GDR.[47] Although the leaders of most radical right groups came from the West, the rank and file was mostly from the GDR itself. But by 1993, overall radical right membership was estimated to have risen to between 36,000 and 40,000 in the eastern *Länder*.[48] Seventy percent of radical right adherents were between the ages of 16 and 21, and 27.5 percent between the ages of 21 and 30. A majority of them were living in economically depressed areas.[49]

The first highly-publicized incident of far right violence against foreigners following the collapse of the GDR occurred in the small town of Hoyerswerda, in Saxony, in November 1990. On this occasion, some

400 foreign contract workers were roughed up, even though their contracts were scheduled to expire the following month. Hoyerswerda was again the scene of troubles when, in September 1991, ". . . a large assembly of neo-Nazis, including many skinheads but vocally supported by numerous local inhabitants, attacked a hostel for asylum-seekers that housed Romanian Gypsies--forcing the authorities to evacuate them from the town."[50] There were further anti-foreigner incidents in Hoyerswerda in mid-November 1991, resulting in the evacuation of Vietnamese and Mozambican locals from the town. Official reports noted that the police had been slow to respond and that two police cars on the scene failed to intervene when a group of 12 skinheads began hurling objects at an asylum shelter. The police eventually called for back-up, but only after the violence had already escalated. Moreover, the reinforcements only arrived four hours later.[51]

The following day, neo-Nazi and skinhead groups from across the eastern part of Germany descended upon Hoyerswerda, along with left-wing anarchist groups like the *Autonoms*. A battle ensued in front of two apartment blocks inhabited by asylum-seekers. Eventually, 500 police managed to cordon off the buildings and stop the riot. The following night, the groups once again appeared in force, launching yet another attack on the asylum shelter. They were dispersed by police armed by truncheons and water cannons. Finally, the refugees were evacuated after a citizens' committee recommended that they be moved to another city. By this time, the buildings were no longer inhabitable.[52] Hoyerswerda had become *Ausänderfrei*--free of foreigners.

Three people were convicted for their roles in the Hoyerswerda attack and given suspended sentences. The judge was reported to have described their behavior as brutal, but to have ruled that their crime was a common one rather than one with political overtones.

Subsequently, on the night of 22 August 1992, rightwing skinheads gathered at a foreigner hostel-complex in Lichtenhagen-Rostock. The crowds of skinheads and on-lookers and sympathizers grew each night for the next few days, throwing stones and Molotov cocktails, and shouting slogans. About 100 rioters were injured in battles with 150 police on 22-23 August. On 24 August, the 200 asylum-seekers in the shelter, mostly Romanian Gypsies, were evacuated, but 150 Vietnamese guest workers were left in the complex. The violence continued, with rioters setting the complex on fire and preventing fire-fighters from reaching the fire. It was later established that between 500 and 600 police had been at the scene for almost six hours before making any move to stop the attack. They had never received authorization to move in.[53]

Organizational Structures and Current Trends

The decay of the GDR resulted in a quickening of the formation of far-right organizations in eastern Germany. Among neo-Nazi organizations formed there since 1989, two of the best known were the *Deutsche Alternative*, created by Frank Hubner in Cottbus on 5 May 1989, and the *Nationale Alternative*, established by Ingo Hasselbach, Andre Riechert, and others in East Berlin on 1 February 1990.[54] Local initiatives were, moreover, reinforced by the expansion of West German radical-right parties into East Germany immediately after the opening of the Berlin Wall. Already in late January 1990, a NPD-subsidiary organization was set up in Leipzig, under the name, *Mitteldeutsche Nationaldemokrate*. Again, on 1 May 1990, Michael Kühnen (1955-91),[55] one of the leaders of the *Aktionsfront Nationaler Sozialisten/ Nationale Aktivisten* and author *of Das politische Lexikon der Neuen Front* (1987), together with a group of adherents, staged a neo-Nazi celebration in a hall in Neukirchen (near Eisenach), singing, *inter alia*, the Horst-Wessel song.[56] The *Republikaner*, still enjoying full liberty of political action at that time, contested local elections in the new *Bundesländer* in October 1990, but attracted only between 0.6 and 1.2 percent of the vote.[57]

The radical right found an audience not merely among the indigent and the unemployed, but also, increasingly, among factory workers and educators.[58] The radical right emphasizes the importance of both physical and psychological conditioning. Konrad Weiß reports,

The new right rejects any type of anarchy and exercises self-discipline. Physical training and healthy life-styles are part of their political program; generally they are extremely fit. Other important values are a personality cult and a pronounced sense of comradeship--and here again the historic role models are undeniable. Weekly meetings serve as forums where members educate one another in absolute adherence to the idea and the idols. The new right deliberately promotes elitism and confidence in rightwing beliefs. Each member has to submit to certain test rituals, in which he proves his willingness to use force; inhibitions to do so are gradually dismantled. Cowardly ambushes on passersby are usual as a test of courage. Some groups spend weekends in camps where battle strategies or paramilitary exercises are practiced. It is no accident that military values are cultivated--discipline, obedience, perseverance, trustworthiness, and especially the sense of Wehrmacht comradeship. An integral aspect of the personality cult of the right is the view that those convicted of violent crimes are heroes. . . . For the faschos and the skinheads, those who have been convicted are real martyrs of the movement.[59]

Most of the extreme-right groups functioning in eastern Germany are small, numbering 10-14 members. The small size is an advantage in enabling these groups to maintain secrecy and control information leaks. Seventy-eight percent of radical-right perpetrators of violent acts are between 14 and 20 years of age.[60]

Beginning in 1992, FRG authorities took a number of measures designed to toughen the fight against rightwing extremism, ranging from the establishment of new police units and agencies to measures designed to make the response of police, prosecutors, and judiciary more effective.[61] Where the eastern provinces are concerned, police actions during 1996 alone included: the arrest (in February) of two rightwing extremists on charges of having attacked a Turkish dormitory; the confiscation of bombs and poison gas in Saxony (February); the arrest of seven neo-Nazis in Berlin who were preparing to establish an association to be called the *White Aryan Opposition* (also February); the arrest of 71 young persons in the Thuringian town of Neuhaus in May on charges of planning an unauthorized march; the arrest of 10 rightwing extremists in the area around Wurzen, near Leipzig, in June; the identification of the assailants involved in an attack on an asylum home in Frohburg in early August, placing 13 persons aged 16-23 under arrest (in September); the confiscation of weapons accumulated by rightwing extremists in Berlin and Brandenburg (November); the breaking up of an evening of song in Oberhavel, in which some 95 persons from Berlin, Brandenburg, Saxony-Anhalt, and Thuringia were to have taken part, arresting 15 of this number (December); house-searches of the residences of rightwing extremists in Jena and its environs in December, resulting in the confiscation of propaganda material; and the obstruction of a planned radical-right demonstration in the town of Kloetze in Saxony-Anhalt also in December.[62]

Unable to destroy the roots of radical right extremism, authorities have concentrated on cutting its branches. In Leipzig, a special commission known by its nickname "Soko Rex" has used mobile strike forces to obstruct and break up radical-right marches and rallies with some efficiency, and in the course of 1997, police units carried out preemptive strikes against rightwing extremists in Berlin, Magdeburg, Halle, and elsewhere in eastern Germany.[63] But despite the incarceration of growing numbers of offenders and a possibly transient decline in the number of violent acts committed by rightwing extremists during 1995 and 1996 (as indicated in Table 4-3), authorities have failed to achieve a breakthrough, as betrayed in authorities' repeated calls for a tougher line against the radical right.[64]

Moreover, even the decline in the number of violent acts between 1993 and 1996 (being most marked during 1995 and 1996) cannot be read at face value, because most of the overall decline occurred in the western provinces. In Hesse, Bavaria, Baden-Wurttemberg, and elsewhere in the West, the number of far right acts of violence declined between 1994 and 1995,[65] thus. But in the eastern provinces, the results were more mixed. While the number of punishable acts committed by adherents of the radical right declined in Brandenburg and Saxony during this period,[66] the number increased dramatically during the same period in Mecklenburg and Thuringia and surged upwards in Brandenburg in 1996, as the figures in Table 4-4 indicate.

TABLE 4.3 Violent Acts Committed by Rightwing Extremists Against Non-Germans

Year	Number
1991	1,483
1992	2,584
1993	2,232
1994	1,489
1995	837
1996	781
Jan.-June 1997	985

Sources: Ekkart Zimmerman, "Xenophobic Movements in Contemporary Germany," paper presented to the Conference on Political Extremism, Hostility, and Violence Toward Foreigners and Other Marginalized Groups, Ljubljana, 22-24 March 1996; *Süddeutsche Zeitung*, (Munich), 23 May 1996, on Nexis; *Neue Zürcher Zeitung*, 25-26 May 1996, p. 3; *Süddeutsche Zeitung*, 5 September 1996, on Nexis; *Die Welt* (Bonn), 9 April 1997, p. 1; and *Die Welt*, 23-24 August 1997, p. 4.

TABLE 4.4 Punishable Acts Committed by Rightwing Extremists in Mecklenburg, Thuringia, and Brandenburg

	1994	*1995*	*1996*
Mecklenburg	483	644	N/A
Thuringia	250	733	N/A
Brandenburg	225	77	517

Sources: Süddeutsche Zeitung, 22 March 1996, 19 April 1996, and 12 October 1996; and *Die Tageszeitung* (Berlin), 22 March 1997--all on Nexis.

Although, at least in the short run, the tougher line seems to have resulted in increased security for non-Germans, it is probably too early to make any estimate of the long-range efficacy of the government's strategy. Much will depend, inevitably, on the government's success in educating both young and old about rightwing extremism and its consequences. Thus, in January 1996, the Munich daily newspaper, *Süddeutsche Zeitung*, warned that it was premature to speak of a general decline in the strength of the radical right in Germany; that judgment would hold true likewise today.

Conclusion

Although numerous people have attributed the rise in rightwing xenophobic violence to feelings of insecurity and stress among east German young people, rightwing extremism and anti-foreigner feelings had been present before the fall of the GDR. Throughout the 1980s, there were rightwing extremist movements in East Germany, enjoying the approval of a certain contingent of the population.

The increase of German nationalism at the time of reunification was unmistakable, however. The mass demonstrations preceding the fall of the German Democratic Republic saw a change in rhetoric toward a nationalist basis for reunification. "We are the people!" became "We are one people!"[67] The common German nationality and origin became the justification for reunification in spite of differences in many other areas. Indeed, in many ways, west Germans and east Germans had grown apart--as they would acknowledge soon enough, as the terms "Wessis" and "Ossis" came into common parlance.[68]

The GDR cast a curious spell on rightwing extremists. On the one hand, the SED carried out a partial policy of de-Nazification. On the other hand, the anti-"Zionist" campaigns provoked by Stalin in the early 1950s had their reflections in the GDR, where officially endorsed anti-Semitism found a resonance among unreconstructed Nazis.[69] But there were other sources of ambivalence, most importantly the very authoritarianism of the SED regime. Even West German neo-Nazis are said to have felt a certain fascination for the East German communist system. Thus, in its October 1990 issue, *Aufbruch*, an internal publication of the Nationalist Front, commented: "The GDR no longer exists. Is that reason to rejoice? Absolutely not!"[70]

Notes

1. Thomas Schmid, "Rightwing Radicalism in the Unified Germany," in Ulrich Wank (ed.), *The Resurgence of Rightwing Radicalism in Germany: New Forms of an Old Phenomenon?*, trans. from German by James Knowlton (Atlantic Highlands, N.J.: Humanities Press International, 1996), p. 80.

2. Regula Heusser in *Neue Zürcher Zeitung* (10 July 1993), on Nexis; *Süddeutsche Zeitung* (Munich), 12-13 August 1995, p. 21; and Die Welt (Bonn), 4 January 1996, p. 2.

3. *Financial Times* (9 April 1997), p. 1.

4. *Berliner Zeitung* (8-9 November 1997), p. 26.

5. *Süddeutsche Zeitung* (18-19 October 1997), p. 7.

6. *Die Welt* (Bonn), 31 May 1996, p. 6.

7. *Die Tageszeitung* (Berlin), 25 June 1997, p. 10, 30 May 1997, p. 2, and 26 March 1997, p. 1.

8. *Der Morgen* (4 June 1991), p. 3, trans. in FBIS, Daily Report (Western Europe), 8 July 1991, p. 23.

9. Bernd Siegler, "Rechtsextremismus in der DDR und den neuen *Ländern*," in Jens Mecklenburg (ed.), *Handbuch Deutscher Rechtsextremismus* (Berlin: Elefanten Press, 1996), p. 617.

10. For more discussion and documentation, see Sabrina P. Ramet, "The Radical Right in Germany," in Sabrina P. Ramet (ed.), *The Radical Right in Central and Eastern Europe since 1989* (University Park, Pa.: Penn State Press, forthcoming).

11. Peter Ködderitzsch and Leo A. Müller, *Rechtsextremismus in der DDR* (Göttingen: Lamuv Verlag, 1990), p. 17.

12. Siegler, "Rechtsextremismus in der DDR," p. 618.

13. Konrad Weiß, "Skinheads and Faschos in East Germany: The New-Old Danger of Fascism," trans. from German by Luise von Flotow, in *Cross Currents*, No. 10 (1991), p. 151.

14. *Ibid.*, p. 619; and Ködderitzsch and Müller, *Rechtsextremismus in der DDR*, p. 19.

15. *Süddeutsche Zeitung* (24 February 1994), p. 6.

16. Paul Hockenos, *Free to Hate: The Rise of the Right in Post-Communist Eastern Europe*, Revised ed. (London and New York: Routledge, 1994), p. 40.

17. *Der Morgen* (4 June 1991), p. 3.

18. Ingo Hasselbach was later the most prominent person to abandon the neo-Nazi scene. In retaliation, an explosive was shipped to his house, falsely identified as the book, *Das Lexikon des Rechtsradikalismus* [The Lexicon of the Radical Right]. By sheer chance, his mother was not injured or killed when she opened the package. See *Süddeutsche Zeitung* (Munich), 16 January 1994, p. 3, on Nexis. See also Ingo Hasselbach with Tom Reiss, *Führer-Ex: Memoirs of a Former Neo-Nazi* (New York: Random House, 1996).

19. Hockenos, *Free to Hate*, pp. 78-84.

20. *Der Morgen* (4 June 1991), p. 3.

21. Holly Carter, *"Foreigners Out": Xenophobia and Rightwing Violence in Germany* (New York: Human Rights Watch, 1992), p. 3.

22. Report by the Federal Government's Commissioner for Foreigners' Affairs on the Situation of Foreigners in the Federal Republic of Germany in 1993 (Bonn, March 1994), pp. 32-33.

23. Hockenos, *Free to Hate*, p. 36.

24. Klaus J. Bade, "Immigration and Social Peace in United Germany," in *Daedalus*, Vol. 123, No. 1 (Winter 1994), p. 92.

25. Bade, "Immigration and Social Peace," p. 92.

26. *Report by the Federal Government's Commissioner*, p. 33.

27. *Focus* (Munich), 19 September 1994, p. 38, on Nexis.

28. *Deutsche Presse-Agentur* (Hamburg), 20 September 1990, trans. in BBC Summary of World Broadcasts (25 September 1990), on Nexis.

29. *Report by the Federal Government's Commissioner*, p. 33.

30. *Süddeutsche Zeitung* (11 April 1994), on Nexis.

31. *Süddeutsche Zeitung* (22 July 1995); and Neue Zürcher Zeitung (22 July 1995)--both on Nexis.

32. Reuter Textline (21 July 1995), on Nexis.

33. *Süddeutsche Zeitung* (22 July 1995), on Nexis.

34. *Neue Zürcher Zeitung* (22 July 1995), on Nexis.

35. *Grundgesetz für die Bundesrepublik Deutschland*, Article 16 (2) (Bonn: Bundeszentrale für politische Bildung, April 1985), p. 29.

36. Heinz Lynen von Berg, "Rechtsextremismus in Ostdeutschland seit der Wende," in Wolfgang Kowalsky and Wolfgang Schroeder (eds.), *Rechtsextremismus. Einführung und Forschungsbilanz* (Opladen: Westdeutscher Verlag, 1994), p. 112.

37. Maryellen Fullerton, *"Germany for Germans": Xenophobia and Racist Violence in Germany* (New York: Human Rights Watch/Helsinki, April 1995), pp. 31-52.

38. *Ibid.*, pp. 31-42.

39. *Ibid.*, p. 45.

40. Cartner, *"Foreigners Out,"* pp. 9-10.

41. *Daten und Fakten zur Ausländersituation* (Bonn: Beauftragte der Bundesregierung für die Belange der Ausländer, October 1994), p. 33.

42. Cartner, *"Foreigners Out,"* p. 2.

43. *Ibid.*, pp. 33-35.

44. Christopher Husbands, "Militant Neo-Nazism in the Federal Republic of Germany in the 1990s," in Luciano Cheles, Ronnie Ferguson, and Michalina Vaughan (eds.), *The Far Right in Western and Eastern Europe*, 2nd ed. (London: Longman Group, 1995), p. 334.

45. *Neue Zürcher Zeitung* (15 May 1996), p. 3.

46. Ködderitzsch and Müller, *Rechtsextremismus in der DDR*, pp. 8-9.

47. *Ibid.*, p. 29.

48. Jillian Becker, *Neo-Nazism: A Threat to Europe?* (London: Alliance Publishers, Ltd., for the Institute for European Defence and Strategic Studies, 1993), pp. 20-21.

49. *Die Zeit* (Hamburg), 8 January 1993, p. 2; and *Der Spiegel* (Hamburg), 7 June 1993, p. 25. See also Uwe Backes and Eckhard Jesse, *Politischer Extremismus in der Bundesrepublik Deutschland* (Berlin: Verlag Ullstein, 1993), pp. 267-68.

50. Husbands, "Militant Neo-Nazism," pp. 334-35.

51. Cartner, *"Foreigners Out,"* p. 17.

52. Becker, *Neo-Nazism*, pp. 27-28.

53. Cartner, *"Foreigners Out,"* p. 19.

54. von Berg, "Rechtsextremismus in Ostdeutschland," pp. 115-18; and "Rechtsextreme und neofascistische Gruppen, Organisationen und Parteien," in

Mecklenburg (ed.), *Handbuch Deutscher Rechtsextremismus,* pp. 231-33, 286-87.

55. "Lexikon--Deutschland rechtsaussen: Personen," in Mecklenburg (ed.), *Handbuch Deutscher Rechtsextremismus,* pp. 484-85; and Ködderitzsch and Müller, *Rechtsextremismus in der DDR,* p. 31. For further discussion of Kühnen, see Michael Schmidt, *The New Reich: Violent Extremism in Unified Germany and Beyond,* trans. from German by Daniel Horch (New York: Pantheon Books, 1993).

56. von Berg, "Rechtsextremismus in Ostdeutschland," pp. 119-20. For further discussion of the new *Bundesländer,* see Thomas Lillig, *Rechtsextremismus in den neuen Bundesländern* (Mainz: Hausdückerei der Universität Mainz, 1994).

57. Weiß, "Skinheads and Faschos," p. 152.

58. *Ibid.,* pp. 152-53.

59. *Die Tageszeitung* (14 April 1997), p. 21.

60. For details, see Fullerton, *"Germany for Germans,"* pp. 53-69.

61. *Süddeutsche Zeitung,* 14 February 1996, 19 February 1996, 21 February 1996, 7 June 1996, 5 September 1996, 2 November 1996, 16 December 1996, 20 December 1996, and 30 December 1996--all on Nexis; and *Neue Zürcher Zeitung* (15 May 1996), p. 2.

62. *Die Welt* (21 August 1997), p. 2; *Neue Zürcher Zeitung* (17 February 1997), p. 2; *Die Tageszeitung* (20 March 1997), p. 5; and *Süddeutsche Zeitung* (8 August 1997), p. 6.

63. Most recently in November 1997. See *Welt am Sonntag* (23 November 1997), p. 4.

64. *Süddeutsche Zeitung,* 29 February 1996, 8 March 1996, and 8 June 1996- all on Nexis.

65. Regarding Saxony, see *Süddeutsche Zeitung* (17 August 1996), on Nexis.

66. See Dirk Philipsen, *We Were the People: Voices from East Germany's Revolutionary Autumn of 1989* (Durham, N.C.: Duke University Press, 1993).

67. Lutz Hoffmann, *Das deutsche Volk und seine Feinde: die völkische Droge-- Aktualität und Entstehungsgeschichte* (Koln: Papy-Rossa, 1994), p. 11.

68. Siegler, "Rechtsextremismus in der DDR," p. 623.

69. Quoted in *Ibid.,* p. 619.

5

The Shadow of the Stasi

David Childs

Very many people outside Germany have heard of the Gestapo, and many outside Russia know what the KGB was, but few would know what is meant by the Stasi. Only in specialist circles is the term common currency. Few books about the GDR written before 1989 mentioned the Ministry for State Security *(Ministerium für Staatssicherheit, MfS)* or the State Security *(Staatssicherheit, Stasi)*.[1] This was partly due to the fact that the GDR did not put out statistics on the work of the MfS, preferring to bombard visitors with endless material designed to convince them of its achievements in health care, education, book production, sports, and even housing. Established in 1950 as the successor to various secret departments, the MfS was a vital part of the cement, which held the GDR together. Most East Germans were painfully aware of the MfS.[2] Its existence was in no way secret. It existed openly in the same way as the FBI and the CIA in the United States or the BfV and BND in what was West Germany. The SED (Socialist Unity Party) party line was that all states have secret security organs and the GDR was simply defending itself in its fight to build socialism. In provincial towns, one could see car park spaces bearing the inscription, "reserved for vehicles of the MfS." The anniversary of the founding of the MfS was celebrated in the media each year, and *Armeegeneral* Erich Mielke, deputy minister 1955-57, minister for state security from 1957 to 1989, was given prominence.[3]

If East Germans were clear about the existence of the MfS/Stasi and clear that it was present from Rostock to Suhl and from Madgeburg to Frankfurt am Oder and widely represented in GDR institutions, they were nevertheless shocked by revelations after November 1989 about the scale of its activities. The MfS was one of the GDR's top employers with roughly 100,000 full-time employees. This worked out to about one full-time operative per 165 inhabitants in 1989. According to the official statistics, the GDR claimed there was one medical practitioner per 400 of population in 1988. In reality, the effective number of doctors was certainly lower.[4] In Karl-Marx-Stadt (Chemnitz) the MfS employed one full-time operative per 500 of population, in Rostock one per 300 of population. Worse still, it has been estimated that, proportionate to population, the density of the Stasi informer network in the GDR was seven times that of the Gestapo in the Third Reich. In 1986 there was on average one informer per 120 inhabitants of the GDR. The administrative regions *(Bezirke)* Cottbus and Schwerin had the highest number. There were only 80 inhabitants per informer in Cottbus and only 94 in Schwerin. In Berlin, there were 148 inhabitants per informer. At the other end of the scale, Erfurt had 149 inhabitants for every informer and Karl-Marx-Stadt 134.[5]

The informers or IM were not evenly spread within a *Bezirk*. Obviously, it depended in part on ease or difficulty of recruitment, the priorities of the Stasi, and so on. East Germans expected there to be strict security in anything connected with defense, including defense industries. They also realized that *all* ministries and the SED would be awarded top security ratings. Some knew that this was true of the media, regional and local government, and higher education. The chain of Interhotels and other bodies normally reserved for foreigners were known to be subject to Stasi scrutiny. It was clear that dissidents would soon have the Stasi after them, as would the churches. Less expected, was Stasi coverage of trains. However, visitors found East Germans were far less talkative on trains than were West Germans. Even many members of the SED were appalled to find out that the Stasi had attempted to cover the "allied parties," all schools and hospitals, cultural clubs, sports organizations, blocks of flats, merchant ships and airliners, and virtually everything else.

The SED, it must be remembered, had a membership of 2.3 million out of an adult population of about 12 million. Many ordinary members were stunned by the first revelations of collaborations with the Stasi, which came when the GDR was still in existence. Erich Mielke was forced to resign as minister for state security on 7 November 1989 when Egon Krenz was still SED general secretary. Mielke was accused of abusing his office, personal enrichment and corruption, and was eventually expelled from the party. Krenz watched as Mielke was first stripped of all his positions and then, on 7 December, was arrested. The day before, Krenz had himself been forced to resign. By then, details of Stasi abuse had reached the public. But some in the SED still did not want to acknowledge the truth. Christina Wilkening's book *Staat Im Staate Auskünfte ehemaliger Stasi-Mitarbeiter*[6] caused something of a minor sensation when it appeared in Berlin in the first half of 1990. Herself a member of the GDR "Establishment," she interviewed 12 former Stasi operatives with ranks ranging from colonel down to non-commissioned officer. "Rainer," 47, from *Hauptabteilung VIII* told his readers that "Es wurden Mann und Maus überwacht." The term *flächendeckende Überwachung*, meaning roughly, total surveillance, became part of the vocabulary of the 1990s. After 10 November 1989 *Der Spiegel* became available to East Germans and was read avidly. It exposed many aspects of the Stasi and its activities. Markus Wolf, the acceptable face of the Stasi, who had retired in 1986 and became a Gorbachev fan, published his story in 1991. His book was entitled *In eigenem Auftrag* (On my own Account).[7] This catchy title was less than accurate given his decades of service first for the Soviets, and later for the MfS of which he was a deputy minister for state security. He became something of a media star and attempted to distinguish his own "clean," "professional" espionage activity from the main internal security function of the Stasi.

It must be remembered that the exposure of the Stasi was not happening in isolation. There was the exposure of the privileged lifestyle of the Politburo members. There was the revelation about the top medical facilities available to the leading politicians of the GDR, but not to the masses. There were the revelations about the inadequacies of normal medical care. There was the shock of finding that West German levels of choice and consumption were even higher than East Germans had believed. For the SED faithful, there were shocks to come from what was still the Soviet Union. Among many other shocks was the rehabilitation of Trotsky and the confirmation that all that had been said about Stalin's crimes in the West was true. One horrific crime, which had been blamed on the Nazis, the massacre of over 15,000 Polish officers in the Katyn Woods, was admitted on 13 April 1990 by the Soviet news agency Tass. Nearer home, there was the exposure of Stalinism within the Soviet Zone before 1949 and the GDR after that date. Walter Janka's autobiographical book *Schwierigkeiten mit der Wahrheit* (Difficulties with the Truth)[8] published in West Germany in 1989 soon became available to East Germans. It shamed and dismayed many in the SED as this former KPD-SED comrade, literary figure, and International Brigade anti-Fascist told of his torture at the hands of the Stasi in the 1950s. In particular he accused Mielke and exposed the cowardice of some other SED comrades. In the GDR itself, Elfriede Brüning had her book *Lästige Zeugen? Tonbandgespräche mit Opfern der Stalinzeit* (Troublesome Witnesses? Taped Interviews with Victims of the Stalin Era), published in December 1989.[9] A communist before 1933, the writer Elfriede Brüning had remained in Germany and, after briefly being incarcerated in 1935 in Berlin's Barnim Street women's prison, had a quiet Third Reich. In 1945, she renewed her political, journalistic, and writing activities on behalf of Soviet and German communism. In her introduction, she confesses her earlier naiveté in the way that she had written about Germans in the Soviet Union. Through recorded interviews, her book tells of the suffering of German communists who went to the Soviet Union to escape Nazism only to become Stalin's victims. Interestingly enough, Brüning remained a communist and GDR loyalist.[10]

Collaboration with the Stasi

Political Figures

Another terrible legacy of the Stasi were accusations against leading East German *Wende* politicians that their hands were not clean, that they had supped with the Stasi and had taken the 40 pieces of silver. The first politician to fall was Wolfgang Schur, a lawyer who had defended dissidents. He had been a co-founder of *Demokratischer Aufbruch* (Democratic Awakening) but was exposed already in 1989. Ibrahim Böhme looked like a rising star in the Social Democratic Party that he had helped to establish. He became the chairman of the SDP/SPD in the GDR and a member of the democratically elected *Volkskammer* in March 1990. In the following month, he was forced to give up his leadership functions. Under the code name "Maximillian" he had worked for the Stasi. In June 1992, he was expelled from the SPD. Another category of politician involved those who had not been known as opponents of the SED regime; on the contrary, they had held official positions, but had attempted to save their careers during *Die Wende*. These included any number of members of the so-called "allied parties," e.g., the Liberal Democratic Party (LDPD) and the Christian Democratic Union (CDU). A notable case was that of Gerhard Lindner, alias "Hans Reichert," an important member of the leadership of the LDPD. He had worked with the Stasi from the 1950s and was known to foreign visitors to the GDR through his membership in the Peace Council of which he became a vice-president and the *Liga für Völkerfreundschaft*. Another of his functions was president of the GDR-UK Friendship Society. He was sent abroad and reported back to the MfS about developments in the peace movements in Britain, Denmark, the USA, and Austria. On 15 September 1987, the UN awarded him a medal for his activities as a worker for peace! He attempted to present himself as a *Wende* politician, eventually being admitted to the Free Democratic Party (FDP) which was part of the government in Bonn.[11]

Another sad case was that of Lothar de Maizière. A long-standing yet lowly member of the CDU of the GDR, he was elected minister president (head of government) by the democratically elected *Volkskammer* in March 1990. He took the GDR into union with the Federal Republic in October 1990 and became a minister in Kohl's coalition. He too was accused of being a Stasi informer, a charge that he has continued to deny.[12] He resigned from the government and the *Bundestag* in 1991. De Maizière's colleague in the CDU Martin Kirchner was also forced to give up all his offices on 2 August 1990. He had been deputy chairman of the Evangelical-Lutheran Church Office in Thuringia and was elected general secretary of the CDU at its special conference on 16 December 1989.[13] The minister president of Brandenburg, Manfred Stolpe (SPD), another leading church figure, has fought a long battle in his attempt to clear his name of being a Stasi informer. He acknowledges that he had contact with the Stasi but claims this was necessary to carry out his activities for the Protestant church. These are very sad cases because the people of the new *Bundesländer* need heroes from among themselves or at least politicians of their own whom they can respect.

The successor party to the SED, the Party of Democratic Socialism (PDS), can only gloat at such embarrassment among its political opponents. Accusations against its own members have less impact. Many of its own hard-core clientele were officials of the SED, the mass organizations, the media, the government ministries, the armed forces, and indeed the Stasi itself. For them there is no disgrace in having worked for the MfS either openly or undercover. Ilja Seifert, a PDS member of the *Bundestag*, 1990-1994, openly proclaimed that he had worked for the Stasi out of conviction.[14] Nevertheless, several members of the PDS have been forced to retire from various functions. So far, Gregor Gysi has resisted attacks on his past. He stands accused of having worked for the Stasi when defending dissidents Rudolf Bahro and Robert Havemann. He came to prominence during *Die Wende* being elected Chairman of the SED/PDS in December 1989. He retained this function up to December 1992. At the time of this writing, he leads the PDS group in the *Bundestag*.

Church Figures

At least as damaging as the accusations against politicians are those made against prominent church figures and against members of the old GDR literary establishment. It came as no surprise to some that Hanfried Müller was exposed as Stasi informer "Michael." Appointed professor of theology at Humboldt University in 1964, this churchman had campaigned all his adult life for the communist cause. He was a "refugee" from West Germany, which he had left in 1952 after taking a leading part in the Moscow-orientated peace movement. He served as a member of the Synod of the Evangelical Church in Brandenburg and of the Union of Evangelical Churches of the GDR. He was active in the Peace Council of the GDR and the Christian Peace Conference and worked tirelessly to bring the churches around to the SED's position. After 1990, Müller remained firmly on the old SED line.[15] Friedrich-Wilhelm Krummacher (1901-1974) was another well-known SED party-liner. Bishop of Greifswald and chairman of the Conference of Governing Church Bodies, he had been a member of the Nazi party and had collaborated with the Soviets after capture when serving as a German army chaplain. "Günter" was the Stasi's code name for Günter Krusche, who held various church positions. He was chairman of the study commission of Lutheran World League from 1977. Krusche retired in 1992 after he was accused of Stasi activities. Overall, a significant number of churchmen had been recruited by the Stasi. In Saxony, the church concluded that of 1,050 main office holders "about two dozen" had collaborated with the Stasi.[16] These informers were often significant figures who had considerable influence. An example of this was the election of the Bishop of Berlin-Brandenburg in 1981. Of the 110 electors, 12 were Stasi informers.

Cultural Figures

Writers and artists were given prominence in the GDR and were awarded material privileges in return for toeing the party line. The SED expected their work to make a contribution to its version of the building of socialism. While supporting the socialist system, many writers felt they needed more freedom to experiment with their writing and to present in a realistic way the problems of society and not just its achievements. Probably more than 80 writers turned their backs on the GDR during its existence.[17] Some simply moved to the West before the Wall was built in 1961, like Uwe Johnson and Theodor Plivier. Others, like Erich Loest and Roger Loewig, left after imprisonment, and others were allowed to leave like Thomas Brasch and Hans-Joachim Schädlich. Some, like Wolf Biermann, were deprived of their right of return while outside the GDR. The Stasi put a great deal of effort into ensuring that creative artists remained loyal. They recruited writers and artists as informers. They also sought the services of individuals occupying important positions in publishing houses, journals, and magazines and literary editors of newspapers. To a degree, this is more surprising as all outlets for any literary work were owned by official organizations of one kind or another and subject to official censorship. Mielke and his generals were leaving nothing to chance in the fight against corrupting influences! An example of this was the recruitment of Armin Zeißler, deputy chief editor of the prestigious literary journal *Sinn und Form*, 1963 to 1988. He worked for *Hauptabteilung II* of the MfS from 1984 to 1988.[18] Likewise, *neue deutsche literatur*, the monthly journal of the GDR writers' organization, was heavily infiltrated by the Stasi.[19] Key positions in publishing houses like Aufbau-Verlag, Verlag Philipp Reclam jun., Leipzig, and Eulenspiegel Verlag Berlin were held by Stasi informers. The Eulenspiegel Verlag, was the leading publisher of satire and humor in the GDR. Mielke wanted his subjects to have a good laugh, but only at the things he found funny!

It was known before the fall of the Stasi and the GDR that manuscripts were subject to censorship, but it was usually thought that this was merely an SED matter. The archives reveal that the Stasi played an essential role in vetting manuscripts independent of the party.[20] One famous case of a Stasi cultural commissar was Klaus Gysi, the father of Gregor Gysi (see above). The 45-year-old, "old" communist Gysi worked as informer "Kurt" from 1957, having been recruited by a 22-year-old Stasi non-commissioned officer, Peter Heinz Gütling. Gysi worked as head of the Aufbau-Verlag from 1957 to 1966. Before that, he had served as head of the department for the history of German literature at the Verlag Volk und Wissen. He went on to serve as Minister for Culture, 1966-1973, Ambassador to Italy and Malta, 1973-1978, and State Secretary for Church Affairs, 1979-1988. Gütling crept up the ladder in the Stasi, reaching the rank of major in 1980. He continued in his attempts to keep GDR literature clean until the Stasi was abolished in 1989.[21]

After reunification there were those who felt that despite its many shortcomings, the GDR could be proud of its writers, both those who had left and those who had stayed. It was a bitter disappointment to this constituency to find that some of the writers they had admired were tainted with Stasi connections. One of the first to be exposed was Sascha Anderson who came quickly to prominence in the GDR at the end of the 1970s, when he was still in his twenties. He had wide connections in intellectual and cultural circles from the DEFA film studios to the churches. In 1986, he was allowed to move to West Berlin. In 1991, he was exposed by Wolf Biermann and Jürgen Fuchs as a Stasi informer. He had worked for the MfS from 1975 onwards, collecting information on fellow writers and opposition figures.

Far more devastating was the exposure of the GDR loyalist Heiner Müller, the best known East German dramatist. Although he had had his difficulties with the SED over his plays, he was given the chance to visit the USA and Mexico in 1975. Shortly after this, he worked for the Stasi as "Heiner." He did not deny or regret his contacts, but argued they were inevitable and even productive.[22]

Worse than either of these cases and others, was that of icon, Christa Wolf. Wolf was the best-known woman writer in the GDR. She had been a member of the SED and, for a period, of its Central Committee. She had stepped out of line on several occasions, but it was revealed that in the 1950s she had operated as an informer known to the Stasi as "Margarete." Apparently she had given her case officer little of value.[23] Her Stasi activities did not stop her picking up honors abroad in the 1990s. In 1991, she was elected Honorary Member of the American Academy and Institute of Arts and Letters. In 1993, she was elected Scholar of the Getty Center in Santa Monica. She attempted to come to terms with her Stasi past in her *Akteneinsicht Christa Wolf. Zerrspiegel und Dialog* published in 1993.

Less surprising than the above-mentioned Stasi informers were Hermann Kant and Dieter Noll. They served the Stasi respectively, 1963-1976, and, with interruptions, 1954-1989. Both were regarded as orthodox supporters of the regime.[24] Kant had contacts with the Stasi going back to the 1950s. These continued until 1976 when the Stasi regarded him as too important in GDR life to continue as an informer. They gave him a medal and said, 'Farewell'. By this time, he was a member of the SED Berlin leadership and a successful author. Perhaps best known for his novel *Die Aula*, he was president of the GDR Writers' League, 1978-1990, and member of the SED's Central Committee, 1981-1990. Noll had served as a member of the Berlin SED's leadership team, 1964-1967, and had later played a leading role in 1976 denouncing Biermann and other dissidents (Wolf had supported Biermann). His main work, *Die Abenteuer des Werner Holt* (The Adventures of Werner Holt), based on his youth in Nazi Germany, was compulsory reading in GDR secondary schools. Another author whose books were widely read in schools was SED Central Committee member Gerhard Holtz-Baumert, alias "Villon," who collaborated with the Stasi over a long period and even sought their help with material for his books.[25]

Not surprisingly, the Stasi was active in the film studios and in the electronic media. One of the most famous GDR documentary filmmakers, Gerhard Scheumann, was recruited in 1975. He was responsible for something like 66 documentary films, many of which were shown around the world. Perhaps best known was *Piloten im Pyjama* (1968), which was made up of interviews with American air crews who had been unlucky enough to fall into the hands of the North Vietnamese. Many, if not all, of the Americans had been tortured, and the interviews were not given freely. This did not of course come out in the film. The "pyjamas" were the prison uniforms worn by the US aviators. One of Scheumann's key functions was to collect information of interest to the MfS in diplomatic circles in East Berlin and no doubt on his trips abroad. His reports were regarded as important enough to go directly to General Bruno Beate, first deputy minister for state security until his death in 1982. Scheumann later appears to have become disillusioned with some GDR policies and was demobilized from service in 1984.[26]

The Stasi Administration Leadership

What about those who organized all these activities, the top echelons of the Stasi? Mielke himself was, as we have seen, arrested for misuse of office in December 1990. That was when Hans Modrow (SED/PDS) led the GDR. With brief interruptions, Mielke remained in custody until he was sentenced on 26 October 1993 for the murder of a police officer in Berlin in 1931. He was then part of the military wing of the Communist Party of Germany (KPD). He has since been released and can be seen occasionally hobbling around Berlin Hohenschön-hausen.

Major General Rudi Mittag, deputy minister for state security from 1975 onwards, was removed with Mielke in December 1989, after which he lived as a pensioner until his death in August 1994. Major General Gerhard Neiber, a deputy minister from 1980, also fell with Mielke. From May 1993, he was remanded in custody for having allegedly attempted to kidnap and kill a frontier soldier who had deserted to the West. Major General Wolfgang Schwanitz served as deputy minister between 1986 and 1989. He then served for a few weeks as head of the Bureau for National Security before that body was abolished in January 1990.

General Heinz Keßler, GDR minister of defense, 1985-1989, was arrested for misuse of office by the Modrow government. He was also expelled from the SED/PDS. The first member of the Politburo to be convicted and sent to prison, he received seven years and six months imprisonment in 1993 for his part in the shootings along the Berlin Wall. Aged 77, he is granted 60 hours leave a month from his West Berlin prison.[27] General Fritz Streletz, Deputy Minister of Defense, was charged with commissioning manslaughter and sentenced in Berlin to five years and six months imprisonment in September 1993. An appeal against this sentence was rejected by the Federal Constitutional Court. Markus Wolf, who entered the GDR intelligence service on 1 September 1951, was deputy minister for state security and head of intelligence (HVA) from 1958 to 1986. He was in charge of East German foreign intelligence from December 1952.[28] Wolf was sentenced on 6 December 1993 to six years' imprisonment for high treason. The sentence was suspended pending an appeal to the Federal Constitutional Court at Karlsruhe. In May 1995, the Constitutional Court gave its verdict. It decided that former GDR inhabitants who pursued espionage against the Federal Republic from *within* the GDR should not be prosecuted for this activity. West Germans who worked for the Stasi could be prosecuted with the full vigor of the law. This judgment cleared Wolf and his successor as Stasi intelligence chief, General Werner Großmann, from threat of prosecution for their main Stasi activity.

The SED Empire

Given the massive burden of German reunification which the old Federal Republic is having to bear, the *Bundestag* is particularly interested in recovering the vast financial reserves of the SED, the MfS, and other former GDR bodies. Apart from financial considerations, there is also the fear that some kind of SED Mafia could use financial means to gain new influence in the united Germany. As with Nazi gold, it is doubtful whether the full story will ever emerge about SED gold. There is no doubt that the MfS had accounts and companies it controlled in Austria, Belgium, Denmark, France, Holland, Italy, Liechtenstein, Luxembourg, Switzerland, West Germany, and other countries. These appear to have been held by the so-called KoKo organization of Dr. Alexander Schalck-Golodkowski, himself a Stasi colonel. He reported directly to Mielke about his activities. The KoKo companies were not subject to the normal rules and regulations for other GDR enterprises. In 1997, Wolf testified that his organization received DM 1.5 million annually to finance HVA operations.[29] This is likely to be a conservative figure, but even so, such an amount could finance the yearly pay of at least a couple dozen spies in West Germany. These operations were by no means the main source of

HVA funds. Schalck, aged 65, a member of the SED Central Committee, was expelled in December 1989. Although a number of attempts have been made to convict him on a variety of charges, he has managed to beat off attacks and lives in some style in Bavaria. It is widely believed his contacts with West German politicians have helped him. Another part of the SED empire, the import-export firm Novum, was thought to have transferred DM 530 million to accounts in Austria and Switzerland.[30] The full story will not emerge due to missing files, memory loss by essential witnesses, and the death or disappearance of others.

The Stasi Archives

Destruction of Files

The storming of the Stasi headquarters in the Normannenstraße of Berlin on 15 January 1990 and in other regional centers like Leipzig (4 December 1989) was a godsend for some Stasi officers and informers. Files were destroyed by the demonstrators. This could have been a deliberate ploy with Stasi agents among the demonstrators, as the Stasi had been destroying files before this. Certainly hundreds, perhaps thousands, of Stasi informers and covert members were saved from the consequences of exposure by the destruction of their files at this time. These were often individuals who had direct access to Mielke or Krenz who could have their files destroyed by a verbal order covering a few individuals rather than a written order covering a particular category. In November 1989, for instance, General Wolfgang Schwanitz gave the order to destroy the files on all parliamentarians of the so-called "allied parties," the satellite parties of the SED, and on individuals who were having love affairs with citizens of capitalist states.[31] As a consequence of this destructive activity, it is more than likely that some informers who did little damage will pay a price while others, who worked for many years for the Stasi and ruined other people's lives, will not be confronted with their pasts.

Access to Stasi Files

The Stasi did not have the opportunity to destroy all its files and, in the end, six million dossiers were found. Of these, four million were files on East Germans and two million were files on West Germans and foreigners.[32] Joachim Gauck, himself an East German dissident, was put in charge of the files after the fall of the Stasi. The freely elected *Volkskammer* of March 1990 passed a law entitling every individual to see his or her file. After reunification in October 1990, the *Bundestag* renewed this right. Under the law (*Stasi-Unterlagen-Gesetz*) passed by the *Bundestag* on 20 December 1991, Section 1, paragraph 3, gives every individual the right to information from the commissioner (Gauck) as to whether there is a file on him or her. If there is, he/she has the right to see the file and obtain a copy of it.[33] Gauck reported 30 June 1995 that his office had received 2.7 million requests for information. In the central archive in Berlin (in the former Stasi headquarters) and in the 14 branch archives, 180 kilometers of documents had been found. These included 35.6 million card indexes containing brief personal details and hundreds of thousands of photographs, tape recordings, and videos.[34]

Investigations

Many of those accused of various crimes after reunification were charged in connection with activities for the Stasi. Up to the summer of 1997 over 20,000 investigations had been carried out in Berlin, the main center for such investigations. Of these, 17,460 did not lead to court proceedings. The remainder, led to 406 individuals being charged, 113 found guilty, and 47 acquitted (30 of these in Wall shooting cases).[35] One can agree with the SPD vice chairman Wolfgang Thierse, himself an East German, that these figures show that the accusation of "victor's justice" is absurd.[36] It must be remembered that almost all of the Politburo of Erich Honecker and around 200 leading personalities of the GDR were arrested for misuse of office and corruption when the SED was still in office. Had the GDR continued to exist, most of those who were fit to stand trial would have been convicted and sent to prison. East German courts would probably have been harder on them than post-unification courts have been. The anger among the East German people, including many in the SED, was so great at the time that it is likely that higher sentences would have been handed down. They would also have faced harsher prison conditions than those prevailing in Germany today.

West German Collaborators

West Germans who have been accused of being Stasi agents have not fared as well as those in the former GDR. One of the many sensational cases that came to light in the 1990s was that of Gisela Gast, known to some American academics for her book on the political role of women in the GDR. She had worked in a senior capacity for the West German intelligence service, the BND, from 1973 to her arrest on 29 September 1990. She had been involved with Wolf's HVA since 1970! Wolf risked going to Yugoslavia to meet the former student who had been recruited through a romantic entanglement.[37] As the figures for arrests show, the opening of the files has proved decisive in exposing former Stasi agents. There were 32 arrests in 1988 of suspected spies, ten of them suspected of having worked for the Stasi and 16 for the Soviets. In 1989, 11 arrests were made of persons suspected of having spied for the Stasi. Another six were arrested for activities on behalf of the Soviet Union. In 1990, 82 persons were arrested for alleged work for the Stasi, and only 11 for spying for the Soviet Union. In 1992, 38 were arrested as Stasi agents, four as Soviet agents. In 1994, 30 individuals were arrested as Stasi agents and two as Soviet agents. Finally, in 1996, only one person was arrested as a probable Stasi agent and one other as a Soviet agent.[38]

How many former Stasi agents remain undetected in Germany? In 1991, the Ministry of Interior believed there had been between 6,000 and 7,000 Stasi agents operating in West Germany in 1989. Only 600 had by that time been exposed. The belief was that up to 400 well-trained agents, many of them in sensitive positions, were still at large.[39] With the opening of the Stasi archives, the West Germans had to face the truth that virtually every organization and every ministry in the Federal Republic had been infiltrated by the Stasi and that many of those enlisted were not just bogus refugees like Günter Guillaume who brought down Chancellor Willy Brandt.[40]

Continuing Issues

The scandals surrounding disclosures from the Stasi archives have inevitably led to accusations of victimization and claims that not all the entries are accurate. Some believe that, in a sense, the Stasi is being allowed to set the agenda in that its former officers act as witnesses in investigations and court cases. In any case, as mentioned above, some individuals of importance to the Stasi or well connected to the old SED leadership were able to get their files destroyed. Is it fair to expose those whose files have survived particularly if they did not harm individuals? There is also the argument that many of those who co-operated with the Stasi were either blackmailed or were the victims of their schooling in the GDR or of their SED/MfS family backgrounds. Finally, there are those who argue that the healing progress can only be complete when the Stasi is finally banished to the past.

All these considerations have led to calls for the Stasi archives to be closed. The majority of Germans still do not agree with this view. A poll in 1997 revealed that, overall, 37 percent of Germans favored closing the files, but 57 percent wanted them to remain open. Among west Germans 36 percent favored closing and 56 wanted the files left open, while 38 percent of east Germans were for closure and 60 percent wanted the files to remain open. Even among PDS voters, 21 percent favored open files, but 79 percent favored closure.[41] Clearly, among PDS voters and more so among party members there is the feeling that the capitalist west Germans have taken over the GDR and are persecuting those "who only did their duty."

Whether the files remain open indefinitely or not, the Stasi will continue to haunt Germany. Unless the law is changed, many of those who have feared prosecution for Stasi activities could stop worrying at the end of 1997. At that time, all crimes that carried a maximum sentence of up to five years lapsed. But revelations about Stasi activities could still prove very damaging in many circles. Far worse than this are the suspicions that still lurk among neighbors, friends, and families. Many will never know whether someone close to them betrayed them to the Stasi, and this must affect the quality of human relations in the former GDR for some time to come. Meanwhile, on 29 October 1997, Joachim Gauck presented his third report to the *Bundestag* about his authority's activities. He revealed there had been 3.7 million requests for information, of which more than 1.3 million were from citizens requesting to view their own files. In 1.07 million cases, these requests had been dealt with. Gauck highlighted the increased interest from west Germans who now made up 20 percent of those requesting information. According to Gauck, Mielke's MfS had recruited 20,000 to 30,000 Germans living in West Berlin or West Germany to work as informers. The problem of the Stasi's shadows was, he said, by no means just an East German problem.[42]

Notes

1. A few examples: Peter Christian Ludz, *The German Democratic Republic From The Sixties To The Seventies: A Socio-Political Analysis* (Cambridge, MA. Center for International Affairs, Harvard, 1970) does not mention Mielke or his Stasi. They were left out of his projections for the future of the GDR power system. Kurt Sontheimer and Wilhelm Bleek, *The Government and Politics of East*

Germany (London: Hutchinson, 1975). They mention the ministries on p. 85 including culture, elementary education, defense and so on, but not state security. Martin McCauley, *The German Democratic Republic Since 1945* (London: Macmillan, 1983) mentions Mielke as Minister for State Security but does not attempt to discuss his ministry. David Childs, *The GDR: Moscow's German Ally* (London: Allen and Unwin, 1983) devotes one-and-a-half pages to the MfS and the same to the *Kampfgruppen*. Mielke gets frequent mentions. Henry Krisch, *Politics And Culture in the German Democratic Republic* (Ann Arbor: The University of Michigan, 1988) does not include anything on the Stasi.

2. See comments of Robert Darnton, *Berlin Journal 1989-1990* (New York and London: W.W. Norton & Co, 1991), pp. 132-33.

3. For Mielke see Jochen von Lang, *Erich Mielke eine deutsche Karriere* (Berlin: Rowohlt, 1991).

4. Statistisches Bundesamt, *DDR 1990 Zahlen und Fakten* (Stuttgart: Metzler-Poeschel, 1990), p. 25.

5. David Childs and Richard Popplewell, *The Stasi: The East German Intelligence and Security Service* (London: Macmillan, 1996), p. 85.

6. Christina Wilkening, *Staat Im Staate Auskünfte ehemaliger Stasi-Mitarbeiter* (Berlin and Weimar: Aufbau-Verlag, 1990).

7. For a useful biography of Wolf see Alexander Reichenbach, *Chef der Spione. Die Markus-Wolf-Story* (Stuttgart: Deutsche Verlags-Anstalt, 1992).

8. Walter Janka, *Schwierigkeiten mit der Wahrheit* (Reinbek bei Hamburg: Rowohlt, 1989).

9. Elfriede Brüning, *Lästige Zeugen? Tonbandgespräche mit Opfern der Stalinzeit* (Halle-Leipzig: Mitteldeutscher Verlag, December 1989).

10. David Childs interviewed Brüning in 1994. Brüning's own autobiography is *Und außerdem war es mein Leben* (Berlin: Elefanten Press, 1994).

11. Joachim Walther, *Sicherheitsbereich, Literatur, Schriftsteller, und Staatssicherheit in der Deutschen Demokratischen Republik* (Berlin: Ch. Links Verlag, 1996), p. 272. This book is a remarkable feat of research based on the Stasi files.

12. David Childs interviewed de Maizière in 1994.

13. Bernd-Rainer Barth, Christoph Links, Helmut Müller-Enbergs, and Jan Wielgoths, *Wer war Wer in der DDR. Ein biographisches Handbuch* (Frankfurt am Main: Fischer Taschenbuch Verlag, 1994), p. 371. This is a very useful publication.

14. Childs and Popplewell, *The Stasi*, p. 195.

15. Barth *et al.*, *Wer war Wer*, p. 522.

16. *Die Welt*, 5 April 1994.

17. *Ibid.*, p. 90.

18. *Ibid.*, p. 529.

19. *Ibid.*, p. 817.

20. *Ibid.*, pp. 773-93.

21. *Ibid.*, pp. 262-3.

22. Childs and Popplewell, *The Stasi*, p. 104.

23. Walther, *Sicherheitsbereich*, p. 21.

24. *Ibid.*, p. 647.

25. *Ibid.*, p. 281.

26. *Ibid.*, p. 529.   Childs met Scheumann in 1968.

27. *Der Spiegel*, No. 36 (1 September 1997), p. 38.

28. *Woche im bundestag*, 8 October 1997.

29. *Ibid.*

30. *Ibid.*, 1 October 1997.

31. Joachim Gauck, *Die Stasi-Akten* (Reinbek bei Hamburg: Rowohlt, 1991), p. 89.

32. *Ibid.*, p. 11.

33. *Ibid.*, pp. 118-40 for full text.

34. *Woche im bundestag*, 5 July 1995, p. 9.

35. *Das Parlament*, 10 October 1997.

36. *Ibid.*

37. See Childs and Popplewell, *The Stasi*, for details.

38. These figures are taken from the annual reports to the Federal Office for the Protection of the Constitution, Der Bundesminister des Innern, *Verfassungsschutzbericht*, Bonn.

39. See Childs and Popplewell, *The Stasi*, for details.

40. Guido Knopp, *Top Spione Verräter im Geheimen Krieg*, (Munich: C. Bertelsmann, 1994), gives a good summary of the Guillaume case.   Peter Richter and Klaus Rösler, *Wolfs West-Spione. Ein Insider-Report* (Berlin: Elefanten Press, 1992), write as former HVA members.   Childs interviewed Rösler in 1994.

41. *Der Spiegel*, No. 36 (1 September 1997), p 38.

42. *Das Parlament*, 7 November 1997, and *woche im bundestag*, 5 November 1997.

6

The Illusory Economic Miracle: Assessing Eastern Germany's Economic Transition

Patricia J. Smith

During the period following the fall of the Berlin Wall in 1989, Germans from East and West looked toward unification with optimism. After all, the Federal Republic of Germany anchored the European Union and possessed one of the strongest economies in Europe and the world. For its part, the German Democratic Republic (GDR) represented the strongest economy in Eastern Europe. West German Chancellor Helmut Kohl confidently predicted a repeat of West Germany's post-world war II "economic miracle," promising that east Germany would flourish within five years.[1] However, this was not to be. The economic upswing has stalled. Despite more than DM 1 trillion ($600 billion) in aid from western Germany, economic self-sufficiency eludes eastern Germany, viable firms are scarce, and high unemployment persists. In the midst of these economic pressures, even the future of the Federal Republic's long-standing social market economy has come under discussion.

Several questions guide this research. What is the state of the economy in eastern Germany now, more than seven years after unification? How well off are east Germans economically? What went wrong? And what are the prospects for the future?

The argument of this chapter is: misconceptions concerning the magnitude of the project and the tasks to accomplish plus mistakes in implementation have handicapped the economic transition in eastern Germany. Providing a largely negative model for other East European transitions, the east German case cautions that quick transitions and rapid privatization without adequate protection can have disastrous consequences for developing or transitioning economies. Both governments and markets play roles in transitions to market economies, and governmental choices can help or hinder the process.

This chapter uses several types of comparisons to provide a context for understanding the east German economic transition. These include comparisons of the current east German situation with conditions in the former GDR, in western Germany, and in Eastern Europe. The post-world war II transition of the Federal Republic of Germany supplemented by Marshall Plan assistance furnishes additional insights.

The Objectives and Costs of German Economic and Monetary Union

The continuing exodus of workers from East to West Germany prompted a quick resolution of the status of the two Germanies. In February 1990 West German Chancellor Helmut Kohl raised the possibility of a rapid economic and monetary union, although most economists and politicians favored a gradual transition.[2] Support for rapid monetary union grew throughout the GDR, and the overwhelming support in the East German *Volkskammer* elections of 18 March 1990 for parties supporting Kohl's proposals provided new impetus. Under this pressure German economic and monetary union took place 1 July 1990, considerably earlier than initially planned.

The treaty of 18 May 1990 provided that the social market system of the Federal Republic would become the common economic system of the two Germanies. Key elements included "private ownership, competition, free pricing, and . . . freedom of movement of labour, capital, goods and services."[3] At the time of monetary union the East German *Ostmark* was converted to the strong West German *deutsche Mark* at a rate of 1:1 for personal savings up to $4000. However, the remainder of East German savings were converted at a rate of 2:1, so profitable East German firms saw their capital cut by half. Some difficult issues, including property ownership, initially remained unresolved, but a primary objective was for East Germany to move as quickly as possible away from central planning and toward privatization and the social market economy.

Privatization

The successes and failures of privatization efforts in eastern Germany lay primarily with *Treuhandanstalt,* the state privatization agency and holding company. Created initially under the Hans Modrow GDR government in early March 1990, the initial objective of *Treuhand* was "to preserve economic assets and protect them against arbitrary take-over and to enable them to adjust to market economy conditions."[4] However, both the new East German *Volkskammer,* elected 18 March 1990, and the unification treaty changed the objective of *Treuhand,* placing new emphasis on restructuring and privatizing firms in line with conditions of the social market economy.[5] Stressing rapid privatization rather than restructuring, *Treuhand* succeeded in privatizing its inventory of firms quite rapidly, but often at the expense of their economic s`urvival.[6]

In July 1990 when economic and monetary union occurred, *Treuhand* controlled 8,482 large state industrial enterprises with more than four million employees (plus about 25,000 small shops, hotels, restaurants, other small firms). *Treuhand's* charge included privatizing about 6,100 of the large enterprises, with the remainder intended for transfer to local authorities.[7] By 31 December 1993, just three-and-a-half years later, *Treuhand* had privatized 92 percent of its firms, but after privatization many remain marginal and a number have closed. Critics abound, charging that *Treuhand* had no restructuring strategy other than rapid privatization and that the overall effect has been massive unemployment and the "deindustrialization" of eastern Germany.[8]

Although *Treuhand* conditions of sale required buyers to maintain specified employment levels for a number of years, by the end of 1993 only 1.5 million jobs remained out of the 3.9 million jobs initially provided by privatized firms,[9] despite a penalty of DM 15,000 to DM 40,000 per job lost.[10] Extremely high subsidies maintained other jobs, but at excessive costs. For example, total subsidies for the Norwegian firm Kvaemer, which purchased the Warnow shipbuilding yard in Mecklenburg-West Pomerania, amounted to DM 709,300 (almost $475,000) per guaranteed job. These included subsidies from *Treuhand,* the state of Mecklenburg-West Pomerania, and the German fund for old liabilities.[11]

Relatively few east Germans could amass the capital necessary to purchase the old state firms. In part, the decision at the time of economic and monetary union to convert savings in excess of 4,000 Marks per person (16,000 Marks or just over $10,000 for a family of four) at a rate of 1 West German Mark (DM) to 2 East German Marks disadvantaged potential entrepreneurs from eastern Germany, reducing their

capital available for investment.[12] Although *Treuhand* had envisioned management buyouts by east German employees as a suitable means
for privatizing many of the 3,000 small firms with less than 250
employees, this did not occur to any great extent.[13] Nor did many
foreigners invest in east German firms. Rather, the vast majority of
assets in eastern Germany were purchased by Germans from the West.
Potential east German buyers were often treated more harshly by the
financial evaluation process, with 75 percent of those involved in
management buyouts forced to assume the firms' "old liabilities" and 95
percent assessed on the value of the firms' assets rather than their
profitability. West German buyers were not subjected to the same
conditions.[14] Although *Treuhand* reports show 80 percent of the shops
owned by east Germans as well as 1,256 of the 6,000 privatized firms
going to east Germans through management buyouts, Harry Nick reports
that "the major concerns, prestigious shops and housing property" did
not pass to east German hands.[15] Sinn calculated the ownership of
firms privatized by *Treuhand*, figured on the basis of jobs, as less than
six percent for east Germans, under ten percent for foreign investors, and
almost 85 percent for west Germans.[16]

Costs of Unification

Since unification, eastern Germany has received massive financial
transfers from western Germany, totaling approximately DM 1 trillion
(more than $600 billion). This amounted to almost 80 percent of the
east German national product[17] and 5 percent of the west German Gross
Domestic Product.[18] In comparison, Marshall Plan aid after world war
II to the Federal Republic of Germany constituted less than two percent
of GDP.[19] Since unification, public sector payments to eastern Germany
have averaged DM 150 billion a year ($100 billion at 1993 exchange
rates).[20] With Germany currently experiencing a recession and with
eastern development proceeding much more slowly than anticipated,
the Kohl government has proposed to continue funding at the level of
DM 140 billion per year. The government plans to target aid toward
creating jobs and improving conditions for private investment.[21]

Infrastructure improvements represented a priority for aid to eastern
Germany, and by the end of 1995 DM 109 billion had gone toward infrastructure improvements and an additional DM 28 billion for rail. These
efforts have produced a number of tangible results in improved roads,
rail transportation, and communication networks. Privatization efforts
consumed an additional DM 121 billion.[22]

Critics of the massive aid programs contend that too much has gone toward consumption and far too little toward investment. According to a study by Deutsche Bank, from two-thirds to three-fourths of the transfers from East to West go toward consumption programs, primarily for welfare benefits.[23] Although Germans in both East and West are reluctant to abandon such social support programs, the current recession throughout Germany is calling the high levels of support provided by the social market economy into question, and the eastern *Länder* are far from achieving economic self-sufficiency. At least for the short-term, it appears that massive public aid will remain the engine of the east German economy.[24] State government authorities in eastern Germany warn that without continuing aid, "economic disparities between east and west could become permanent" and result in "a long-term two-class economic system that would endanger Germany's inner unity."[25]

The European Union (EU) has also provided aid for eastern Germany, treating the new German states like other poorer regions in member states and placing the new eastern states in the category with highest priorities for aid and west Berlin in the second-highest category, at least temporarily. Mecklenburg-West Pomerania in northeastern Germany ranks number seven on an EU list of 25 structurally weak regions.[26] From 1991-93 the EU contributed DM 6 billion in aid to eastern Germany and planned to provide an additional DM 20 billion between 1993 and 1999.[27] In April 1996, prime ministers of the east German states jointly appealed to the European Union Commission not to end EU regional development fund aid in 1999 and thereby jeopardize eastern Germany's modernization efforts.[28] Nevertheless, joining the European Union and receiving EU aid has its price. Eastern Germany must adhere to EU standards, and many economic decisions must receive European Union approval. In some cases, particularly in ship-building and in agriculture, this has had negative consequences for the east German economy.[29]

The State of the Economy in Eastern Germany

Almost eight years after economic and monetary union significant weaknesses continue to characterize the economy in eastern Germany. This holds true for most economic sectors. Moreover, the productively of all eastern states lies far below that of even the poorest state in western Germany. Eastern Germany contributes only about seven percent to the gross domestic product (GDP) of the Federal Republic, but contains about 20 percent of the population.[30]

Objectively assessing the condition of the east German economy presents numerous difficulties, and different reports describe widely varying conditions. For example, government reports on the "upswing East" have consistently presented a rosy picture of developments, while other reports bemoaning the loss of East German industry have painted a picture of deindustrialization and destruction and characterize the former GDR as a colony.[31] Economic assessments of eastern Germany also differ considerably in terms of the starting point. For example, German Finance Minister Theo Waigel argued in late 1992 that a reassessment showed the GDR economy in much worse condition than originally anticipated. The government of GDR Prime Minister Hans Modrow had valued state assets at DM 1,365 trillion ($900 billion), but a reappraisal using market economic criteria showed the value of assets dramatically reduced. In fact, when the debt of GDR firms (which had lived off capital for years) and other factors such as environmental clean-up costs were taken into consideration, German officials estimated that the holding company *Treuhand*, charged with the privatization of GDR firms would have a *deficit* of DM 209 billion ($140 billion) when it ceased operation in 1994.[32] Others dispute such a negative valuation of the GDR economy and assets, suggesting that political arguments and the need to discredit anything associated with the communist era and the GDR may color perceptions and result in unrealistically negative valuations of GDR economic assets.[33]

Growth and Productivity

In terms of productivity, eastern Germany still trails the old *Länder* by a wide margin in most sectors, although in a few sectors productivity has almost reached west German levels.   Per capita gross domestic product (GDP) in the five eastern states, excluding Berlin, exhibit little variation, ranging from DM 22,540 in Mecklenburg-West Pomerania to DM 24,830 in Brandenburg. In the west, the city-state of Hamburg leads in per capita GDP with DM 78,830, compared with a low in Rhineland-Palatinate of DM 38,180, a much larger variation.[34] This means that the GDP of the state in eastern Germany with the highest level stands at only two-thirds of the lowest state GDP in western Germany, and at less than one-third of the western state with the highest GDP. Despite attempts to equalize conditions throughout the FRG, as mandated in the Basic Law, wide variations still exist.

Although per capita GDP almost doubled in the East between 1991 and 1995, it increased only 13 percent in the West, thereby reducing the gap between the two areas.[35] However, these increases are measured from a quite low base, because immediately after economic and monetary union the GDP in eastern Germany dropped dramatically, *declining* 14.5 percent in 1990 and 30.3 percent in 1991.[36] (In 1992 the GDP in eastern Germany still lay below the level of 1990--DM 93.2 billion as compared with DM 111.5 billion.[37]) As resources have flowed to eastern Germany since unification, the GDP has increased, growing seven percent annually from 1991 through 1994 but only five percent in 1995.[38] In 1996 the growth rate in eastern Germany stood at only 2 percent, with projections for 2.5 percent growth in 1997. With the current low growth rates, eastern Germany no longer continues to catch up with the West.[39]

Continuing Problems

While about 500,000 new businesses have started since economic and monetary union, bankruptcies have increased dramatically in recent years, and only about 300,000 firms survive.[40] In the first five months of 1993, east German business failures resulted in a financial loss of DM 5 billion and the loss of 40,000 to 50,000 jobs. An estimated 1,200 firms declared bankruptcy in the first six months of 1993. Business startups did create 65,000 new jobs during that period, but that represented a slowdown in the rate of new starts.[41] The rate of bankruptcies continued to increase, with 5,874 east German businesses filing in 1995, a 46.2 percent increase from the previous year. In the hard-hit construction industry, bankruptcies increased by 82 percent.[42]

At this point, even optimistic scenarios argue that it will take decades for eastern Germany to catch up with western Germany in economic terms.[43] These projections stand in contrast to Chancellor Kohl's campaign pledges and other arguments prior to economic and monetary union in 1990 that, given the Federal Republic's economic strength, in only a few years the East would catch up with the West. Recent statements by government officials admit that major tasks remain in rebuilding the East. As Johannes Ludewig, secretary in the economics ministry and commissioner for the new *Länder,* stated, "In five to ten years east Germany must have an economy that stands on its own legs without subsidies and transfers."[44] Implicit in his statement is the necessity for subsidies and transfers in the interim period. Arguing that western firms would not have been able to privatize and become competitive in the post-war period without foreign investment, he pointed to the need for investment from west German firms to make east German firms competitive, noting that German firms have not invested enough in eastern Germany and are conspicuous by their absence.

Economic Sectors in Eastern Germany

The strength of the east German economy varies considerably from sector to sector. Since 1989 east Germany has moved toward a service society, as the manufacturing, mining, shipbuilding, and agricultural sectors have all declined substantially. (See Table 6.1.) Currently, services, banking, and insurance represent the strongest sectors of the east German economy. Initially increasing with the building boom after 1989, construction earlier represented another bright spot but has declined more recently. Although trade was a strong economic sector in the GDR, east German trade with western Germany and Eastern Europe has not yet rebounded to pre-1989 levels.

TABLE 6.1 East German Employees by Sector (in percentages)

Year	Service Sector	Manufacturing Sector	Agriculture and Fishing Sectors
1991	50.9	42.3	6.8
1995	60.2	35.9	3.9

Source: "Service Industries," *Deutschland*, German Information Service, No. 6 (December 1996), p. 21.

Manufacturing. As the foregoing discussion of privatization suggests, the manufacturing sector in eastern Germany has suffered a disastrous decline, and many observers point to the "deindustrialization" of eastern Germany. Critics have argued that the transition process and the incorporation of the GDR into the FRG should be described as a "benign takeover" or "a rapacious exploitation of the GDR's assets and the ruthless de-industrialization of a once advanced industrial state."[45] Prior to unification, East Germany's economy was viewed as the strongest in Eastern Europe and manufacturing made a major contribution, but after unification the situation changed rapidly. For example, in the first quarter of 1990, manufacturing provided DM 22 billion of the DM 79 billion quarterly economic value in the GDR, or more than one-fourth (28 percent). However, in the first quarter of 1991, manufacturing provided only DM 6.1 billion (of the DM 45.4 billion total value), just 13.4 percent, and less than one-third of the previous year's manufacturing value.[46] Currently manufacturing in eastern Germany contributes only a small fraction to the total German economy. Although containing one-fifth (20 percent) of Germany's population, eastern Germany accounts for only one-sixteenth (6 percent) of the united Germany's manufacturing output (industrial value-added) and one-fiftieth (2 percent) of her goods exports.[47]

The rapid adoption of the structures of a market economy and one of the world's strongest currencies, the powerful West German *deutsche Mark* (DM), intensified the problems of the East German industrial sector. With economic and monetary union, East Germany's attractiveness as a manufacturing center immediately decreased. In comparison with west Germany, eastern manufacturing plants suffered from outdated technology, environmental problems, delays in resolving property ownership issues, and low productivity.[48] A major cause of east Germany's economic difficulties stemmed from the fact that the government and industry within Germany failed to make a commitment to saving east German firms. With little emphasis on restructuring, the initial strategy favored fast privatization of east German firms, even if it meant that the firms could not survive in the competitive market climate. Since many west German plants had excess capacity, it was much easier to increase production there and sell the goods in the East than to restructure or create new plants in the East. Western plants supplied machine tools, automobiles, chemicals, and many other products, as east German plants in these fields closed down. In other words, initially east Germany served primarily as a market for the West, with relatively little western investment flowing to the East. Several years after unification, the government (belatedly) introduced policies to stimulate the development of industry in the East, but at this time few firms can survive the competition of the market economy without continued subsidies.

With the adoption of the West German Mark (DM) and the movement toward wage and salary equalization mandated by economic and monetary union, east Germany's competitiveness in relation to her former trading partners in the east bloc has decreased. Prior to 1989 an extremely high proportion of the GDR's trade had been with the Soviet Union and other eastern partners within the Council of Mutual Economic Assistance (CMEA), the east bloc trading system, e.g., in some sectors such as oil refining equipment and microelectronics the GDR provided between 50 and 90 percent of the Soviet Union's imports.[49] The GDR was an industrial leader within the east bloc, and high technology and intelligence-related industries constituted 45 percent of the GDR's production.[50] These industries, along with steel construction and machine tools, were assessed as having good chances for survival within the new system, in contrast to large proportions of industry which were outdated or had serious environment problems.[51] However, after economic and monetary union and with the disappearance of the barter economy, her former partners could no longer afford east Germany's markedly more expensive products. Since her products were not yet competitive in the West, east Germany's high technology sector collapsed.[52]

In comparison with many other East European states, east Germany's manufacturing has fared poorly. Relatively high wages and the strong DM make east German products very expensive in comparison with other countries in Eastern Europe, and German industrial firms are increasingly moving to lower-wage areas, especially in border regions in the Czech Republic and Poland.[53] For example, the area around Zittau in southern Saxony near the border with the Czech Republic recently had a 22 percent unemployment rate and no firm in the area employed more than 500 workers. At the same, time just across the border in the Czech Republic, the unemployment rate stood at 1.5 percent, and twelve firms in the Limerec region had more than 1000 employees.[54] Prague and the Czech Republic in general, with their well-educated and skilled labor force and relatively low labor costs, have been attractive sites for investment, and the Czech government has instituted strict wage controls, linking wage increases to increases in productivity. Wages there are only approximately ten percent of those in western Germany or Austria.[55]

In comparison, in a few industrial sectors, east German wages have already reached west German levels, although in most industries productivity has lagged far behind.[56] In recognition that with such high wages eastern Germany cannot compete with the rest of Eastern Europe and other areas, contracts in some sectors have been renegotiated, and east Germans have accepted lower wages in hopes of saving their jobs. Some recent news paints a more optimistic picture of east German industry in the future. A 1996 survey of 300 east German manufacturing firms revealed that two-thirds now consider themselves competitive after laying off workers since unification, and two-thirds reported growth in the past year. The bad news is that less than half of these firms considered their work force stable, and most foresaw laying off more workers.[57]

Construction. Since unification the construction sector has provided the primary impetus for growth, as funds flowed into eastern Germany for infrastructure and construction projects and rehabilitation of residential housing. Almost every east German city provides evidence of the construction sector's vital role in the economy since 1989. As older buildings are rehabilitated and modern new skyscrapers arise, the skylines and the character of east German cities are changing.

Since unification, construction has constituted a disproportionately large share of the east German economy, more than 15 percent, as compared with only 5 percent in the West.[58] Since construction represents such a large proportion of the economy, the recent decline in demand for construction has intensified concerns of economists and others about the weakness of the entire east German economy. Moreover, because financing was so readily available, buildings may have been constructed with little regard for demand, and revenues may not be adequate for the repayment of loans. For example, in Leipzig, which experienced a major construction boom immediately after unification, thirty percent of the office buildings remained empty for months after completion of construction, and the vacancy rate has continued to increase.[59]

In recent years the building boom has slowed and with it the entire economy. In the first quarter of 1996 new orders for construction decreased 15 percent and for furnishings 22 percent, and orders have continued to fall in 1997.[60] As construction orders have declined, the number of workers in this sector has also declined and their wages have been reduced. For example, in 1996, 70,000 fewer workers were employed in firms with twenty or more employees than in 1995, and employee wages in these firms averaged 20 percent less than the previous year.[61] Pressure for wage reduction continues. In late 1996, forty percent of the workers in small firms worked for less than the industry-wide union wage, and two-thirds of the firms that paid union level wages were considering abandoning their collective bargaining agreements and paying lower wages.

On a positive note, the construction sector has been viewed as relatively efficient. Productivity is much higher than in other sectors, estimated at 75 percent of the western level already in 1993, and with little variation from state to state.[62] In 1996, construction wages averaged 91 percent of those in west Germany, but effective pay including non-wage benefits was only 74 percent of the western level.[63]

Prospects in the construction sector remain fair because housing construction continues to receive tax advantages, and most housing units in eastern Germany had deteriorated during the communist period. Nonetheless, the boom for infrastructure and commercial building has ended,[64] and continuing bankruptcies and reduction in staffs are anticipated. With construction no longer providing the engine of growth, no other sector has yet emerged to provide the impetus.

Services. The private service sector's proportion of the total east German economy has expanded considerably since unification, particularly in light of the deindustrializtion of eastern Germany. Nonetheless, services in eastern Germany still constitute a smaller proportion of the economy than in western Germany (and in most other western countries), in 1996 representing respectively about 20 percent and 25 percent of total employment.[65] While some aspects of the service sector, such as banking and insurance, have been among the most successful in eastern Germany, others, such as retailing, have experienced more difficulties.

The service sector has attracted considerable investment as west German firms targeted the new east German market with its 16 million people. With the advent of economic and monetary union in 1990 a number of west German banks and several foreign ones expanded into eastern Germany, and already by the end of 1991 these banks had opened several hundred branches in the East. Some formed joint ventures with eastern banks, e.g., Deutsche Bank (FRG) with Deutsche Kreditbank (GDR) and Dresdner Bank (FRG), also with Deutsche Kreditbank (GDR).[66] Far fewer east Germans work in banking than west Germans, 34 and 76 of every 10,000, respectively, but banking and insurance are among the most productive sectors of the east German economy, with productivity rates standing at almost 90 percent of western levels in 1995.[67]

In the retail sphere, big west German firms moved east at the time of economic and monetary union, providing fierce competition for the new or newly-privatized east German firms. Initially, a number of west German firms entered the east German market, seemingly with the objective of removing east German goods from the market. East Germans leveled charges of unfair competition, as large western firms with access to capital and other supports attempted to drive struggling east German firms out of business. For example, the two major GDR grocery chains, Konsum and HO, initially signed agreements with west German suppliers requiring that they carry almost exclusively west German goods,[68] and when shops opened 1 July 1990, the day of economic and monetary union, east German products disappeared from the shelves, replaced by western goods. Birgit Breuel, president of the privatization agency *Treuhand*, criticized the "shocking imbalance" in intra-German trade. In 1992 the equivalent of DM 234 billion in goods and services flowed from West to East, but only DM 33 billion from East to West. Breuel and *Treuhand* feared that western firms would dump cheap goods in the East, in an attempt to drive east German competitors out of business.[69]

In the years following unification, east Germans began demanding more eastern products. According to a 1992 survey by the Central Marketing Association of German Agriculture, 60 percent of east Germans preferred foodstuffs from the East in 1992 as compared to only 21 percent in 1990.[70] Now a market for eastern products may be emerging in western Germany. A 1996 survey by the Institute for Market Research in Leipzig indicated that 84 percent of west Germans would like to see more east German products on their shelves, as compared with only 63 percent in 1992.[71] But in actuality, only a small proportion of east German goods reach western Germany: east German products have constituted just over one percent of west German sales.[72]

Trade. Trade has served as the engine of growth in the united Germany since the most recent recession, but with eastern products representing such a small proportion of Germany's total trade, the eastern states have participated to a lesser extent in the small economic upturn of recent years. East German trade now constitutes 5.1 percent of total German foreign trade,[73] up from 1.7 percent in 1994,[74] and trade represents only 14.1 percent of eastern Germany's GDP but 33.3 percent of western Germany's.[75] While east German trade with west Germany and with other countries has increased in recent years, volume, value, and related employment still stand far below GDR times. In 1988 GDR exports totaled 90 billion *Ostmarks*, or $30.6 billion,[76] and 600,000 jobs depended on Soviet trade.[77] Of total exports before unification, 37 percent went to the former Soviet Union, 28 percent to other East European states, 12 percent to West Germany, and 13 percent to other West European states.[78]

Nonetheless, in 1991 the value of east German trade had dropped to $11.9 billion,[79] and in 1993, exports still totaled only one-third of the previous volume.[80] Trade with East Germany's former east bloc partners dropped precipitously. Indeed, by 1992 trade between east Germany and Hungary, Romania, and Bulgaria had virtually stopped, and trade with Poland, the former Soviet Union, and the Czech Republic and Slovakia had declined by 70 to 80 percent since 1989. Despite this drastic reduction, Central and East European states continued to represent important trade partners for the new German states. In 1992 more than half of eastern Germany's exports went to the region, as compared with only five percent of western Germany's exports, and almost 50 percent of eastern Germany's imports came from Central and Eastern Europe. However, by 1995 trade with Central and Eastern Europe had declined substantially to 35.5 percent of eastern Germany's exports and 40.8 percent of imports, as eastern Germany's trade with Western Europe expanded.[81]

After the initial downturn in east German production and trade, several programs were launched to promote economic growth. In 1991 a number of west German businesses developed an initiative to buy east German products, thereby stimulating the small east German private sector. When this program was introduced, orders of west German firms stood at around DM 25 billion, but by the end of 1995 the 86 participant companies had signed contracts to buy east German goods totaling DM 150 billion (US $100 billion). In 1995 a new initiative was launched to stimulate research in eastern Germany, and a public-private "export offensive" launched in 1996 seeks to help eastern firms expand foreign trade and develop cross-border ties.[82] The most recent initiative of business and trade union leaders intends to create 100,000 new jobs per year in eastern Germany, to subsidize investors, and to purchase more east German products. Labor leaders have agreed to changes in east German contracts in an effort to increase the competitiveness of east German firms,[83] but economic experts view the plan to create 100,000 jobs under the currently poor economic conditions as unrealistically optimistic.[84]

The Economic Well-Being of the East German People

The geopolitical location of East Germany during the twentieth century leads east Germans to make multiple comparisons when they assess their economic situation. They tend to ask how they are doing now compared to in GDR times, compared with East Europeans, and compared with west Germans. And each of these comparisons involves both objective and subjective responses. In contrast to the weak state of the economy in eastern Germany, as described in the previous sections, the economic situation of some east German citizens is good when measured by economic indicators such as wage levels, benefits, and availability and affordability of goods and services. However, high levels of unemployment and underemployment, along with their removal from many decision-making positions, have caused most east Germans to assess their economic well-being quite negatively.

Unemployment

Continuing high levels of unemployment represent by far the most negative aspect of the economic well-being of east Germans. This has led to a two-class society in eastern Germany--those with jobs and those without. In the German Democratic Republic, unemployment was practically unknown, but since economic and monetary union, one-third of all east German jobs have been eliminated.[85] From the currently high level, unemployment continues to rise in eastern Germany. In May 1997 the official unemployment rate stood at 18.2 percent, a percent increase from the previous year, with 1,295,400 persons without jobs. At that time the unemployment rate in western Germany was 9.6 percent, an increase of just over one percent from the previous year.[86] By November

1997 the unemployment rate in eastern Germany had risen to 19.6 percent, with 1,473,000 persons unemployed in the eastern states.[87] Although layoffs in east Germany's manufacturing sector have decreased recently, cutbacks have increased in the service sector among health-care workers, social workers, teachers, and other public service employees.[88] The east German unemployment rate compares unfavorably with rates in most East European states. For example, in the Czech Republic unemployment stood at 3.9 percent in March 1997, up less than one percent from the previous year. Poland's unemployment rate was 13.0 percent, down from the previous year's rate of 15.4.[89]

TABLE 6.2   Unemployment Rates in Central and Eastern Europe May 1996 and May 1997 in Percent

State/Region	May 1996	May 1997
Eastern Germany	15.2	17.2
Western Germany	8.7	9.6
Czech Republic	3.0	3.9
Estonia	2.0	4.5
Poland	15.4	13.0
Romania	7.2	9.8
Russia	9.0	9.7

Sources: "Monthly Update," *Business Central Europe* (June 1997), p. 65; "Little Change in Job Market: 4.2 Million Jobless in May," *The Week in Germany* (13 June 1997), p. 4. Unemployment rates for Germany are for May 1996 and 1997. Rates for other countries are for February, March, or April 1996 and 1997.

Unfortunately official unemployment figures do not present the full picture in eastern Germany, and a variety of other measures conceal the true extent of unemployment or underemployment. In 1989 more than 9.95 million people worked in paid employment,[90] but in 1997 only 6,120,000 people had jobs, plus another 93,000 who worked reduced hours.[91] Early retirement, training courses, and job creation programs keep a large proportion of the population off the unemployment rolls,[92] and a number of east Germans also commute to jobs in the West. A study by the Institute of Economic Research in Halle in 1993 estimated that when persons in these programs were added to the regular unemployment figures, approximately 34 percent of the potential east German workers were unemployed or employed outside the "normal" labor market.[93] Helmar Drost provides similar figures, arguing that an adjusted unemployment rate for eastern Germany in 1992 would have been 28 percent, taking into consideration these other categories, as compared with a registered employment rate of 14.7 percent.[94] In 1993 the Federal Labor Agency reported that 1.7 million people in eastern Germany took part in federal job programs, worked reduced hours, or had taken early retirement.[95] Adding this figure to the 1.3 million persons in the East officially reported as unemployed, the total unemployed rises to almost three million.

Unemployment hits some portions of the population harder than others. After unification a number of older workers who lost their jobs were offered early pre-retirement payments--at age 55 for women and 57 for men--in order to keep unemployment levels down, and in 1991 the government proposed to lower the retirement age to 55 for both women and men in eastern Germany. The unemployment level for women and for youth has also been higher than for adult males.[96] (See chapter 9 by Irene Dölling for more on the employment problems of east German women.)

Although all east German states have experienced high unemployment levels, rates have varied from state to state, and some sectors of the economy have been particularly hard hit.[97] The highest levels of unemployment have been in Mecklenburg-West Pomerania, where in GDR times the major employers were agriculture and shipbuilding, two sectors experiencing severe difficulties since unification. Largely due to the loss of jobs in the heavily polluted chemical industry, in 1997 Saxony-Anhalt had the highest unemployment rate in eastern Germany at 21.3 percent.[98] In the early years after unification Saxony had lower levels of unemployment than the other new *Länder*, in part because of the boom in construction, but with the decline in this sector, unemployment rates there have also jumped. In the academic community, another sector in eastern Germany with high unemployment, 47,500 were without jobs in 1996.[99] Numerous east German intellectuals lost their positions when east German academies of science closed, and many university professors were replaced by west Germans who crossed over to take jobs in the East. In general, the unemployment picture in eastern Germany remains poor for 1998, with research institutes predicting an unemployment rate of 19.6 percent[100] and with jobs created continuing to lag behind those lost.[101]

Income, Purchasing Power, and Relative Prosperity

Because equality constituted an integral part of the unification agreements, east German wages and salaries increased regularly during the first several years after unification. In some sectors such as metalworking, east Germans achieved wage parity with their counterparts in the West,[102] although benefits tended to remain lower. However, as more and more employers and employees recognized that high wages were pricing east German products out of the global market, pressures developed to lower wage levels. On average, wages rose from 44 percent of the western level in 1990 to 69 percent in 1994.[103] Nevertheless, full equality continues to escape east Germans. A recent study by the German Institute for Economic Research predicts that "average wages in Germany's new states will stand at only 93 percent of western wages, even if the economy picks up and does well over the next decade and a half."[104]

In comparison with their counterparts in other east bloc states, East Germans lived well prior to unification. Per capita income in the GDR led the other East European states, and, depending on the source, East Germans had a living standard two to three times as high as Poles, twice as high as Hungarians, and almost 20 percent as high as their closest competitor, the Czechoslovaks.[105] The East German government focused on material well-being, and in relation to their eastern neighbors, East Germans viewed themselves as relatively prosperous. However, high quality products were in short supply, variety was limited, and most East Germans resented the perks available to party officials but not to ordinary citizens. When GDR citizens looked west to the Federal Republic, they saw another picture. In comparison with West Germans, East Germans were poor relatives, and the economic prosperity and opportunity represented by the West contributed to the exodus of East Germans to West Germany and to the fall of the Berlin wall, as hundreds of thousands crossed from the GDR to the FRG in the 1980s.[106]

Now, after unification, how do we assess the relative economic status of east Germans? In comparison with GDR times, some east Germans are better off today, in terms of real income and standard of living, if they have jobs.[107] Between May 1990 and March 1992, 65.3 percent of east Germans experienced a gain in real income (based on the concept of equivalent income) even after adjusting for a 29.6 percent cost of living increase, including the loss of free childcare and skyrocketing rents. However, almost two-thirds of east Germans experienced a drop in income during at least one of the two years of the study period, and 12.8 percent experienced a drop in income both years. In a large minority of the households studied (38.3 percent), at least one family member was without work, and these families experienced a significant decline in income. For the minority of families where participation in the labor force increased (10 percent), incomes also increased substantially.

Some studies suggest that the number of east Germans living in poverty has also increased since unification. Based on east German average income data, the poverty rate rose to 6.1 percent in 1992 from 2.5 percent in 1990. On the other hand, using west German income figures as a base, the poverty rate of east Germans declined from 25 percent in 1990 to 15 percent in 1993.[108]

In comparison with their neighbors in Central and Eastern Europe, the economic position of east Germans has improved since unification and the gap has widened as east Germans today generally enjoy a much higher standard of living today, having participated to a degree in the prosperity of the West. Working east Germans have benefited from programs to raise wages toward equality with west German levels, and those without jobs have received a higher level of support from social service programs and through a wide variety of transfer payments intended to develop the eastern *Länder* than have their East European counterparts. Data comparing post-communist countries shows Czechs have only 45 percent of east German purchasing power, Hungarians 32 percent, and Poles 25 percent.[109] According to a survey of persons with paid employment, 86 percent of east Germans receive sufficient income to live adequately on the official economy, compared with only 58 percent of Czechs, 43 percent of Poles, 34 percent of Hungarians, and 15 percent of Russians.[110] To get by, those in other countries turn to multiple jobs and the unofficial economy. In contrast, even without jobs most east Germans receive adequate resources to support themselves from income maintenance or other official sources, a situation not enjoyed by many other East Europeans.

Nevertheless, in contrast with west Germans, east Germans see a different picture. In a 1996 survey by Emnid reported in *Der Spiegel*, only 9 percent of east Germans and 19 percent of west Germans viewed the economic situation in eastern Germany as "good" or "very good."[111] However, this does not mean that east Germans disapprove of the Federal Republic's social market system. Survey research indicates that only 36 percent of east Germans approved of the economic system of the GDR, but 75 percent viewed the social market system of the Federal Republic positively.[112]

Job Satisfaction, Competence, and Expectations

Despite their relatively good financial situation, at least compared with their counterparts in Eastern Europe, most east Germans view their work situation or lack of employment very negatively. The vast majority express dissatisfaction with their income and standard of

living, and researchers have concluded that the drop in satisfaction
level between 1990 and 1992 represents one of the largest ever observed
in any country.[113] The authors of the study suggest that east Germans
were dissatisfied because persons holding equivalent jobs in the West
were better paid and had much higher living standards, because the
revolution and unification raised expectations, because they
experienced increased job insecurity, and because the media portrayed
the situation in eastern Germany negatively.   Others attribute the
dissatisfaction in large part to the marginal position of east Germans in
united Germany. As Detlef Schubert characterizes it, east Germans
have gained prosperity but lost competence.[114] Large numbers of east
Germans who had previously played important roles in government and
politics, the economy, and society found themselves excluded from
participation in the transition, by early retirement, unemployment,
and/or relegation to positions lacking authority. Their previous work
and life experiences were discounted, as west Germans moved in to fill
mid- and upper-level positions and to implement laws, regulations, and
procedures from the West. This discounting of east Germans and their
experiences resulted in a loss for many east Germans personally and for
society as a whole. As Helmut Wiesenthal argues, in contrast to other
East European states where lack of resources and political skills
hindered the transitions, east Germany suffered from "the
predominance of external actors and their neglect of--or insensitivity
to--'local' views and preferences."[115]

Assessing Eastern Germany's Economic Transition

*Some people may have believed that once communism was removed
the free play of market forces would create a miracle in the East. It is
now patently obvious that this belief was completely mistaken.*
                                         --Gerlinde Sinn and Hans-Werner Sinn[116]

The Role of Government

The east German transition demonstrates that transitions from centrally planned economies to market economies are not (and cannot be)
simply *economic* transitions. Rather, these transitions involve the complex interplay of political/governmental and economic forces. Governmental decisions shape economic transitions as states create frameworks and institutions, determine fiscal and monetary policies, regulate

competition and trade, and provide assistance for infrastructure development, struggling firms, and citizens disadvantaged by the transition processes. A fundamental question in all modern-day transitions is not should governments be involved in the transition processes but, rather, how should governments be involved? To what extent should governments protect struggling firms, national economies, and citizens from the ravages of the market? For governments are involved in economic and business decisions today, just as they were in the past. Both shock therapy and the gradual transition to the market involve decisions by governments which set the direction and pace for changes and influence outcomes.

The following brief comparison of eastern Germany's recent transition with the Federal Republic's post-world war II transition provides insights into the roles of governments, highlights reasons for difficulties in the current German transition, and helps explain the failure to create a second "economic miracle." The comparison also highlights the very different starting points and situations of the two periods. Even though many aspects of the east German transition differ from those in other East European states, the experience nevertheless provides some valuable lessons that contribute to a better understanding of the post-communist transitions.

Comparing Transitions

The recent German transition has not resulted in a second "economic miracle" in large part because conditions shaping the two transitions differed dramatically. In the post-war period the German occupation governments as well as the subsequent Federal Republic of Germany encountered a Europe in ruins, but since all European economies were weak, Germany entered the rebuilding phase among similarly disadvantaged states.[117] Moreover, the starting point for this economic transition was not fundamentally different from the goal of a market economy. Germany had had a capitalist system during the Weimar period only a few years earlier, and the economic system in the Nazi period, even though an authoritarian and corporate war economy, was "still based upon private property and predominant market forces, technical innovation and efficiency."[118] As Claus Offe has argued, "Capital just happened to be partially destroyed as a physical entity, not capitalism as an institutional reality."[119]

In contrast, with economic and monetary union in 1990, eastern Germany immediately entered into competition with economically strong and technologically advanced market economies, with no real adjustment and modernization period. The centrally planned economy of the German Democratic Republic differed fundamentally from the market economies of the West, and after almost fifty years of communism, almost no east Germans in the 1990s had had any experience with a market economy. East Germans had created almost totally new systems in both the post-world war II period and after 1989. And the quick method of transition adopted after 1989 did not allow sufficient time for east Germans or the economy to adapt to the new system. The east German transition was further disadvantaged by an international recession and fundamental economic problems facing the whole of Germany in the 1990s.

The twentieth century German economic and political transitions were shaped by government decisions, and these decisions affected outcomes. Several political/governmental decisions in the context of the European Recovery Program or Marshall Plan helped the war-torn West German economy develop and thrive in the post-war period. First, the German mark (DM) was undervalued, which helped make German exports competitive.[120] Also, austere wage controls were implemented, low labor costs kept prices down and contributed to the competitiveness of German products,[121] and Marshall Plan aid emphasized increasing productivity, both in terms of overall production and output per worker.[122] Refugees from the East available for jobs further depressed wages.[123] Financial transfers from the Marshall Plan provided crucial capital for infrastructure and capital development, including roads, bridges, canals, railways, and electrical facilities.[124] Moreover, the state provided protection for the domestic economy from the forces of the market and foreign competition.[125] Finally, in terms of decision-making, the Marshall Plan gave Germans and other Europeans considerable authority for designing and carrying out programs in their respective states.

East Germany's transition to a market economy in the 1990s was "state-led,"[126] but, viewed in retrospect, a number of ill-advised decisions regarding shape and speed of the transition determined the outcome and hindered the repeat of an "economic miracle." Pressured by the continuing exodus of East German workers to the West after the borders opened,[127] Chancellor Kohl promised East Germans rapid unification, monetary union along with the coveted West German Mark, and living standards on par with West Germany within a few years. Despite good intentions and the transfer of more than a trillion DM from West to East, these choices eliminated any competitive advantage that east German products might have enjoyed and led to the deindustrialization of the eastern region.

First, the decision in favor of early economic and monetary union, the exchange of the East German *Ostmark* with the DM at a ratio of 1:1, and the requirement that east German goods be purchased with hard currency contributed to the collapse of the market for east German products. The GDR's traditional trading partners to the East could not pay hard currency for east German goods, and east German products were not yet competitive in western markets. Lessons of these decisions concern the needs of states to control their currency rates. Overvalued currencies inhibit trade, and devaluation of the currency to more reasonable levels can promote the competitiveness of the state's products.

Second, the political and social decision to quickly raise wages to western levels made east German goods non-competitive, both in her traditional markets to the East as well as in the West, because quality and productivity had generally not achieved western standards. Both in the FRG after world war II and in the most competitive East European states today, low wages have enabled developing/transitioning states to compete with states with more developed economies. In eastern Germany, wage increases were not based on productivity but rather on political and social objectives. The laudable decision to help Easterners to achieve political, economic, and social equality with Westerners as soon as possible--backed up by the Basic Law of the Federal Republic--led to devastating consequences for the east German economy. In retrospect critics argue that these objectives could have been achieved more easily with social support and guaranteed income programs rather than through economically unjustifiably high wages which drastically increased production costs.

A third lesson of the East German transition concerns the potential role of government to protect fragile economies from market forces. In the transition period, eastern Germany was disadvantaged by isolation, weak infrastructure, poor technology, poor quality, and low productivity, but the Federal Republic failed to protect east German industries and adequately support their products. Despite the examples of protecting developing or transforming industries provided by the German government in 1948,[128] by the European Union for new and/or economically weaker members, and currently by other East European governments, the Federal Republic failed to provide protection for and to adequately promote east German products. With economic and monetary union, east German products were immediately subjected to competition from western Germany and the European Union, just as her traditional markets in Eastern Europe shriveled. Trade and marketing practices of west German firms, unhindered by government regulation, also contributed to the demise of east German products and firms, as eastern Germany was transformed into a market for western products.

Initial polices and practices of the German privatization agency *Treuhand* contributed to the deindustrialization of eastern Germany, particularly the emphasis on privatization instead of restructuring which resulted in the sale of non-competitive firms. And the priority given to west Germans and to mergers, rather than to foreign or to east German investors, provided more established west German firms with essentially monopoly positions in the East.[129] Belatedly, the German government and *Treuhand* shifted gears and designed programs supporting industrial development in the East and incorporating the cooperation of west German firms. However, by then the bulk of east German production had disappeared. East Germany, previously a powerhouse of the Soviet bloc, became an importer of food and industrial products.

Another mistake in retrospect concerned decision-making. The decision to superimpose almost all FRG structures on the former GDR and to import west Germans for most management positions had negative effects, particularly on east German elites. In contrast to other former east bloc states where the former opposition or lower level bureaucrats filled most managerial positions, in east Germany most elites were pushed aside in favor of west Germans.[130] The result was a loss of competence, among many of those working but especially among those not working or working minimal hours or in "make work" positions. Since employment dropped from about 9 million jobs in GDR times to only 6 million now[131]--this translates into a major loss in productive abilities and competence. These moves devalued the experience of east Germans, resulted in unnecessarily antagonistic relations, and contributed to the feeling among east Germans that they were second-class citizens.

Despite the generally negative outcome of the economic transition, a few positive factors emerge. After making a decision in favor of early unification, the German government quickly took steps to improve the standard of living of east Germans, aiming to equalize conditions between the two parts of Germany as rapidly as possible. As a consequence of government actions, the objective economic conditions for many east German citizens improved, with a much wider variety of goods and services immediately available and intentions to provide both wages and social benefits approaching west German levels. This stands in positive contrast to many East European countries where the standard of living has declined precipitously and a growing number of families fall below the poverty level.[132] However, it should be remembered that East Germans were also viewed as relatively prosperous in GDR times, both by themselves and by other East Europeans.

Prospects

The outlook for the future is mixed. On the positive side, the good intentions of the German government to eliminate disparities between West and East and the vast economic resources of the Federal Republic of Germany suggest that economic self-sufficiency and relative equality will be achieved in eastern Germany, probably not in five years, but perhaps in twenty. On a more pessimistic note, the deindustrialization which has already taken place in eastern Germany plus the loss of economic potential and competence by a large proportion of the east German population argues for a much longer transition--perhaps generations. Today almost no one speaks of another economic miracle occurring in just a few years. A study by a group of economists analyzing the failure of economic integration suggests that full integration will take 30 to 40 years, and that in the meantime continuing financial transfers from East to West will be necessary. The authors also argue that German economic integration provides insights into some of the difficulties that will undoubtedly occur with the economic and monetary union set to take place in the European Union in 1999.[133]

Nevertheless, some reasons for optimism about the future of the economic transition in eastern Germany do exist. Massive investments in infrastructure have resulted in a much improved transportation system and the most modern communications system in the world.[134] Also, eastern German firms and workers have already made a number of adjustments in an effort to meet west German standards and to become more competitive. Some observers suggest that these changes may help east German firms adapt more easily than their west German counterparts to changes required by the upcoming European economic and monetary union, including the replacement of the D-Mark by the *Euro*. East Germans experienced converting from one currency to another at the time of German economic and monetary union, and eastern firms are already adjusting accounting practices in conformance with the standards of European currency union.[135] Workers in eastern Germany have also demonstrated more flexibility concerning wages and work hours than their western counterparts, and in some sectors have developed a strong service mentality. As the *Süddeutsche Zeitung* recently reported,

> The eastern Germans have learned quickly, at least more quickly than the western Germans, who persist with the feeling of economic superiority and shirk before necessary changes. The hold-up to reforms (*Still-Standort Deutschland*) lies in the west; things are moving in the east. The new states are, out of necessity, going down the difficult path to economic renewal and joining world markets.[136]

Notes

1. *Der Spiegel* (19 March 1990), p. 20.

2. See Mike Dennis, *Social and Economic Modernization in Eastern Germany from Honecker to Kohl* (New York: St. Martin's Press, 1993), Chapter 3, for a discussion of economic and monetary union and the events preceding it.

3. "Treaty on the Creation of a Monetary, Economic, and Social Union, 18 May 1990," Chapter 1, Article 1 (3), translated in Konrad H. Jarausch and Volker Gransow (eds.), Allison Brown and Belinda Cooper (trans.), *Uniting Germany: Documents and Debates, 1944-1993* (Providence, RI: Berghahn Books, 1994), p. 155.

4. Hans Modrow, "Die Treuhand: Idee und Wirklichkeit," in Horst van der Meer and Lothar Kruss (eds.), *Vom Industriestaat zum Entwicklungsland?* (Frankfurt am Main, Dieter Joester Vertriebsgemeinschaft GmbH, 1991), p. 197, translated in Harry Nick, "An Unparalleled Destruction and Squandering of Economic Assets," in Hanna Behrend (ed.), *German Unification: The Destruction of an Economy* (London and East Haven, CT: Pluto Press, 1995), p. 92.

5. When first created, *Treuhand* was a small agency, but by April 1991 it had 3000 employees and was the largest holding company in the world, Gerlinde Sinn and Hans-Werner Sinn, trans. by Juli Irving-Lessmann, *Jumpstart: The Economic Unification of Germany* (Cambridge, MA and London, England: The MIT Press, 1992), p. 97.

6. Harry Nick, "Destruction" [note 4], p. 92.

7. *The Economist* (Sept. 30, 1995), p. 22, says 15,000 privatizations. The number of firms for privatization increased over time as large *Kombinate* were broken up into smaller units. See Sinn and Sinn, *Jumpstart*, p. 96; Nick, "Destruction," p. 93; Karl H. Kahrs, "Treuhand: The Privatisation of a Planned Economy," in Peter H. Merkl (ed.), *The Federal Republic of Germany at Forty-Five: Union without Unity* (Washington Square, NY: New York University Press, 1995), p. 169; and Helmar Drost, "The Great Depression in East Germany: The Effects of Unification on East Germany's Economy," *East European Politics and Societies*, Vol. 7, No. 3 (Fall 1993), pp. 452-81.

8. Mike Dennis, *Social and Economic Modernization*, p. 129, and Karl Koch, "The German Economy: Decline or Stability?" in Derek Lewis and John R.P. McKenzie (eds.), *The New Germany: Social, Political, and Cultural Challenges of Unification* (Exeter: University of Exeter Press, 1995), p. 138. See also Claus Offe, *Varieties of Transition: The East European and East German Experience* (Cambridge, MA: The MIT Press, 1997), p. 153.

9. Nick, "Destruction," p. 102.

10. *Ibid.*, p. 99.

11. *Berliner Zeitung*, 23 September 1993, cited in Nick, "Destruction," p. 103.

12. Sinn and Sinn, *Jumpstart*, p. 69.

13. Dennis, *Social and Economic Modernization*, p. 129.

14. Nick, "Destruction," p. 103.

15. *Ibid.*, p. 112.

16. Hans-Werner Sinn, *Wirtschaftswoche*, No. 1-2 (7 January 1994).

17. Horst Siebert, *Das Wagnis der Einheit. Eine wirtschaftspolitische Therapie* (Stuttgart: Deutsche Verlags-Anstalt, 1992), p. 142.

18. "Germany Survey," *The Economist* (9 November 1996), p. 9.

19. Siebert, *Das Wagnis der Einheit*, p. 142.

20. Payments have ranged from a high of DM 172 billion in 1993 to an estimated low of DM 135 billion in 1997, Barbara Beck, "Germany's Long Pull," *The World in 1997* (London: The Economist Publications, 1996), p. 41.

21. "Cabinet Plans to Continue High Level of Aid to Eastern Germany," *The Week in Germany* (4 April 1997), p. 4.

22. "Rebuilding Eastern Germany: The Flow of Funds from West to East 1991-1995," compiled from *Süddeutsche Zeitung*, *The Week in Germany* (23 June 1995), p. 5.

23. Reported in "Germany Survey," *The Economist* (9 November 1996), p. 9.

24. Emil Nagengast, "Eastern Europe and Germany's *Treuhandanstalt*," *East European Quarterly*, Vol. 29, No. 2 (June 1995), p. 199.

25. "Eastern Ministers Urge Bonn and the EU to Continue Financial Help," *The Week in Germany* (21 February 1997), p. 5.

26. "EU Aid for Western German States; Mecklenburg-Vorpommern Seeks Further Help," *The Week in Germany* (14 February 1997), p. 5.

27. "European Community to Increase Support for Eastern Germany," *The Week in Germany* (7 May 1993), p. 4. The new German states rank behind Greece and Portugal in terms of economic development, the poorest European Union member states, "Osten braucht Auslandsinvestoren," *Die Welt* (4 June 1996), p. 13.

28. "Eastern German Finance Ministers Call on Bonn to Continue Financial Aid to their States," *The Week in Germany* (12 April 1996), p. 4.

29. See Kahrs, "Treuhand," pp. 177-78, on shipbuilding, and Patricia J. Smith, "German Economic and Monetary Union: Transition to a Market Economy," in Sabrina P. Ramet, *Adaptation and Transformation in Communist and Post-Communist Systems* (Boulder, CO: Westview Press, 1992), p. 53, on agriculture.

30. Dennis, *Social and Economic Modernization*, p. 80.

31. See, for example, Peter Christ and Ralf Neubauer, *Kolonie im eignenen Land: Die Treuhand, Bonn und die Wirtschaftskatastrophe der fünf neuen Länder* (Berlin: Rowohlt, 1991) and Hannah Behrend (ed.) *German Unification: The Destruction of an Economy* (London and East Haven, CT: Pluto Press, 1995).

32. "Waigel Calls Stocktaking of East German Economy 'Sobering,'" *The Week in Germany* (October 23, 1992), p. 4.

33. For example, see Harry Nick, "Destruction," pp. 108-10.

34. "Economic Performance of the Federal States: Hamburg Leads the League," *Deutschland*, No. 4 (August 1996), p. 43..

35. "Economic Performance," *Deutschland*, No. 4 (August 1996), p. 43.

36. Koch, "The German Economy," p. 137.

37. Dennis, *Social and Economic Modernization*, p. 81.

38. The Economist Intelligence Unit, *Country Report: Germany* (1st Quarter 1997), p. 23.

39. The Economist Intelligence Unit, *Country Report: Germany* (2nd Quarter 1997), p. 21.

40. "Germany Survey," *The Economist* (9 November 1996), p. 17.

41. "Private, Business Bankruptcies on the Rise in Germany," *The Week in Germany* (11 June, 1993), p. 5.

42. "Statistics Bureau: Bankruptcies Reached Record High Last Year," *The Week in Germany* (15 March 1996), p. 5.

43. "No Quick End to Germany's East-West Economic Gap, Study Argues," *The Week in Germany* (20 September 1996), p. 5. See also Rudiger Dornbusch and Holger Wolf, "Economic Transition in Eastern Germany," Brookings Papers on Economic Activity (1992), pp. 235-61.

44. "Osten braucht Auslandsinvestoren," *Die Welt* (4 June 1996), p. 13.

45. Dennis, *Social and Economic Modernization*, p. 80.

46. *Ibid.*, p. 76.

47. The Economist Intelligence Unit, *Country Report: Germany* (2nd Quarter 1997), p. 21.

48. Property claims represented a political issue with extremely negative economic effects. The FRG decided to follow a policy of restitution, with property or compensation going to the original owners where ownership claims could be traced. Many property claims were tied up for years, and it was difficult for firms to get clear title to land.

49. Günter Hedtkamp and Hermann Clement, "Treuhand und Osteuropa," in Wolfram Fischer (ed.), *Treuhandanstalt: Das Unmögliche wagen* (Berlin: Akademie Verlag, 1993), pp. 510 and 512.

50. Dennis, *Social and Economic Modernization*, p. 84

51. Nick, "Destruction," p. 85

52. Of the 2000 computer and microelectronics firms, 30 percent collapsed, 20 percent were taken over by *Treuhand* for privatization, and the remaining 50 percent with five or fewer employees had little chance of survival, Martin Flug, *Treuhand-Poker: Die Mechanismen des Ausverkaufs* (Berlin: Links Verlag, 1992), p. 144, cited in Dennis, *Social and Economic Modernization*, p. 84.

53. "Poll: More and More German Companies Relocating Abroad," *The Week in Germany* (12 November 1993), p. 5.

54. *Die Welt* (1 March 1994), p. 12, cited in Nagengast, "Germany's *Treuhand-anstalt*," p. 198. However, recent developments suggest that Czech reforms have not gone quickly enough, and the Vaclav Mercier government fell in November 1997, amidst charges that he failed to institute significant reforms, *New York Times*, 30 November 1997, p. A1, and 1 December 1997, p. A1.

55. In 1993 wages, for one worker in Bremen in western Germany a firm could hire ten in Budapest, fifteen in Warsaw, or seventeen in Prague, but only one and one-half in Dresden in eastern Germany, Nagengast, "Germany's *Treuhandan-stalt*," p. 193.

56. In 1993, productivity in manufacturing in eastern Germany was estimated at 40 percent of the level in the West, with productivity ranging from 49 percent of the West in Saxony-Anhalt to 34 percent in Saxony, "Association Expects Productivity in Six Years," *The Week in Germany* (16 July 1993), p. 5.

57. "Institute: Eastern Germany's Manufacturers Continue to Grow," *The Week in Germany* (23 February 1996), p. 5.

58. "Germany Survey," *The Economist* (9 November 1996), p. 4; *Der Spiegel*, No. 25 (17 June 1996), p. 108.

59. *Der Spiegel*, No. 25 (17 June 1996), p. 108.

60. *Ibid.*, p. 108; The Economist Intelligence Unit, *Country Report: Germany* (2nd Quarter 1997), p. 22.

61. "Eastern Construction Industry Breaking with Wage Agreements," *The Week in Germany* (20 December 1996), p. 5.

62. "Association Expects Productivity in Six Years," *The Week in Germany* (16 July 1993), p. 5.

63. "Eastern Construction Industry Breaking with Wage Agreements," *The Week in Germany* (20 December 1996), p. 5.

64. The Economist Intelligence Unit, *Country Report: Germany* (1st Quarter 1997), p. 23.

65. "Germany Survey," *The Economist* (9 November 1996), p. 4.

66. *New York Times* (2 July 1990), p. A5; *Business Eastern Europe* (17 September 1990), p. 312 and (1 October 1990), p. 328, and Patricia Smith, *German Economic and Monetary Union*, p. 58.

67. "Institute: Financial Services Lead in Eastern Productivity," *The Week in Germany* (29 November 1996), p. 4.

68. See Patricia Smith, "German Economic and Monetary Union," p. 53.

69. "Treuhand: Purchasing Initiative to Support Eastern German Economy and Early Success," *The Week in Germany* (17 September 1993), p. 5.

70. *Berliner Zeitung* (6 August 1992), p. 30.

71. "Western Germans Increasingly Interested in Eastern Products," *The Week in Germany* (29 November 1996), p. 4.

72. "Western Stores Stock Few Eastern Consumer Goods, *The Week in Germany* (12 February 1993), p. 5.

73. "Eastern German Exports on the Rise," *The Week in Germany* (12 December 1997), p. 5.

74. "Eastern German Trade with Western Nations Increasing," *The Week in Germany* (17 May 1996), p. 5.

75. "Eastern German Exports on the Rise," *The Week in Germany* (12 December 1997), p. 5.

76. "Eastern German Trade in Decline since 1989," *The Week in Germany* (2 July 1993), p. 5.

77. Dennis, *Social and Economic Modernization*, p. 94.

78. "Survey: The New Germany," *The Economist* (30 June 1990), p. 20.

79. Matthias Greulich, "Außenhandel 1991," *Wirtschaft und Statistik*, No. 1 (1992), p. 97.

80. "Eastern German Trade in Decline since 1989," *The Week in Germany)* (2 July 1993), p. 5.

81. "Eastern German Trade with Western Nations Increasing," *The Week in Germany* (17 May 1996), p. 5.

82. "New Export Initiative to Aid Eastern Firms," *The Week in Germany* (1 November 1996), p. 5.

83. "New Initiative to Spur Job Creation in Germany's Eastern States," *The*

Week in Germany (23 May 1997), p. 4.

84. *Die Welt* (Bonn), 22 May 1997, p. 13.

85. "The Reconstruction of Eastern Germany: Interim Balance and Prospects for the Future," Part I, Special, No. 4464 (13 September 1996), http://www.bundesregierung.de/ausland/news/bpaspecial/special4464.html.

86. "Little Change in Job Market: 4.2 Million Jobless in May," *The Week in Germany* (13 June 1997), p. 4.

87. From *Reuters*, reported in *The New York Times*, 10 December 1997, p. C1.

88. "Marginal Drop in Unemployment; Labor Agency Sees Signs of Turn-around in the West," *The Week in Germany* (7 November 1997), p. 4.

89. "Monthly Update," *Business Central Europe* (June 1997), p. 65. The Czech Republic followed a route of gradual privatizing, protecting jobs and industry, while Poland represents a quicker transition.

90. Dennis, *Social and Economic Modernization,* p. 96.

91. The Economist Intelligence Unit, *Country Report: Germany* (2nd Quarter 1997), p. 23. Fifty percent of those in short-time positions worked less than half-time and one-fourth did not work at all, Dennis, *Social and Economic Modernization,* p. 99.

92. See statistics on early retirement, short-time works, and other labor creation measures in Dennis, *Social and Economic Modernization,* p. 235.

93. "Ostdeutschland 1992 und 1993. Zwischen Skepsis und Hoffnung," *IWH-Kurzinformation*, No. 11 (19 January 1993), p. 2.

94. Helmar Drost, "The Great Depression in East Germany: The Effects of Unification on East Germany's Economy," *East European Politics and Society*, Vol. 7, No. 3 (Fall 1993), pp. 459-60.

95. "Number of Jobless Hits Three-Million Mark as 1992 Drew to a Close," *This Week in Germany* (15 January 1993), p. 4.

96. Patricia Smith, "German Economic and Monetary Union," p. 62. See Chapter 9 by Irene Dölling in this volume for a discussion of employment patterns for women.

97. See Dennis, *Social and Economic Modernization,*" pp. 96-97 and 232-33.

98. "Unemployment Levels Off in February, But Remains at Record High," *The Week in Germany* (7 March 1997), p. 4.

99. "Institute: Joblessness in Academia at All-Time High," *The Week in Germany* (14 June 1996), p. 5.

100. "Institutes Predict Stronger Growth for 1998 but See No Improvement in Jobs," *The Week in Germany* (31 October 1997), p. 4.

101. "Marginal Drop," *The Week in Germany* (7 November 1997), p. 4.

102. "Institute: East-West Wage Disparity to Continue," *The Week in Germany* (20 September 1996), p. 5.

103. Rüdiger Pohl, "Five Years of Upturn East--or the Refounding of an Entire Economy," *Deutschland* , No. 4 (August 1995), p. 24.

104. "Institute: East-West Wage Disparity to Continue," *The Week in Germany* (20 September 1996), p. 5.

105. Richard Rose and Christian Haerpfer, "The Impact of a Ready-Made State: East Germans in Comparative Perspective," *German* Politics, Vol. 6, No. 1

(April 1997), p. 105.

106. See Norman M. Naimark, "'Ich will hier raus': Emigration and the Collapse of the German Democratic Republic" in Ivo Banac (ed.), *Eastern Europe in Revolution* (Ithaca, NY: Cornell University Press, 1992), pp. 72-95.

107. See Bruce Headey, Peter Krause, and Roland Habich, "East Germany: Rising Incomes, Unchanged Inequality, and the Impact of Redistributive Government, 1990-92," *British Journal of Sociology,* Vol. 46, No. 2 (June 1995), pp. 225-43.

108. "Institute: 15 Percent of Eastern Germans Live in Poverty," *The Week in Germany* (7 January 1994), p. 4.

109. Richard Rose and Christian Haerpfer, "Ready-Made State," p.108, based on European Comparison Programme date, 1993, as published by Europestat, Luxembourg, *Statistics in Focus: Economy and Finance,* No. 4. (1996).

110. Rose and Haerpfer, "Ready-Made State," p. 109.

111. *Der Spiegel* (24 June 1996), p. 39.

112. Rose and Haerpfer, "Ready-Made State," pp. 112-13.

113. Headly *et. al.,* "Rising Incomes," p. 239-40.

114. Detlef Schubert, "Between Gain in Prosperity and Loss of Competence: Reflections on the Social and Political Situation of the East German People after German Reunification," *German Monitor,* No. 33 (1994), pp. 31-48.

115. Helmut Wiesenthal, "East Germany as a Unique Case of Societal Transformation: Main Characteristics and Misconceptions," in Andreas Pickel and Helmut Wiesenthal (eds.), *The Grand Experiment: Debating Shock Therapy, Transition Theory, and the East German Experience* (Boulder, Co.: Westview Press, 1997), p. 60.

116. Sinn and Sinn, *Jumpstart,* p. 180.

117. Stephen Padgett, "The New German Economy," in Gordon Smith *et. al.* (eds.), *Developments in German Politics* (London: Macmillan Press, 1992) p. 189.

118. Offe, *Varieties of Transition,* p. 171.

119. *Ibid.,* p. 172.

120. Padgett, "The New German Economy," p. 189.

121. Nagengast, "Germany's *Treuhandanstalt,*" p. 201.

122. "Introduction to Part II," Charles S. Maier (ed.), *The Marshall Plan and Germany: West German Development within the Framework of the European Recovery Program* (New York and Oxford: Berg, 1991), pp. 221-22.

123. Padgett, "The New German Economy," p. 189.

124. See Charles S. Maier, "Introduction: 'Issue Then is Germany and with It Future of Europe,'" pp. 34-39, and Alan S. Milward, "The Marshall Plan and German Foreign Trade," pp. 474-87, in Maier (ed.), *The Marshall Plan and Germany.*

125. Nick, "Destruction," p. 115.

126. Padgett, "The New German Economy," p. 204.

127. To a large extent politicians may have felt forced into this decision by the continuing exodus of east German workers to the West. Approximately 400,000 persons moved from the GDR to West Germany between November 1989 when the wall came down and July 1990 when economic and monetary union occurred.

128. Nick, "Destruction," p. 88.

129. Padgett, "The New German Economy," pp. 196-97, 204.

130. Schubert, "Gain in Prosperity," p. 41.

131. Some assessments view this even more negatively. Schubert, "Gain in Prosperity," p. 37, points to 10 million jobs in the GDR as compared with 5.5 million in eastern Germany in 1992.

132. Schubert, "Gain in Prosperity," p. 35.

133. A.J. Hughes Hallett and Yue Ma, "East Germany, West Germany, and their *Mezzogiorno* Problem: A Parable for European Economic Integration, *Economic Journal*, Vol. 103, No. 417 (March 1993), p. 417.

134. "Eastern Germany's Telecom Network Complete," *The Week in Germany* (28 November 1997), p. 5.

135. "Bank: Eastern Firms Better Prepared for the Coming of the Euro," *The Week in Germany* (14 November 1997), p. 5.

136. *Süddeutsche Zeitung* (Munich), 2 October 1997, translated in *The Week in Germany* (3 October 1997), p. 3.

PART TWO

Culture, Society, and Religion

7

Shock Therapy and Mental Walls: East Germany as a Model for Post-Communist Political Culture?

Laurence McFalls

"Keine Experimente! [No experiments!]" Brandishing this quintessentially conservative slogan, Christian Democratic (CDU) chancellors have twice in the past half century subjected Germans to social experiments of the most radical kind. In the late 1940s and 1950s, Konrad Adenauer and his economics minister (and immediate successor) Ludwig Erhard pushed the still shell-shocked West Germans into the liberal democratic, capitalist, western alliance, whereas the rival Social Democrats (SPD) had proposed a more conservative program of a mixed economy and the pursuit of national unity through neutrality. The CDU's radical experiment worked: not only had the Federal Republic by the late 1950s experienced an "economic miracle" and anchored itself in the western alliance, but by the late 1970s it had consolidated a liberal democratic political culture. After the fall of the Berlin Wall and in the first free East German elections in 1990, Helmut Kohl promised he would reapply the proven West German formula. His CDU revived the *"Keine Experimente"* slogan, distributed copies of Ludwig Erhard's writings on the social market economy, and went on to defeat the opposition parties, which, again more conservatively, warned of the social and economic costs of rapid unification.

Kohl's proven formula turned out, of course, to be the most radical social experiment since Stalin's communizations of Russia and Eastern Europe. More quickly and more completely than any other post-communist society, East Germany witnessed the collapse and restructuring of its economy, the recasting of its political and social institutions, and the replacement of its elites. From the perspective of its eastern neighbors, East Germany's new position was and still is enviable: virtually overnight it acceded to the European Union, NATO, and the club of wealthy democracies. East Germans, however, remain unconvinced of the success of Kohl's experiment in radical transformation.

Whatever East Germans' subjective opinions of unification may be, it is of course too soon to judge "objectively" whether the experiment of German unification has succeeded. Living standards and communications infrastructures have greatly improved in the East, but the structural conditions for self-sustaining growth have not emerged. Institutional transfer from the West is by and large complete, but political parties (with the notable exception of the communist successor Party of Democratic Socialism [PDS]), unions, and civil society as a whole remain weak; and while the worst abuses of western carpet-baggers and of failed western careerists at the helm of virtually everything in the East have receded, a large number of competent, educated eastern elites have suffered enormous status decline. At the mass level, few if any East Germans sincerely wish to turn the clock back on Kohl's experiment, but, as opinion polls repeatedly confirm, most had hoped for better; and although some quip that the Poles, the Czechs, and the Hungarians at least still have their own countries, few would want to change places with their post-communist neighbors.

If East Germany is indeed the best case scenario for the post-communist transformations to date, that is, if it represents a desirable intermediate if not end-point to the transition process, then we might ask what lessons the East German case holds for other post-communist transformations. More specifically, if, despite the relative structural successes of the unification process, East Germans continue to express discontent with their new political, economic, and social order and to regret the disappearance of aspects of their socialist past, then might we not expect subjective, or cultural, resistance to the transformation to be at least as great in the other post-communist societies?

The comparability of the East German case to other (post)communist societies has raised methodological questions since even before 1989.[1] Because the East German state was an artifice of the Cold War, it faced greater problems of legitimation than any of the other imposed East European regimes, but with the end of the Cold War, East Germany found itself in the most privileged position. To be sure, the peculiarities of the East German case set it apart from its eastern neighbors; yet precisely these particularities make it useful for comparison. In this chapter, I shall argue that because the East German post-communist transformation occurred through national unification with West Germany, it can be more or less instructive for understanding the evolution of post-communist political culture elsewhere, depending on the level of society. Specifically, on the basis of my own and other studies of the evolution of political culture in East Germany since 1989 and drawing on the sociological theory of Pierre Bourdieu, I shall contend that while particularities of the unification process have predominantly conditioned East German elites' attitudes, at the mass level East German post-communist political culture has responded to the challenges of the transition from state socialism to liberal capitalism in a manner perhaps more generalizable to societies that did not experience such radical cultural shock therapy.

The Wall in Whose Head?

German unification on 3 October 1990 came with confusing speed. Even just a year before, no one had expected it, and since then the Germans themselves are not certain what consequences it will yet entail. With the serendipitous fall of the Berlin Wall on 9 November 1989, some form of unification became a foregone conclusion: without the repressive mechanism of the Wall, the state socialist regime could not survive, and without socialism, the German Democratic Republic (GDR) had no further *raison d'être*. The rapid, radical form unification took emerged from a combination of high politics--Kohl's seizure of the strategico-diplomatic moment to persuade Mikhail Gorbachev to cede the GDR--and low politics--ordinary East Germans' voting with their feet and at the ballot box for immediate monetary union. Thus, by the early summer of 1990 and before the negotiation of the unification treaty, Gorbachev's agreement to NATO annexation of the GDR[1] and the destruction of the East German economy through one-to-one conversion of East German wages, assets, and debts made it clear that unification would take place through a simple enlargement of the existing Federal Republic. As a technical problem, unification became one of the unilateral transfer of western institutions to the East. As a cultural problem, unification was one of the unilateral adjustment of Easterners to western institutions.

Initially, in the euphoric phase of unification which lasted until Kohl's triumphant re-election as the "Chancellor of Unity" on 2

December 1990, it appeared that East Germans would have a relatively easy time adjusting to their new order. Opinion pollsters, led by their Christian Democratic doyenne Elisabeth Noelle-Neumann,[2] marveled at the striking similarities between East and West Germans' attitudes and values despite more than forty years of division. Not only did East and West Germans share general outlooks on life, but more remarkably the East Germans, who had not participated directly in the development of a democratic political culture in the West, expressed political attitudes sometimes even more liberal and democratic than their experienced western compatriots. Such findings contradicted the assumptions of classical political culture theory,[3] which holds that political culture generally lags behind structural change as people gradually, through experience with new institutions, adjust their attitudes and values. Russell Dalton, who had traced this gradual process in the democratization of West German political culture over some thirty years,[4] thus scurried to save classical political culture theory's assumptions by arguing that East Germans, thanks to western television viewing and personal contacts, had been "vicariously socialized" into the Federal Republic's democratic order.[5]

Subsequent developments, however, proved that Dalton and others had been too quick to judge early opinion data, for the initial euphoria of mutual rediscovery quickly gave way to the perhaps psychologically necessary phases of disenchantment, denial, differentiation, and with luck maybe yet recognition and reconciliation.[6] My own survey work with ordinary East Germans,[7] which I chose to begin the day after Kohl's triumphant re-election on 2 December 1990, showed that the reality principle had suddenly sunk in as respondents admitted that their belief in Kohl's campaign promise of "flourishing landscapes" and a quick equalization of living conditions had been wishful thinking. By the end of my initial interviews with 202 randomly selected East Germans in the spring of 1991, many were already expressing a certain nostalgia for the GDR and resentment of Westerners. Indeed, the idea that East and West Germans after forty years of separation would reach harmonious understanding on the basis of a shared cultural heritage was yet another egregious example of wishful thinking, particularly in light of the fact that the two German states had actively constructed their postwar political cultures on the basis of mutual recriminations about the perpetuation of the crimes of their recent common past. While the GDR accused the FRG of maintaining the social system and elites that had brought the Nazis to power, the FRG depicted the GDR as the prolongation of German totalitarianism under a different name.[8] The explosion of xenophobic violence in the East in 1991 and 1992, most notoriously in Hoyerswerda and Rostock-Lichtenhagen, lent credence to the western prejudice that old German authoritarian and racist values lingered in the East alone, at least until the incendiary murders of Mölln and Solingen and the brief-lived electoral success of far-right parties in the West suggested the need to think twice.

Nevertheless, because of the East's allegedly atavistic attitudes, modernization theory enjoyed a revival even among critical intellectuals in the East as well as the West of Germany for a few years in the early 1990s.[9] The mass mobilizations of the fall of 1989 became a "catch-up revolution," [10] a world-historic lurch forward of the stagnant, relatively undifferentiated societies of the eastern bloc. From this perspective, East Germans' cultural assimilation to the West depended not only on their integration into the economic and social structures of a cosmopolitan, information-based society but on the development of the (post-)modern capacities for individual self-realization and self-expression that had been suppressed by socialist authoritarian paternalism.[11] This theoretical language was echoed in popular usage through the rise of the monikers *Besserwessis* and *Jammerossis*, with the former term describing Easterners' annoyance with Westerners' alleged false sophistication and attitude of superiority and with the latter expressing Westerners' impatience with Easterners' supposed complaints about and resistance to change. Indeed, the level of misunderstanding between East and West Germans quickly reached the point where the only point of agreement was that a "Wall in the heads" continued to divide them. Paradoxically, this mental Wall seemed to be growing even as eastern Germany began to stabilize in the mid-1990s after the most radical phase of political, economic, and social transformation. As Jens Reich, co-founder in 1989 of the New Forum and one of the few eastern voices still to enjoy legitimacy in the German public sphere, lamented: "Je besser es administrativ geht, desto schwieriger wird es mental [The better things go administratively, the worse they get mentally]."[12]

The idea that a cultural barrier persists, if not grows, between East and West Germans has perhaps taken on the quality of a self-fulfilling prophecy. Still, there remains the question of how and why the widespread belief in the "Wall in the heads" emerged. In my analysis of the survey I conducted of 202 randomly selected East Germans in 1990-1991, I postulated that the lingering of cultural values that had stabilized the East German regime before 1989 and that were therefore largely incompatible with life in a capitalist, liberal democratic order would hamper East Germans' adjustment and create potentially violent cultural conflicts within reunified Germany.[13] To test this hypothesis that the survival of GDR values in the East explained the persistent cultural division of Germany, or the "Wall in the heads," I returned to eastern Germany in 1994 to reinterview a representative subsample of 40 of my original 202 survey respondents. Contrary to my expectations, where I had anticipated finding economically dissatisfied individuals rallying around their eastern identity and values in opposition to western arrogance and to growing inequality, I discovered generally satisfied consumers acceptant of the competitive, individualistic social order and identifying with the enlarged Germany while retaining a certain loyalty to their GDR pasts. Mass surveys conducted around the same time and since have confirmed that East Germans claim to have little difficulty in their subjective adjustment to the new order, though they tend to continue to identify themselves, depending on survey question wording, as former GDR-citizens, East Germans, or second-class citizens.[14] Thus, like the mass surveys, my interviews (to which we shall return below) found that the so-called "Wall in the heads" is not built upon East Germans' cultural resistance to their new social structures.[15] Instead, the interviews raised several questions: Does such a Wall exist at all? If so, in whose heads does it exist if not in those of the ordinary East Germans I surveyed? And if the latter claim not to have difficulties in culturally adjusting, why do they continue to identify with the East?

Elites and Masses in the Construction of East German Identity

It is neither redundant nor a tautology to recall that the "Wall in the heads" is quite literally an intellectual construct. In fact, this observation may hold the key to understanding where and how the mental barrier between East and West arose, namely among intellectual elites and through their efforts to protect their social standing. Although the metaphor of the "Wall in the heads" is immediately or intuitively comprehensible to all Germans (and others), its connotative resonance as a communicative symbol within German political discourse resides in its reflexive elaboration by intellectual elites.[16] That is, the very idea that the (partial) absence of common values, symbols, and meanings impedes communication and understanding between East and West Germans presupposes that at least some Germans in both East and West, "intellectuals" by definition, have reflected upon their own values, symbols, and meanings and compared and contrasted them with those of the "other" Germans. The recognition and metaphorical articulation of difference, as with the "Wall in the heads," does not usually alone make for an effective, resonant political symbol, though.

Like any product, a symbol, whatever its intrinsic, intellectual merit, must appeal to its potential consumers to succeed.   Whether metonymous or metaphorical, an effective symbol must evoke an entire complex context in order to rally cognitive recognition among individuals with a diverse range of experiences within that context. Thus, although symbolic interaction defines cultural groups, common symbols do not have precisely the same meaning for different members of the group; they are polysemic.

In the contemporary German context, for instance, the "Wall in the heads" effectively symbolizes the communicative difficulties experienced between East and West Germans, but different groups of Germans experience the "Wall" in significantly different ways. For the mass of West Germans with little contact with the East, about whom I shall say no more here, the "Wall in the heads" accurately describes their quite understandable inability to empathize with East Germans' historical and contemporary life experiences. The "Wall in the head" clearly signifies something else for East Germans, who have less difficulty understanding the values and norms governing life in the West (and increasingly in the East), but the expression also means something different for intellectual elites and for "ordinary" people in the East. As I shall argue, the former have cultivated the symbol of the "Wall in the heads" as a strategy for recognition in their competition with western elites whereas the mass of East Germans have accepted the term as a description of the cultural ambivalence they are experiencing in the transition process.

Although I contend that a broadly defined intellectual elite has cultivated the discursive use of the "Wall in the heads," I am not concerned here with attributing the authorship or explicit use of the symbol to any individual or group. The concept of a mental Wall between Germans arose well before the concrete Wall fell, perhaps even as soon as the Wall's erection in 1961. Novelist Peter Schneider, for example, elaborated on the idea of a "Wall in the heads" in the *Mauerspringer*, published already in 1982. Whatever the term's precise origins, its use in public discourse has clearly mushroomed since the early 1990s, with everyone from the federal president to popular journalists invoking it to lament the cultural difficulties of unification. The problems it describes, however, vary according to social context: among intellectual elites in the East--be they artists, academics, managers, or dissidents--it refers to an explicit critical stance towards some or most West German values, whereas among ordinary East Germans, such as the ones I interviewed, it refers to an ambivalent posture in which they seek to reconcile past and present values.

East German elites do not, of course, hold in common the same attitudes towards socialism as it existed in the GDR, towards the revolutionary events of 1989, or towards the new social order within the enlarged Federal Republic. What they do share, though, is a loss of relative if not absolute social standing. While East German workers had nothing to lose but their jobs thanks to unification, elites faced not only unemployment but irreversible status decline. To understand why eastern elites have therefore had to adopt explicitly critical positions against (aspects of) unification and western values, i.e., why they have had to construct a "Wall in the heads," we can translate their social situation into the language of a simplified version of Pierre Bourdieu's "genetic structuralist" sociological theory.[17] According to Bourdieu, structured social relations are essentially ones of competitive domination and can be divided into as many "fields" as there are forms of competitive interaction between social actors drawing on various material, intellectual, and social resources. Extending the logic of marxist structuralism through analogy, Bourdieu calls these resources diverse forms of "capital," which can be not only economic (including money, material goods, and techniques) but also social (family ties, friendships, obligations, etc.) and cultural (knowledge, experience, competence, etc.). Within each field (be it industrial production, literary criticism, or gang warfare), actors seek to preserve or increase their relevant form of capital, though capital acquired in one field can sometimes be converted into capital in another, with economic capital usually being the most easily convertible (so that the wealthy generally end up with good social connections and at least a veneer of cultural sophistication as well). Every individual participates more or less consciously in the structured interactions of countless fields, acquiring various capitals and internalizing experiences that constitute the individual's "habitus." Members of the same social milieu, i.e., individuals who tend to participate in the same fields and to have the same amounts of capital and life experience, also share a habitus.

Bourdieu's sociology and vocabulary can make sense of East Germans' experience with unification and particularly of the elite's insistence on its cultural distinction from the West. With unification East Germans suddenly found themselves thrust into entirely new economic, political, social, and cultural fields, in which the capital they had acquired in GDR times was either devalued absolutely or relatively in comparison with West Germans in the same fields. In economic fields, East Germans for obvious reasons brought along little or no capital: the two-to-one conversion of most savings gave them a small cushion in the harsh new economy, but the one-to-one conversion of wages at low productivity levels took away whatever competitive edge they might have had in labor markets. Previous formal political capital, e.g., party membership, in many cases became a liability, though the social capital of personal connections sometimes proved convertible in the new context. Thus, those without useful connections denounced the post-unification *Seilschaften*, or networks of influence that allowed powerful people from before 1989 to retain positions of authority. The one form of capital that East Germans might have expected fully to conserve and to convert in unified Germany, however, was their cultural capital.

Intellectual elites in particular might have thought, though not necessarily in these terms, that, despite their lack of wealth, power, and connections, they had the habitus and the cultural capital to retain their standing within their respective fields. Critical artists especially had reason to believe that they would retain their social status since they had won reputations and respect in the West with publications and performances there. Similarly, dissidents who had won admiration in East and West for their moral courage in voicing opposition to the communist regime might have hoped to be heard even more in a liberal democracy. More generally, well educated East Germans who had demonstrated competence in their academic, scientific, administrative, or managerial functions must have expected their intellectual capital to retain much of its value, at least if they were not unduly politically compromised. Very quickly and not unexpectedly from a Bourdieusian perspective, however, East German intellectual elites learned that even when they enjoyed equal or superior cultural capital compared to Westerners, neither their habitus nor their "portfolio" of capital enabled them to compete in fields with which West Germans were already familiar and in which they could mobilize other forms of capital. In short order, artists previously considered critical of the regime found themselves labeled apologists; dissidents dismissed as hopelessly utopian; academics replaced with their western evaluators' former students; and managers and administrators supplanted by careerists from the West, initially often of dubitable qualifications. These developments were not only theoretically predictable, but as I shall illustrate with a few concrete examples, they have obliged East Germans intellectual elites to adopt the only available strategy for preserving what remains of their cultural capital: the rejection of West German values, or the construction of the "Wall in the heads."

The devaluation of East Germans' cultural capital occurred neither slowly nor silently. Instead, it began promptly and noisily with the so-called *Literaturstreit*.[18] Launched in June 1990 in *Die Zeit* with Ulrich Greiner's denunciation of Christa Wolf as the GDR's poet laureate

(*Staatsdichterin*), this debate between West German literary critics had the effect of a strategic surgical strike that decapitated the East German intelligentsia. Echoing the more famous and more clearly political *Historikerstreit* of the mid-1980s, the *Literaturstreit* pitted conservative defenders of a "purely literary" aesthetic against advocates of the morally and politically engaged aesthetic that had dominated postwar German literature in East and West. Although the title of an edited volume on the debate summarized "Es geht nicht um Christa Wolf [It's not about Christa Wolf],"[19] Wolf was the debate's principal victim. Previously admired on both sides of the Wall as a critical voice but a sincere defender of socialist ideals, Wolf, who admitted having briefly supplied information to the Stasi, saw herself dismissed as a hypocrite, a Stalinist, or at best a hopelessly naive utopian. Thus deprived of her legitimate voice on the German literary scene, Wolf, like other East German authors who found themselves judged not on the merits of their work but on their biographies, had little recourse but to denounce unification as colonization by a foreign power. In other words, to salvage her remaining cultural capital, Wolf had to abandon the all-German literary field, though the western critics have pursued her even in her retreat: as Anna Chiarloni has shown with a lexicographic analysis of the critiques of Wolf's latest novel, *Medea*, western critics continue to attack not only Wolf but her eastern readers for their compromised pasts.[20] Thus, East German authors and the reading public have had to throw up cultural walls to preserve their capital, be it in the form of literary reputation or reading pleasure.

The educated elite in East Germany has suffered a devaluation of its cultural capital not only because its literary leaders have been decapitated but because it now finds itself in immediate professional competition with West Germans from a different habitus. The Leipzig sociologist Michael Hofmann has studied administrative and managerial elites in the new *Länder*, examining their social origins and value orientations.[21] Whereas East German elites tend to come from the traditional literary and philosophic German *Bildungsbürgertum*, the West German managers and administrators who have supplanted them in leadership positions usually belong to the more modern rationalistic-technocratic socio-cultural milieu. Having lost their leadership through a shift in fields for which their habitus did not prepare them, eastern elites, according to Hofmann, have tried to preserve their status at least as culturally superior intellectuals by exercising moralistic critiques of the technocratic unification process; they have become the *Warner und Mahner* [warners and admonishers] of unification. East German intellectuals' adoption of a moralistic tone has not, however, been an entirely successful strategy in their battle to conserve their cultural capital since the attempt to seize the moral highground requires ambivalent self-justification on the part of East Germans who wish to be critical of unification without appearing to be apologists for the *ancien régime*. Linguists who have conducted conversation analyses of interactions between East and West Germans, be they television talk shows or community encounter sessions, have shown that East Germans must use ambiguous or awkward linguistic formulations in order to reconcile their potentially compromised pasts with their present critical attitudes.[22] They thus come across as inarticulate, confused, or communicatively incompetent and suffer a loss of linguistic cultural capital even as they struggle to preserve their moral intellectual capital.

While East German intellectuals in general have lost their voice in the all-German public discourse and have therefore had to retreat into cultural separatism behind the "Wall in the heads," one particular group of intellectuals, namely the dissidents, could have expected its political and moral capital to appreciate with unification. The leaders of political opposition in the GDR also largely came from the traditional *Bildungsbürgertum* and had accordingly exercised a moral- istic critique of the state socialist regime. Although some turned out to have collaborated with the Stasi, most came into unified Germany with untarnished pasts and could claim some credit for toppling the odious regime. As Detlef Pollack has shown with an on-going study of former GDR opposition group leaders, however, only a few have converted their old political capital into new positions within the party system, and even these former dissidents complain of a loss of effectiveness within the larger, more complex, and morally more ambiguous political system of the Federal Republic.[23] All of the former dissidents he has interviewed experienced the opening of the political system as a loss of the sense of community they enjoyed as a network of outsiders trapped behind the Wall. These losses of voice and commun- ity have thus led to a depoliticization of most former dissidents and to their apparent withdrawal behind the "Wall in the heads" alongside other members of the intellectual milieu.

The cultural isolation of East German dissidents is not a new phe- nomenon, however. Despite their public visibility during the momentous events of 1989-90, they never held significant political or social capital in the GDR and were hardly representative of mass cultural values.[24] If today, like the rest of the intellectual elite, they cultivate the "Wall in the heads" as a means of retaining some cultural legitimacy or capital, their pursuit of cultural distinctiveness from the "colonizing" West does not necessarily reflect the subjective orientation towards unification of the broad mass of East German society. Indeed, former dissidents as well as intellectuals (partially) defensive of the communist regime have been disdainful of ordinary East Germans, who allegedly traded in their country for bananas and fell for Kohl's patently false promises of *blühende Landschaften* (flourishing landscapes). Such moralistic condemnation reeks, of course, of a domination strategy in which intellectual elites seek to augment their cultural capital by affirming their moral and intellectual superiority over the East German masses while at the same time they defend their capital by professing their cultural separation from the West. Ordinary East Germans, however, have little cultural capital at stake in the unification process and therefore have equally little interest in asserting their cultural distinctiveness from the West. Dominated in the GDR, dominated they remain in the FRG, though probably in a morally more acceptable way. As one woman whom I interviewed summarized the difference, today ordinary East Germans feel powerless, but it is *Ohnmacht ohne Angst* (powerlessness without fear).

Although ordinary East Germans in unified Germany pursue no strategy of capital conversion or conservation, they nonetheless find themselves subordinated in the economic, political, social, and cultural fields in which their inherited habitus, or culture, can handicap (or perhaps help) their action possibilities. Thus, whereas intellectual elites must defend their cultural differences, ordinary Easterners must adapt their culture as well as they can to their new fields. The second round of interviews that I conducted with forty East Germans in 1994 sought to assess this process of cultural adaptation at a time when the forms that the new social order was taking were becoming evident in the new *Länder*. [25] As I mentioned above, these interviews initially revealed that my forty respondents were having little difficulty adjusting to the new order, though I had expected that their GDR habitus would leave them ill-equipped or at least uncomfortable in the expanded FRG; they had, over many years after all, internalized behavioral norms that had facilitated their survival in and the reproduction of the state socialist system. Was it possible that within five years they had constructed an entirely new habitus, that they had shed a lifetime of experiences, values, and habits?

As I listened to my interview partners more closely, I realized that the relative ease with which they claimed to be adjusting to a competitive, individualistic consumer society did not signal a miraculous transmutation of their solidaristic, modest and frugal habitus. [26] Increasingly I noticed a disjuncture between individuals' discursive evaluation of the new social order and their own experiences within it. They noted, for example, that social relations had all become more competitive and instrumental yet maintained that their own friends, colleagues, and acquaintances had remained as solidaristic as before. Similarly, regardless of their age, they insisted that those younger than they had abandoned GDR attitudes and values whereas they themselves were too old to change. Most telling was a young day-care worker in Apolda, Thuringia, who, after extolling the individual opportunities she had found in unified Germany, said she would not be comfortable in her new country until she could go to work without feeling guilty since others did not have the same opportunity. She, like my other interview partners, seemed to be clinging personally to old egalitarian GDR cultural values that intellectually she knew had been supplanted.

In other Bourdieusian words, ordinary East Germans seem to understand and even accept the "doxa," i.e., the organizing principles or rules of the games, of the new, westernized fields in which they must act while necessarily retaining their old, eastern habitus. Because they have little or no economic, social, or cultural capital acquired in GDR times, they have no interest in assuming heterodox positions in their fields or in withdrawing from them as do intellectual elites. Therefore they need not participate in the construction of the "Wall in the heads." At the same time, however, their lifelong socialization into a GDR habitus constitutive of their identity and action repertoire leaves them attached to their old identity and values but not in an instrumental or consequential manner. They may wish to validate their GDR past but they do not wish to live in it. Their "Wall in the head" does not prevent their integration into the new social order. Thus, without in any way contradicting themselves, they can espouse nostalgic opinions and claim an East German identity at the same time as they voice satisfaction with unification.

I have argued elsewhere that East Germans' desire to validate their pasts without refusing their unified present expresses itself in part through widespread acceptance of a legitimate political role for the Party of Democratic Socialism (PDS) if not outright electoral support for the communist successor party.[27] While the mainstream (western) parties CDU and SPD (as well as the alternative Alliance 90/Greens, in which former East German dissidents still have a visible presence) have tended to treat East Germans' GDR past as highly compromised or, at best, as an embarrassment to be forgotten, the PDS and its candidates have skillfully exploited biographical continuity as a campaign theme, thus appealing to Easterners' wish to salvage their pasts. To be sure, with the notable exception of East Berlin with its large concentration of elites, the PDS has not (yet) garnered even a plurality of East German votes; a majority of Easterners appreciates its role as a defender of their interests and identity, but most still overwhelmingly prefer one of the mainstream parties, especially the party of unification, the CDU.

Such simultaneous acceptance of the PDS and support for the CDU is consistent with my Bourdieusian interpretation of ordinary East Germans' somewhat ambivalent cultural dispositions. Also consistent with my analysis is the fact that support for the PDS is not strongest among the so-called "losers of unification," i.e., among those with the least capital of various forms, but rather among the relatively well-off and well-educated--precisely among the intellectual elites, whose efforts to preserve their cultural capital require that they reject or criticize unification. Those who have profited most in absolute terms from unification but who have suffered the greatest relative status decline tend to vote for (and lead) the party that has most strongly opposed and criticized unification. Thus, the PDS emerges as the perfect political manifestation of the "Wall in the heads." It gives intellectual elites a mouthpiece to express their political cultural separateness, and it offers the mass of ordinary East Germans a defense of their pasts without threatening their present integration into unified Germany since the party is structurally assured of a permanent minority position in German politics.

Political Cultural Lessons of the East German *Sonderfall*

The structural peculiarities of the East German case of post-communist transformation that prevent the PDS from posing a serious challenge to the emerging liberal capitalist order also raise the question of the relevance of the East German experience as a model for other transitions. In the neighboring advanced post-communist societies of Central Europe, a certain nostalgia for the certitudes of the communist past has followed the euphoria of liberation, and communist successor parties have resurged--even returning to power, first in Hungary and then in Poland--by vaunting their political experience and appealing to welfarist ideological sentiment.[28] But are these phenomena comparable in a meaningful way to the rise of the "Wall in the heads" and of the PDS in the former GDR? Two fundamental differences--most importantly, the GDR's unification with the large, wealthy, and powerful Federal Republic and, as a consequence of the first, the much greater speed and extent of change--make any comparison difficult. The Bourdieusian theoretical model that I have applied to the East German case here, however, logically suggests some similarities and differences that we might expect in the evolution of political culture in the former GDR and in neighboring post-communist societies.

At the elite level, with the exception of a few unreconstructed Stalinist leaders and their cronies in the secret police, the intellectual, political, and economic elites of Central and Eastern Europe beyond the GDR came through the collapse of communism with their various forms of cultural, social, and economic capital intact or enhanced. Unlike the East Germans, they did not come into competition with a large, alternative elite; a handful of returning expatriates, even millionaires, could not really challenge their social power, though a few dissidents, like Vaclav Havel and Lech Walesa, did rise to prominence. Whereas East German elites quickly found themselves excluded from political, economic, and cultural power and reduced to seeking to salvage their cultural capital by rejecting or criticizing the post-communist order, other East-Central European elites not only preserved their leadership positions but were free to experiment with or to embrace new cultural and ideological values, or culturally to recapitalize, in the absence of an alternative elite with a higher cultural capital endowment. In fact, even before 1989, East-Central European elites enjoyed relatively greater cultural and ideological latitude than those in East Germany because the latter could justify their existence independent of the West German elite only through communist orthodoxy.[29] Since 1989, however, the former enjoy relative freedom (within the constraints of the international social fields to which they belong) to adopt any cultural values that might enhance their capital. For example, the Polish and Hungarian communist successor parties under new-old elite control can, unlike the PDS, promote purely reformist social democratic or even neo-liberal programs.

At the mass level, by contrast, the East German case may hold some lessons for neighboring societies which have not yet undergone as much structural transformation. As we have seen, ordinary East Germans do not face immediate or direct competition with West Germans as their elites do. What is more, they have little cultural capital acquired in the GDR at stake in their new fields of social competition. For them the challenge of unification lies in drawing on their GDR habitus as best they can in fields of action which they have neither the hope nor the interest to contest or to change. Their "Wall in the heads" is not a refusal of the transformation process but an expression of the values and identity from their old habitus, which they would like to preserve even as they internalize their new subordinate position. Because the structural position of masses in other post-communist societies is similar, we might expect them to adopt a similarly ambivalent cultural posture in which they accept radical structural change even as they hold onto old identities and values. In East Germany, however, such ambivalence is sustainable because the rules of the game of various cultural, economic, political, and social fields are clear, namely those established in West Germany.

Thus, we might conclude that mass cultural resistance to or acceptance of structural change in East-Central Europe beyond the former GDR will depend on elites' ability to impose clear and stable rules of the game. In East Germany, rapid and radical social transformations have provoked little cultural resistance because unification not only socially disempowered elites but forced them into cultural separatism, leaving the mass without a credible cultural leadership in the new system. It would thus be a mistake to assume that East German elites' criticisms of unification reflects mass opinion. (For example, many East Germans admire informal PDS leader Gregor Gysi for his biting wit but lament that he is "in the wrong party," i.e., they recognize that his charisma and criticisms ultimately carry no effective weight.) Elsewhere in post-communist Europe, indigenous elites still enjoy social power and can play their "natural" roles as cultural leaders. In those societies we might therefore expect a greater overlap between elite and mass political culture, depending of course on the dynamics of elite competition, but speculations on the cultural consequences of those dynamics are clearly beyond the theoretical scope of this essay.

Notes

1. See Andreas Pickel and Helmut Wiesenthal, *The Grand Experiment: Debating Shock Therapy, Transition Theory and the East German Experience* (Boulder, CO: Westview Press, 1997), introduction.

2. Elisabeth Noelle-Neumann, *Demoskopische Geschichtsstunde: Vom Wartesaal der Geschichte zur Deutschen Einheit* (Zurich: Edition Interfrom, 1991).

3. See, for example, the classic formulation of political culture theory in Gabriel Almond and Sidney Verba, *The Civic Culture: Political Attitudes and Democracy in Five Nations* (Princeton, NJ: Princeton University, 1963).

4. Kendall Baker, Russell Dalton, and Kai Hildebrandt, *Germany Transformed: Political Culture and the New Politics* (Cambridge, MA: Harvard University Press, 1981).

5. Russell Dalton, "Communists and Democrats: Democratic Attitudes in the Two Germanies," *British Journal of Political Science*, Vol. 24, No. 4 (October 1994), pp. 469-493.

6. Social psychologist Wolf Wagner in *Kulturschock Deutschland* (Berlin; Rotbuch, 1996), p. iii, organizes his study of post-unification communications problems between East and West using these phases.

7. Laurence McFalls, *Communism's Collapse, Democracy's Demise? The Cultural Context and Consequences of the East German Revolution* (New York: New York University Press, 1995).

8. See Anne-Marie LeGloannec, *La nation orpheline* (Paris: Calmann-Lévy, 1989), ch. 1.

9. See, for example, Michael Brie and Dieter Klein (eds.), *Umbruch zur Moderne,* (Hamburg: VSA-Verlag, 1991).

10. Jürgen Habermas, *Die nachholende Revolution,* (Frankfurt am Main: Suhrkamp, 1990).

11. Some East German sociologists have argued, however, that the contradictions between socialist authoritarianism and paternalism created the space for individuals to cultivate these cultural values. See, for example, Rudolf Woderich, "Mentalitäten zwischen Anpassung und Eigensinn," *Deutschland Archiv,* Vol. 25, No. 1 (January 1992), pp. 21-31.

12. Jens Reich, "Die Einheit: gelungen und gescheitert," *Die Zeit* (international edition), Vol. 50, No. 38 (22 September 1995), p. 16.

13. Laurence McFalls, "Une Allemagne, deux sociétés distinctes," *Revue canadienne de science politique,* Vol. 23, No. 4 (December 1993), pp. 721-43.

14. See, for example, the surveys cited in Richard Rose and Edward C. Page, "German Responses to Regime Change: Culture, Class, Economy, or Context?" *West European Politics,* Vol. 19, No. 1 (January 1996), pp. 1-27.

15. Laurence McFalls, "Political Culture, Partisan Strategies, and the PDS: Prospects for an East German Party," *German Politics and Society,* Vol. 13 , No. 1 (Spring 1995), pp. 50-61.

16. For a seminal discussion of the role of elites in the production and competitive manipulation of political symbols for mass consumption, see Lowell Dittmer, "Political Culture and Political Symbolism: Toward a Theoretical Synthesis," *World Politics,* Vol. 29, No. 4 (July 1977), pp. 552-83.

17. The simplified version of Bourdieu's theory, on which I draw here primarily for the suggestive power of its vocabulary, may make his theory appear unduly mechanistic when in fact it seeks to avoid structuralism's excessive determinism. For good introductions to Bourdieu's sociology, see: Pierre Ansart, *Les sociologies contemporaines* (Paris: Seuil, 1990), chapters 1, 5, and 9; Alain Acardo and Philippe Corcuff (eds.), *La sociologie de Bourdieu* (Bordeaux: Le Mascaret, 1986); Pierre Bourdieu, *Questions de sociologie* (Paris: Éditions de Minuit, 1984); Pierre Bourdieu, *Raisons pratiques: sur la théorie de l'action* (Paris: Seuil, 1994).

18. For an analysis of the broader literary and political repercussions of this debate as well as its scapegoating of Christa Wolf, see Claudia Mayer-Iswandy, "Between Resistance and Affirmation: Christa Wolf and German Unification," *Canadian Review of Comparative Literature,* Vol. 22, No. 3-4 (1995), p. 813-35.

19. Thomas Anz, ed., *"Es geht nicht um Christa Wolf": Der Literaturstreit im vereinten Deutschland* (Munich: Spangenberg, 1991).

20. Anna Chiarloni, "Zur Rezeption Christa Wolfs *Medea. Stimmen,*" unpublished manuscript (University of Torino, Italy), presented to the 22nd New Hampshire Symposium, Conway, NH, 19-26 June 1996.

It is not only East German authors (and readers) who fell victim to the *Literaturstreit*. The debate's principal target in the West was Günter Grass, whose politically engaged novels had contributed greatly to the West German public's confrontation with its Nazi past in the 1960s and 1970s. His publication of a novel problematizing unification, *Ein Weites Feld*, in 1995 provoked a second round of the *Literaturstreit*, in which virulent West German criticism assured Grass of the top place on the East German best-seller list for months.

21. Michael Hofmann, "Die Warner und Mahner der Vereinigung," unpublished manuscript (University of Leipzig), presented to the 22nd New Hampshire Symposium, Conway, NH, 19-26 June 1996.

22. See Cf. Grit Liebscher and Heinz Kreutzer, "Ost-West-Kommunikation in deutschen Talkshows," unpublished manuscript (University of Texas at Austin and Monash University, Australia); Ricarda Wolf, "'Reden, ohne auf den Punkt zu kommen': Doppelorientierung als Selbstdarstellungsproblem ostdeutscher Frauen in Gesprächen mit westdeutschen Frauen," unpublished manuscript (University of Potsdam); both papers presented to the 22nd New Hampshire Symposium, Conway, NH, 19-26 June 1996.

23. Detlef Pollack, "Zum Wandel von Sprach- und Kommunikationsformen in ostdeutschen Bürgerbewegungen und Oppositionsgruppen seit der Wende," unpublished manuscript (Europa-Universität Viadrina, Frankfurt/Oder), presented to the 22nd New Hampshire Symposium, Conway, NH, 19-26 June 1996.

24. Pollack, *ibid.*, has shown that they were never particularly representative of East German society or culture. Christian Joppke, *East German Dissidents and the Revolution of 1989* (New York: NYU Press, 1995), also argues convincingly that the utopian and intellectual tone of the East German elite opposition estranged it from mass discontent.

25. I conducted these interviews in July and August 1994 with a subsample representative of the 202 randomly selected persons whom I had interviewed in 1990 and 1991 in eastern Mecklenburg-Vorpommern, East-Berlin, southern Thuringia, and the Halle-Leipzig-Jena industrial triangle. I shall be interviewing the entire survey sample again in 1997-98.

26. In McFalls, *Communism's Collapse*, ch. 4, I present modesty, solidarity, and equality as the trio of values that best summarized East German political culture before 1989. These were values that paradoxically emerged from--and rendered bearable--the system's vices of penury, dependence, and political privilege.

27. See McFalls, "Political Culture," pp. 55-61.

28. See Barnabas Racz and Istvan Kukorelli, "The 'Second-generation' Post-communist Elections in Hungary in 1994," *Europe-Asia Studies*, Vol. 47, No. 2 (June 1995), pp. 251-79; Frances Millard, "The Polish Parliamentary Election of September, 1993," *Communist and Post-Communist Studies*, Vol. 27, No. 3 (September 1994), pp. 295-313; Georges Mink and Jean-Charles Szurek, "Europe Centrale: La Revanche des Néo-communistes," *Politique internationale*, No. 67 (Spring 1995), pp. 157-68.

29. See Joppke, *East German Dissidents*, ch. 1.

8

The Situation of Religion in Eastern Germany After 1989[1]

Detlef Pollack

During the forty years of communist rule churches were politically oppressed, ideologically stigmatized, and largely excluded from public life in the German Democratic Republic. Many Christians had to suffer from disadvantages in their education and their professional careers. Although the legal status of the church was guaranteed by the constitution, church life always depended on arbitrary decisions of the communist rulers and was restricted in many respects. After the *Wende* (the radical changes accompanying the collapse of communism in the German Democratic Republic) churches and religion were no longer excluded from society but became more and more integrated into it. Now, churches have the right to provide religious instructions in schools, they are present in the media and in public life, their work for charity is generously subsidized by the state, and because of their enterprising role during the *Wende*, they are widely appreciated and acknowledged.

In order to describe the current religious situation in eastern Germany three questions will be raised. What are the main features of the religious situation in eastern Germany compared with those in western Germany? Was the diminution of church parishes in eastern Germany connected with the development of a new type of church membership, a more engaged and committed one? Did new forms of religiosity outside the church emerge which are suited to compensate for the loss of church

members?   For answering these questions I will refer to some
representative polls, church statistics, and several studies carried out
by sociologists and the churches themselves.

The Process of Separating from the Church in Eastern Germany

Membership

In assessing the situation of the church in eastern Germany following
the *Wende,* a comparison of church membership in eastern and western
Germany can be illuminating. In the western German states, more than
80 percent of the population are members of one of the two major
churches, their number being divided almost evenly between the Roman
Catholic Church and the Lutheran Churches.[2] In 1950, some 96 percent
of the total population of the Federal Republic of Germany were church
members.[3] The number of those not belonging to any denomination has
trebled in the course of 45 years, having risen from four to well over
twelve percent.[4]

In the eastern German states, by contrast, combined membership in
the Lutheran Church and the Roman Catholic Church does not even
account for 30 percent of the population: just under 25 percent belong to
the Lutheran Church and 3 percent to the Roman Catholic. Here, those
not belonging to any denomination--close to 70 percent--make up the
largest group.[5] In 1950 they accounted for about 7 percent of the
population.[6] In other words, their numbers have risen tenfold within
the last 45 years.

Church membership is, of course, a comparatively superficial
feature of the situation with regard to churches and religion. However,
the following will show that the different church membership figures
in eastern and western Germany represent an astonishingly accurate
reflection of the underlying religious and ecclesiastical differences.

Rituals

Service attendance as an indicator of church practice, for example,
shows that the differences between the eastern and the western German
states in terms of church membership figures are also evident with
regard to participation in church life.   Some 21 percent of western
Germans say they never attend church services. In eastern Germany,
those who say they never attend make up 60 percent of the population.
Conversely, 24 percent of western Germans say they go to church once a

month, as against a mere 7 percent of eastern Germans.[7] Just under 40 percent of western Germans do not participate in any way in church activities. In the East, 72 percent say that they do not take part in church life.[8] Of those interviewed in western Germany, well above 90 percent say that their children have been baptized; 86 percent say they would have their children baptized if they had any. In eastern Germany, those whose children have been baptized account for only a good third. Forty-eight percent of those interviewed there who do not have any children yet would be willing to have their children baptized.[9] As to the frequency of prayer, 28 percent of those interviewed in the western German states say they never pray; in eastern Germany, this figure is 70 percent.[10]

Looking at actual rituals, one must say that the differences between eastern and western Germany are rather profound. With regard to religious practice one would think that these are two different societies. Are these differences reflected in the subjective dimension of an individual's faith and experience?

Beliefs

How many say that they believe in God depends to no small degree on the wording of the question. In western Germany, 10 percent of the population deny any form of belief in God, while in eastern Germany, this figure is 49 percent. In the west, 80 percent profess at least some vague faith in God or in some supernatural being as against 37 percent in the the East.[11] If the survey refrains from presenting the notion of God in explicit terms and if no allowance is made for different degrees of certainty, people saying they believe in God account for about 70 percent of western Germans and for about one-third of eastern Germans.[12] When asked briefly and succinctly: "Does God exist?" fewer people answered in the affirmative in both East and West: 61 percent in the West and 21 percent in the East.[13] Regardless of the wording of the questions, the differences in the distribution of the belief in God between East and West remain consistent. Similar East-West differences occur if people are asked how close to God they feel as a rule. In western Germany, 46 percent answered "very close" or "rather close," while in eastern Germany, only 15 percent marked these answers.[14] Similarly, belief in life after death is far more widespread in the West than in the East; here, 54 percent positive answers in the West contrast with 14 percent positive answers in the East.[15] Inquiring about religious self-assessment helps best in recording the extent of religious convictions and views molded outside the church. In the answers to such questions, differences between East and West remain undiminished. While only 13 percent of western interviewees describe themselves as not religious at all, this figure tops 50 percent in the East.[16]

Accounting for Differences

How can these enormous East-West differences with regard to religiosity and church affiliation be accounted for? At first sight, one could assume that what is involved are so-called secondary effects, i.e., that the differences are not of a religious or ecclesiastical nature, but that they rather result from differences in age, social structure, or educational level. Indeed, life expectancy in western Germany is higher than in the East,[17] and it is a fact that religiosity and church ties get stronger with advancing age.[18] On the other hand, the formal level of education of the population in the western German states is higher than that of the eastern German population,[19] and people of a higher educational level are, on average, more critical of faith and the churches.[20] Moreover, the tertiary sector (the service sector) in western Germany is far more advanced, at the expense of industry and agriculture, than in the East.[21] Traditionally, farmers have been a major stay for the stability of church life, while in modern technical fields, science, teaching, and research professions support for religion and the churches is particularly weak.[22] Urbanization, which is further advanced in the West than in the East, also strengthens the trend towards withdrawal from the churches.[23] Looking at socio-structural differences, the western German states, on account of their higher degree of modernization, ought to be far more secularized and dissociated from the church on the whole than eastern Germany. However, the contrary is true. Pointing to socio-structural differences, therefore, does not help explain the differences with regard to religion and the churches.

A far more significant factor is the higher proportion of Roman Catholics in the West in contrast to in the East. Compared to Protestants, Roman Catholics are known to be more committed to their church, to participate in church life--in particular in Sunday services-- to a larger extent, and to be stronger in their belief in God and in their conviction that religion is important in daily life.[24] Consequently, the higher proportion of Roman Catholics in western Germany directly affects the East-West differences presented here. But these denominational differences do not suffice to explain the religious differences; in GDR times, the Roman Catholic Church also had to accept losses which, proportionally speaking, were at least equal to those of the Lutheran Churches.[25]

The decisive factor is the difference in the numbers of people not belonging to any religious denomination. Why this figure is so high in the eastern part of Germany has been the subject of much debate. Many observers point to the political repression to which churches and Christians had been subject in GDR times.[26] This is a correct observation. The largest number of people leaving the churches coincides with the period of the most severe political repression of the churches and greatest discrimination against Christians: the second half of the 1950s.[27] At the time, church resignation figures sky-rocketed within a matter of three years, and with the introduction of the *Jugendweihe* (youth dedication: in the GDR, a non-religious ceremony replacing confirmation in which fourteen-year-olds were given adult social status) the proportion of those confirmed dropped from more than three-quarters to about one-third. The number of baptismal ceremonies also dropped by one-third.[28]

Political repression apart, a number of other factors must also be held responsible for the church's loss of significance, as membership also shrunk in the 1960s, 70s, and 80s, when the trend to leave the churches had ebbed. By the 1980s, the number of those leaving the Lutheran Churches was only slightly higher than those joining. Prominent among the reasons for the drop in membership during this period was no longer the high number of withdrawals but rather a diminishing willingness to have children baptized.[29] While church members were no longer encouraged to leave the church by the state's offensive anti-church policy, religion and the churches did remain ideologically stigmatized and socially excluded. A clever policy of passive repression denied the churches' integration into society. Obviously, this was sufficient reason for many people to lose contact with the church and for many others to shrink from visible relations with the church or, while not leaving the church themselves, to not send their children to church anymore.

In addition, forced shifts in social structure destroyed traditional environments and broke the socio-structural backbone of Protestantism in both urban and rural areas. Those shifts resulted from political pressure towards the end of the 1940s and in the 1950s; the expulsion of the propertied classes and of many educated middle-class intellectuals, higher civil servants, and large numbers of teachers; the collectivization of farming; the nationalization of industry; and the formation of tradesmen's and craftsmen's cooperatives. The political mobilization of society led to a profound rupture in tradition and culture which cut the churches to the quick.

And finally, another factor in the process of alienation from the church is the fact that in the nineteenth century ties with the church were already extremely weak in large parts of central Germany. Segments of the working classes and even quite a number of country people had developed a "Let-us-be-Christians-without-going-to-church" approach,[30] a kind of inner secularization while remaining church members and continuing to rely on christening, wedding, and burial rituals.[31] This inner secularization met with exterior political pressure--a process which began not under the SED regime but in the Third Reich--and the effects of both components mutually reinforced one another.[32]

Of course, there was also a considerable wave of people leaving the churches in western Germany. The trend of withdrawals set in at the end of the 1960s in connection with the student unrest and the cultural upheaval of the young at the time, reached its peak in early 1970s, and died down noticeably towards the end of the seventies.[33] Today, the surge of resignations in the late sixties and early seventies is often linked with the simultaneous change in values from order, security, and authority to self-realization and participation.[34] Ronald Inglehart and others argue that in the 1960s the United States, the Federal Republic of Germany, and other Western European countries reached a level of prosperity that for the first time allowed the population to shift the emphasis of their practical activities from the pursuit of material interests (like prosperity, work, performance, diligence, etc.) to the pursuit of post-materialist values (like freedom, emancipation, self-realization, etc.).[35] The churches' decline in membership could thus be interpreted as part of a general process of cultural modernization. One should add, however, that the wave of withdrawals in West Germany in the 60s and 70s never reached the East German high. While the highest annual withdrawal rate in the Lutheran Churches in the West was 0.8 percent in 1974,[36] it was as high as 2.5 percent in the East in 1958.[37] In West Germany, the churches enjoyed a position protected by law: they had a say in the running of social organizations, radio stations, and television broadcasting corporations; they had the right to provide religious instruction in schools; and they were socially integrated. This difference in socio-political conditions also helps to explain the differences between eastern and western Germany in terms of alienation from the church and secularization. All in all, the following statement can be made: even though denominational affiliation may be a rather superficial and formal criterion, it is a clear indicator of the differences in the religious environments of eastern and western Germany.

National Church or Voluntary Church?

In societies in which we are confronted with a national church almost the entire population belongs to the church. In these societies church membership is regarded as traditional or a matter of course. This kind of church membership is, however, often not connected with personal commitment to the church or with a high level of personal belief. In the absence of a national church, belonging to the church ceases to be a matter of course, and it becomes necessary to decide personally for or against church membership. In these cases, a voluntary church often provides the opportunity for a more personal engagement in spirituality and elicits a higher degree of participation in church life.

Have the shrinking congregations in eastern Germany led to an intensified commitment among the remaining parishioners? Here again, let us compare eastern and western Germany. This time, we look only at the situation within the church, confining ourselves to the Lutheran Church.[38] Our comparison is therefore restricted to the behavior and attitudes of the members of the Lutheran Church in East and West.

Church Practice

Looking at the *church practice* of Protestants, one can say that the church behavior of eastern Germans almost completely tallies with that of western Germans. According to church statistics and to information provided by interviewees, service attendance was somewhat higher in the West than in the East until shortly after the *Wende*. Church offices say that in the early nineties, some 5 percent of congregation members attended services on an ordinary Sunday in the West--a figure slightly lower than in the early eighties[39]--while in the East, the figure ranged from 3 to 6 percent.[40] In 1992, according to church members surveyed, 13 percent went to church at least once a month in the West, and 11 percent in the East.[41] Since 1991-1992, the number of churchgoers among congregation-members has, however, increased in the East[42] while it dropped further in the West, so that now the percentage of service attendance in eastern Germany is slightly above the western German level. Outside church services, 72 percent of church members in the western German states do not take part in church life, while in the eastern German states this figure is 68 percent.[43] The figures are, as one can see, very close indeed. A larger difference is to be observed in the christening figures. In the West, the rate is 95 percent, but in the East, a mere 75 percent.[44] The proportions of Protestants who would be willing to have their children baptized if they had any are similar in the East and West--some 90 percent would do so.[45] Similarly, differences are not too great between eastern and western German Protestants with regard to the frequency of prayer; the figure is only slightly higher in the West than in the East.[46]

Indicators measuring *conviction* present a similar picture. Figures for eastern German Protestants are similar to figures for Protestants in western Germany. However, questions concerning belief in God, the feeling of being close to God, and the self-assessment of one's own religiosity always elicit somewhat more positive answers in the West than in the East.[47] Belief in the continuation of life after death is also higher among Protestants in the West.[48]

Attitudes Regarding Churches

To ascertain the attitude of Protestants vis-à-vis their churches, it is not sufficient to depict only the ritual-practical and the faith and conviction dimensions of religiosity. Survey questions must also analyze *Protestants' attitude vis-à-vis the church and church activities, expectations concerning the church, and motives for membership*. What then comes to light is an astonishing similarity in the answers given by eastern and western Germans. Asked how close they felt to the church, one-third of interviewees in both East and West replied that they felt rather or very closely linked, another third said they felt somewhat linked, and the last third answered that they felt hardly any or no links to their church.[49] Although the proportion of those feeling very closely linked is somewhat higher in the East than in the West, on the whole, the patterns of answers differ only insignificantly.

A similar pattern is also evident in what is expected of the church. In East and West alike, the church is first and foremost expected to be active in the field of charitable service; to commit itself to the care of the aged, sick, and disabled; and to look after the needy. The church is further expected--in the East somewhat more so than in the West--to fulfill its fundamental religious functions: to preach the gospel, to relate it to every-day life, to hold engaging services, and to provide a space for peacefulness and for prayer.[50] Active help for fellow human beings who have become destitute and spiritual communication are other tasks the church is expected to fulfill. Expectations, therefore, tend to center on the church's traditional tasks. Less welcome are the church's opinion on political issues; its participation in the upbringing of children and in marriage and family counseling; its commitment to women's equal rights; its range of cultural opportunities; and the church's involvement in everyday working life.[51] The church is expected to concentrate on its genuinely religious and charitable tasks-- this holds for East and West alike.

We find a similarly conventional approach with regard to people's reasons for being church members. "Because I am a Christian" and "because I agree with the Christian doctrine" are the most frequent answers given in both East and West. Almost as many people say "I am a member of the church because I do not want to do without a church wedding and a church burial" and "because my parents were church members too."[52] The church's commitment to justice in the world, the kind of fellowship it offers, and the opportunities for meaningful parish work are less important reasons for membership.[53] People are members of the church because of a concurrence of values, for reasons of tradition, and because they are interested in rites of passage or life-cycle rites; their desire to commit themselves in the church or to seek the fellowship of other believers is less significant.

The conventional nature of church membership is also evident in replies to a question about the essence of being a Protestant. Participatory aspects such as church attendance, reading the Bible, or being informed about church life are items very rarely marked as important. Interviewees think the essentials are christening, confirmation, and membership in the Lutheran Church[54]--characteristics that are to a high degree specific to the institution itself. Being a Protestant, they say, also means that one has to follow one's conscience and that one should be a respectable and reliable person.[55] In other words, it means meeting humanistic criteria. With regard to this question, it can be observed that eastern German Protestants are somewhat stronger in accepting participatory features and somewhat weaker in accepting institutional features than western German interviewees. Differences in this respect are, however, slight.

The conventional nature of church membership becomes particularly evident in interviewees' attitudes vis-à-vis confirmation. This ceremony, which is by theologians usually seen as an occasion for the adolescent to reaffirm his church membership by way of a personal decision, is interpreted by Protestants in both East and West as the ceremonious closing of childhood and entry into a new period of life, as a rite of passage. Among all the options offered as possible answers, the statement that "confirmation is a personal decision on whether or not to remain a church member" meets with the least acceptance in both East and West.[56]

On the whole, then, neither eastern nor western German Protestants in their majority can be said to excel by determination, consciousness or high commitment in their relationship with their churches. The characteristics of a voluntary church have hardly emerged in the East, and neither the percentage of people making use of what the church has to offer nor the acceptance of statements concerning faith is noticeably higher than in the West. While eastern Germans' attitudes vis-à-vis the church may at times not have as conventional an appearance, they differ from the attitudes of western Germans only in degree. The characteristics of a national church have largely reproduced themselves in eastern Germany, albeit on a qualitatively lower level. The small group of committed, mature, conscious Christians has always been more a model for church leaders and pastors than reality.

The only exception to this pattern is the group of adolescents and young adults in eastern Germany. Their readiness to participate is greater than that of older church members; on average, they attend services more often, and they are even more readily prepared to shoulder further tasks, provided these are limited in time and provide scope for self-realization.[57] In their readiness to participate, young Protestants in the East not only differ from older church members in eastern Germany but also from young Protestants in the West, who as a rule keep a greater distance from church life than their parents.[58] Moreover, young Protestants in the East are interesting insofar as in contrast to their west German counterparts of the same age, they prefer unconventional life-styles, they stand out by their political and social openness, and--also in contrast to young Protestants in the West--as a rule, they are better educated than the group of their non-denominational peers.[59] But in church life on the whole, young eastern Protestants' greater readiness to commit themselves is hardly noticeable, as they account for a negligible percentage of the total number of church members, while older members are clearly over-represented.

Reviewing these results, the reader will no doubt be surprised to note that after forty years of separate social and, to a large extent, church-related development, the profiles of church members are so similar in East and West. In part, this is attributable to the high proportion of older people in eastern German congregations. That the parochial structures of the GDR were not given up in spite of decreased membership numbers also plays a major role. With the church leadership adhering to the principle of exhaustive coverage,[60] members felt no need to change their church behavior, and people not forced to change their behavior are hardly likely to give up their cherished habits. The conventional attitude of the majority of church members can thus be interpreted as a consequence of a lack of boldness on the part of the church's governing bodies. But the question should also be asked whether a radical restructuring of the traditional church organization would not have resulted in a much more dramatic drop in membership and participation.

What happened after the *Wende* was a certain strengthening, however weak, of national church features in eastern Germany. For example, the baptism rate in Lutheran Churches doubled between 1989 and 1991. Although the number of christenings remained quite stable in absolute terms, the ratio of Protestant christenings to total births rose from 15 to just under 30 percent, partially as a result of the drastic drop in the birth rate. In part, this was only a form of catching up, as is evident from the comparatively high number of children between the ages of one and fourteen years baptized after the *Wende*[61] and from the drop in the baptism rate after 1993. The rise in the baptism rate is, however, not completely attributable to this catch-up effect.[62] Participation in confirmation classes has likewise grown. Another astonishing development is the relatively large participation in religious instruction in schools, even though to some extent this has been at the expense of participation in catechism classes organized by the church. The number of people joining the church has risen: new memberships trebled between 1989 and 1991. This increase, however, in no way offsets withdrawal figures, which have remained high. So there is a slight consolidation towards a *national church*, a situation whose durability cannot yet be predicted.

To explain the existence of a national church in eastern Germany, it should be pointed out that for many people church and religion provide a traditional background which they would not like to lose, but on which they fall back only in times of difficulty. This subordinate function of the church and religion has applied to large sections of the population for quite a long time. The hope that a lively, highly active, voluntary church might develop is perhaps asking too much of people who have to fill roles in many fields of society and who reject having their entire lives controlled from just one field, particularly in our modern society with such differentiated functions. Perhaps the national church thrives more in a social climate of empathy than on the committed support of all its members.[63] Looking at the case of the German Democratic Republic in which churches were stigmatized and had to cope with the anti-church policy of the state, one can see what becomes of a church deprived of supportive social surroundings. In any case, the church's stability depends to an extraordinarily large degree on its social environment.

Forms of Religiosity Outside the Church

Have the losses in church-related religiosity been offset by religiosity outside the church, outside Christianity? This is the question that we shall pursue in conclusion by means of another comparison between eastern and western Germany. Let us begin with eastern Germany.

After the collapse of socialism quite a few people expected an enormous boost in new religious sects, which eastern Germans--in their search for orientation in the midst of the severe upheavals they were facing--would get hooked on all too easily.[64] In actual fact and in spite of claims to the contrary on the part of a few officials in charge of monitoring sect activity, interest in sects has largely failed to boom in eastern Germany.[65] Interest in new religious practices is markedly lower in eastern than in western Germany. A representative poll among east and west Berlin school students showed that in the east of Berlin, the proportion of students who had been involved at least once in an occult practice was 50 percent lower than in western Berlin. In the East, some 12 percent of the adolescents said they had already had experience in occult practices; in the West, about a quarter admitted so.[66] After the *Wende*, there was neither a major trend back to the church, nor a turn towards alternative religious practices.[67]

One of the reasons for this is that many eastern Germans are already alienated from Christianity to such an extent that they find *any* religious idea or concept suspicious and odd. But the path towards alternative religious ideas and practices is often, as in the West, a path via Christianity, in other words, through some stage of gradual separation from the church.[68] Secondly, any orientation along forms of alternative religiosity, be it meditation, yoga, theosophy, mysticism, or new age, does not tally with the widespread aversion in eastern Germany to everything conspicuous, extravagant, flashy or eccentric.[69] And lastly, in recent years eastern Germans have had to concentrate on securing their material existence, on retraining or furthering their vocational training, and on their social re-orientation. And obviously many felt they could solve these problems without resorting to any form of transcendency. As for an upswing in religiosity *outside the church*, there is hardly anything of the sort.

In eastern Germany, religiosity still is mainly defined in terms of church (although this may be beginning to change now[70]). Religiosity, measured for example in terms of belief in God or one's self-assessment as being religious, and church affiliation, measured for example in terms of service attendance or the attachment one feels to the church, are closely connected. Those attending church services more frequently tend to consider themselves religious. The closer an individual feels to the church, the greater the probability that he or she also believes in God. If the churches decrease in importance, religion does as well--at least at the present time.

The situation is similar in western Germany. While in recent years interest in non-church forms of religiosity has grown immensely,[71] this increased interest cannot make up for the decline in traditional attachment to the church that has occurred since the 1960s. Nor is it possible to establish any statistical correlation between declining attachment to the church and growing acceptance of alternative forms of religion.[72] In view of the dimensions involved, such a correlation would be extremely unlikely. In the 1970s, when new religious movements were quite popular in West Germany and in Western Europe in general, the Lutheran Churches in West Germany lost 1.5 million members and the Roman Catholic Church over half a million.[73] Optimistic estimates placed membership in new religious movements at no more than 30,000,[74] not even 2 percent of the membership lost by the large churches, in the late 1970s. It is equally true of western Germany, although not quite as strictly so as in the East, that the more frequently church services are attended and the greater the attachment to the church, the stronger the individual religiosity.

Even if one allows a loose definition of religion and asks whether "marveling at the miracles of nature," "a cheerful confidence without any external reason," "holding an inner dialogue," "being deeply moved when listening to a certain type of music" or "experiencing a sense of fellowship" is associated with religion, it again will be those who are closer to the church rather than those who are at a distance from it or non-affiliated who can produce such associations more readily.[75] Religiosity and attachment to the church, while not identical, are very closely connected indeed. In other words, the validity of Thomas Luckmann's thesis[76]--that what is diminishing is the importance of the institutionalized social form of religion rather than that of subjective religiosity--has to be strongly qualified. Of course there are various forms of religiosity--Christian and non-Christian--outside the church, but what prevails is the trend under which, along with the decline in institutionalized forms of religion, the importance of individual religiosity diminishes as well.

This is by no means a coincidence, as every religious concept needs visualization and concretization, and it is the very institutions of religion that are in the best position to provide pictures, symbols, space, time, roles, and stories in order to vividly portray the not so lively aspects of religion. The large membership decline the churches are currently experiencing affects not only the churches themselves, but also is indicative of a cultural change that goes far beyond the churches. The motive mentioned most frequently by church-leavers in the West and relatively frequently in the East as well--the church tax --should be seen in close connection with other motives for leaving. These include, in both East and West, the statement that faith does not mean anything to the person concerned and that he or she does not need any religion in his or her life and does not care for the church.[77] The number of church leavers is not merely a critical attitude vis-à-vis the church or an expression of annoyance over church statements, even though these motives also exert some influence. Rather, the number of church leavers is an expression of a growing distance from the Christian faith and of a decline in religiosity.

Notes

1. This chapter was translated by Nicole Gentz and Peter Kleinhempel.

2. Zentralarchiv für Empirische Sozialforschung (ed.), *Allgemeine Bevölkerungsumfrage der Sozialwissenschaften (ALLBUS 1994): Codebuch* (University of Cologne: Zentralarchiv für Empirische Sozialforschung, 1994), variable 321. Since the mid-1980s, the number of Roman Catholic members has been slightly higher than Lutheran Church members, Statistisches Bundesamt (ed.), *Statistisches Jahrbuch 1992 für die Bundesrepublik Deutschland* (Stuttgart: Metzler/Poeschel, 1993) , p. 104f.

3. Wolfgang Pittkowski and Rainer Volz, "Konfession und politische Orientierung: das Beispiel der Konfessionslosen," in Karl-Fritz Daiber (ed.), *Religion und Konfession: Studien zu politischen, ethischen und religiösen Einstellungen von Katholiken, Protestanten und Konfessionslosen in der Bundesrepublik Deutschland und in den Niederlanden* (Hannover: Lutherisches Verlagshaus, 1989), pp. 93-112, here p. 95.

4. Some six percent belong to an Evangelical Free Church or to another Christian or non-Christian denomination (*ALLBUS 1994* [note 1], variable 321). This accounts for the discrepancy between the combined number of religious adherents and persons professing no religion and 100 percent.

5. *ALLBUS 1994* [note 1], variable 321.

6. *Statistisches Jahrbuch der DDR*, Vol. 1 (1955), p. 33.

7. *ALLBUS 1991* [note 1], variable 316. To characterize the situation with regard to belief and ritual, I am quoting from the data provided in *ALLBUS 1991* since that paper focusing on religion covered all the indicators in pertinent poll questions. By way of comparison I am also quoting the ALLBUS 1994 figures since the pertinent variables were included. On the basis of the 1994 figures,

changes that have taken place in religious attitudes and behaviour can be seen. As for service attendance, a slight decline is to be observed in both western and eastern Germany. The proportion of churchgoers who attend service at least once a month has gone down to 23 percent in western Germany and to 6 percent in eastern Germany, and the proportion of those who never go to church has risen to 23 percent in the west and to 64 percent in the east of Germany.

8. *ALLBUS 1991* [note 1], variable 493. This question was not asked in 1994.

9. *ALLBUS 1991* [note 1], variables 318 and 319.

10. *ALLBUS 1991* [note 1], variable 492. In 1994, 25 percent of those interviewed in the West said they never prayed, compared to 75 percent in the East (*ALLBUS 1994*, variable 323).

11. *ALLBUS 1991* [note 1], variable 465.

12. Renate Köcher, "Gottlos," in *Rheinischer Merkur/Christ und Welt*, No. 28 (September 1990), p. 26. According to another study made in 1993, 71 percent of western Germans said they believed in God as against a mere 27 percent in the East (Sabina Platzer, "Verlieren die Deutschen den Glauben?," in *Reader's Digest Das Beste*, Vol. 46 (November 1993), pp. 41-49, here p. 42.

13. "Das Profil der Deutschen," in *Spiegel Spezial*, No. 1 (1991), p. 74. According to a *Spiegel* poll conducted in 1992 by the Bielefeld Emnid Institute, 56 percent of western Germans believe that "God exists," another 17 percent believe in the existence of a "supernatural being," and 25 percent believe neither. In the East, according to the same poll, 27 percent believe that "God exists," *Der Spiegel*, 15 June 1992, pp. 36-57, here p. 37 and p. 41.

14. *ALLBUS 1991* [note 1], variable 466.

15. *ALLBUS 1991* [note 1], variable 468. In the above-mentioned 1992 *Spiegel* poll, 50 percent of the western Germans surveyed believed in "life after death," *Der Spiegel* [note 12], p. 37.

16. *ALLBUS 1991* [note 1], variable 494.

17. Gunnar Winkler (ed.), *Sozialreport 1992: Daten und Fakten zur sozialen Lage in den neuen Bundesländern* (Berlin: 1993), p. 57.

18. Karl Gabriel, *Christentum zwischen Tradition und Postmoderne* (Freiburg: Herder, 1992), pp. 32ff.

19. Rainer Geissler, *Die Sozialstruktur Deutschlands: ein Studienbuch zur Entwicklung im geteilten und vereinten Deutschland* (Opladen: Westdeutscher Verlag, 1992), p. 216.

20. Rüdiger Schloz, "Das Bildungsdilemma der Kirche," in Joachim Matthes (ed.), *Kirchenmitgliedschaft im Wandel: Untersuchungen zur Realität der Volkskirche; Beiträge zur zweiten EKD-Umfrage "Was wird aus der Kirche?"* (Gütersloh: Gütersloher Verlagshaus, 1990), pp. 215-30.

21. Geissler, *Die Sozialstruktur Deutschlands* [note 18], p. 117.

22. Johannes Hanselmann, Helmut Hild, and Eduard Lohse (eds.), *Was wird aus der Kirche? Ergebnisse der zweiten EKD-Umfrage über Kirchenmitgliedschaft* (Gütersloh: Gütersloher Verlagshaus, 1982), pp. 143ff. See also the results of a Swiss study, Alfred Dubach and Roland Campiche (eds.), *Jede(r) ein Sonderfall? Religion in der Schweiz* (Zurich: NZN Buchverlag, 1993), pp. 74, 80; Franz-Xaver

Kaufmann, Walter Kerber, and Paul M. Zulehner, *Ethos und Religion bei Führungskräften* (Munich: Kindt, 1986).

23. The trend towards dissociation from the churches grows in proportion to the rise in population figures, Hanselmann *et al.*, *Was wird aus der Kirche?* [note 21], pp. 143ff.; Volker Steckhan, "Kirchenmitgliedschaft in der Großstadt," in Matthes, *Kirchenmitgliedschaft im Wandel* [note 19], pp. 231-47.

24. Karl-Fritz Daiber, *Religion unter den Bedingungen der Moderne: die Situation in der Bundesrepublik Deutschland* (Marburg: Diagonal, 1995), pp. 124ff.

25. In the GDR in 1950, 11 percent of the population were members of the Roman Catholic Church (*Statistisches Jahrbuch der DDR*, Vol. 1 (1955), p. 33); in 1989, the figure was about 4.5 percent (median of the figures given in Bernd Hannemann and Helmut Franke, "Kirchenmitglieder wollen schnelle Einheit," in *Übergänge*, Vol. 16 (1990), pp. 139-143, here p. 139, and of those in *ALLBUS 1991* [note 1], variable 315. While in the course of the GDR's history, membership in the Lutheran Churches shrank to just under one-third, that of the Roman Catholic Church dropped to about two-fifths.

26. Karl-Fritz Daiber, "Kirche und religiöse Gemeinschaften in der DDR," in Franz-Xaver Kaufmann and Bernhard Schäfers (eds.), *Religion, Kirchen und Gesellschaft in Deutschland* (Opladen: Leske + Budrich, 1988), pp. 75-88, here p. 80; Ehrhart Neubert, "Von der Volkskirche zur Minderheitskirche - Bilanz 1990," in Horst Dähn (ed.), *Die Rolle der Kirchen in der DDR: eine erste Bilanz* (Munich: Olzog, 1993), pp. 36-55, here p. 39ff.

27. Detlef Pollack, *Kirche in der Organisationsgesellschaft: zum Wandel der gesellschaftlichen Lage der evangelischen Kirchen in der DDR* (Stuttgart: Kohlhammer, 1994), p. 425.

28. Pollack, *Kirche in der Organisationsgesellschaft* [note 26], pp. 381f., 384ff., 414f.; see also p. 150.

29. Pollack, *Kirche in der Organisationsgesellschaft* [note 26], pp. 382f., 426f.

30. Daiber, *Kirche und religiöse Gemeinschaften in der DDR* [note 25], p. 81.

31. Helmut Obst, "Zwischen Geistheilung und Konsum: Religion nach dem einst existierenden Sozialismus," in *Lutherische Monatshefte*, Vol. 31 (1992), pp. 8-11, especially p. 8.

32. Kurt Nowak, "Historische Wurzeln der Entkirchlichung in der DDR," in Heinz Sahner and Stefan Schwendtner (eds.), *Gesellschaften im Umbruch: 27. Kongreß der Deutschen Gesellschaft für Soziologie*, Kongreßband II (Opladen: Westdeutscher Verlag, 1995), pp. 665-69.

33. Petra Thinnes, "Sozialstatistik zum religiösen und kirchlichen Leben in der Bundesrepublik Deutschland," in Kaufmann and Schäfers, *Religion, Kirche, und Gesellschaft* [note 25], pp. 203-17, here p. 211ff.

34. Gabriel, *Christentum zwischen Tradition und Postmoderne* [note 17], pp. 59f.

35. Ronald Inglehart, *The Silent Revolution: Changing Values and Political Styles Among Western Publics* (Princeton, N.J.: Princeton University Press, 1977); id., *Kultureller Umbruch: Wertwandel in der westlichen Welt* (Frankfurt am Main, New York: Campus, 1989); Helmut Klages, Hans-Jürgen Hippler, and Willi

Herbert (eds.), *Werte und Wandel: Ergebnisse und Methoden einer Forschungstradition* (Frankfurt am Main and New York: Campus, 1992).

36. *Amtsblatt der EKD: Statistische Beilage*, Vol. 80, No. 10 (1987), p. 21.

37. Pollack, *Kirche in der Organisationsgesellschaft* [note 26], pp. 381f.

38. Attitudes and behaviour of members of the Lutheran Churches have been the subject of an EKD study, Studien- und Planungsgruppe der EKD (ed.), *Fremde Heimat Kirche: Ansichten ihrer Mitglieder; dritte EKD-Umfrage über Kirchenmitgliedschaft* (Hanover: EKD Kirchenamt, 1993). No comparable study has been made with regard to Roman Catholics.

39. According to *Statistischer Bericht TII 90-91, Statistische Beilage Nr. 88 zum Amtsblatt der EKD*, No. 11 (15 November 1993), p. 15, service attendance on a normal Sunday averaged 4.9 percent of the members of the Lutheran Churches in western Germany in 1990, and 4.8 percent in 1991. In 1984, church service attendance on an ordinary Sunday still averaged 5.6 percent, a percentage which had been stable since the mid-1970s and declined only after 1984 (*Statistischer Bericht TII 90-91*, p. 15).

40. In the eastern German states, the situation with regard to the availability of data is precarious. Annual data are not available from all the provincial churches, which is why it was not possible to ascertain an eastern German average figure covering church service attendance. One rather has to look at the various member churches separately. The statistical report of the Evangelical Lutheran Church in Saxony (*Statistischer Bericht über die Verhältnisse in der Evangelisch-Lutherischen Landeskirche Sachsens im Jahr 1991*, p. 12), for example, says service attendance averaged 4.4 percent in 1990 and 4.9 percent in 1991. In Berlin-Brandenburg in 1991, 2.9 percent of the church membership attended service, and in Thuringia in the same year the figure was 5.8 percent. Taking into account weak (in terms of participation) provincial churches in Mecklenburg-Western Pomerania or in the Kirchenprovinz (covering roughly the state of Saxony-Anhalt), the total number of churchgoers in the East during that period can be assumed to have been somewhat lower than in the West.

41. *ALLBUS 1992* [note 1], variable 306 (analysis as per denomination: Wolfgang Lukatis).

42. This is easily evidenced by developments in Saxony. While the number of churchgoers on a normal Sunday in 1990 accounted for 4.4 percent of church members, in 1992 the figure was 5.0 percent, and in 1993, 5.2 percent (*Statistischer Bericht über die Verhältnisse in der Evangelisch-Lutherischen Landeskirche Sachsens im Jahr 1993*, p. 14). The increase in the ratio of those attending services to the number of church members--provided that the Saxon figures are taken as representative of the whole of eastern Germany--exceeds the western German average level but is, however, not attributable to an absolute increase in service attendance (in absolute terms, there has in fact been a slight drop in Saxony). Rather it is the result of the strong decline in church membership. In Saxony in the 1980s, those attending service accounted for just 3 to 4 percent of church membership, a figure markedly lower than the West German percentage. Wolf-Jürgen Grabner, *Religiosität in einer säkularisierten Gesellschaft: eine*

Kirchenmitgliedschaft-untersuchung in Leipzig 1989 (Frankfurt am Main: Lang, 1994), p. 210. The data provided in ALLBUS confirm that meanwhile, proportionate to church membership, the number of those attending services is higher in the East than in the West. While, according to their own statements, 13 percent of Lutheran Church members went to church at least once a month in western Germany and 11 percent in eastern Germany in 1992, the figures for 1994 were 12 percent and 15 percent respectively (*ALLBUS 1994* [note 1], variable 322).

43. Studien- und Planungsgruppe, *Fremde Heimat Kirche* [note 37], p. 31.

44. *ALLBUS 1991*, variable 319. The EKD study, Studien- und Planungsgruppe, *Fremde Heimat Kirche* [note 37], p. 45, gives similar figures.

45. *ALLBUS 1991* [note 1], variable 319. The EKD study Fremde Heimat Kirche (Studien- und Planungsgruppe, *Fremde Heimat Kirche* [note 37], p. 45), in contrast, finds that in the East fewer Protestants than in the West are willing to have their children christened.

46. *ALLBUS 1991* [note 1], variable 492. By 1994, however, the differences between East and West had increased (*ALLBUS 1994*, variable 323).

47. *ALLBUS 1991* [note 1], variables 465, 466, 494.

48. *ALLBUS 1991* [note 1], variable 468.

49. Studien- und Planungsgruppe, *Fremde Heimat Kirche* [note 37], p. 24.

50. *Ibid.*, p. 27.

51. *Ibid.*

52. *Ibid.*, p. 26.

53. *Ibid.*

54. *Ibid.*, p. 28.

55. *Ibid.*

56. *Ibid.*, p. 29.

57. *Ibid.*, p. 37f.

58. In addition to this and to what follows, more details can be found in Wolf-Jürgen Grabner and Detlef Pollack, "Jugend und Religion in Ostdeutschland," in Karl Gabriel and Hans Hobelsberger (eds.), *Jugend, Religion und Modernisierung: kirchliche Jugendarbeit als Suchbewegung* (Opladen: Leske + Budrich, 1994), pp. 91-116, especially pp. 96ff., 110ff.

59. See also Jürgen Eiben, "Kirche und Religion: Säkularisierung als sozialistisches Erbe?," in Jugendwerk der Deutschen Shell (ed.), *Jugend '92: Lebenslagen, Orientierungen und Entwicklungsperspektiven im vereinigten Deutschland*, Vol. 2: Im Spiegel der Wissenschaften (Opladen: Leske + Budrich, 1992), pp. 91-104, here p. 98ff.

60. This was made possible thanks, among other things, to major financial support from the West. See also Armin Volze, "Kirchliche Transferleistungen in die DDR," in *Deutschland Archiv*, Vol. 24 (1991), pp. 59-66.

61. The *Statistischer Bericht TII der EKD* [note 38], p. 8, suggests that about half the number of infant baptism ceremonies were held later than immediately after birth. But already prior to the *Wende*, delayed christening ceremonies accounted for some 25 percent of infant baptism ceremonies. So, if the baptism

rate rose by about 14 percentage points between 1989 and 1991, it is not 7 but maybe 3 to 4 percentage points that should be deducted to account for such delay. Thus, the number of babies baptized during that period must have risen by at least two-thirds.

62. This becomes evident from the fact that in Saxony between 1989 and 1991 the number of late baptisms rose by 8 percentage points as against the overall baptism rate, which rose by 22.4 percent--from 23.2 to 45.6 percent (*Statistischer Bericht über die Verhälnisse in der Evangelisch-Lutherischen Landeskirche Sachsens im Jahre 1993*, p. 7). Since the official baptism rate of the Saxon Church also includes adult baptism figures, the rise by 5 percentage points of the proportion of adult baptism ceremonies must also be taken into account, so that the rise in the number of baptized babies amounts to just under 10 percentage points, or about two-fifths. The mean of this figure and of the growth rate of about two-thirds, as per note 67, suggests that the growth rate in the number of baptized babies amounts to some 50 percent.

63. There is already an obvious discrepancy between such church membership criteria as christening (usually during infancy) or the payment of church tax and commitment in faith.

64. Thomas Gandow, "Jugendreligionen und Sekten auf dem Vormarsch in die DDR," in *Materialien der Evangelischen Zentralstelle für Weltanschauungsfragen (EZW)*, Vol. 53 (1990), pp. 221-33. 253-61, here pp. 226f.

65. Andreas Fincke, "Die geistig-religiöse Lage in den neuen Bundesländern," in *Materialdienst der Evangelischen Zentralstelle für Weltanschauungsfragen*, Vol. 56 (1993), pp. 313-19, here p. 317; Andreas Fincke, *Bericht an die Kirchenleitung*, Berlin 1995, unpublished manuscript, p. 3.

66. See the statistical data in Hartmut Zinser, "Moderner Okkultismus als kulturelles Phänomen unter Schülern und Erwachsenen," in *Aus Politik und Zeitgeschichte*, No. B 38 (1994), pp. 41-42. According to the EKD study Fremde Heimat Kirche, Studien- und Planungsgruppe, *Fremde Heimat Kirche* [note 37], p. 11, about a quarter of those east Germans interviewed, adolescents and adults alike, said they had already had experience with such alternative religious phenomena as astrology, cartomancy, chiromancy, divination by means of a pendulum, anthroposophy, zen meditation, yoga, and the like. After subtracting those whose personal experience is limited to horoscopy and astrology, there are some 15 percent who have come into contact with alternative religious practices. This number differs markedly from the number of those who are members of occult and esoteric groups and who practice alternative cults regularly. The number of the latter is well below the proportion of those who have no more than spot experience with such practices. However, according to the EKD study, the differences between East and West seem to be smaller than the Zinser study would suggest. As the EKD study (Studien- und Planungsgruppe, *Fremde Heimat Kirche*, p. 11) ascertained, 28 percent of the interviewees in western Germany had had experiences with non-Christian religious practices and, after subtracting those involved in astrology, only 18 percent remain who have come into contact with occult practices and esoteric ideas--insignificantly more than in the East.

This result is confirmed by an analysis by Michael Terwey and Alan L. McCutcheon, "Belief and Practice in the Unified Germanies," in *ZA (Zentralarchiv)-Information*, Vol. 34 (1994), pp. 47-69, who found only astonishingly small differences between East and West with regard to belief in occult phenomena. On average, somewhat more than a quarter of western Germans attributed an effect of at least some probability to good-luck charms, fortune-tellers, miracle healers, and the influence of the stars; in eastern Germany, the readiness to accept such phenomena averaged just under one quarter. See Michael Terwey, "Zur aktuellen Situation von Glauben und Kirche im vereinigten Deutschland: eine Analyse der Basisumfrage 1991," in *ZA-Information*, Vol. 30 (1992), pp. 55-79.

67. Only the *Jugendweihe* as a pseudo-religious rite has been enjoying growing popularity. While in the GDR in the late 1980s, some 97 percent of the members of the relevant age-group took part in the *Jugendweihe* ceremony (170,000), their number dropped to 80,000 in 1991 and to 50,000 in 1992. Thomas Gandow, *Jugendweihe: humanistische Jugendfeier* (Munich: Evangelischer Presseverband für Bayern,1994), p. 5. In 1993, however, this number rose to some 70,000 (*Welt am Sonntag*, 21 March 1993), and 86,000 are reported to have taken part in *Jugendweihe* ceremonies in 1995 (Michael Nüchtern, *Jugendweihe und Konfirmation*, Berlin, 1995, unpublished manuscript).

68. Rainer Wassner, "Neue Religiöse Bewegungen in Deutschland: ein soziologischer Bericht," in *EZW-Texte* Information, No. 113 (1991), pp. 25f.; Heiner Barz, "Jugend und Religion in den neuen Bundesländern," in *Aus Politik und Zeitgeschichte*, No. B 38 (1994), pp. 21-31, here p. 25.

69. See Rudolf Woderich, "Mentalitäten zwischen Anpassung und Eigensinn," in *Deutschland Archiv*, Vol. 25 (1992), pp. 21-31.

70. The first results of a study on people entering the church which I am currently conducting together with Eckhart Friedrich and Klaus Hartmann, sponsored by the Forschungsstätte der Evangelischen Studiengemeinschaft (FEST), Heidelberg, seem to point in this direction. In our investigations we have come across a type of catching-up in religious individualization--people who joined the ranks of the church after the *Wende*, became critical of the church, and then turned to some alternative religious content and form.

71. See for example the astonishingly high figures in what is known as the BRIGITTE study quoted in Michael Terwey, "Para-Gläubigkeit," article in G.L. Eberlein (ed.), *Kleines Lexikon der Parawissenschaften* (Munich: Beck, 1995), pp. 112-117, here p. 114.

72. Studien- und Planungsgruppe, *Fremde Heimat Kirche* [note 37], p. 11.

73. Hanselmann, Hild, and Lohse, *Was wird aus der Kirche?* [note 21], p. 24.

74. Frank Usarski, *Die Stigmatisierung Neuer Spiritueller Bewegungen in der Bundesrepublik Deutschland* (Cologne: Böhlau, 1988), p. 110.

75. Studien- und Planungsgruppe, *Fremde Heimat Kirche* [note 37], p. 12.

76. Thomas Luckmann, *The Invisible Religion: The Problem of Religion in Modern Society* (New York: Macmilan, 1967).

77. Studien- und Planungsgruppe, *Fremde Heimat Kirche* [note 37], p. 54. In

addition, the statement that it is possible for the person concerned to be Christian without the church and that he or she feels that the church is not credible is widely endorsed in the West, above the level of acceptance in the East. This shows that those not affiliating with a church in western Germany are much more critical of the churches than their counterparts in the East. At the same time, the non-affiliated in the West show a stronger inclination towards the Christian faith than their counterparts in the East (p. 55), even though their orientation to the values of the Christian faith on the whole is only a weak one. A mere 9 percent in the West and only 3 percent in the East, however, say that they have left the church because they have adopted another religious belief.

9

Structure and *Eigensinn*:[1] Transformation Processes and Continuities of East German Women

Irene Dölling[2]

At the beginning of the 1990s, during the time of the political unification of the two German states, various sociological scenarios were being developed in relation to women. Two assumptions were made in connection with this. First, it was assumed that the restructuring of the job market and occupational fields would transpire in a relatively gender-neutral manner. This assumption was based on the fact that women in the German Democratic Republic (GDR) had worked in full-time jobs over the course of numerous generations and had attained a high degree of professional education. More generally formulated, there was only one broadly accepted model of work and career. The existence of a pronounced gender-specific segregation in the occupational system and the limiting of gender competition in the job market which accompanied it were also seen as favorable prerequisites for keeping women from being driven out of the occupational sphere. Second, based on the "double burden" of GDR women, it was assumed that they viewed professional work *(Erwerbsarbeit)*[3] above all as compulsory and that therefore a large group of women would leave the occupational world relatively quickly and voluntarily. It was presumed that the three-phase model of the female career which was propagated in the Federal Republic Germany (FRG) (gainful employment, a long interruption of this after the birth of children, and later re-entry into gainful employment) would establish itself in the new *Länder* as well.[4]

Neither of these assumptions was born out in the following eight years. East German women, as numerous empirical studies attested to in the meantime, adhered to their previous outlook on life to an astounding degree. These facts have led to a change of perspective in sociological research, especially in the field of so-called transformation research (and there not solely or even mainly in relation to women). The idea that the new *Länder* would adapt themselves to the West German model--in a crash course on "catch-up modernization" via the adoption of institutions and structures--dominated in the early years. Subjective potentials for action *(Handlungspotentiale)*, mentalities, etc. of East German women and men appeared from this perspective generally as deficient, although at best in some individual points they were viewed as "modern."[5]

In recent years the sociological viewpoint has changed insofar as the assumption is now, after the largely completed transfer of institutions and structures from west to east, that the "more deeply established everyday-life orientations of action, cultural schema and norms"[6] of East Germans continue to remain effective. These present themselves as resources or restrictions which shape individual possibilities for action along with institutions and structures.[7] The observable "own ideas" *(Eigensinn)* of East German women as well as their adherence to full-time work and to the compatibility of career and family are not the least of the phenomena which have sharpened the focus of the sociological view concerning the influence of subjective potentials for action on transformation processes. Meanwhile, it is becoming ever clearer that the crisis-like economic and social developments in eastern Germany are not the expression of a short-term phase of transition and adaptation to the (prosperous) West German model. Instead, they are signs of a crisis of the capitalist system, a pending radical reorganization of the economy and in the social welfare state, and in connection with this, a reordering of gender relations.

With this as a background, in this contribution I would like to present some aspects which presently characterize the life-context *(Lebenszusammenhang)* of East German women. This happens in the form of "snapshots" of a process which has begun and is today in no way predictable in its consequences and results. As "snapshots," these aspects also have differing sociological reach and strength of assertions. I will limit myself to the areas of professional occupation, the compatibility of career and family, and demographics. My central focus is on how (changed) structures and the "own-ideas" *(Eigensinn)* of women encounter one another and what outlooks concerning women's possibilities for action or for gender relations can be cautiously concluded from this encounter.

Professional Occupation *(Erwerbsarbeit)*

East German women are characterized in a common slogan as the "losers of German unification." On the one hand, this correctly grasps the fact that East German women are experiencing forms of discrimination in many ways previously unknown to them, and that important conditions of life and social services have changed drastically and to their disadvantage. On the other hand, this slogan conceals the fact that enormous and growing social differentiation exists among East German women, and the slogan pushes women as actors into the background of public perception. In this slogan they are simultaneously made into victims in the forefront.

A view to the developments of the job market in eastern German since unification shows both gender-neutral and gender-specific tendencies. The experience of unemployment is mostly gender neutral. As the *Social Report 1996* establishes, since 1990 "unemployment has already become a personal experience for over half of all citizens between 18 and 60."[8] Also gender neutral, the risk of job loss is no greater for women than it is for men, i.e., no more women's jobs were lost in recent years than men's.

The chance of finding a new job, on the contrary, is gender-specific. The statistics show clear gender-specific differences with regard to unemployment and re-employment since 1990. In 1995, 19.4 percent of women and 11.1 percent of men were jobless in eastern Germany (and the percentage points have risen somewhat in the meantime); the proportion of unemployed women to total unemployed amounted to 62.4 percent. In comparison to their share of unemployment, however, women have fewer chances than men of receiving aid in the form of "political job market measures" (ABM) (52 percent) or of entering into a regular occupational situation (38 percent).[9] A similar picture is produced when the length of unemployment is observed. In 1996, 43 percent of those unemployed in eastern Germany had already been unemployed for longer than 24 months; this affected 57 percent of unemployed women, but only 24 percent of men.[10]

Up to the present time, the proportion of women among the total employed has not significantly changed in comparison to 1989;[11]

however, some developments stand out which (could) lead to a redistribution of employment along gender lines. Hildegard Nickel and Sabine Schenk characterize this in three scenarios. 1. Industries which were typical for women in the GDR, i.e., generally also less attractive and lucrative (e.g., commerce, banking, insurance), will become mixed industries. 2. Mixed industries (e.g., agriculture, transportation, postal services) will tend to become male-dominated industries. 3. Traditionally male-oriented industries (mining, energy, construction, metal and electrical industries) will continue to exclude women.[12] Nickel and Schenk conclude:

> Against this background, the assumption arises that a renewed cementing of gender specific inequalities of opportunity is taking place on at least two levels. First, on the level of the redistribution of scarce good jobs to the detriment of women. Second, on the level of a successive "gender reversal" of occupational fields which leads to women again remaining relegated to the less future-oriented, less secure, and less lucrative developmental paths.[13]

It can be generally ascertained that gender has less influence on employment for the youngest age group (18-25 years) than for the group of those over 50 and that women in the 35-50 age group have relatively good employment opportunities while women between 25 and 35 years of age have fewer chances on the job market.[14] Corresponding to the last point is the fact that men between 20 and 40 years of age have the greatest chances for employment if they live in stable partnerships (marriage/family). Here the preferred model in the old *Länder*--the provider marriage--becomes apparent, structurally. Men, if they are married and have children, are consequently viewed as "providers," and this factor--even more than their qualifications!--influences their percentage of jobs *(Erwerbsquote)*.[15]

Unemployment in the new *Länder* has up to now meant unemployment in relation to the achieved qualification structure of the GDR-- "above all, unemployment of citizens with completed professional or technical training *(abgeschlossener beruflicher Ausbildung)*."[16] In other words, the majority of the unemployed are skilled workers and master craftsmen and women *(FacharbeiterInnen/MeisterInnen)*, while technical/trade school and university graduates, independent of gender, have so far experienced relatively little unemployment. The unskilled and those without vocational training who represented a quite small group in the GDR have relatively low chances of obtaining employment on the newly-formed job market; their share of the unemployed, measured against their share of total employment, is high.

Along with structural influences such as employment sectors and regional location and individual factors such as age, for women who are skilled workers the *level* of professional education plays a decisive role in the chance of finding new employment. Especially for women from 35 to 50, "the level of qualifications is able to compensate for the negative gender effect in this context."[17] Nevertheless, re-employment on the basis of a high qualification level as a rule does not lead to competition with (equally or less qualified) men, but instead works against less qualified women. In other words, there is now, in comparison to in the GDR, a growing social differentiation among women which is, besides structural factors, influenced by individual characteristics such as professional education/level of qualification, age, marital status, and number of children and/or age of children.

The trends outlined here confirm in the first place that the restructuring of the job market in eastern Germany tends to lead to a worsening of the employment and career chances of women. The characterization of women as "the losers of unification" is thus not entirely unwarranted. This impression is also strengthened by the fact that women rarely offer organized resistance to the loss of jobs, in contrast to the many actions which have been and are being undertaken with varying success by men in prestigious job sectors. Instead, women use a "quiet" and individualized form of resistance; that is, they retain with their "own ideas" *(Eigensinn)* certain orientations of action and values against the constraints or pressures of the adopted West German structures which affect their everyday life. This can be seen especially in their "unbroken propensity for gainful employment" *(ungebrochene Ewerbsneigung)*.

In contrast to the presumptions of the *Wende* period, that women in the GDR were employed largely compulsorily and were only waiting for the end of their double-burden, the statistics show an unchanged (and even growing) desire of East German women to be or remain employed. About two-thirds of the women want to be employed full-time and approximately 30 percent would like to work part-time, while only a very small percentage of women want to be housewives.[18] In 1996, 83 percent of East German women considered work to be "very important" and 14 percent "important."[19] The positive valuation of women's work remains undiminished among East German men. (In 1996, 16 percent were of the opinion that women should definitely be working and 71 percent would leave the decision to the woman.[20]) In other words, even women currently unemployed are not voluntarily going back to the "private sphere" ("the kitchen sink") and, above all, they do not want to stay there permanently. Instead, they want to return to the job market, sooner or later. (In reality, however, this will not be possible for all of them, especially not for the older ones.)

For the overwhelming majority of East German women, (full-time) employment is one of the givens in their life plans to which they cling, even under the changed conditions.[21] The reasons why women continue to adhere to life-long careers, despite decreasing chances, are obviously quite complex.   Among them, material factors are not to be underestimated. Wages and salaries remain lower in eastern Germany than in western Germany (the differences, depending on the industry, lie between 10 percent and 35 percent), so that a family can seldom live or maintain its standard of living on a single income.   The general insecurity of the job market leads to a situation in which no one voluntarily leaves her job. In addition, many women fear becoming economically dependent on a husband/man, not only currently but also in a more long-term perspective, i.e., after reaching retirement age. Material necessities are tied to the adherence to a professional occupation by an internalized norm of the compatibility of career and family which defines the self-conception of most women in eastern Germany.   This self-conception,[22] moreover, rests in the practical experiences of a relatively strong position in the household and in the family, a position bolstered by the contribution of women to household income as well as by their hitherto independent position outside the home.[23]

Still, in 1996 over 30 percent of the then employed women expressed the desire to work part-time; (they were mainly women who were married or who had small children[24]). When considering the number of hours they desire to work, however, it becomes apparent that East German women are referring to GDR norms. The majority of them want to reduce their weekly work hours to 25-35 hours (57 percent) or to 35-40 hours, as in GDR times.[25] This desired number of hours is well over the average part-time arrangements in the old *Länder*. It is more of a work reduction than part-time work (which, in addition, usually is tied to cuts in benefits and social services as a result of the reduced work week). Thus, one could also say: East German women certainly want to reduce their work hours, but they think little of part-time jobs with minimal or no insurance or other social coverage. (However, it must be taken into account that, for now, the supply of such part-time jobs in eastern Germany is still very low).

In general, the following can be said of the situation of East German women on the job market. Although tendencies toward a reorganization of the job market along gender differences and to the disadvantage of women exist and cannot be ignored, and women disproportionately belong to the unemployed, the share of women among total employed has not decreased. Women with relatively high levels of professional qualification and with technical school and university degrees generally have, at least in certain age groups, good chances on the job market. The majority of women believe in lifelong full-time work and they develop a multitude of activities in order to find a new job after becoming unemployed.[26] East German women on the whole produce an enormous amount of pressure on the job market through their adherence to full-time employment. What the long-range effects of this will be-- whether East German women will indeed (have to) adapt themselves to the West German structures, whether their adherence to professional occupations will facilitate their remaining in or returning to the job market, whether part-time work will become, as Kreckel predicts, "a potential gateway for the west German job market regime into east Germany"[27]--all this is difficult to foresee today.[28]

Compatibility of Career and Family

One characteristic of the "female life-context" *(weiblicher Lebenszusammenhang)* in modern societies is "double socialization": women must reconcile professional occupation, which has become increasingly a (short- or long-term) part of women's biographies with their--unchanged--duties to household and family. One of the special characteristics of their socialization is thus "society-ization" *(Vergesellschaftung),*[29] the development of full authority, skills, and motivation for both areas of life. The GDR belonged to those modern societies which allowed women to reconcile lifelong professional employment with their familial duties through a broad network of child-care institutions and social policy measures. As we know, there is no immediate connection between the employment rate of women and the possibilities of child care outside the home (as is shown, no less, by the GDR where women already in the 1960s and 1970s exhibited a comparatively high share of employment while the availability of nurseries and kindergartens was well under the need at the time, and many women had to find familial or private solutions). On the other hand, however, it can be said that a large and affordable network of child-care institutions promotes not only continuing professional work with only a short-term interruption after the birth of children, but also achieves a continuity in gender relations which are determined among other things by the model of the dual-earner marriage (or partnership). This model became accepted as the general norm in the GDR, and under current conditions also serves as a resource for East German women to oppose the changed structures and institutions with their "own ideas" *(Eigensinn).*

East German women remain committed not only to (full-time) professional work, but also to the compatibility of career and family-- as well as have a high acceptance of child care outside the home. In a 1992 survey only 12 percent of East German women and 16 percent of East German men favored a longer career pause for women after the birth of children, while in the old *Länder* 41 percent of women and 38 percent of men voted for this option. In the east, one percent of women and three percent of men could envisage women giving up their careers entirely while this was considered an appropriate solution for six percent of West German women and twelve percent of West German men. East and West German women and men voted similarly concerning maternity and parental leave.[30] This survey data makes clear the fact that in eastern Germany the dual-earner model and in western Germany the modernized provider model[31] are accepted and practiced by the majority of both genders. For East German women this consensus proves to be a favorable factor for their adherence to professional work. The majority of men accept women's claim of equal access to skilled, professional work,[32] and they share with them a lifestyle in which both partners pursue a career and the woman interrupts her employment only for a short time after the birth of children. Men also assume responsibilities in the family in order to allow their partners the ability to acquire further qualifications or education outside of working hours, if that will secure their jobs. [33]

It cannot be overlooked, however, that--independent of the subjective outlooks of East German women and men--the conditions for women to practice the model of the compatibility of career and family are becoming increasingly unfavorable. Along with the already outlined setbacks in the job market, the closings of child-care institutions and the rising costs of those that remain are having an increasingly negative effect. Company kindergartens and nurseries were already closed shortly after currency union and the introduction of the market (in July 1990) because they were, from the perspective of the market economy, ineffective. State kindergartens were transferred to local government authorities, and they are being supplemented by private and religious institutions. The total amount of available kindergarten space today is still larger in eastern than in western Germany (where kindergartens are often only open mornings). With the increasing financial difficulties of east German locales and the extreme decline in the birth-rate (see the following section), closings on a larger scale are planned.

In addition, since unification the costs of kindergarten spots, school meals, etc. have continually risen[34] (although from *Land* to *Land* in differing degrees). Child care outside the home thus becomes a cost issue for many women and families who are searching for private solutions, and single mothers are hit especially hard. In addition, financial shortages and the high unemployment level of women lead to fewer children attending the institutions. Already by the end of 1991

> two-thirds of employed women but only every fifth unemployed woman with children under four years of age made use of a nursery school. Of the four to six year-old children, three of four with working mothers but only one out of every two children with unemployed mothers were cared for in kindergartens, a lower figure than in west Germany.[35]

With the closing of child-care institutions because of decreasing demand, a vicious circle develops for unemployed women who want to re-enter the work force: employers demand proof that the children will be taken care of before hiring women, but many kindergartens, due to limited capacity, give spots solely to women who are employed.

On the whole it can be stated that, until now, for East German women the compatibility of career and children is still possible, even though under more difficult conditions, if one takes the level of available child-care facilities as a basis. It remains to be seen whether the 1996 entitlement to a kindergarten spot for all children over three years old, will become a right in 1999 as planned. For East German women, this would at least amount to the preservation of the status quo.[36]

Demographic Development

A discrepancy similar to that which exists for East German women, between their wish for a career and the possibilities of employment can also be established under demographic viewpoints. Although the appreciation of family and the desire for children has not changed for East German women and men in comparison with GDR times, a massive decline in the birth rate since unification can be observed. As Kreckel correctly notes, for women in the GDR it was not the "double burden" which led them to limit the number of children, but it was rather "exactly the opposite: their threatened 'housewifeization' (*Hausfrau-isierung*)"[37] led to a decline in the birth rate after 1990.

While 198,922 children were born in 1989 in the GDR, there were only 80,500 born in 1993. With that, eastern Germany has one of the lowest fertility rates in the world.[38] Although the number of live births in eastern Germany rose slightly in 1996, the "demographic decline" (*demographischer Einbruch*) of recent years is far from overcome. In a 1995 report on the demographic situation in Germany the authors find that "the birth rate in the new *Länder*, with an average of 0.77 children, remains significantly lower than in the earlier Federal Republic . . ."[39]   While in the GDR it belonged to the "normal biography" of a woman to have children,[40] presently two trends in the reproductive behavior of East German women can be seen. First, young women are delaying the birth of their first child longer. They are thus approaching the reproductive behavior of West German women who are on average 28 to 29 at the birth of their first child. Whether or not East German women will also conform to West German women in regards to the growing childlessness currently cannot be predicted.[41]

Second, the number of East German women who opt for sterilization and are thus actively, on the basis of their own decisions, prematurely ending their fertility phase has sharply risen since 1989. In the state of Brandenburg, for example, the only *Land* in Germany which includes complete sterilization records in its statistics, the number of sterilization procedures performed rose from 827 in 1991 to 6,224 in 1993.[42] The numbers in all the new *Länder* are likely to be similarly high. In order to evaluate these statistics it must be borne in mind, for one, that in the GDR sterilization was a seldom-practiced method of birth control (in contrast to in West Germany). In addition, sterilization was coupled with a complicated medical and bureaucratic procedure.[43] A certain "catch-up effect" and "newness effect" must also be considered. In addition, and this is more important, as the empirical studies of Daphne Hornig (now Hahn) show for the *Land* of Branden-burg, only women who are on average over 30 years old and who have completed their family planning with the birth of the desired number of children (one to two, for the majority) have themselves sterilized. In other words, the thesis of the "birth strike" of East German women,[44] continually launched in the press, especially in 1992 and 1993, is doubly wrong. First, the number of very young women who are having themselves sterilized is near zero,[45] that is, these women are not permanently refusing to have children at all. Second, the women who are having themselves sterilized as a rule have already borne children.

Both very young women who are delaying the birth of children, and women who are having themselves sterilized are making their decisions in the context of their desire to remain (fully) employed and/or to continue to combine family and career. Their reproductive behavior can surely be interpreted as a silent, individual form of resistance to the new structures, conditions, and unreasonable demands. Even if one considers that times of high unemployment and widespread social insecurity always negatively affect birth rates, the fact that the decline in births in eastern Germany today is higher than in Germany during the world economic crisis preceding World War II points to complex motivations of women in their current reproductive behavior. Young women know very well that career and family are more difficult to reconcile today than they were in the GDR, and they want to first acquire a relatively secure position in the working world before they begin a family. With their decision to wait before having children they are also resisting the broad danger of being prematurely forced out of the job market as mothers. Furthermore, this corresponds to the fact that only very few East German women interrupted their employment due to the birth of children, at least in the first few years after the political unification. "Hardly any women (0.7 percent) took parental leave from their employment from 1991 to 1992."[46]

Of the women who underwent sterilization, two large groups with different motivations can be ascertained, according to our studies.[47] The first is the group of socially disadvantaged women (unemployed and/or with only a low family income or both partners unemployed) who, above all, do not want to worsen their social situation (their children's chances) through further births. For these women--in contrast to in the GDR--the now costly contraceptives present an unacceptable stress on the family budget. Second is the group of professionally established women who want to make use of their current opportunities on the job market and have concluded their family planning. In contrast to GDR times, when they may have borne an additional, unplanned child and not viewed this as a hindrance to their professional ambitions, under the changed conditions they want to avoid endangering their career through an unwanted pregnancy. It is also interesting that 57 percent of the women surveyed in 1993-94 by Daphne Hahn pointed to the changed abortion law (which limited the possibilities for abortions after unification in eastern Germany) as a central motive for their decision to undergo sterilization. They did not want, as many of them formulated in a similar manner, (old) men in Bonn to dictate to them whether they carried out a pregnancy or not.[48]

Outlook

In this contribution I have tried to show, on the basis of a few examples and trends, that between the adopted West German structures and institutions on the one hand, and the subjective potentials for action and habitual patterns and norms of behavior of East German women on the other, friction and points of conflict are ascertainable. Over the short-term as well as long-term these could influence the professional and social opportunities for East German women and/or gender relations. In concluding I would like to formulate some speculations about the effects the encounter of new structures and the "own-ideas" *(Eigensinn)* of East German women may have for gender relations. In doing this, however, I reduce to a few correlations the complexity of economic, social, and cultural figurations which influence gender relations respectively and give it concrete shape and form.

1. All the facts show that the transformation processes in eastern Germany up to now have not transpired in a gender-neutral manner and that this will also not be the case in the future. Even if certain consequences of the implantation of new economic, legal, and social systems become effective for East German men and women equally, "gender" as an usher in the newly forming society is effective in all respects. Social differentiation presents itself here along gender lines, as it was practiced in "real socialism" (e.g., in the forms of segmentation and segregation in the professional sphere), as "favorable" starting point conditions. That the capitalist, as the "real socialist," systems are two variants of modern society[49] is witnessed, not insignificantly, by the fact that they share the symbolic gender order as characteristic of both their cultures. In this respect, for a limited time gender relations in eastern Germany will exhibit a few differing characteristics from those in western Germany. However, they will not differ from each other qualitatively.

2. The "real socialist" GDR provided for women--in terms of modernization theory--a "modernized" model of the female career. This included access to (qualified) professional work, a broad network of institutions, measures for the compatibility of career and family, and the possibility of self-determined pregnancy, etc.. This "modernized" model was coupled with a "gender contract" *(Geschlechtervertrag)*[50] which, on the one hand, established the responsibility of woman for the "private sphere" and for reproductive work in the family and, on the other hand, replaced the "provider of the family" model with the "dual-earner" model. This gender contract functioned in the GDR in part because social differences were generally not as strongly defined, so "gender" as a factor of social differentiation thus played a subordinate role.

When East German women currently cling to their "modernized female life" *(modernisierter weiblicher Lebenslauf)*, this is possible because, among other reasons, the gender contract remains largely intact. That is, men also accept and practice the norms of this contract. However, this does not exclude the fact that men profit from the "invisible hand" through which "gender" is becoming effective in the reformation of industries in the professional sphere. This means concretely, for example, that men are advancing in careers previously occupied by women, and generally the poorer jobs are open to women. Whether this tendency will destroy the current gender contract, however, is doubtful. The generally observable erosion of the "normal work situation" presently in the developed industrial countries, which was mainly oriented to the male worker and the "provider-nourisher" model, should rather facilitate the continued existence of the "gender contract" taken from the GDR.

3. East German women increase immensely the pressure on the job market by adhering to full-time work (with the remaining forms and institutions for child care outside the home facilitating this). It is conceivable that, in order to reduce this pressure, the supply of part-time jobs will also be increased in eastern Germany. These jobs, in their worst form, will not amount to more than nineteen hours per week, placing them below the minimum hours for benefits and social services coverage. With the ruling passed in March 1997 stating that, after only six months of unemployment, workers must accept even a job below their professional qualifications, the door could be opened for part-time positions in eastern Germany (usually these are the unskilled "everyman jobs")--and that means first and foremost for women. The fewer the opportunities for women on the job market, and the longer, for example, the period of their unemployment, the more inclined East German women will be to take on part-time jobs in order to remain in the work force at all. On the other hand, East German women's adherence to full-time work could also foster tendencies toward a more gender-neutral distribution of the "scarce work" *(knappe Arbeit)*. The fact that in eastern Germany--in contrast to in the former Federal Republic--there has been as yet no gender-specific divisions of the occupational sphere into (male, skilled) full-time work and (female, unskilled) part-time work, which could be carried over into the development of new forms of work, could prove to be favorable for the re-structuring of the job market.

One should also bear in mind that in the current reorganization of the occupational sphere in eastern Germany, drastic rationalization processes are taking place, not the least of which are occurring in the service sector where many women continue to be employed. Here, forms of work organization are being adopted from the industrial sector (e.g., group work) which are characterized by a general breakdown of hierarchies in the work processes. With this, however, the hitherto common "genderization" of work duties or decision-making powers and the previously quasi self-evident hierarchies between men and women are becoming obsolete. It remains to be seen whether the demand of East German women for equal access to qualified work together with the consensus inherent in the (GDR) "gender contract" will produce strong enough pressure to eliminate the hierarchization of gender relations which arise out of the modern organization of work.

It is also conceivable that, with continued structural unemployment, new lines of social differentiation will develop, i.e., between those with and those without jobs--which will run diagonally to differentiation by gender. This could lead--similar to the situation in the GDR, but this time for different reasons--to the weakening of "gender" as a factor of social differentiation as many combinations and other factors of social stratification (age, qualification, familial status, nationality) come to the fore. This could also mean that the forms in which women and men construct their relations will differentiate themselves.

4. Currently the scenario is rather bleak. The crisis symptoms which are observable in all western industrial countries through "globalization" apply completely to the Federal Republic of Germany. These are presently felt even more strongly in the new *Länder* than in the old. This is rather counter-productive for East German women's continued adherence to their "own ideas" *(Eigensinn)*. Even if East German women prove themselves on the job market and continue to adhere to the model of the compatibility of career and family, the losses already sustained in the level of their professional quali-fications cannot be overlooked. These occurred through the disappear-ance of entire industries and professions, as well as through lengthy unemployment and holes in institutional networks and social policy measures for the compatibility of career and family. The result of this configuration, short- and long-term, for the manner of integration of women into society remains to be seen and can only be determined through empirical studies.

Notes

1. This chapter was translated by Michael Kelly. Thanks to the Consulate General of the Federal Republic of Germany, Seattle, for providing financial assistance for this translation.

Translator's note: *Eigensinn* is, in the context of this essay, somewhat of a play on words, or a re-interpretation of a common word. In regular usage, the word means simply "stubbornness," yet in this essay it has been separated into the two words which are used to create it: *eigen* and *Sinn*. Literally, these two words mean "own" and "sense" or "meaning." In this essay, the term is used to describe a particular quality of East German women which affords them a view of life and a form of quiet resistance to the changes their lives are undergoing. Thus, I struggled to find a suitable English translation and have left it in its original in the title. Other occurrences of the term in the text have been translated as "own ideas" and put in quotation marks.

All translations of quotations from other sources quoted by the author originate exclusively from the translator of this essay and not from other published translations in the cases where such do exist.

2. I thank Sylka Scholz for her literature search in preparation of this article.

3. The terms "professional work" and "professional occupations" are used here in the broad sense to denote career or vocation, including those in technical fields.

4. Sabine Schenk and Uta Schlegel, "Frauen in den neuen Bundesländern - Zurück in andere Moderne? in *Berliner Journal für Soziologie*, Vol. 3, No. 3 (1993), p. 374.

5. In an update of theories of modernization, deficits and advantages of modernization in the GDR as opposed to in the FRG were highlighted, whereby the GDR, especially, was acknowledged as having a modernization advantage as compared to the FRG with regard to the social situation of women. See Stefan Hradil, "Die 'objektive' und die 'subjektive' Modernisierung. Der Wandel der westdeutschen Sozialstruktur und die Wiedervereinigung," in *Aus Politik und Zeitgeschichte*, No. 29 (1992), pp. 15-28; Rainer Geißler, "Die ostdeutsche Sozialstruktur unter Modernisierungsdruck," in *Aus Politik und Zeitgeschichte*, No. 29 (1992), pp. 15-28; and Irene Dölling, "Zum Verhältnis von traditionalen und modernen Aspekten im Lebenszusammenhang von Frauen," in *Berliner Debatte. Initial. Zeitschrift für sozialwissenschaftlichen Diskurs*, No. 4 (1994), pp. 29-35, from the perspective of East German women.

6. Peter A. Berger, "Was früher starr war, ist nun in Bewegung oder: von der eindeutigen zur unbestimmten Gesellschaft" in Michael Thomas (ed.), *Abbruch und Aufbruch* (Berlin: Akademie Verlag, 1992), p. 143.

7. See Stefan Hradil, "Die Modernisierung des Denkens: Zukunftspotentiale und 'Altlasten' in Ostdeutschland," *Aus Politik und Zeitgeschichte*, No. 20 (1995), pp. 3-15; Martin Diewald and Karl Ulrich Mayer (eds.), *Zwischenbilanz der Wiedervereinigung. Strukturwandel und Mobilität im Transformationsprozeß* (Opladen: Leske + Budrich, 1996).

8. Gunnar Winkler, *Sozialreport 1996. Sonderheft 1 + 2: Zur sozialen Situation und deren subjektive Reflexion in den neuen Bundesländern* (Brandenburg: Sozialwissenschaftliches Forschungszentrum e. V., 1996), p. 24.

9. See Sabine Schenk, "Neu- oder Restrukturierung des Geschlechterverhältnisses in Ostdeutschland?", in *Berliner Journal für Soziologie*, Vol. 5, No. 4 (1995), pp. 475-76.

10. Winkler, *Sozialreport 1996*, p. 25.

11. The downward tendency cannot be overlooked; however, in 1989, the share of women among the employed amounted to 47 percent, while in 1993 it had sunk to 44 percent, Sabine Schenk, "Erwerbsverläufe im Transformationsprozeß," in Hans Bertam (ed.), *Ostdeutschland im Wandel: Lebensverhältnisse - politische Einstellungen* (Opladen: Leske + Budrich, 1995), pp. 75-76.

12. See Hildegard-Maria Nickel and Sabine Schenk, "Prozesse geschlechtsspezifischer Differenzierung im Erwerbssystem," in Hildegard-Maria Nickel,

Jürgen Kuhl, and Sabine Schenk (eds.), *Erwerbsarbeit im Umbruch* (Berlin: Akademie Verlag, 1994), pp. 265-66.

13. Nickel and Schenk, "Prozesse geschlechtsspezifischer Differenzierung," pp. 266-67.

14. Schenk, "Erwerbsverläufe," p. 77.

15. *Ibid.*, p. 85.

16. Winkler, *Sozialreport 1996*, p. 25. Translator's note: Qualification structure refers to the system of education and practical training which existed in the GDR (and the FRG to some extent) by which one becomes officially qualified for various positions and trades.

17. Schenk, "Erwerbsverläufe," p. 91.

18. Winkler, *Sozialreport 1996*, p. 23.

19. *Ibid.*, p. 20.

20. *Ibid.*, p. 24.

21. See Ina Dietzsch and Irene Dölling, "Selbstverständlichkeiten im biografischen Konzept ostdeutscher Frauen: Ein Vergleich 1990-1994," in *Berliner Debatte. Initial. Zeitschrift für sozialwissenschaftlichen Diskurs*, No. 2 (1996), pp. 11-20.

22. There are studies which view East German women's adherence to the models of full-time work and the compatibility of career and family critically. In these, according to the views of some authors, the wide-ranging harmony of ideal and self-image in East German women, who have internalized and experienced in practice the norm of motherhood and career, functions rather as a hindrance to a critical reflective view of their lives and socialization in the GDR until now. See Heike Ellermann and Katrin Klatt, *Bundesdeutsche Hausfrau? Nie im Leben! Eine Studie zum Selbstverständnis von Frauen in Ost und West* (Berlin: Hoho Verlag Christine Hoffman, 1995), pp. 204ff.

23. Women's contribution to household incomes remains at 43 percent, approximately the same as in GDR times. In comparison, the contribution of women in the old *Länder* to household incomes is 18 percent (1988). See Schenk, "Neu- oder Restruktierung," pp. 484 and 479.

24. Winkler, *Sozialreport 1996*, p. 23.

25. In 1995, 64 percent of all employees in the new *Länder* still had a standard work week of 40 hours, while this applied to only three percent of employees in the old *Länder*, Winkler, *Sozialreport 1996*, p. 22.

26. A method for avoiding unemployment which women have discovered for themselves is that of founding independent companies. These are usually small companies in the service sector. Women in eastern Germany currently profit from state assistance to independent companies equally as much as men, although they usually have relatively little start-up capital available. To what degree these small companies have a chance of survival is currently difficult to say. See Frigga Dickwach and Monika Jungbauer-Gans, "Betriebsgründerinnen in Ostdeutschland," in *Soziale Welt*, No. 1 (1995), pp. 70-91.

27. Reinhard Kreckel, "Makrosoziologische Überlegungen zum Kampf um Normal- und Teilzeitarbeit im Geschlechterverhältnis," in *Berliner Journal für Soziologie*, Vol. 5, No. 4 (1995), p. 492.

28. In 1995, economists at the Institute of Economic Research in Halle put forth the thesis that "the east German job market crisis is *not*," as the sociologist Reinhard Kreckel summarizes, "due foremost to the loss of over 3.5 million jobs since 1989, but rather to the much higher 'inclination to work' of east Germans (in comparison with the old *Länder*)." (See Kreckel, "Makrosoziologische Überlegungen," p. 490.) This "higher inclination to work" in eastern Germany is accounted for, above all, by East German women.

29. Translator's note: The German word here is *Vergesellschaftung* which is otherwise best translated as "socialization." However, as the author is distinguishing between two different types of socialization, it would be misleading and redundant to translate this second form as such. I have thus used the term "society-ization" to impart the author's meaning of socialization *into* a specific society and societal role.

30. Pregnant women in the Federal Republic receive a 14-week paid maternity leave (6 weeks before and 8 weeks after childbirth) with job-dismissal protection of four months. Since 1994 a three year parental leave for mothers or fathers is allowed. For this period there is a guarantee of employment; child-rearing money is received for the first six months (320 ECU per month) and after that the following eighteen months can be financed depending on income.

31. This model is modernized insofar as women, in the old *Länder* too, increasingly are employed. There is still a wide-ranging consensus, however--and this is confirmed by corresponding tax breaks--that employment should be interrupted for a longer period prior to (possible) re-entry after childbirth. The provider model is thus only modified.

32. Dietzsch and Dölling, "Selbstverständlichkeiten," pp. 11-20.

33. Frank Thielecke, *Der Habitus im Veränderungsprozeß eines Versicherungsunternehmens*, Dissertation (Berlin: Humboldt University, 1993), has shown this for the banking and insurance sectors. In these typical occupations for women in the GDR, women had to obtain additional qualifications soon after unification in courses in the old *Länder* which sometimes lasted a period of weeks. Although the majority had children, the women often and seemingly without serious conflicts made arrangements with their husbands for child care and domestic duties during the time of their absence. Even if one considers that this represented an extraordinary situation (by taking the courses the women retained relatively secure jobs and their salaries were quickly brought to the level of those of the west), these findings still speak for the experiences of a practiced everyday division of labor between the sexes which could be fallen back upon. This is not intended to deny results of studies from the GDR, according to which women did three-fourths of all housework. Under such unequal distributions, however, East German men appear to have experience with domestic duties. Unfortunately there are no sufficient empirical studies on this topic.

34. Child-care institutions were practically cost-free for parents in the GDR. Only approximately 30 Marks for food had to be paid. Today for a kindergarten spot in Berlin, for example, costs range from DM 75 to DM 490 per month. As of 1998, a kindergarten spot will cost at least DM 95, if the parents earn less than DM 44,000 yearly. The price rises to DM 140 if yearly income lies between DM

44,000 and DM 55,000 and to DM 240 for yearly incomes between DM 55,000 and DM 66,000. Top earners (over DM 150,000 yearly income) will no longer pay DM 490, but rather DM 560. For this money, however, it is also possible to find private child care, which promotes a further reduction in public child care.

35. Gerhard Engelbrech (1993), quoted in Schenk and Schlegel, "Frauen," p. 378.

36. One must bear in mind, however, that day care in eastern Germany for children in the lower classes and school-based recreational possibilities have largely disappeared. Hence, the entitlement or the right to a kindergarten spot can only partially compensate for the lost network of public child care in the GDR.

37. Kreckel, "Macrosoziologische Überlegungen," p. 494.

38. *Die Zeit*, 10 October 1994, p. 37.

39. Jürgen Dorbritz and Karla Gärtner, "Bericht 1995 über die demographische Lage in Deutschland," in *Zeitschrift für Bevölkerungswissenschaft*, Vol. 20, No. 4 (1995), p. 339.

40. "Desired childlessness" *(Gewollte Kinderlosigkeit)* in the GDR was negligible. In the corresponding studies of the Institute for Sociology and Social Policy of the GDR Academy of Sciences from the years 1982 and 1987, the amount of those who desired no children was merely 1.5 percent and 0.9 percent, respectively. See Sonja Menning, "Geburten- und Heiratsverzicht in den neuen Ländern - Abschied von der Familie?", in Hubert Sydow, Uta Schlegel, and Andreas Heimke (eds.), *Chancen und Risiken im Lebenslauf. Beiträge zum gesellschaftlichen Wandel in Ostdeutschland* (Berlin: Akademie Verlag, 1995), p. 138. While the fertility level tended to fall in the GDR as in all industrialized countries, the rate of motherhood *(Mütterrate)*, *i.e.*, the percentage of women who had borne at least one child during her lifetime, rose. In 1989-90 it stood at 90 percent, according to Winkler, *Frauenreport 1990* (Berlin: Verlag Die Wirtschaft, 1990), p. 27.

41. Dorbritz and Gärtner, "Bericht 1995," p. 339, highlight "the relatively high childlessness in the former Federal Republic" as a characteristic of the demographic situation in Germany. They claim the proportion of childless women born in 1960 is 25 percent. According to their evaluation, this high rate is an "international exception."

42. Daphne Hornig, *Auswirkungen gesellschaftlicher Transformationsprozesse auf das reproduktive Verhalten Brandenburger Frauen unter besonderer Berücksichtigung irreversibler Schwangerschaftsverhütung* (Potsdam: Ministerium für Arbeit, Soziales, Gesundheit und Frauen, 1994), p. 67.

43. Hornig, *Auswirkungen*, p. 62ff.

44. In a research project we have analyzed this press campaign using discourse theory and related it to the motives of East German women for undergoing sterilization. The results of this research will be published in English as Irene Dölling, Daphne Hahn (formerly Hornig), and Sylka Scholz, "Birth Strike in the New Federal States an Act of Resistance?", in Susan Gal and Gail Kligman (ed.), *Gender Transformations: Reproduction as Politics in East Central Europe* (Princeton: Princeton University Press, forthcoming). The German version is titled "Gebärstreik im Osten? Wie Sterilisation in einer Pressekampagne

diskursiviert wurde und welche Motive ostdeutsche Frauen haben, sich sterilisieren zu lassen," by Irene Dölling, Daphne Hahn (formerly Hornig), and Sylka Scholz (1996), Potsdamer Studien für Frauen- und Geschlechtsforschung, Vol. 2, No. 1 (1998).

45. See Hornig, *Auswirkungen.*

46. Elke Holst and Jürgen Schupp, "Perspektiven der Erwerbsbeteiligung von Frauen im vereinten Deutschland," *DIW Diskussionspapier No. 68* (Berlin: Deutsches Institut für Wirtschaftsforschung, 1993), p. 6.

47. See Hornig, *Auswirkungen,* and Dölling, Hahn, and Scholz, *Sterilization.*

48. Hornig, *Auswirkungen,* p. 58.

49. See Zygmunt Baumann, *Moderne und Ambivalenz. Das Ende der Eindeutigkeit,* trans. from English by Martin Suhr (Hamburg: Junius, 1992).

50. In German social science discussion in recent times, the concept of "gender contract" has played a role. See Birgit Pfau-Effinger, "Macht des Patriarchats oder Geschlechterkontrakt? Arbeitsmarkintegration von Frauen im internationalen Vergleich," in *PROKLA,* No. 4 (1993), pp. 633-663. The basic assumption of this approach is that, in all modern societies, a historically developed sociocultural consensus exists on the respective forms of communication and exchange between the sexes. This involves a model and life-pattern for the "correct" form of gender-specific distribution of work, commonly accepted by both men and women, and on the form of the family and the manner of integration of both genders into society, the job market and/or the family." See Schenk, "Neu- oder Restrukturierung," p. 478. In ideal form, two separate models can be differentiated here. One is the model of the male provider marriage, in which women are primarily integrated into society through the family and their roles as housewife and mother. On the other hand, there is the model in which participation in the employment system presents the dominant form of integration into society for both men and women equally and which proceeds from the participation of all employable people in the job market. Without going into concrete formations at this point, one can say that for the former Federal Republic a gender contract according to the model of the male provider marriage is characteristic, and for the GDR, or for the new *Länder,* the model of the dual-earner marriage.

10

Radio and Television in the East: A Continuing Odyssey of Change

Joseph E. Naftzinger

There is nothing permanent except change.
--Heraclitus

The broadcasting landscape in eastern Germany has changed dramatically in the eight years since revolution gripped the German Democratic Republic (GDR). In 1989, as the drama began to unfold, East Germans were accessing a relatively limited array of largely public or state radio and television stations broadcasting from both the GDR and the Federal Republic of Germany (FRG). The number and, for the most part, programming of these stations had changed only gradually over the years. The most significant departure from this slow, decades-long evolution had been the appearance in the mid-1980s of two fledgling private television stations in the West that were broadcasting via satellite.

Today, a still evolving mix of public and private broadcasters is generating a diverse melange of programming in what has become a fiercely competitive pan-German media market. The number and variety of offerings dwarfs that available less than a decade ago. In early 1996, fifty-three public radio stations were competing with 167 private ones on the national, regional, state, or local level.[1] Twenty-eight public and private television stations or networks were offering programs[2] nation-wide, while another 62 were broadcasting regionally or locally.[3] Thirty more foreign or international television stations were included in cable networks or, in border regions, received terrestrially. Satellites provided potential access to almost 80 more channels.[4] The average household accesses 33 channels from this mix, compared with a mere three to five in the mid to late 1980s.[5] Digital transmission, pay-per-view, and specialty programming have arrived, interactive broadcasting "stands at the door," and the pan-German broadcasting market has become the "largest and most competitive in Europe."[6]

These fundamental changes in the broadcasting environment were occurring simultaneously with the political revolution that unified East and West and swept away the GDR and its state radio *(Rundfunk der DDR)* and television *(Deutscher Fernsehfunk* or *DFF)* institutions in the process. They were not a product of that revolution, however. The broadcasting audience in Germany, particularly television viewers, was already essentially unified at the time, and East Germans were already consuming much of the same programming that attracted audiences in the West. East Germans either tuned into western stations directly, especially for news and commentary, or consumed films, shows and serials of western genre that had become a staple of the entertainment programming broadcast by the DFF. The characterization "one nation, one television screen" had already been used in the mid-1980s, and the trend continued as satellite antennas began to sprout in the eastern corners of the country where western broadcasts were difficult to receive.[7] Indeed, the two national television programs produced by the FRG's "public corporations," ARD and ZDF,[8] and the radio broadcasts from West Berlin of RIAS (Radio In the American Sector) were as familiar to most East Germans as were those of their own services. They were the icons of a broadcasting landscape in the FRG that had changed little for decades.

The profound change in radio and television program availability in the East is the result of a revolution of another sort, a fundamental transformation of the broadcasting environment in the FRG that was occurring coincident with, but independent of, the political revolution engulfing the GDR. Even as the Wall was being breached in the East, so too was the sclerosis that had characterized the broadcasting structure in the West. The way for change had been cleared by a November 1986 ruling of the FRG's highest court. That ruling allowed private broadcasters to compete directly with the public stations that, ever since 1949, had a virtual monopoly on broadcasting within the country. Shortly after the court's action, SAT 1 began broadcasting from Mainz, becoming Germany's first privately owned German TV station,[9] and the revolutionary *duale* or dual public-private broadcasting order was launched.

By the time Germany was reassembled, private radio and television broadcasters had secured a solid foothold in the West and were establishing roots in the East as well. And in 1997, as CNN prepared to introduce an all news television program--in German, and the country's first all religious program *Radio Paradiso* completed its initial quarter of broadcasting, the traditional public broadcasting institutions were locked in fierce head-to-head competition with an array of privately owned and operated radio and television stations. The dual broadcasting system is now codified by inter-state treaty among all sixteen *Bundesländer* and has produced a palette of programming in Germany matching or exceeding that available anywhere.

The competition within the public and private sectors has been, and continues to be, fueled by the march of technology. Cable transmission has allowed many more competitors into the race for audience attention. Satellite broadcasting multiplies the competition and enables the consumer to circumvent any local restrictions on program access. Moreover, even as public and private broadcasters jockey to secure political support and audience acceptance in the still developing dual landscape, today's technology is poised to fundamentally change the rules of the broadcasting road yet again. Now, as digital transmission and interactive and on-line programming open a Pandora's box of unexplored capabilities with unclear implications for the future, the talk is of a *Triale* or triad broadcasting system. [10]

The current competition between the FRG's established public broadcasting institutions and their private challengers juxtaposes technology, programming policy, and audience appeal in a manner similar to that which prevailed in the GDR before the revolution. Since the 1950s, the GDR state radio and television services battled against the FRG's public broadcasters for the attention of the eastern audience. As discussed below, the western institutions, or more accurately their programs, swept the field.

From the beginning, the Socialist Unity Party (SED) leaders had viewed East German radio and television as "instruments" of the party and state, and they tightly controlled all aspects of these institutions, including programming. Nevertheless, GDR citizens found a way to watch the programs they wanted to watch, not those their government thought they should watch. By the 1980s, they had largely abandoned East German radio and television as sources of news in favor of western broadcasts. With regard to other programming, the East's political leadership and media struggled against increasingly popular western fare. Largely in vain, they pointed to the social virtues of quality, education, and information in programming as opposed to the western stress on crass entertainment that they viewed as "frivolous" or worse.

Paradoxically, this is the same type of appeal now being marshaled by officials of the FRG's public broadcasting organizations in their struggle with private competitors.

The competition between public and private providers within the FRG's dual broadcasting system is still evolving, with the final outcome uncertain. Private broadcasting now has over half of the primetime television market, up from single digits a decade ago.[11] Nevertheless, the public broadcasters have made significant programming and administrative adjustments and may have stabilized the situation. Future development will reflect political decisions, especially within the sixteen states themselves, but also increasingly at the European Union level. Nevertheless, as in the earlier competition between East and West German broadcasters, it is likely that a pan German audience will, in one way or another, get the programming they want.

The dramatic changes in the broadcasting landscape that affected consumers, especially the explosion of programming choice, had relatively little to do with the political revolution occurring in the East. That revolution did have a significant impact on broadcasting producers, however. Indeed it fundamentally altered the structure and culture of the radio and television institutions operating there. Just a little more than a year after unification, at midnight 31 December 1991, the last vestiges of the GDR's services, which had been distilled into a type of holding company and operated on a provisional basis during the year, ceased to exist. From that point on, broadcasting in the five new eastern states emanated from totally new public broadcasting institutions organized under FRG law that gives the individual states responsibility for media policy. The large bulk of personnel in these newly created broadcasting organizations were former GDR radio and television employees, but most of the top leadership was imported from the western media, and the eastern organizations were produced from the western mold.

Considerable criticism accompanied this process, which of course profoundly affected how radio and television services are produced in the East. It had a direct, often traumatic, impact on the lives of thousands of employees who, for whatever reason, were not able to find work or adjust to the new institutional culture. Some, in both the East and West, even considered the process to be the equivalent of a hostile takeover of the East's indigenous broadcasting operations by Westerners, or a conspiracy to exact "revenge for the GDR media's past actions."[12] More fundamental, however, is the criticism that a unique chance had been missed to create a different type of broadcasting institution and culture, one neither shackled by the GDR's past nor infected with the "deficiencies"[13] that some find in the FRG media.

Thus, two distinct perspectives emerge when viewing the metamorphosis of radio and television in eastern Germany since 1989. One perspective assesses the change from the consumers' point of view; the other from that of the producers. The discussion below sketches the parameters of the change from both perspectives, but does not pretend to be a definitive analysis of either. It begins with a snapshot of the broadcasting landscape in the East as it stood in 1989. It then looks more closely at how the course of the larger political revolution was reflected in broadcasting changes there, first while the GDR government still existed, and then immediately after unification. Finally, it briefly assesses the broadcasting scene today, noting that technology and audience demand appear to be underlying forces driving the competition and direction of change, and that the audience in the East appears to be largely satisfied with the results.

Several broad insights emerge from this discussion. Both consumers and producers of radio and television programming in eastern Germany have experienced profound change since 1989, but that change stems from different roots. For the eastern consumer, the dramatic expansion of available programming results largely from public-private competition leveraged by the advance of technology, and not from the political revolution and subsequent process of unification. On the other hand, unification did profoundly affect the eastern producers by fundamentally transforming the broadcasting organizations in which they worked. That transformation was nothing less than the abolishment of the GDR institutions and of totally new ones based on the existing FRG pattern. This outcome is best seen as stemming from East German citizens demanding unification now and the ensuing turbulent political interaction among the various eastern political parties and groupings, not as a hostile takeover by western politicians. Finally, given the primacy of the individual states in setting broadcasting policy, the prevailing public-private competition in the West, and the advance of technology, viable alternatives to the general pattern of institutional change that took place in the East are not evident.

Radio and Television in East
Germany Before the Revolution

As the 1980s drew to a close, the citizens of the German Democratic Republic were enjoying well-developed and comprehensive broadcasting services. Virtually every house had a television set, and over half of them were color.[14] In addition to normal terrestrial transmission, broadcasts were transmitted over local cable networks and, on an increasing though still limited basis, were received by private satellite dish, particularly in the Elbe valley where it was difficult or impossible to receive western stations directly. On average, East Germans watched more television than their western counterparts and listened to about as much radio.[15]

Much of the programming they watched and listened to was broadcast by the GDR's centralized, state owned and operated television and radio systems. The DFF ran about 170 hours of programming per week over two separate channels, DFF I and DFF II, that had been aligned to provide viewers a continuous choice between program types. For its part, East German radio focused on five national and one international program, although it had also organized fourteen "regional windows," programs tailored to specific locals and broadcast on a restricted, intermittent schedule.

Because of a rare confluence of circumstance, however, most East Germans also watched and listened to the programs of the West German public broadcasting corporations. Indeed, competition with West German programming for audience appeal had been a constant conditioner of broadcasting in East Germany ever since 1956, when the SED Politburo made the decision to change the picture-tone frequency separation of East German television broadcasts from that used by their socialist allies in the East to that used in the West German system. This adjustment removed the last technological impediment to what would soon become an enduring, often bitter struggle with the West German broadcasters for audience attention. Geographic proximity enabled western broadcasts to reach most East German households, compatible technical standards permitted East Germans to receive the signals,[16] and a common language ensured that the broadcasts would be understood.

By the time the dramatic events of 1989 began to unfold, watching West German television and listening to western radio had become staples of life in the GDR. East Germans had come to rely on western broadcasts for news and commentary. Only five to fifteen percent of the population tuned in to the country's prime time, flagship television news broadcast, the DFF's *Aktuelle Kamera*, and the DFF's news journals fared little better.   Further, eastern Germans were avid consumers of western entertainment programs. East German television and radio produced some very well received programming, but apart from sports and an excellent children's program, their most popular fare was entertainment cast in the western model, either produced in-house, or purchased from the West itself.[17]

Thus even before the revolution, the East German consumer or audience accessed radio and television programming that was essentially unified, or at least homogenized, with that viewed in the West. Only the various West German public television programs produced and broadcast on a state-wide or regional basis (the ARD's Third programs),[18] and western radio programs broadcast regionally or locally were not widely available in the East. Most East Germans relied on western broadcasts for their news and information, although the GDR's regionally specific radio programs had relatively little competition from outside the country regarding local events. And entertainment, whether produced in the East or West, was increasingly from the same mold, the West's. One result of this pan-German broadcasting landscape was captured colorfully by an experienced observer, who offered this observation about East German candidates during the heavily televised March 1990 election campaign in the GDR: "Their language was increasingly the same [as the West German officials]; so many little Genschers, Kohls, Brandts springing fully armed out of the television screen. Indeed, most of them had learned the language watching West German television."[19]

While most East Germans welcomed the opportunity to watch West German programs, not surprisingly the SED leadership had long viewed the practice as a serious political problem. The ready availability and widespread public acceptance of western broadcasting had broken the party leaders' monopolistic control over media content and confounded the prescriptions of their Marxist-Leninist mass media doctrine. In the beginning of their struggle, the party leaders had tried to prevent the GDR citizenry from listening to or watching western programs. By 1970, however, they had largely abandoned these efforts which proved to be either damaging politically or, especially in the case of television, too complicated technically. Instead, during the 1970s and 1980s, the leadership emphasized competition for audience appeal. As they did so, however, they were forced to abandon their doctrinaire, blanket condemnation of western style entertainment. Given the competition that is occurring throughout a united FRG today between public and private broadcasters, it is worth briefly sketching this development.[20]

In the SED's mass media concept, entertainment was to help instill a "higher socialistic moral quality" in the state's citizens. In the 1960s this was to be achieved through good "humanistic" socialist programs. "Capitalistic decadence," "trashy literature," "hot music," and "the ecstatic songs of an Elvis Presley" were condemned in the drive to steer television viewers "away from simple artistic enjoyment and toward creative participation in cultural and spiritual life."[21] "Educate entertainingly, entertain educatedly" was the initial slogan. Gradually, however, in the face of competing programming from West Germany, the doctrine shifted, placing less stress on "educate" and more on "entertain." In 1973, Erich Honecker acknowledged a carefully prescribed place for "light entertainment." Finally, in the 1980s, western style entertainment programs were embraced wholesale. The East German audience had let their desires be known by tuning into the West German competition and, with regard to entertainment, the party leadership was flexible enough to bend their doctrine and give the public what they wanted.[22]

The party leadership did not alter its stance with regard to news and journalistic broadcasts, however. Such programs operated within a rigid system that strictly enforced the "party line" and were tightly and personally controlled by Erich Honecker and other top SED leaders until the day of their resignations. Consequently, news broadcasts strained to project a positive image of the East German socialist state and generally excluded any information which might reflect negatively upon it. Problems of concern to citizens were usually not broached unless solutions were in sight. In practice, this translated into propagation of a message that was increasingly divorced from the realities of everyday political and social life. As a result, by 1989, the party leaders had essentially abrogated the competition for audience attention in this genre, and most East Germans turned to West German broadcasts for their news and information.[23]

The Producers and the Impact of Unification

Thus the Germans in the East and West consumed generally homogenized programming. They watched the same type of entertainment and, for the most part, the same news broadcasts. On the other hand, the GDR broadcasting services, the producers, were organized and run very differently from those in the FRG. Distilled to its essence, the East German system was an archetype of the communist model featuring a state-owned and centralized structure operating under strict party control.[24] The West German system reflected the pluralistic structure and divorce from government control that underpins the media of most western democracies. Additionally, and especially important to the process of change that was about to begin, media policy in the FRG was anchored at the state, not the federal level.

The impact of unification on broadcasting in eastern Germany is essentially the story of the abrupt and complete transition from the GDR's institutional broadcasting model to the FRG's radio and television system--and the individual and institutional cultural struggles engendered by that transition. A substantial amount of literature already addresses this transition and raises several relevant issues. To what extent was the final outcome of this transition a dictate from western politicians? Under the circumstances, what other outcomes were possible? Were chances missed to erect different institutions that would have provided the audience in eastern Germany with programming better attuned to their desires?[25]

When one considers this transition of the broadcasting structures in the East, two stages become apparent. The first stage lasted roughly from November 1989 until unification in October 1990 and the second from unification until 31 December 1991. The first stage was initially characterized by the development of liberalizing reform within the existing GDR broadcasting institutions themselves. This was then followed, after the 18 March 1990 GDR national elections, by the attempt of the de Maizière government to pass legislation that would establish new or reformed broadcasting structures in the still existing GDR, structures that would be legally and operationally compatible with those in the FRG. The second stage embraced the brief afterlife of the former GDR structures that were consolidated within a unified FRG in accordance with the unification treaty, and the concurrent effort to establish the foundations for the totally new institutions that would follow.

Attempts at Reform Within the GDR

Internal reforms within the broadcasting institutions had begun almost immediately after Honecker resigned his party post. By the time of the 18 March elections, SED party control of broadcasting policy and content had been stripped away, along with much of the top leadership and the party apparatus itself, and the beginnings of independent regional radio were evident. Further, a political consensus had developed within the GDR that its state-owned and -operated radio and television institutions should become public service corporations removed from state control. Initial legislation to this end was developed by the Modrow government's Media Law Commission, and the *Volkskammer* had incorporated it into a "Decision on the Media" (*Medienbeschluss*). However, consensus could not be reached on the details necessary to establish the final legal basis for such reform of the broadcasting institutions.[26]

Additionally, it had become clear to those responsible for the GDR's radio and television operations that the existing state structures were hopelessly over-staffed and inefficient. There was consensus that financial self-sufficiency would require advertising revenues to supplement the radio and television taxes. They also recognized the need for modern, efficient equipment and for large personnel reductions.[27]

The popular mandate of 18 March introduced an element of true revolution into the unfolding dynamic of change for the broadcasting services as well as for the state itself. Unification "now" meant not simply reform, or even "growing together," but direct accession into the FRG via Article 23 of the Basic Law, essentially a blanket adoption of its laws and institutions. For the GDR broadcasting media, this meant transferring the responsibility for mass media policy to the yet to be created new states and acceptance of the dual public-private broadcasting system.

Shortly after assuming power in April, the de Maizière government established a Ministry for Media Policy. The ministry was tasked with developing the legislation necessary to establish new or reformed broadcasting structures that would generally fit into the West German model. It relied heavily on West German advisors for information and ideas and attempted to build on the consensus for reform that had developed within the East German government and broadcasting media itself. There was general agreement that, in addition to divorcing the media from the state, the new structure would need to be compatible with the FRG's federated model. Political agreement ended, however, with these broad goals for media reform, and the consensus necessary to achieve them within a still existing GDR via a comprehensive media law did not materialize.[28]

Several factors contributed to this lack of consensus. First there was deep-rooted political and ideological disagreement over whether to retain some aspects of the old central broadcasting institutions, or to start over completely on a federated basis with new institutions. Typically, those arguing the former view believed that retaining some elements of the existing institutions would provide for some continuation of East German identity and true diversity in cultural themes and political opinion. On the other hand, those easterners arguing the latter position considered the existing institutions and their personnel so hopelessly compromised that only a completely new start would do.[29] Of course there were varying mixtures and gradations of these views, and the debate was not confined to East Germans.

Secondly, regardless of political orientation, all who wanted to preserve some elements of the existing broadcasting systems and not abolish them totally faced very real practical and legal hurdles. Not the least of these was the conundrum that, while the unified Germany would be a federated republic with media policy vested in its component states, the "new states" being created out of the GDR were not yet legal entities, and governments with the competence to determine such policy were not in place. Thus, whatever would be decided by the then still existing GDR government would be subject to approval and possible change after unification.[30]

Finally, all these difficulties were exacerbated by the accelerating pace of unification. Formal work on the unification treaty was already underway, and the first "Two plus Four" talks began in May. The astonishingly swift and successful conclusion of the international framework for unification and the necessity to stop the hemorrhaging of East Germans to the West combined to propel unification at break-neck speed. By mid-summer, it became clear that the time remaining to establish new broadcasting institutions in East Germany that could be carried over into a united Federal Republic would be measured in months or weeks, rather than years.[31]

As the pace of unification accelerated, the effort to agree on the details necessary to establish new broadcasting institutions in the still existing GDR became increasingly futile. A last attempt within the GDR to pass legislation that would have reformed its institutions and regulated the transition of the media upon unification foundered in the *Volkskammer* in July. From then on, time simply did not permit resolution of the numerous practical issues and legal entanglements, even if the basic political and ideological differences in approach to broadcasting reform could have been reconciled. It was now clear that the question of broadcasting reform in eastern Germany would be carried over into the unified FRG. The mechanism established to do this was Article 36 of the unification treaty, an article designed to insure that the impasse would be overcome and the issue resolved quickly.

Article 36 and the Einrichtung

Article 36 came into force with the rest of the unification treaty on 3 October 1990. It emphasized that the "responsibility" to "provide broadcasting services" for the population living in the territory of the former GDR lay directly with the five new states and a reunified Berlin that had been established there. Until these states could prepare themselves to execute this responsibility, however, the *Rundfunk der DDR* and *DFF* as they existed on 3 October were consolidated into one legal, public service institution independent of the federal state (*gemeinschaftliche staatsunabhängige, rechtsfähige Einrichtung*)--referred to simply as the *Einrichtung*. The *Einrichtung* was either to be "dissolved" through a joint treaty between the six eastern states compatible with the federated nature of FRG media laws, or "transferred" to public broadcasting corporations established by these states acting singly or in groups. If neither occurred by 31 December 1991, the *Einrichtung* was to be disbanded and its tangible assets (real estate and property) distributed proportionally among the new states.

The *Einrichtung* was placed under the control of a broadcasting executor *(Rundfunkbeauftragter)*. Advised and assisted by a broadcasting council *(Rundfunkbeirat)*, the executor was tasked to direct the operations of the *Einrichtung*, represent it in all external matters, and insure a balanced operating budget. Further, the executor was to guarantee necessary broadcasting services for the population in the former GDR until the states could assume this responsibility. The executor's responsibilities would end on 31 December 1991 at the latest when the *Einrichtung* was dissolved through one of the paths identified above.

Thus, Article 36 established the two key criteria that would determine the fate of broadcasting services in the eastern states. In one way or another, the former GDR radio and television institutions would be dissolved and, in the end, the eastern states alone would decide what would take their place. The executor was vested with broad powers to ensure the necessary continuity of operations for a brief, clearly defined interim period, but after that, the six eastern states would be on their own. Although elements of the old GDR structures continued to function, they were now under the executor's direction and the course leading to their final dissolution was set unambiguously. The political debate on what would take their place was now shifted largely from the federal to the state level.[32]

Article 36 also stipulated that the executor was to be nominated by the Minister President of the GDR and approved by the *Volkskammer* before 3 October. If that did not occur, the executor was to be selected by majority vote of the heads of government from each of the five new states and Berlin after unification. In fact, the de Maizière government did not nominate, and the *Volkskammer* did not approve, a candidate before unification. Thus the task fell to governments of the five new states and Berlin, and they appointed Rudolf Mühlfenzl to the position on 15 October 1990. Active in broadcasting operations and policy in Bavaria, Mühlfenzl was a conservative and a firm supporter of the Kohl government. It is clear that the Bonn government engineered his appointment,[33] and that he was expected, and intended, to "end the former GDR state broadcasting [institutions] and to prepare for a new broadcasting order in the new states."[34]

Mühlfenzl and a staff of twelve--all but one from the West--lost no time in taking up his responsibilities. The broadcasting council selected by the new states, all but one were easterners, was formed and joined in steering the operation several months later. The remainder of the personnel in the *Einrichtung* were all members of the GDR's radio, television, or technical broadcasting services who were carried over into the new organization. They included Christoph Singelnstein and Michael Albrecht who had been appointed as the new directors for GDR radio and television respectively by the de Maizière government. Their work continued for fourteen months until 31 December 1991, when the *Einrichtung* was dissolved.

Mühlfenzl's direction of the *Einrichtung* has been the target of much criticism and has lead to the judgment of some that western politicians essentially "colonized"[35] the eastern broadcasting system. Certainly, many of the East German personnel who continued to produce and broadcast the programs and administer the *Einrichtung* resented being directed by a transplant from the West, especially one who was personally unknown to them and a conservative to boot. Leaving aside the criticism directed personally at Mühlfenzl, however, it is important to take a summary look at the substantive results of the odyssey of change that occurred during the *Einrichtung's* fourteen month existence. Those outcomes can be considered in the three generic tasks implicit in Article 36; management and liquidation of the *Einrichtung*, provision of broadcasting services to the eastern states, and the establishment of new broadcasting services in these states.

Management and Liquidation. This task had the most immediate, direct personal impact of all. The GDR state broadcasting services had employed about 14,000 full-time workers as change swept over the country in 1989. Because the remnants of these services would cease to exist when the *Einrichtung's* authority expired on 31 December 1991, all would have to find employment elsewhere, accept pension, or join the ranks of the unemployed. About 4,000 of these employees were cut while the GDR still existed, and the *Einrichtung* inherited about 10,000 upon unification. The number was progressively reduced until about 3,500 personnel were left during the final months of operations.

Complete data on the fate of all 14,000 former employees of the *Rundfunk der DDR* and *DFF* are not published. In general, technicians and administrators found it easier to adjust to the new conditions and find employment than editors and journalists.[36] Similarly, as in most other sectors of the economy, those under forty-five years of age generally fared better than those who were older. Mühlfenzl estimated in 1995 that "a good two thirds" (or close to seven thousand) of the employees who were in the *Einrichtung* had found jobs elsewhere. Most of these were employed in the new public and private broadcasting organizations created by the eastern states, and their contributions there are taken up later.[37]

A second personnel action, also traumatic for some, was the screening of employees to identify those who might not be considered fit for leadership or other responsible positions in the media because of their past relations with the SED regime. An initial questionnaire, modeled on the one used by the state of Brandenburg, was submitted to about 9,500 employees in February 1991. On the basis of the completed questionnaires, 1,677 employees were referred to a small commission of east Germans for further evaluation. After their review, the commission recommended that 600 employees not be permitted to keep their leadership positions within the *Einrichtung*, largely because they had advanced to them solely because of their SED party affiliations and lacked the necessary training and experience. Immediate dismissal was recommended for another 198 who, after individual hearings, were confirmed to have worked for the *Stasi*.[38] While criticized by some, similar procedures were undertaken for all civil servants and employees in public institutions throughout the five new states and Berlin, and the action seems to have been accepted as appropriate by the majority of employees.[39]

In addition to the fate of individual employees, the future of unique and popular radio and television production units and groups was a priority concern. Despite the disappearance of their parent organization, a number of the most successful were, in one way or another, kept intact and transferred into the new media organizations. These include the well received radio and television programs that had been directed toward youth, *DT-64* and *Elf 99* respectively, the critically acclaimed radio station *DS-Kultur*, and the children's television teams producing the popular *Sandmännchen*. Additionally, the *DS-Kultur* symphony orchestra and chorus, the television ballet, and most performers from another nine musical ensembles were absorbed into the remodeled broadcasting landscape.

Article 36 specified that the *Einrichtung* would operate on a balanced budget, and this was accomplished. In fact, the books were closed with a surplus of over DM 300,000. This was used to fund two administrative entities formed to dispose of the real estate and other property left after the *Einrichtung* ceased its organizational existence. In all, Mühlfenzl estimated that the *Einrichtung* provided a total of more than one half billion DM toward the development of new broadcasting entities in the eastern states.[40]

Finally, the disposition of the uniquely valuable archives of the former East German television (DFF) and radio services deserves mention. Responsibility for securing and maintaining this material was given to the ARD's *Deutsches Rundfunkarchiv* (DRA) with headquarters in Frankfurt. After the *Einrichtung* was dissolved, the effort to collect, index, and preserve this archival material continued under DRA direction using largely the same employees who had worked in the East's central archives before unification. That work is now complete, and most of the material is in a facility termed *"DRA-Ost,"* located in Berlin and administered from Frankfurt.

The material collected and archived there dates from 1945 and includes tapes and recordings of virtually all radio and television programs produced in the East until 1991, some 350,000 musical recordings alone. It also includes over 3,000 running meters of documents from all sectors of radio and television operation. An historical archive that supported the DFF contains over 2.3 million negatives, 260,000 pictures, and 100,000 slides, and the DFF research section includes a comprehensive inventory of the "competition," that is, West German broadcasts. All of this material is now available to support the research and programming of both FRG and foreign broadcasters.[41]

Provision of Broadcasting Service to the Eastern States. The major change made within the *Einrichtung* from the broadcasting pattern that had existed in the GDR immediately before unification dealt with television. Four central radio programs broadcast by the GDR were continued,[42] and emphasis was placed on continuing the development of regional programs. On the other hand, the most successful programs from DFF's two channels were combined into one called the *Deutscher Fernsehfunk Länderkette,* and the freed frequency was allocated to the ARD for direct broadcasting in the East. The ZDF received a (previously unused) DFF frequency that they used for direct broadcasting there as well. Thus from the consumer's perspective, dramatic changes in the structure of the broadcasting environment were not evident, although ARD and particularly ZDF programs were now easier to receive in some areas than they had been before the frequency reallocations, and the DFF was offering one, not two programs.

The content and tone of radio and television programs, particularly the news and journalistic magazines, had changed significantly, however. Change began to emerge in the late Fall of 1989 as SED party control dissipated in the wake of Honecker's resignation and the abdication of the Politburo's old guard. It was noticeable in DFF television reporting when the Wall was breached in the night of 9 November. Change progressed unevenly within the radio and television institutions and at first it remained constrained within an institutional culture still dominated by a (reformed) SED. Then, as 1989 turned into 1990, editors and reporters found a new measure of journalistic license which they began to pursue more energetically.[43]

Increased journalistic freedom was accompanied by a clear increase in popular acceptance of the GDR broadcasting media. This was particularly true with regard to news and journalistic programs, and the DFF became a major player alongside the ARD and ZDF in covering the governments and elections in 1990. For the most part, the same journalistic freedom was carried forward into operations under the *Einrichtung*, although the circumstances within the organization and the disestablishment looming on the horizon attenuated the élan and esprit there.

Despite the expanded journalistic freedom that prevailed within the former GDR broadcasting services as they functioned within the *Einrichtung*, the response of the eastern audience to their programming presents a mixed picture. Regional radio broadcasts increased in appeal and surveys indicated that the *DFF Länderkette* was an important "orientation" help for eastern viewers. On the other hand, the DFF *Länderkette* trailed both the ARD and ZDF in general audience share. And, while its prime time newscast, which had been renamed *Aktuelle,* had drawn equal to that of the ZDF's *Heute,* it still trailed ARD's established *Tagesschau,* sometimes by a two to one margin. A similar pattern is evident when comparing the ratings of the journalistic magazines. Just as importantly, however, eastern television viewers, along with their western counterparts, were turning increasingly to private broadcasters for their television entertainment. And the combined market share in the five new states and Berlin of the three major private broadcasters equaled that of the ARD, making it three times that of the *Länderkette's.*[44]

Establishment of New Broadcasting Services. The most far-reaching task associated with Article 36 was the establishment of new broadcasting services in the East. Here, although the executor had important influence in the beginning, ultimate responsibility lay collectively with the governments of the five new states and Berlin. Formed following the state elections in October, these governments represented a spread of political orientations as well as regional outlooks, and the interplay among them determined in large measure the nature of the outcome.

One obvious option would have continued the operations of the re-formed and slimmed down GDR broadcasting services, now consolidated under the *Einrichtung,* as a public law utility established, supported, and operating within common guidelines set by the six eastern states (including Berlin) acting cooperatively. Variations on this theme ranged from a type of third national public broadcaster, similar to the ARD or ZDF, to a large regional utility that would have been integrated into the federated ARD structure. Such an arrangement would have carried with it a distinct inheritance from the GDR. Not surprisingly, this was the favorite of a number of former GDR media professionals and, for a time, was advanced by Mühlfenzl himself.

Mühlfenzl has been criticized by some for not pressing this option more vigorously with the state governments,[45] but there is no indication that the common political ground necessary to launch such a cooperative venture could have been created among the states. In fact, events point in the opposite direction. The three CDU-governed states in middle Germany--Saxony, Saxony-Anhalt, and Thuringia--were ready to cooperate with each other, but they could not reach agreement on media policy with the CDU/FDP coalition governing Mecklenburg-West Pomerania, let alone the SPD government in Brandenburg or the "grand coalition" in Berlin.[46] It soon became clear that a treaty among the six states that would have provided some type of a unified after-life for the former GDR broadcasting services collected within the *Einrichtung* was not a viable political option.

Attention therefore turned to the second alternative envisioned in Article 36, that of forming regional public broadcasting corporations by groups of states to which the *Einrichtung*'s assets could be transferred. An initial concept envisioned creating two such regional entities, one embracing the northern two new states plus Berlin, and the second the three new states in the South. This concept was embraced by the executor and others and made progress at first. Tentative agreement to establish a *Nordostdeutsche Rundfunkanstalt* or NORA was reached by government representatives from Mecklenburg-West Pomerania, Brandenburg, and Berlin in April 1991, and in May the governors from the three southern states of Saxony, Saxon-Anhalt, and Thuringia signed a treaty forming the *Mitteldeutscher Rundfunk,* or MDR.

The *Mitteldeutscher Rundfunk* was a natural evolution. Bearing the name of the second oldest radio station in Germany (which began broadcasting in March 1924), it services a cohesive regional population of sufficient size (about 10.5 million) to make it economically viable. Just as importantly, however, the governments of the three states that formed it were politically compatible, being in general center-right and reflecting the mandate for swift and total union with the West. Consequently, the MDR developed expeditiously. Dr. Udo Reiter, who had held important broadcast policy and operational positions in Bavaria, was imported from the West to establish the organization and direct its operations. The MDR began broadcasting on 1 January 1992, operating two radio stations and producing a full Third television program within the ARD structure.

NORA foundered, however. In July 1991, the Mecklenburg-West

Pomeranian state legislature voted not to join Brandenburg and Berlin in forming a common corporation. Instead they opted to join the existing *Norddeutscher Rundfunk* (NDR) formed from the other north German states (minus Bremen). This decision left Berlin and Brandenburg. The logic and economic benefit of joint broadcasting operations between the two was evident to most observers, but disagreement on the modalities prevented combining institutions and operations. West Berlin itself already had a robust broadcasting capability in their *Sender Freies Berlin* (SFB) and, reinforced somewhat with assets from the *Einrichtung*, its operations were extended to formally embrace the entire city. Brandenburg opted not to join Berlin in a joint broadcasting organization. It established the *Ostdeutscher Rundfunk Brandenburg* (ORB) instead, tapping Hansjürgen Rosenbauer, also a Westerner, to set up the quite small operation. Given the state's small size and the heavy competition from Berlin which it surrounded, ORB was destined to operate on the margin financially and cooperates with SFB in many areas.

On 31 December 1991, as the *Einrichtung* broadcast its last television program, a New Years Eve gala, the final curtain rang down on what remained of the former GDR's broadcasting services. Since then, MDR has served the southern tier of states in the East and ORB the state of Brandenburg. Both are members of the expanded ARD system that now encompasses eleven state and regional broadcasting institutions throughout an enlarged FRG. Mecklenburg-West Pomerania's broadcasting effort is combined with those of its northern neighbors within the NDR, and SFB continues to serve the, now united, city-state of Berlin.

Assessment. As indicated earlier, a good deal of criticism has been leveled at the transition sketched above. Certainly for the Easterners who lost their jobs it was a traumatic life experience. Additionally, for the more senior GDR broadcasting professionals who continued work within the *Einrichtung*, it was a bitter pill to be in the second rank, behind Westerners during the process of disestablishing the old and creating the new institutions. And it seems evident that the executor's *modus operandi* did little to assuage these feelings; indeed it might well have exacerbated them.

On the other hand, criticism that the transition was simply a concerted takeover of the process by conservative, western politicians, who squandered or blocked chances to create other outcomes better suited to the eastern audience, misses the mark. During the tumultuous year leading to unification, the still functioning GDR government was unable to achieve internal consensus and pass the legislation necessary to comprehensively reform the country's broadcasting services while they still existed as such. Consequently, the March 1990 popular mandate for the quickest, most complete form of unity possible determined the fate not only of the GDR, but also of the state institutions it had created. Article 36 of the unification treaty was no more or less than the formal application of this mandate to the broadcasting sector. Wholesale conversion to the western model, not reform of the eastern, was the clearly mandated course.

Further, ultimate responsibility for the institutional arrangements that would mark the outcome of the conversion lay not with the executor of the *Einrichtung*, but with the governments of the six eastern states themselves. The outcome that was preferred by those who wanted to retain a vestige of GDR identity in the new broadcasting services, essentially establishing a single large operation consolidated from the old, was simply not feasible politically. Indeed, it proved impossible to achieve the interstate agreement necessary to establish joint operations among the three northern states themselves (Mecklenburg-West Pomerania, Brandenburg, and Berlin), an outcome that most considered the next best. Mühlfenzl tried hard to bring about NORA and to find a home for many of the most popular and successful GDR radio and television units.

On balance, the transition is best seen as being driven by the larger political dynamics underpinning and surrounding the revolution itself, dynamics created by the former GDR citizens themselves. Similarly, the reconstruction and configuration of the broadcasting services in the East after unification largely reflect the course of politics within and among the five new states that were formed on its territory, not decisions taken in Bonn. Western officials were involved in dismantling the old and creating the new broadcasting structures, but in the end it was the eastern voters themselves who set the terms for the transition. And, as discussed below, by and large they seem satisfied with what they got.

The Consumers--Competition and Technology

While the producers of broadcasting services in the East were profoundly affected by unification, the fusion of East and West itself had relatively little impact on what the radio and television audience consumed. What did have an impact, however, was the explosion of private broadcasting and the competition it generated. The dual broadcasting system, launched in the late 1980s, was in take-off mode as the 1990s began and it rapidly gained velocity. With it came dramatic change to the broadcasting environment throughout Germany. Before reviewing the outlines of this development and closing with an evaluation of how well the entire broadcasting effort has met the desires of the eastern audience, it is useful to further track the development of public sector broadcasting in the East.

The legal basis that formally incorporated the public broadcasting organizations and efforts in the five new states into that of a unified FRG was the "Interstate Treaty on Broadcasting in United Germany." Signed in August 1991 by representatives of all sixteen German states, it took effect on 1 January 1992, the day after the *Einrichtung* ceased to exist as a legal entity. Its provisions included agreements that added important policy flesh to the existing legal skeleton that established the dual public-private broadcasting system and coordinated the funding of all public broadcasting organizations.[47] At the same time, the five new states formed the state media institutions (*Landes-medienanstalten*), essentially state committees established to monitor and regulate broadcasting diversity in general and private broadcasting in particular.[48] In addition, Brandenburg and the three southeastern states organized broadcasting councils to oversee the new broadcasting services they had created, ORB and MDR respectively.[49]

As noted above, the states responsible for ORB and MDR had called on Westerners to direct their establishment and operations, and the new directors general, Hansjürgen Rosenbauer and Udo Reiter, brought with them selected advisors and assistants from the West as well. The policy of both, however, was to absorb as many Easterners as possible. Thus, for example, in October 1992, about ten months after beginning operations, ninety percent of MDR's 1,700 full-time employees were Easterners, as well as all of the trainees in the newly established apprentice program.[50] Although comprehensive, detailed data are lacking, the ninety percent eastern, ten percent western division of personnel appears to have been the rule in ORB as well--and this percentage appears to have remained relatively constant as the organizations grew in size, now about 600 for ORB and 2,100 for MDR.[51]

Thus, ORB, MDR, and SFB (serving a united Berlin) are the three public broadcasting corporations located in the eastern part of the country. Fully integrated into the ARD network, ORB and MDR contribute to its nationwide First television program and produce their own Third programs as well, as SFB continues to do. All three institutions produce or contribute to a range of radio programs broadcast nationally as well as within their respective regions or states. Meanwhile, ZDF, the centrally organized public corporation headquartered in Mainz and broadcasting the Second (public television) program, has extended its production facilities into the East, establishing a studio in each of the five new states. The cites selected were Magdeburg, Schwerin, Erfurt, Potsdam, and Dresden, and the practice was to renovate and use buildings protected as monuments because of their architectural or cultural value.[52]

The most significant changes in the broadcasting landscape were not primarily the result of the new public institutions, however. Rather, they were produced by the dramatic advance of private broadcasting and the competition it engendered. In 1990, less than a dozen privately produced radio programs were broadcast nationally in Germany along with six privately produced television programs. By mid-1996, the numbers had jumped to 34 and 18 respectively.[53] In addition to these nationally broadcast programs, 150 private radio, and 62 private television, stations are now broadcasting on a regional or local basis.[54] Not only has the number of private programs increased, but so has their diversity. Although weighted in the entertainment and sports sectors, the palette of programming offered by private broadcasters now embraces essentially all of the major program types, such as children's, all-news, travel, weather, and all-music programs.[55]

The consequences of this rapid growth of private broadcasting are profound. The audience share of public versus private television broadcasts (in the "old" FRG) dropped steadily from about seventy percent in 1990[56] to about forty percent in mid-1996.[57] The metamorphosis in radio was similar, though not as dramatic. Sensing a "war of annihilation,"[58] the major public broadcasters have reacted vigorously to this development. Publicly and politically they plead the case for continued public broadcasting that would not be held hostage to the market and the Mark; broadcasting that would guarantee a "wide offering of informative, educational and entertaining programs for majorities and minorities" that would be "freely accessible and receivable for everyone"[59]

Operationally, the two public broadcast networks have slimmed down budgets and increased cooperation. ARD and ZDF now collaborate in the programming and operation of four separate, specialized channels, as well as individual programs broadcast over their main channels.[60] In some cases, such as ARD-ZDF children's channel launched in 1997 and PHOENIX (similar in format to C-SPAN in the United States), they met private broadcasting head-on by adding channels designed to appeal to specific, limited segments of the potential audience.

Two diverging themes mark the continuing public debate and political contests throughout the FRG that are associated with the competition between public and private broadcasting. One theme emphasizes the responsiveness of private broadcasters to citizen demand. The other underscores the responsibility of public broadcasting for the broader societal good. Politically, the public-private issue is played out primarily at the state level and has resulted in a major revision to the 1991 state broadcasting treaty that took effect on 1 January 1997. Among a range of other provisions, the revision ensures continued public financing of the ARD and ZDF while, subject to a thirty percent audience share cap, removing the limits to the number of private radio and television stations or networks in which a single corporation can participate. Further, the individual state media committees are the source of private broadcasting licenses and determine which programs will be carried on the still generally limited capacity (23 channels) cable networks in their states. [61] Thus they have a strong influence on the public-private broadcasting mix within their jurisdictions.

In fact, the individual states reflect a diversity of approach to the public-private mix, but the differences do not appear on an East-West divide. With regard to radio, for example, the most competitive private markets are in Bavaria and Berlin-Brandenburg, and Brandenburg and Saxony have joined Baden-Wurttemburg, Bavaria and North Rhine-Westphalia in adopting a dual system of local and state-wide stations, while the other states envision adopting state-wide networks of stations.[62] Similar state-to-state differences reflecting the inclusion of private versus public television channels in state cable networks are evident. In this regard, however, the rule generally followed is to give first priority to stations that are receivable in the local area via terrestrial transmission without special antennae and second priority to those that can be received with improved antennae. The remaining capacity is then available for the inclusion of other stations.

Regardless of the orientation of individual state governments and media committees, technology is clearly conditioning the competition. While state governments can regulate terrestrial and cable transmission, there is little they can do to restrict citizens' access to programs broadcast by satellite. Further, as fiber-optic cable replaces the existing metal, the number of channels that can be included in the feed will expand dramatically, and consequently, it will be difficult for controlling bodies to justify excluding popular programs. Thus, as in the former GDR, regardless of politics or policy, the television audience in Germany, East as well as West, will get to watch the programs they want to watch.

The Eastern Audience:
Essentially Integrated and Satisfied

The world hates change, yet it is the only thing that has brought progress.
--Kettering

Change is one thing, progress another.
--Russell

How have eastern Germans reacted to the restructuring of public broadcasting institutions and to the onset of public-private competition? There was an initial flurry of individual protest at the loss of "our radio," and some observers arrived at the initial judgment that, with the possible exception of Brandenburg, the population in the East was being ill-served by the new broadcasters.[63] Nevertheless, the weight of evidence contradicts these assessments and indicates that eastern consumers are generally satisfied with the product offered by public broadcasters in their states, certainly as much, if not more so, as their countrymen to the West.

ORB had incorporated senior personnel from the former GDR broadcasting services into many of its top operational positions[64] and developed a reputation as the "Red Socks Broadcaster" in "Red Brandenburg,"[65] particularly in contrast to MDR formed in majority CDU states. On the other hand, MDR took in the production units of a number of the GDR's most successful radio and television programs and integrated them into its own efforts, some with more difficulty than others. For example, the struggle to retain the radio program *DT-64* became a *cause celebre* during the transition.[66] In any event, by 1995, MDR's Third television channel was by far the most successful in the area it served of the eight regional public channels in the FRG, while ORB's Third channel ranked sixth.[67]

More generally, the regionally produced Third television programs capture a larger percentage of the audience in the East than in the West,[68] and proportionally more eastern than western Germans (twenty-nine versus seventeen percent) identify them as their favorite stations.[69] Indeed, a broad examination of audience habits and opinions in the East[70] revealed positive opinions in 1994 of both ORB and MDR with, for example, 80 percent agreeing that both broadcasters produce "above all, programs by East Germans, for East Germans."[71] Similarly, 83 percent of eastern Germans surveyed thought that the public broadcasting stations informed them "completely and thoroughly about the day's developments," and 70 percent (versus only 60 percent in the West) agreed that the public stations had reporters and moderators who understood their work.[72]

The greater affinity for the regional, or Third, public television channels in the East is one of several clear differences between the television audience there and that in the West. Easterners continue to watch more television than Westerners,[73] a phenomenon noted during the GDR years, and a significantly greater percentage of Easterners receive their programs over satellite,[74] carrying forward a development that began in the late 1980s. And finally, it was noted that Easterners watched the ARD's and ZDF's main public channels less than

Westerners,[75] while evidencing a slightly greater preference for private television programs.[76]

Commentary accompanying the examination commissioned by ARD and ZDF that developed much of this data suggested that the viewers in the new states have a "greater requirement for entertainment; for programs that make life lighter and let one escape from every day life into the entertainment and fictional word of television."[77] Nevertheless, it is difficult to separate objective causes from such imputed psychological ones. For example, the population in the East is more rural and retired than that in the West and, for the most part, the data presented do not allow comparisons between these and other sociological groups. Moreover the data in the study disclosed numerous strong similarities in the opinions and preferences of the eastern and western audience. Significantly, it is clear that the primary cause for the decline in acceptance of public television's main programs in both the East and West was the strong competition from increasingly numerous and aggressive private broadcasters, a consideration that greatly overshadows a simple East-West division when describing the pan-German television audience.[78]

The picture of popular satisfaction with locally-produced public broadcasting is apparent in radio as well. For example, ORB's *Antenna Brandenburg* is by far the most popular radio station in the state, as is MDR's *Radio Sachsen* in Saxony,[79] and a 1993 study underscores the quick acceptance by youth of MDR's locally produced radio broadcasts.[80] Differences in audience acceptance of public versus private radio programs also reflect influences other than the East-West factor. Thus, while most states where public radio holds a higher market share than private stations are in the West, Saxony's is roughly equal to that in the Rheinland-Palatinate (respectively 54.7 and 56.1 percent) and the market share of Thuringia equals that of Hesse (53 percent).[81]

On balance, and apart from the lives of those east Germans who were directly and personally caught up in the disestablishment of the GDR institutions where they worked, the books can be closed on the impact unification has had on broadcasting in eastern Germany. The modalities of production there have been transformed and are fully integrated with those in the rest of the country. If unique "socially valuable" qualities were lost in the process,[82] they do not seem to have been missed by most, and eastern consumers appear satisfied with the outcome. As before the *Wende*, Easterners are listening to and watching essentially the same programming as their fellow citizens in the West, and differences in the eastern and western audiences are overshadowed by the commonalties.

The major issues associated with broadcasting in Germany today do not stem from an East-West divide. They are rooted in the explosion of communications technology and the advent of public-private competition in the country at large. Technology and public-private competition have introduced revolutionary change in the broadcasting landscape over the past decade, and the synergism between them, together with the increasing importance of the international dimension in broadcasting politics, will frame the next chapters of broadcasting change within the country.

Notes

1. Arbeitsgemeinschaft der öffentlich-rechtlichen Rundfunkanstalten der Bundesrepublik Deutschland, *ARD Jahrbuch 96* (Hamburg: Hans Bredow Verlag, 1996), p. 173.

2. When used with regard to radio and television, the German word *"Programm"* and the English word "program" can cause confusion. The German *Programm* is more nearly equivalent to the English channel or station, which of course broadcasts a number of individual "programs." This paper generally uses "channel," "station," or "network" where a German text would use *Programm*.

3. As of July 1996. Ten of the stations with programming available nationwide were public, including six producing regional "Third" programs that were also available nationally via satellite. Eighteen were private broadcasters. The regional or local stations include the other two public Third programs and sixty-two private ones. Arbeitsgemeinschaft der Landesmedienanstalten in der Bundesrepublik Deutschland (ALM*)*, *ALM Jahrbuch der Landesmedienanstalten: 1995-1996* (Munich: Verlag Reinhard Fischer, 1996), pp. 251-252, and 343.

4. *Ibid.*, pp. 253, 257; 254-255.

5. As of 1 December 1996. On average, the approximately 27 percent of households with satellite antennae have access to 60 channels, the 57 percent with cable 29, and the remaining 17 percent that depend on terrestrial transmission, 7 channels. Arbeitsgemeinschaft der öffentlich-rechtlichen Rundfunkanstalten der Bundesrepublik Deutschland, *ARD Jahrbuch: 97* (Hamburg: Hans Bredow Verlag, 1997), pp. 162, 378.

6. The framework of the FRG's broadcasting (and print) media is sketched in Georg Hellack, Basis-INFO 13-1996: Press, Radio, and Television in the Federal Republic of Germany (Bonn: Inter Nationes, 1966), in English and German versions. Hermann Meyn's, *Massenmedien in der Bundesrepublik Deutschland* (Berlin: Wissenschaftsverlag Volker Spiess, 1996), covers essentially the same ground but in greater depth, highlighting associated political and sociological issues and debates. The operations of the state and regional public broadcasting corporations, the nation-wide public television corporation, and private broadcasters are reviewed in considerable detail in annual "yearbooks" published by the ARD, ZDF, and ALM (see notes 1, 52 and 3 respectively). These

annual publications also include considerable data on audience reaction and technical developments and address the key policy issues facing each group of broadcasters. Additionally, both ARD and ZDF have www. home pages. ARD's connects to those of its state-regional components, which vary considerably in quality and usefulness. *Medienbericht '94*, [note 9] published by the FRG Press and Information Office, the latest of four that have been published since 1970, is a massive compilation of data and legal information addressing all aspects of the broadcast and print media.

7. *Die Tageszeitung* (Berlin), 5 September 1985.

8. ARD is the commonly used abbreviation for the nationally organized co-operative of the eleven regional and state public broadcasting corporations (the *Arbeitsgemeinschaft der öffentlich-rechtlichen Rundfunkanstalten der Bundesrepublik Deutschland*) in the FRG. Six of these organizations operate their own regional television channel, known as the local Third Program, while the other five cooperate to produce two more. They also pool their efforts to produce the programming broadcast nationally over the ARD network, known as the First Program, and they operate the country's public radio stations. The ZDF (*Zweites Deutsches Fernsehen* or Second German Television) is a public broadcasting corporation organized in 1961 and headquartered in Mainz that operates a nation-wide television network known as the Second Program.

9. The court case arose from pilot television cable projects that were launched in Ludwigshafen, Munich, Dortmund and Berlin in 1994-95. Presse- und Informationsamt der Bundesregierung, *Medienbericht '94* (Bonn: Bonner Universitäts-Buchdruckerei, 1994), p. 144.

10. The *Triale* concept embraces public broadcasters financed by public funds and advertisement, commercial private broadcasters, and broadcasters offering specialized services for a fee to small groups, Albert Scharf, "Vernetzen statt versparten," *ARD Jahrbuch: 1996*, p. 14.

11. Average for 1996, *ARD Jahrbuch: 1997*, p. 377.

12. Richard L. Merritt, "Normalizing the East German Media," *Political Communication*, Vol. 11, No. 1 (January 1994), p. 52

13. Richard Kilborn, "The New Face of German Broadcasting," *Debatte*, No. 2 (1994), p. 119.

14. The GDR Academy of Sciences *et. al., Information GDR*, Vol. 2 (New York: Pergamon Press, 1989), p. 561.

15. In 1990, East Germans watched, on average, just over one-half hour of television more per week than Westerners, *Medienbericht '94*, p. 262.

16. The DFF followed the lead of the Soviet Union when it adopted the French SECAM color system, and West German television used their own PAL system. By the 1980s, however, the technical incompatibility introduced by these different systems was largely overcome in that East German citizens could, if they wanted, buy converters as well as sets with dual system capability. West German television was also reformatting some of its color programs for broadcast to the East. See for example Rolf Geserick, *40 Jahre Presse, Rundfunk und Kommunikationspolitik in der DDR* (Munich: K.G. Saur Verlag, 1989), p. 373. Even by 1985

less than forty percent of East German households were equipped to watch color programming, Staatliche Zentralverwaltung für Statistik, *Statistishes Jahrbuch der Deutschen Demokratischen Republik*, Vol. 38 (Berlin: GDR, 1986), p. 281.

17. For example, Helmut Hanke provides a succinct overview of the reasons why audiences in the GDR "used" the FRG's radio and television programs "more than the eastern programs," in "Kommunikation in Aufruhr--Medien im Wandel," *Rundfunk und Fernsehen*, Vol. 38, No. 3 (1990), pp. 299-322. Kurt R. Hesse in "Ständiges Puzzlespiel" addresses the use by East Germans of West German news and journal programs, "up to 85 percent were regular viewers," and Dieter Wiedermann analyzes the heavy predominance of western type entertainment programming broadcast by the DFF in "Westprodukte auf Ostkanälen," both in *Unsere Medien; Unsere Republik, 1987: Auf ewig gute Nachbarn*, No. 7 (October 1993), pp. 34-36 and 37-39 respectively.

18. See note 8. Since unification, viewers throughout the FRG can access multiple Third programs from different regions via cable and satellite.

19. Timothy Garton Ash, "East Germany: The Solution," *The New York Review of Books*, 26 April 1990, p. 14.

20. The GDR leadership's effort to cope with West German television over the years is examined in detail in Rolf Geserick, *40 Jahre Presse*, and Joseph E. Naftzinger, "Policy-Making in the German Democratic Republic: The Response to West German Trans-border Television Broadcasting," Ph.D. diss., University of Maryland, 1994.

21. Walter Ulbricht quoted in Hans Müncheberg and Peter Hoff (eds.), "Experiment Fernsehen: Vom Laborversuch zur sozialistischen Massenkunst," *Podium und Werkstatt*, Vol. 15, No. 16 (Berlin: Verband der Film und Fernsehschaffenden der DDR, 1984), p. 87.

22. A succinct overview of this metamorphosis from an insider's view point is in Peter Hoff, "Von 'Da lacht der Bär' über 'Ein Kessel Buntes'--ins 'Aus,' " in Heide Riedel (ed.), *Mit uns zieht die neue Zeit . . . 40 Jahre DDR-Medien* (Berlin: VISTAS Verlag, 1994), pp. 86-94.

23. Paradoxically, when it changed the picture-tone frequency separation in 1955, the SED leadership actively sought and encouraged the ensuing competition, confidently seeking to propagate their message to as many Germans as possible. Peter Ludes (ed.), *DDR-Fernsehen intern* (Berlin: Wissenschaftsverlag Volker Spies, 1990), provides a multifaceted view of the DFF's struggles with news and journalistic programs just before the revolution.

24. A good thumbnail sketch of the East German broadcasting media in the late 1980s is in Gunter Holzweissig, *Massenmedien in der DDR* (Berlin: Verlag Gebr. Holzapfel, 1989).

25. The outlines and tone of the debate are apparent in the transcript of "Workshop 11.1.1993: Einrichtung and Abwicklung" in Riedel, *Mit uns zieht die neue Zeit*, pp. 286-99, and in the articles and discussion in Walter A. Mahle (ed.), *AKM-Studien: Medien im vereinten Deutschland: Nationale und internationale Perspektiven* Vol. 37 (Munich: 1991). Summary views in English include Merritt, "Normalizing the East German Media;" Kilborn, "The New Face of German

Broadcasting;" and John Sandford, "The Transformation of the Media in East Germany since the *Wende*," *Journal of Area Studies*, No. 2 (1993), pp. 25-36.

26. See for example Heinz Odermann, "Der Umbruch und die Mediengesetz-gebung in der DDR," *Rundfunk und Fernsehen*, Vol. 38, No. 3 (1990), p. 378. Of the numerous sources addressing this development, the collection of documents and statements in Ingrid Pietrzynski (ed.), *Radio im Umbruch: Oktober 1989 bis Oktober 1990 im Rundfunk der DDR* (Berlin: Funkhaus Berlin, October 1990), is particularly informative.

27. For example, in June 1990 the deputy director of the Rundfunk der DDR saw the need for a "*drastic* personnel reduction," (italics added). Quoted in Walter A. Mahle (ed.), *AKM-Studien: Medien in Deutschland: Nationale und internationale Perspektiven*, Vol. 32 (1990), p. 77.

28. Documented in Walter J. Schütz, "Der (gescheiterte) Regierungsentwurf für ein Rundfunküberleitungsgesetz der DDR: Chronik und Dokumente," in Arnulf Kutsch, *Rundfunk im Wandel: Beitraege zur Medienforschung* (Berlin: VISTAS Verlag, 1992).

29. For example, Wernfried Maltusch, then director of *Radio DDR*, "It follows, that the old top echelon in the central radio can only be eliminated by liquidating this radio," quoted in Kurt R. Hesse, "Fernsehen in Revolution: Zum Einfluss der Westmedien auf die politische Wende in der DDR," *Rundfunk und Fernsehen*, Vol. 38, No. 3 (1990), p. 341.

30. A thumb-nail sketch is in Wernfried Maltusch, "Deutsch-deutsche Inter-dependenzen bei der Demokratisierung des Rundfunks in der DDR" in Mahle, *AKM-Studien*, Vol. 32 (1991), pp. 77-83.

31. For example, the East German journalist Helmut Hartung reported, "[In early 1990] the majority of the journalists even in television argued for a measured approach to German unity, for a process spanning several years." Then after the 18 March elections, "We proved that we were no less useful than ARD or ZDF, when we used the chances and possibilities. But time was too short to pursue this change in all areas, and with all consequences." In Ludes, *DDR-Fernsehen intern*, pp. 345 and 348.

32. The irony of creating a highly centralized instrument to "dissolve centralized institutions" was not lost on some observers. Edith Spielhagen, "Öffentlich rechtlicher Rundfunk in den neuen Bundesländern," in Mahle, *AKM-Studien*, Vol. 37 (1991), p. 47.

33. See Sandford, "The Transformation of the Media," p. 32, for details of how the FRG government put its man in the position.

34. Rudolf Mühlfenzl, "Auftrag und Wirken der *Einrichtung*," *BARO-MEDIA*, No. 1 (1996), p. 9.

35. Peter Schiwy, "Verpasste Chancen--Neue Sender in alten Schuhen," Mahle, *AKM-Studien*, Vol. 37 (1991), p. 37; and Kilborn, "The New Face of German Broadcasting," pp. 102 and 103.

36. Almost all East German journalists had graduated from the University of Leipzig, where the "party line" was the basis for instruction and study. Consequently, the collapse of the socialist system was a difficult psychological

challenge for many and elicited an almost infinite variety of individual responses. A good introduction to the considerable literature that addresses this topic is the collection of interviews broadcast in a 1996 series by *Deutschland-Radio Berlin* in Willi Steul (ed.), *Genosse Journalist: Eine Sendereihe im Deutschland-Radio Berlin* (Mainz: Donata Kinzelbach Verlag, 1996).

37. Mühlfenzl, "Auftrag und Wirken," BAROMEDIA, p. 11.

38. Rudolf Mühlfenzl in "Rundfunk im Aufbruch: Erste Bilanz," brochure produced by Pressesprecher des Rundfunkbeauftragten (Berlin, 1991), p. 11.

39. The interview with Günter Gaus in *Berliner Zeitung*, 23-24 November 1991, p. 35 provides a sample of the critique.

40. Mühlfenzl, "Auftrag und Wirkung," p. 13.

41. Joachim F. Leonhard, "Programmvermögen und kulturelles Erbe: Die Rundfunkarchive Ost im Deutschen Rundfunkarchiv," *Deutschland Archiv*, Vol. 28, No. 4 (April 1995), pp. 404-10. One exception to the DRA's former GDR broadcasting holdings is the archive of press clippings which is at Leipzig University's institute for communication and media science.

42. A fifth, Radio Berlin International, designed to represent the GDR to foreign audiences, ceased operations the day before unification. Its frequencies were given to West German stations, which hired twenty-one of RBI's employees. *Medienbericht, 94*, p. 148.

43. A detailed discussion of the evolving changes in the news and journalistic efforts of the DFF from October 1989 to October 1990, is in Ludes, *DDR-Fernsehen intern*. In Ludes' view, November 1989 marked the beginning of significant change in direct influence by the party leadership, p. 55. Pietrzynski, *Radio im Umbruch*, documents similar change in the East German Radio establishment.

44. Data are from Reinhard Schlinkert, "Mediennutzung in den neuen Bundesländern," in Mahle, *AKM-Studien*, Vol. 37 (1991), pp. 62 and 66.

45. Including Singelnstein in Riedel, *Mit uns zieht die neue Zeit*, pp. 292 and 293.

46. A detailed examination of the state-level politics surrounding the creation of the new broadcasting institutions, especially the failed NORA project is in Gunnar Tödt, "Das gescheiterte Drei-Länder-Rundfunk-Project, NordOstdeutscher Rundfunk," *Diplomarbeit*, presented to the political science faculty of the Free University, Berlin (1 September 1995).

47. Among the more important provisions, the continued existence of the public corporations was "guaranteed" while private broadcasters were granted the sender capacity and advertising potential necessary to compete with public corporations, Meyn, *Massenmedien in der Bundesrepublik Deutschland*, p. 118.

48. These state institutions are intended to represent a diversity of societal groups and most contain twenty or more representatives. Brandenburg and Berlin, however, decided to pool their institution, with each state electing three representatives, and a seventh by two-thirds majority of both legislatures. Thus there are fifteen such institutions in the FRG, *Medienbericht*, p. 156.

49. Both the state media institutions or committees and the broadcasting councils are ultimately responsible to the elected state governments. Consequently, this has raised the charge of political influence. See, for example, Meyn, *Massenmedien in der Bundesrepublik Deutschland*, p. 116. It should be also pointed out, however, that the influence of political parties nation-wide is mitigated by the diverse party governments of the sixteen state governments that form these bodies.

50. Mitteldeutscher Rundfunk, press release, "Hier Sender Leipzig - Absichten und Erfahrung beim Aufbau" (19 October 1992).

51. Arno Kappler (ed.), *Facts About Germany* (Frankfurt: Societäts-Verlag, 1996), p. 443.

52. Zweites Deutsches Fernsehen, *ZDF Jahrbuch: 95* (Mainz: Zweites Deutsches Fernsehen, 1996), p. 178.

53. *ALM Jahrbuch: 1995-96*, pp. 251, 385.

54. *Ibid.*, pp. 343, 385.

55. Well beyond the scope of this chapter, the explosive growth in private broadcasting in Germany from essentially a zero start a decade ago is a story that deserves careful examination. Two major themes to that story are the noticeable concentration of private broadcasting within a few highly competitive media conglomerates and the strong ties to foreign, especially U.S., broadcasting and entertainment firms such as the Disney corporation.

56. Landesmedienanstalten, *DLM Jahrbuch der Landesmedienanstalten 1993-94* (Munich: Verlag Reinhard Fischer, 1994), p. 536

57. *ALM Jahrbuch: 1995-96*, p. 261. However, indications are that the public broadcaster's loss of market share, particularly in radio, has stabilized.

58. Dieter Stolte, "Von Markt zur Marke," *ZDF Jahrbuch: 1995*, p. 45.

59. Albert Scharf, "Vernetzen statt versparten," *ARD Jahrbuch: 96*, p. 14.

60. ARTE, the European cultural channel has been operated by ARD, ZDF, and French television since May 1992.

61. There are significant exceptions to the general cable pattern in the FRG, particularly in the new states. For example, in Saxony-Anhalt the majority of cable networks are owned by middle-sized private corporations and are of significantly greater capacity than those laid by German Telekom. *ALM Jahrbuch: 1995-96*, p. 226.

62. *Ibid.*, p. 52.

63. See in particular, Kilborn, "The New Face of German Broadcasting," pp. 111 and 115.

64. Notably Christoph Singelnstein, who had been director general of the GDR radio and became chief editor of Radio Brandenburg, and Michael Albrecht, the last chief of the DFF, who directed television production. (In 1997, Albrecht became the executive responsible for guiding ARD's digital television efforts.)

65. Hannelore Steer, in an interview with Norbert Wassmund, in Steul, *Genosse Journalist*, p. 159.

66. Born as a special service radio program that played 99 hours of non-stop, live, and internationally popular music for the all-German youth festival hosted by the GDR in 1964, *DT-64* developed a reputation as being more "modern" and

less doctrinaire than the norm for East German radio. It did survive the *Wende* and, under the name *MDR-Sputnik,* now broadcasts nationally over satellite in digitized format from a studio in Halle. A detailed chronology is available from their world wide web site.

67. In terms of market share of viewers older than three years, *ARD Jahrbuch: 96,* p. 96

68. *Ibid.,* p. 397.

69. Edith Spielhagen, "Ergebnisse der Ost-Studie der ARD/ZDF-Medien-kommission," *Media Perspektiven,* No. 8 (1995), p. 382.

70. "Ost-Studie: Zuschauererwartungen und -reaktionen in den neuen Ländern." The results are reported in *Ibid.,* pp. 362-392 .

71. *Ibid.,* p. 389.

72. *Ibid.,* pp. 370, 389.

73. The difference in 1996 was forty-five minutes, *ARD Jahrbuch: 97,* p. 379.

74. Sixty-three percent to fifteen percent in 1994, *DLM Jahrbuch: 1993-94,* p . 491.

75. *ARD Jahrbuch: 96,* p. 175.

76. In the East, 57 percent identified an ARD or ZDF program as one of their (three) favorites, versus 63 percent of the Westerners. Similarly, a private program was among the three favorites of 79 percent of Easterners contrasted with 67 percent of Westerners. Spielhagen, "Ost-Studie," p. 882.

77. Hansjürgen Rosenbauer, "Die doppelte Öffentlichkeit," *Media Perspektiven,* No. 8 (1995), p. 358.

78. *Ibid.*

79. *Radio Sachsen's* sisters, *Radio Thüringen* and *Radio Saxon-Anhalt,* are in essentially two- and three-way ties in their states, however, *ALM Jahrbuch - 1995-96,* pp. 412, 421, 423, and 425.

80. In 1987, in Saxony and Saxon-Anhalt, only eighteen percent of 13-to-17 year-olds identified at least one program "from the new lands" (meaning the former GDR) as their favorite. Already by 1992 that percentage had increased to sixty-three. Closer analysis of the data shows that the great bulk of the increase stemmed from MDR broadcasts. *DLM Jahrbuch: 93-94,* p. 166.

81. *ALM Jahrbuch: 1995-96,* p. 427.

82. Merritt, "Normalizing the East German Media," p. 63.

11

Literature as Social Memory: On the Role of Literature in the New German States[1]

Klaus   Hammer

Christoph Hein, when asked what he now considers himself, an ex-GDR writer or a German writer, answered:

Hein: Anna Seghers and Heinrich Böll were all-German writers. With the beginning of my generation, something else has developed. Botho Strauß, for example, my age, has different experiences, a different background than I. That did not change on October third. We will come closer to each other; we, of course, more so than they over there. I will collect a few West German experiences. Botho Strauß, on the other hand, will probably not make any East German ones. Regardless, I will most likely go to my grave as a GDR writer. Or as an East German writer. The year 1968 simply formed us differently in the East and in the West. What were the student revolts in the West compared to the events in Prague?
Interviewer: Was there such a thing as GDR literature, or was it just a branch of German literature?
Hein: GDR literature was a branch of German literature. Nonetheless, I think that a West German as well as a GDR literature, i.e., an East German literature, existed, and that among those living now there will continue to be such a difference as long as there are differences between these parts of the country. Of course, West German authors do not feel as if they form a special branch of German literature. They always understood themselves as Germans.[2]

The Debate Surrounding the German Question

"There will always be problems. The debate surrounding the German question is just beginning," predicted Ulrich Greiner in *Die Zeit* already in December 1989. The literature debate was sparked by Christa Wolf's story *Was bleibt* (Engl. *What Remains)* and was given further life by the Stasi (state security service) entanglements of authors of the autonomous literary scene of the eighties. There are the experiences of those who left, or had to leave the GDR, and of those who stayed and tried to withdraw themselves from the ideological demands. The experiences of the older authors who had to abandon their ideals and utopias, and those of the young ones who had no interest in these ideals.

Did a literary opposition and autonomy actually exist in the GDR? Could the concept of abandoning the language of the state as well as no longer reacting antipodally to it succeed as an alternative concept in this closed circle, (not) knowing that the Stasi was always present? Were not authors who remained available to their audience virtually irreplaceable in understanding one's own identity and gaining sense from the life of waiting. Did not literature also create unrest and implant doubt and contradictions so that without it the fall of 1989 would not have transpired at the same speed and with the same consequence? Should literature in this part of Germany disappear into an anonymity which levels all its exceptional qualities, or should it remain recognizable as it is, the memory and conscience of East Germany?

Literature Will Expose the Blind Spots

In her acceptance speech for an honorary doctorate from the University of Heidelsheim in 1990, Christa Wolf stated: "Literature will have to accomplish what it always and everywhere has to achieve. It will have to expose the blind spots in our past and accompany the people into the new conditions. Every attempt at self-denial would destroy creativity at its roots."

To call one example to memory: Volker Braun's novel *Hinze und Kunze,* already printed, had to be repressed at first. Then, despite resistance "from above," it came out in 1985 with the "reader's assistance" of a well-known GDR literary scholar--a masterpiece of literary diplomacy. However, the still available copies (there were none, however) already delivered to the bookstores, had to be returned to the Leipzig commission and the wholesaler. In the novel, the worker

Hinze, a chauffeur *(der Fahrer)*, drives the car of Kunze, the driven *(des Gefahrenen)*, a party member with a high position. Hinze waits outside in the car for Kunze "like an insect in the shiny box," while he is inside practicing politics. "Hinze, with whom we are waiting outside, withdrew himself from anything further to be on the safe side (for our readership is numerous, uncontrolled, and not completely competent)." Movement happens only externally. Braun is interested in the distanced model of a relationship between the driven *(dem Geführten)*, Hinze, and the driver *(dem Führenden)*, Kunze. Possible movements can be derived from this model, but exclusively by the reader, if she proves knowledgeable, mature, and integrated into the movement and not in the stagnation of real, existing socialism. Then, strong protest is possible where the novel is concerned, above all with regard to the pair of characters, one of whom allows everything to be done to him.

In his novel, Braun keeps tabs on the critic, Ms. Professor Messerle, and the literature she defends. The critic demanded a book from author B that author N had just written. "She couldn't get enough similar books, exemplary ones. She likely put them in the living room nearby, a secure bastion against the insecure reality." The author N, argues the critic, had the right pattern *(Strickmuster)*. He showed, namely, that the conditions were good and that the people simply had to be adjusted to them, for which all means were justified.

Braun, who already in his early poetry exposed the open ends of history (discovered through his prose in the 1970's as one of the first) the "most stirring contradiction" which had developed between the political leaders and the led. He arrived early at the core of social and political contradictions which he tried to capture with his conflicts. He wanted to strengthen the appetite for democracy of those who had little power. That led him, like others, into constantly new involvements with the powers, and these required much cunning to withstand. The old contradiction between spirit and power *(Geist und Macht)* which run through German history had not only regenerated itself once again, but it came even more pointedly to light than at many other times. But it was exactly these social tensions which challenged the authors who did not want to abandon their ideal, their utopia of all people living together with equal rights.

The situation often bordered on the unbearable. It destroyed authors like Werner Bräunig who, in 1959, coined the phrase "Take to the pen, friends!" and was terribly discriminated against at the eleventh SED (Socialist Unity Party) plenum because of his unvarnished representation of the world of miners. Authors like Christa Wolf, Volker Braun, and Erwin Strittmatter created their aesthetic by withstanding these contradictions. With Christa Wolf it was entwined around the attempt to change the individual morally, and thus to change society. For Braun, the individual was to arrive at a changed behavior, while Strittmatter put the focus on insight into the nature of man. As different as these individual writers are, they all lead to an aesthetic of resistance and to the protection of individual rights.

The Strategies of "Writing the Truth"

Volker Braun wanted to be humorous in his brilliant philosophical satire--"in the lightest manner of our existence, art." But art, it continues, does not directly follow life: "one has to read around the corner." The artistic strategies in "writing the truth" (Bertolt Brecht) varied in the literature of the GDR. The art of both speaking with a disguised voice and reading around the corner were connected with the moral duty of replacing "gagged" journalism and restrained public discourse with art. According to Jurek Becker, all GDR literature was created under censorship. Ties through friction serve as motivation for Christa Wolf's writing, and, for Fritz Rudolf Fries as well, writing is always criticism of the conditions. Thomas Brasch remarks sarcastically: "One either follows the censorship and goes under the borders, or one fools them. Then you become the superfool." "Writing in the GDR was and is a kind of steeplechase," said Stefan Heym when asked about his experience working on his autobiography *Nachruf* (lit. "Obituary," trans.). "If you write something that the reader understands and the censor cannot find anything which gives reason for intervention, that is art, and that is fun." Many authors made it their goal to use the language of power only in its superficial structure, and thus to have made fools of the instruments of the power apparatus and brought "secret messages" to the people, as Fritz Rudolf Fries describes. The author, dissimulated and puzzled, constructed his work according to the model of anagram or palimpsest, labyrinth or rebus, and the initiated reader puzzled over and deciphered them.

The need for "getting rid of contradictions" motivated the writing of Heiner Müller. "If one is an object of the story, one needs other figures in order to speak about problems." Doing that required a form which made expression possible through roles and masks: the "dramatic" text and, increasingly, the "theatrical" text. "I can say one thing, and I can say the opposite." Christoph Hein, though, rejected the attempt at a functionalization of literature to the ends of a conspiratorial communication through the "slave language." He insisted on the desire to write and demanded this freedom--unlimited publicity (*uneinge-*

schränkte Öffentlichkeit)--for all. His piece, *Der Ritter der Tafelrund* (Engl. The Knights of the Round Table), which appeared in Spring 1989, was understood in East and West as a farewell to the aged round table of surviving SED rule. And yet the myth of King Arthur and his courtly community did not serve as a cloaked "hideout" for the author. What was to be shown was the fall of a myth which consisted only of the clichés and set pieces of a standardized ideal. Destruction is heralded as the prerequisite of freedom, the abandonment of all viewpoints, even the renunciation of previous literary principles. The future demands an oath of disclosure and is uncertain in the literal sense.

Literature, which was subsidized like a basic food in the GDR, always ran the risk of singing the song of those whose bread it ate. The responsible speaking and writing, indeed the over-responsibility of the authors, did not exclude over-identification with the state--with a state which saw itself as anti-fascist and socialist, in other words, as a moral state which strove to integrate its population into its morals. And there was indeed also--who would want to deny it--the perfectly honest attempt to partially bring to life the dream of the community of socialist solidarity which lived in many works of art. In a space, argued Rolf Schneider, "which was guarded by overanxious censors and mistrustful rulers," art was attributed "an importance it did not have." Schneider is speaking directly of a complicity of the arts with the dictatorship: "The public delegated to the arts its spiritual need. The arts served the public in that they more or less clearly formulated this need and offered help in articulation. Such a partnership of convenience . . . was created with need and lie as its background and, as a result, could be little more than a doubtful provisional arrangement."

Ulrich Plenzdorf also sees himself as standing before the ruins: "We were used for the image of the GDR in the same way as the top athletes and, in return, we raked in material wealth and privileges." He sarcastically commented on the unspoken but established "rules of the game:" at a reading, Schelte followed the state censor, who, in turn, was used for literature, and this found resonance in East and West. Was such a double game, a paradoxical strategy which simultaneously created as well as restricted freedom, the only chance for an author who wanted to remain in the GDR?

A Special Personality Type:
Full of Neuroses and Lacking in Deed

From Volker Braun's *Unvollendete Geschichte* (lit. "Unfinished Story," trans.), written already in 1974, through Christoph Hein's *Der Fremde Freund* (Engl. *The Distant Lover*) to Christa Wolf's *Sommer-*

stück, GDR literature tried its hand in analyses of real, everyday life processes. It problematized and took leave of previous ways of life and life concepts. The deficiencies of their life situations were brought to the readers' consciousness, and surely the articulation of loss of meaning aroused defenses (most texts saw themselves in this warning capacity). These stories--experiment descriptions, test reports, artificial games-- could be read as nightmares and imaginary fears, alienation and loneliness, concern and threat, longing for happiness and missed happiness. They were like micro-sociological stock-taking, the results of which revealed largely unfulfilled life plans. People recognize the "insignificance of their existence" (Helga Königsdorf), the (East) German full of neuroses and lacking in deed. Those, who like Luisa in Christa Wolf's *Sommerstück,* are forced to mimetically become like any common person *(einer jeden Natur),* see their identity disappear into an external appearance. The mask, the disguise, be-comes nature again, becomes the only weapon they possess with which to defend themselves. But does not this mask only protect their own appearance, or is there really, as Ellen feels, an "intangible remnant" that eludes every intervention, even that of the infinitely repeated destruction?

Thinking in the category of negation took the place of the demand for new movement. Heiner Müller's *Bildbeschreibung* (lit. "Description of a Picture," trans.) contains a sequence whose semantic describes the horror of repetition, the déjà-vu-experience, the illusory movement in the eternal sameness. Müller ends this passage with a linguistic "emergency exit": "the gap in the development, the other in the repetition, the stuttering in the speechless text, the perhaps liberating mistake." The discovery of a mistake in the mechanism, standstill, or development would be the chance for the subject's own liberation and the chance of art for freedom.

Works of GDR literature have not only yielded results and analyses, but have also helped prepare the future, contribute to the change and renewal of life, and promote courage for taking risks, for following new paths, and for pursuing unfamiliar ways of thinking. At the extraordinary Writers' Congress in March 1990, Christa Wolf spoke retrospectively of how writers spoke on behalf of others "because no other institution expressed the contradictions which ever deeper tore this country, and because it often would have cost the others more dearly than the writers if they had spoken." In order to form their own opinions, many people obtained their information from the art and literature in which they found their difficulties and hopes articulated. That lent many authors their significance as the mouthpieces of their readers. With their literature they contributed to creating among the people a consciousness of societal contradictions. Without this common consensus the events of Autumn 1989 would not have taken place with the same consequence and at the same breath-taking speed.

Günter de Bruyn sees the preparatory function of literature in this way:

> For years literature has performed preliminary work in its--the intellectual--field. The strength of its effect is naturally difficult to measure but it was there. That other phenomena were at work in triggering the actual events in October and November (1989) does not at all speak against this perhaps necessary groundwork. The French writers of the eighteenth century also did not storm the Bastille, but that they helped sound the horn, for the storming cannot be disputed.

During the "peaceful revolution," when they placed themselves at the forefront of the protest movement and the people listened to their words with hot hearts, East German authors were still considered to have moral authority. Soon enough they lost their position as the heralders of repressed truths, their function as representatives, their role as mouthpieces--to the public *(an der Öffentlichkeit)*.

The people of the GDR had reconquered the right to speak for themselves, and they seemingly had no use for their writers anymore. The theaters and galleries were empty, the books of the authors were no longer sold, the literati became mute and silent. They were now once again alone with themselves and their pieces of paper. Thomas Brasch said that writers are not duty-bound to be morally impeccable people, but rather much more "to write about the rift which is going through society and through themselves." If no one expects anything of writers anymore (and until now too much was expected of them, readers expected something different than "authority"), if there is hardly a word spoken about the political and moral norms of an author, if the author is once again fully alone with himself and his imagination, then this does indeed represent a significant change in the social function of literature, a change which occurred long ago in West Germany.

If the sworn community of those secretly exchanging messages--the image of writers' readings before the *Wende* in 1989--had been discharged into the public sphere, then this sworn society could reconvene under different circumstances than as a team of knowledgeable literary specialists. Then it would no longer be the censor and the political dictatorship which unified them, but rather literary communication at a high level. The poetic quality of works could then be reevaluated, and not only the political statements of authors. In their texts which were published after the *Wende*, the "examination of conscience" *(Gewissensprüfung)*--of victim, perpetrator, and accomplice--took place. This occurred in stories of people with their contradictions and their meanness; in the many examples of composure, human dignity, and solidarity; and in their illusions and horrible tragedies. The painful process of reckoning has long begun.

Can One Write in a New Language?

Christa Wolf's *What Remains,* the story of a writer under Stasi observation, was taken by many critics in the West to be a complaint against the privileged system in the GDR after the fall of that system--a system which had particularly honored her. For the critics, it was not Wolf, but rather the rigorously persecuted who had a right to speak. Was this text, however, which had originated in 1979, but was reworked only in 1989 and published in Spring 1990, really an autobiographical report, a document of justification to which the sharp edges were belatedly added? The narrating figure is a fictitious person, not to be confused with the author, Christa Wolf.

The personal assurance at the beginning, to not be afraid, is tied to the hope of being able to write in a new language which opposed the power of the institutions and thus retained a human future. These imploring words are part of a fictional text. They should transplant the reader into a fictive present in which fear rules to a "morning in March." The observation had already begun more than two years before the day portrayed and serves as an opportunity for the narrator to remember back to the beginnings of her desperate loss of orientation. On this day, however, when the alienation, hopelessness, and emptiness become particularly perceptible, a new language cannot yet be found. For that, certain attitudes must first change: for instance, the certain "arrogance" tied to her privileged status which simultaneously protects her from and makes her susceptible to the extortions of the system; "the alienation which separated me from the masses," but at the same time "separated the masses from themselves;" and other things. In addition, there are characters that contrast with the narrator, such as the young woman who is herself a writer and has already been in jail as a result of her convictions. She "did not belong to the blackmailable" and "did not ask petty-mindedly: "What remains."" She has no status that protects her and spares her from much.

Volker Braun Ruthlessly Settles Accounts

No East German author accused himself more ruthlessly of prolonging the catastrophe as a "social romantic" *(Sozialromantiker)* than Volker Braun in his dialog prose text, *Der Wendehals* (lit. "The Neck-Turner," trans.).[3] The Brechtian theorem that one should not present us with finished works, but rather that we (the audience) should be forced to participate, finally becomes caught in the bitter truth that "all art was in vain." Braun's works were repeatedly censored by the GDR authorities and already in Spring 1988 his play *Die Übergangsgesellschaft* (lit. "The Transitionary Society," trans.) provided a foretaste of the mass demonstrations of the *Wende* Autumn. In hindsight Braun had to realize: "The provocation crashed in the idyll." He separates the real from the false revolutionaries, speaks of politics' betrayal of art, and observes unmoved the "neck-turning" comrades bawling and rolling in the dust of the crumbled systems.

Heiner Müller Plays with the Ruins of History

The suspicion of opportunism fell on every author who stayed in the GDR. But if an author like Heiner Müller really thought as a communist, then there was hardly anyone who more sharply viewed the misery of "real existing socialism" than he. Müller's uncompromising aesthetic subjectivism appropriated the forms of language and historical experiences of his world as "material," loaded it with tradition, and carried his inner convictions to extremes. In his monologic long poem *Mommsen's Block* (1993), perhaps the most rigid reckoning with himself and the world since the collapse of the GDR, Müller adopts the view of historian Theodor Mommsen on the late period of antiquity. He makes the point that the modern history of the unified world civilization of money-changers and traders has just as little representational value as the age of Nero had for Mommsen. How can one describe the experience of a dictatorship if there is only one "information flow" which extinguishes the individual? Müller admits that he could no longer write about history: "No dialogs occur to me anymore. There are now only quotes." He compares his writing block, which was brought on by his "disgust with the here and now" of rampant capitalism, with that of Theodor Mommsen. According to Müller's suspicions, Mommsen found the time of Nero, which was probably the happiest time for the Roman people--"They had their bread and their games"--devoid of any greatness and dishearteningly boring. The ironic link to Müller's poem was the fact that in the entrance hall to Berlin's Humboldt University, Karl Marx was taken from the pedestal and Mommsen was moved from the side court and returned to the main court. The author plays with the dust of the rubble of history like a clown who cuts out the heart of the other, the co-clown. "But that is just a brick. Her heart is a brick," says "Two" in the short skit *Herzstück*.   And "One" answers, "But it beats only for her."

Writers as Agents of Simulation

Wolfgang Hilbig set his novel *Ich*   ("I"), which became an all-German best seller, against the newspaper dispute about the downfall of the GDR and the Stasi monstrosities which were thus set free. Is it a social novel about the last days of the GDR?   The reverse of a *Bildungsroman?*[4] For here the identity of a self is produced through non-identity.   The self-realization of a young person begins as self-extinguishing. This young man named "M.W." is an aspiring writer, and if he is going to write at all, then he can also write reports for the Stasi.   Through seduction, pressure, hidden intrigue, and revealed intelligence, he becomes someone who writes "inofficial literature" *(in-offizielle Literatur)* and simultaneously an "informal collaborator" *(in-formelle Mitarbeiter)*. Between "IL" and "IM"[5] in the alphabet lies only a tiny empty space.

Hilbig transforms the destroyed landscapes of East Germany into paranoid Kafkaesque dream-labyrinths.   The darkness spreads in the subterranean passageways under the eastern part of Berlin, in a branching system which hollows out the city: tunnel shafts of the subway, sewers, the basement passageways of apartment houses which served as air raid bunkers in World War II. This is the cellar-underground of the East Berlin scene which gathers here and does not suspect that the eye of the Stasi is nevertheless watching over them.   Even M.W., codename "Camembert" observes and is himself observed. All important people in the novel turn out to be Stasi informers involved in a game which no one has complete control of, yet which still results in a state.

Without considering even his own illusions about the power of writing, Hilbig develops the idea of similar structures in which writers function just as the protectors of the state.   The Stasi needs the opposition just as the opposition needs the state security services. Both live with their paper outlines in the world of symbols; both replace the real with arbitrary inventions of the intellect; both are agents of simulation. Games for the game's sake. In his novel *Das Napoleon-spiel* (lit. "The Napoleon Game," trans.) Christoph Hein shows us, in the West Berlin attorney Wörle, a man who is trying to compensate for inner emptiness, lack of personal bonds, and loss of values with the activities of his changing game. If success and profit become apparent too quickly and routine and superiority minimize the thrill and the danger, then the game has lost its meaning, and it becomes necessary to search for something new. These are "games out of self-defense," games for the game's sake which are unhesitating and which stop at nothing.

The explanation of his philosophy of life, the game, often interrupts Wörle's narrated biography and creates strong delaying elements in the epistolary monologue. Wörle's digressing monologue is clearly motivated by the pressure to talk his way out of it *(zum Sicherhausreden)*. The obsession with the always new, which is not satisfied by fulfillment but instead simply redirected to new objects, here becomes a metaphor for the everyday existence of an industrial society no longer harnessed by social ideologies. Hope, or even utopia, no longer appears; the dimension of history is broken away. Politics is now no longer historical action in the old style, but is instead understood as a post-modern game of risk. In contrast to a "closed" society that is constantly provoking the individual to overstep her bounds, in an "open" society the use of freedom always also encompasses its abuse. Even if the life stories of the doctor Claudia in *The Distant Lover* from 1982-1983 and of Dallow in *The Tango Player* (1989) show specific GDR offenses, they are tied to Wörle through boredom, the symptom of a deformed state of modern civilization. Yet while Claudia and Dallow have sunk into apathy, reacting with excess pressure and coldness to the loss of values and relationships, their western relative Wörle attempts to numb himself with his "game actionism" *(Spielaktionismus)*. He is even more invulnerable, more clever and cold-blooded than both figure variations from the East. And according to Hein, "He still has enough games in stock." For the author, writing has a lot to do with games. He writes role-prose because the most terrible truths, even about oneself, are easier said with a mask.

Fries' Ideogram of the German Present

Fritz Rudolf Fries wrote a modern picaresque novel with the *Nonnen von Bratislava* (lit. "The Nuns of Bratislava," trans.). "Hitler won World War II New Year's Eve 1989 at the Brandenburg Gate. That is the situation," announces a certain Dr. Kerb, founding member of the revolutionary council which constituted itself not far from Petershagen by Berlin, where Fries lives. A six-member revolutionary army storms the Palace of the Republic because "the people are corrupted in this Toyota-imperium" and incapable of making a revolution. The turbulent story with its multifarious analogies and allegorical associations through centuries, languages, and identities reflects in an exemplary manner the intellectual climate in East Germany--disappointments, bitterness, retreats, and enmities--an ideogram of the German present whose empty West German chapters are more eloquent than words.

The game of hide-and-seek with words, motifs, and meanings for which his prose is known is taken up once again here: the technique of interspersed omissions, leaps, hints, barely expressed truths. Enlightenment exercised through distributed roles. With Fries, literature appears as a continual game with his own life story. The relentlessness of Fries' role analyses actually always includes himself. It is the radical self-exposure of the *journal intime*. Lived literature versus a literary life. In his *doppelgänger*-figures--Arlecq, Paasch, Alexander Retard, Ole Knut Berlinguer, and Mateo Alémán, the master of the Spanish picaresque novel--Fries mirrors himself. He plays his own round in the small world game where the state of the game always simultaneously reflects the state of time--that of the GDR past as well as the "new German" present. Maybe this is also, but naturally not only, an explanation for Fries' role-play with the Stasi.

A Story of Subjective "Differentness" (*Andersartigkeit*)

Seldom have such succinct continuities and breaks in German history been pointed out as in Brigitte Burmeister's praised novel of German unification *Unter dem Namen Norma* (lit. "By the Name of Norma," trans.). Just as the first-person narrator invents her identity as "IM Norma," the secondary figures also contain their own picture puzzles, fantasies of fantasies. Collectively these make up the heroine: "Marianne Arends, staircase B, fourth floor" in that section of central Berlin (*Berlin-Mitte*). This was once the "outskirts," "no man's land, beyond, firearms were used," and today once again rightly bears its name. For the author this story of subjective "differentness," of the confrontation with unknown societal codes, and of the still divided and dividing sky is cause for disseminating a whole host of unbelievably sensitive observations and extremely subtle linguistic images.

Fritzleben

In 1994 the "novel of a *Wende* " was put out by the publishing house Volk und Welt with the title *Fritzleben*. Was this the great Wende epic that was anxiously awaited in the literary scene? The Berlin publisher heated up the rumor mill. It was preparing the longed-for monumental work of the hitherto unknown newcomer Lutz Tilgner for publication. *Fritzleben* told of the sensational and successful novel of the same name that, for its part, dealt with the less sensational small East German town of Fritzleben and whose 521,612 already-sold copies, complete with print documents, stock, and manuscript fell victim to a mysterious catastrophe on 13 July 1994. Retained and published in the new work was merely a number of reviews of *Fritzleben*. That is not all. The author Lutz Tilgner, who is as little a reality as the novel, assumes the guise of sixteen German language critics in style and name. In this manner, under the names of the--actually existing--reviewers, he simulates their comments on the lost bestseller. It can easily be assumed that the sixteen actual critics invented their own author, Tilgner, whom they let write in their names and thus play a prank on their peers. But that does not simplify matters. When sixteen critics congregate under the guise of a fictive author whom they use--via reviews--to create a novel which does not exist, the result is a narrative perspective which is at least as broken as the relationship of Germans to their nation. Is that which is summarized by the term "German unity" not so complex that only one narrator is no longer enough to narratively unravel history? *Fritzleben*, indeed, creates a sixteen-fold original short version of the great *Wende* epic; it is a brilliant parody of the literature business of the post-*Wende* period. The publisher describes it as a picaresque novel.

The Parsifal of Our Time

Thomas Brussig's *Helden Wie Wir* (lit. "Heroes Like Us," trans.) (1995) quickly received enormous popularity; even the stage took hold of his topic. Born in 1965, Brussig never participated in the yearning projections of the generation of Erich Loest, Christa Wolf, Wolf Biermann, and Volker Braun. What he has his comic hero Klaus Uhltszcht say applies to himself as well: "But I never, in total innocence, participated in their naive enthusiasm of the years of construction. I cannot claim to have sacrificed myself for the people! I also cannot dream of Socialism. . ." Karl Marx--that was for Uhltszcht "the guy on the hundred Mark bill," Friedrich Engels "the guy on the fifty Mark bill." One so completely unburdened can tell the history of the last twenty years of the GDR as pure farce as well as treat the "peaceful revolution" of Autumn 1989 without respect.

The author's medium for this is Klaus Uhltzscht who first saw the light of day on 20 August 1968 on a living room table in the Saxon *Erzgebirge* as the troops of the National People's Army rolled into Prague and his mother's water broke out of fear--a fitting entrance for a novel hero reminiscent of Günter Grass' Oskar Matzerath and occasionally also of François Rabelais' Gargantua and Pantagruel. The boy Klaus is ashamed of the smallness of his member and is persuaded by his Stasi father and hygiene inspector mother that it is only there for passing water. As an idiotic fool, he stumbles through an authoritarian (and thereby constantly becoming more grotesque) late-GDR and ends up, finally, with the Stasi. The employees there appear in Brussig's work as so ignorant, petty, and mindless that the fall of the GDR appears to the reader as indeed a necessary consequence. The crucial point and the constant, eerie center of the whole picaresque novel is, however, the penis of the hero, on which, so to speak, his entire educational history takes place. Towards the end of the novel, on the legendary 4 November 1989, the hero suffers a fall down some stairs and his member swells to a considerable size--and that in turn impresses the border guards so much that they open the wall. Thus, instead of the search for historical authenticity, comical distortion, and grotesque super-elevation are implemented in order to drive the false pathos out of the mythologized *Wende* events. The author wants just as much to expose the socialistic raptures and moving speeches of his compatriots to laughter.

A Cheerful *Treuhand*[6] Fairy Tale

Franz Franska, the youngest member in the long chain of town mayors in the seven-town community of Salow, formerly the Cordialisch-Anomenische Earlship (county), grabs the *Wende* by the hair, makes the previously state-run property of the people the real property of the people of Salow, and, together with the farmers, founds the "Land and Forest AG Earlship." The Sorbian-German author Jurij Brezan opens his new novel, *Die Leute von Salow* (lit. "The People of Salow," trans.) (1997), with this mayoral trick in 1989. The novel quickly unfolds as a saga of cunning resistance. A country people takes what is theirs?

The high-ranking *Treuhand* authority, abbreviated BAAAL *(Befugte Anstalt für Ab- und Auflösung)* for "authorized institution for eliminations and dissolutions,"[7] gets wind of this "public annoyance through complete disregard of the situation" and makes the case a matter of major importance. Complete communal land-restructuring is the maxim at *Treuhand*. As the helicopter with the director Maria Maader lands on the sports field in Salow, she is given a reception such as Erich Honecker had never experienced: "Two-hundred-thirty-seven children were cheering freely; it was incomprehensible, and with all the power in their lungs the fireman's band played *Heil dir, die du uns erschienen* (lit. "Praise to you, that you have appeared to us," trans.). Maader also has to hear the Radetzky March and various *Ave Marias* as well as listen to the pastor's speech on what the convert Paul had to say about property: "Give to the emperor what is his, but retain what is your own, so that you and your children are well."

The residents of the moor do not complain; they assert their existence. Ceremonial hindrances trade off with organized troubles. Grinding her teeth, the *Treuhand* president acknowledges that her armored vehicle cannot reach Salow and BAAAL cannot use the castle as its operation's building. Where could they go with the museum of local history and the handicapped workers in the side-wing? The *Treuhand* authorities refer to the unification agreement that demands the privatization of state property and the sale of the castle and the agricultural enterprises. The Salowans fear a break-up and, with the town mayor at the fore, lead a resistance movement within the bounds of the law. With cunning and malice they scare off potential buyers and acquire important sections themselves--secretly for the community. That they finally succeed in putting the monetary idols of BAAAL on their backs is attributed to their home advantage: Self-confidently they bring their knowledge of the town and their consciousness of history and tradition to bear. The BAAAL employees succumb, one after another, to the unfamiliar rural charms--the moor landscape, the town teacher, the rustic native cuisine.

The almost 81 year-old author surprises the reader with a cheery *Treuhand* fairy tale. It deals with the humor and the honor of a small folk who has turned its self-assertion in centuries-old struggles into a culture of living and surviving. From the *Leute von Salow* we learn how beautiful history could have been.

The Humanization of a Woman-Monster

The experience of exclusion forms the background of the "Medea" novel by Christa Wolf. Medea, the daughter of the King in Kolchis who is also the Priestess of the Hecate, declared herself for Jason and set herself against her own father and his politics in Kolchis, not out of love for Jason but out of the desire to break out, and thus she had to flee. The Kolchians who went with her are also exiles in Corinth. Hence the myth is made useful for the present, for from the exodus of the Jews to the mass migration in the Balkans, flocks of refugees have been part of the basic experiences of our century. The author had to endure exclusion as well.

One can also read *Medea* as an allegory of the German situation at the beginning of the 1990s. The people who came from the backwards Kolchis to the advanced Corinth can find room only on the outer edges in the world of prosperity. No place on earth: that is the tragedy of women and of Christa Wolf's characters in general. Like them, Medea also lives between the times. She knows "that we cannot proceed with the fragments as we like, putting them together or tearing them apart, whatever suits us at the moment." Christa Wolf investigates the "destructive roots" of our civilization and the "mechanisms of the production of a scapegoat."

In Medea she sees misunderstandings and unjust harassment. She created the motives for Medea's actions because the myth, passed down in patriarchal form by Euripides, covered up the old sources and motives: Medea is no raving avenger bent on destruction, but rather a victim of a masculine defamation of character which is meant to destroy her right to autonomy. A central motive of Creon's followers for eliminating Medea is that she discovered a closely-guarded secret of the kingdom when she finds the bones of Creon's first daughter, Iphinoe, in a vault. Thus it becomes clear that Creon's power in Corinth is based on a lie, indeed a murder, and Jason is supposed to continue this deception with Glauke, the epileptic daughter of the King of Corinth. Iphinoe and Absyrtos, Medea's brothers, are both victims. One wanted to save Corinth, the other Kolchis, and both were murdered for it. Through her knowledge of this, Medea becomes a threat to the empire. She rebels when expected to assume the submissive posture of those who were colonized, supposedly for their own good. Does she not possess an older knowledge, thoughts which flow out of feelings, does she not have the ability to heal, and can she not help her fellow humans to be themselves? She still has memories of the matriarchy, when there was no infanticide by mothers. Did Christa Wolf domesticate the raging Medea? If the patriarchal world wronged her, what can one see then? For indeed, everyone sees only what they can see or want to see. In the proclamations of Medea's adversaries, the network of intrigue that is constantly tightening around the hunted takes shape, a breathtaking story of social ostracism. A retreat into herself is the only thing that remains for Medea: "Where should I go? Is a world or a time conceivable into which I would fit? There is no one there whom I could ask. That is the answer." When, after being banished from Corinth, she learns of the murder of her children by a crazed mob of Corinthians, the only thing left her is the powerless curse. She no longer believes the power of the word. Is this the end of utopia? Of literature?

Literature is Now Only a Matter for the Well-Versed

All this is highly explosive material, as if tailor-made for the readers, provoking them to critically examine the past and present. And yet the stories of Christa Wolf, the long poem of Heiner Müller, or the picaresque novel of Fries hardly concern society as a whole anymore. These works perhaps want to capture the general in the concrete, the absolute in the most mundane. The fact that they have long been communicated only to a secluded group of literary-versed people shapes them in their substance. But was it not exactly the East German reader who knew the game of hide-and-seek in the metaphor through which dangerous contents were expressed? Was the reader not a practiced decipherer? Yet no one gets the idea anymore that literature could mesh with the symbolic processes by which a modern community organizes itself. Literature is a highly complex, historically over-determined art form. Its enjoyment is conveyed in so many ways that finding a way from one's reading back to the daily reality of life is no longer so simple for the reader. Literature has become a concern of the minority. The public interest in their current appearance has gotten so low that they allow themselves practically everything. Hardly anyone speaks of political or moral norms today.

Literature has always tried to illustrate aesthetically what political interests have tried to palm off on us as historically important. Yet the task of literature is not to wring aesthetic pictures out of current events or to duplicate political pictures of the world and reality. Such attempts degenerate into principled trash, to an indication of the hostility toward art which obligates literature to external appearances and would like to conceptually discipline all phenomena. The Stasi debates surrounding various writers were and are also only an attempt to evaluate the political facts aesthetically, and vice versa. Not what one writes makes the work good or bad, but how one writes.

If there were previously an unfulfilled demands for the great social novel in East and West German literature, now the expectations are for the great all-German novel, the novel of the unification or--as some subtitles promise--the novel of the *Wende*. But it is not literature's job to copy reality and to reproduce opinions. Rather, literature should expose the fictional nature of reality and dismantle the illusion that all reality is truth. Literature holds the possibility of distancing itself from the announcements and lies which determine our political existence and of understanding human relationships, behaviors, and experiences which are not to be found in rule and regulation, prohibition and administration. For does not the task of literature begin only there where rational discourse fails?

Literature as Social Memory

The function of literature as social memory remains irreplaceable, however. Particularly the literature being written in the eastern part of Germany will be recognizable as such, at least for the generation of Christoph Hein. It will be memory and conscience. Literature will both raise East German history with its specific experiences in the conscience of (West) German readers (who else should give them to understand that it is also about their own history) and prevent the all-German history with its specific experiences from falling victim to the frightening tendency towards amnesty which can currently be observed. Whoever touches on the past will find an eye, whoever forgets it will lose both, goes a common saying. Authors can still be trouble-makers today. In teaching the responsible citizen to walk upright, literature can continue to be--or henceforth return to being--an indispensable companion to its readers.

Notes

1. Translated by Michael Kelly. Thanks to the Consulate General of the Federal Republic of Germany, Seattle, for providing financial assistance for this translation.

2 . Christoph Hein, "Ich werde als DDR Schriftsteller in die Grube fahren" in *Freitag* (Berlin), 28 May 1993.

3. The term *Wendehals* is a derogatory term used in the GDR during the period of the *Wende,* and it referred to those who were deemed to be political opportunists, constantly changing positions and views according to the prevailing political winds.

4. A psychological novel.

5. In the German original, the terms "inoffizielle Literatur" and "informeller Mitarbeiter" gives this a meaning that is otherwise lost in translation, trans.

6. The *Treuhand* is a much-criticized institution which was established in Berlin to carry out the privatization of all formerly socialized industries and state property of the GDR. It will not be translated in this essay, trans.

7. Translator's note: My notes on the terms *Treuhand* and *Wendehals* have been paraphrased from the glossary section in Richard T. Gray and Sabine Wilke (eds. and trans.), German Unification and its Discontents: Documents from the Peaceful Revolution (Seattle: University of Washington Press, 1996). All other translations of quotes from other sources originate exclusively from the translator

of this essay and not from other published translations in the cases where such exist.

Primary Literature

Braun, Volker. *Hinze-Kunze-Roman.* Halle: Mittledeutscher Verlag, 1985.

_____. *Der Wendehals. Eine Unterhaltung.* Frankfurt am Main: Suhrkamp, 1995.

Brezan, Jurij. *Die Leute von Salow.* Leipzig: Gustav Kiepenheuer, 1997.

Brussig, Thomas. *Helden Wie Wir.* Berlin: Volk und Welt, 1995.

Burmeister, Brigitte. *Unter dem Namen Norma.* Stuttgart: Klett-Cotta, 1994.

Fries, Fritz Rudolf. *Die Nonnen von Bratislava.* Munich: Piper, 1993.

Hein, Christoph. *Die Ritter der Tafelrunde. Eine Komödie.* Berlin: Henschel-verlag, 1989.

_____. *Das Napoleonspiel. Ein Roman.* Berlin: Aufbau-Verlag, 1993.

Hilbig, Wolfgang. *Ich.* Frankfurt am Main: S. Fischer Verlag, 1993.

Müller, Heiner. *Bildbeschreibung.* Graz: Droschl, 1985.

_____. *Mommsens Block in Drucksache.* Berlin: Berliner Ensemble (private print), 1993.

Tilger, Lutz. *Fritzleben. Roman einer Wende.* Berlin: Volk und Welt, 1994.

Wolf, Christa. *Was bleibt. Erzählung.* Berlin: Aufbau-Verlag, 1990.

_____. *Medea. Stimmen.* Hamburg: Luchterhand, 1996.

Secondary Literature

Adel, Kurt. *Die Literatur der DDR - ein Wintermärchen?* Wein: Braumüller, 1992.

Anz, Thomas (ed.). *"Es geht nicht um Christa Wolf." Die Literaturstreit im vereinten Deutschland.* Munich: Ed. Spangenberg, 1991.

Arnold, Heinz Ludwig (ed.). *Die andere Sprache. Neue DDR-Literatur der 80er Jahre.* Munich: Ed. text + kritik, 1990.

Böthig, Peter and Klaus Michael (eds.). *Macht Spiele. Literatur und Staats-sicherheit.* Leipzig: Reclam-Verlag, 1993.

_____, *Literatur in der DDR. Rückblicke.* Munich: Ed. text + kritik, 1993.

_____. *Feinderklärung. Literatur und Staatssicherheit.* Munich: Ed. text + kritik, 1993.

_____. *Macht Apparat Literatur. Literatur und "Stalinismus."* Munich: Ed. text + kritik, 1990.

Deiritz, Karl and Hannes Krauss (eds.). *Der deutsch-deutsche Literatur-streit oder "Freunde, es spricht sich schlect mit gebundener Zunge."* Hamburg and Zürich: Luchterhand-Literaturverlag, 1991.

Emmerich, Wolfgang. *Kleine Literaturgeschicthe der DDR. Erweiterte Neu-ausgabe.* Leipzig: Gustav Kiepenheuer, 1996.

Fröhlich, Jörg, Reinhild Meinel, and Karl Riha. *Wende-Literatur. Bibliographie und Materialien zur Literatur der Deutschen Einheit*. Frankfurt am Main: Suhrkamp, 1996.

Hein, Christoph. "Ich werde als DDR Schriftsteller in die Grube fahren" in *Freitag*. Berlin: 28 May 1993.

Mayer, Hans. *Die Turm von Babel. Erinnerung an eine Deutsche Demokratische Republik*. Frankfurt am Main: Suhrkamp, 1991.

Schwilk, Heimo. *Wendezeit, Zeitenwende. Beiträge zur Literatur der 80er Jahre*. Bonn: Bouvier, 1991.

Vom gegenwärtigen Zustand der deutschen Literatur. Munich: Ed. text + kritik, 1992

Walther, Joachim (ed.). *Protokoll eines Tribunals. Die Ausschlüsse aus dem DDR-Schriftstellerverband 1979*. Reinbek bei Hamburg: Rowohlt Taschenbuch Verlag, 1991.

_____. *Sicherungsbereich Literatur. Schriftsteller und Staatssicherheit in der Deutschen Demokratischen Republik*. Berlin: Links, 1996.

PART THREE

Foreign Policy and Security

12

The German Soldier
and National Unity

Donald   Abenheim

The demise of the German Democratic Republic (GDR) in October 1990 brought the end of the *Nationale Volksarmee* (NVA), the second leading army of the Warsaw Pact alongside the Soviets. The *Bundeswehr* entered the former GDR as the largest, most powerful organization of the Bonn state.[1] For those figures in the federal government who prepared for this unexpected contingency, the fate of the soldier in unity would reveal the efficacy of West German statecraft amid the unprecedented and improbable trial of national unification.

In their own time, makers of policy in the GDR had imagined the German soldier-in-unity as the harbinger of catastrophe. In the overheated realm of state-socialist propaganda and myth, the *Bundeswehr* marched into the GDR again and again, crushing the border fortifications in clouds of radioactive rhetoric and flashes of ideological hot steel.[2] Recalling the SED regime's justification for 13 August 1961 as a pre-emptive blow against NATO, East German theoreticians warned of a West German revanchist onslaught under the NATO compass and black-red-white Nazi war flag. Once the atomic fires had subsided, the West German imperialists would emerge from their *Bundeswehr* armored personnel carriers to enslave the workers and peasants of the other Germany and once more erect the gallows and charnel houses of the Nazi People's Community.

In the event, as unification became a real possibility in 1989-1990, observers among Germany's neighbors generally feared national unity as a redux of the wars of unification of 1864-1871. Once united, Germany would overturn the balance of power in Europe and lead to a renewed push for world power by means of military strength. Speculative accounts of the military future of a united Germany conjured up images of "German rearmament," and a resort to nuclear blackmail in a drive to the East. The reality of events in 1990 and after proved to be quite different and suggested how little such anxious observers really understood the military institutions and defense policy of the Federal Republic of Germany and the North Atlantic Treaty Organization.

The actual progress of the *Bundeswehr* in 1990 into the GDR/new states unfolded differently from the propagandists' fantasies of carnage and from the fears of certain Anglo-Americans about a re-emergence of a neo-Wilhelmine or neo-Nazi Germany. Nowhere did men on the march in the fall of 1990 hold aloft torches to the sound of drums and fifes, nor did a scene of unity-in-martial-triumph unfold as interpreted by the Prussian academician Anton von Werner in his heroic canvas of Bismarck's proclamation of the Empire in Versailles in 1871. The few hundred *Bundeswehr* soldiers who moved into the headquarters, garrisons, and training areas of the former NVA in early October proceeded in near silence and with none of the military pathos of the German past--and not a shot, to say nothing of a nuclear-laden shell, was fired.

Indeed, the advance of West German institutions of leadership, command, morale and obedience among the NVA veterans in *Bundeswehr* olive uniforms, which forms the subject of this chapter, corresponded to the communist "image of the enemy" in only one crucial aspect. Unity did, in fact, bring about the enlargement eastward of the Atlantic area referred to in Articles VI and X of the Washington Treaty. This process as it spread beyond a united Germany fostered cooperation between formally mortal opponents that grew over the decade. The accession into the *Bundeswehr* of tens of thousands of NVA veterans in 1990 formed the prelude to the rising tide of military-to-military contacts of the North Atlantic Cooperation Council/Euro-Atlantic Partnership Council (1991-97), the "Partnership for Peace" (1994), and NATO Enlargement (1995-99). This general defense reform, soldierly collaboration, and re-orientation of professional military ideas and practices spread presently from German territory outward. In so doing this process altered substantially the civil-military customs and practices of command, leadership, morale, and obedience in the armies of Central and Eastern Europe. The transfer of western military institutions to the armies of the expiring Warsaw Pact (what by the middle of the 1990s were called, in NATO parlance, "Partner Countries") began in its most dramatic form in Germany in mid-1990.[3]

The soldierly dimension of unity meant something very different from the merger of two German armies as intact institutions on equal terms; rather, one army ceased to exist, while its former opponent took over its personnel, equipment and installations. The night before the unification ceremonies in front of the Reichstag, at the sound of twelve, the NVA vanished with the striking of its hammer and compass colors; yet the soldiers remained at arms, now to serve the opponent state. The next night, as the black-red-gold flag rose on the mast in the Platz der Republik before the assembled crowd of notables and common folk, the men and women of the former NVA became citizens of the Federal Republic. Granted the provisions of the unity treaty, many of them also became soldiers of the federal armed forces. Ninety-thousand NVA veterans underwent this metamorphosis at midnight on 3 October.

Only a fraction of these troops, however, could eventually (that is, by 1993) become career soldiers in the *Bundeswehr*. The diplomacy of unification--which assured Germany's many neighbors of the united country's peaceful demeanor--required a 370,000 strong *Bundeswehr* by the end of 1994. This limit signified a vast reduction from the nearly 600,000 soldiers of East and West in garrison at midnight of 3 October 1990.[4]

The present chapter relates the most vital aspect of the German military-in-unity: the transformation of the ideals of military professionalism in the midst of drastic political upheaval. How could the institutions of command and morale in the old *Bundeswehr* (as it was called after 3 October 1990) adapt to the challenges of its vanishing opponent in the process of unification? How did the so-called "inner structure" of the armed forces change as a result? In the second instance, far less obvious in 1990 to the strategic planners of the German ministry of defense, was how the unification of Germany heralded the advent of a period of general strategic change and turmoil. The present work seeks to place this German experience of unification and arms within the general transformation of NATO and military institutions in Central and Eastern Europe in the 1990s.[5]

Military Plans and Obstacles to Their Realization: The Past German-German Dimensions of the Soldierly Ethos

During September 1990, the German ministry of defense announced the role of the *Bundeswehr* in unity.[6] The ministerial effort toward this goal had started formally only a few weeks earlier. Planning of a circumscribed kind began in early-1990, while the Kohl cabinet only gave the green light for full preparations for unity in the summer of 1990. Such an enterprise could rely upon no previous staff-studies. At best, those in charge had incomplete information about the shape, size and character of the NVA.

As the GDR passed into a political coma in early 1990, the leaders of the NVA hoped that their army might endure until the end of the decade as a territorial force. Western critics of such a policy argued that the FRG should dismiss all East German soldiers out of hand. Embracing neither extreme, the leadership of the ministry of defense chose to abolish the NVA de-jure with unification, while retaining the soldiers on hand in a staged system of reductions-in-force and administrative re-organization that would require the expertise and aid of former-NVA soldiers. The armed forces of a united Germany would shrink drastically to only 370,000 peacetime-actives on the territory of a united Germany by the end of 1994. Some 25,000 career soldiers of the former NVA would be integrated into the *Bundeswehr* after a period of probation and assessment. Conscription would be retained without pause for all of Germany, with a period of service of some twelve months. Adhering to custom, the NVA would muster recruits on 1 September (unlike the annual 1 October mustering date in the FRG), but these conscripts would soon become *Bundeswehr* draftees. In a staged program that would require nearly four years to complete fully, most of the bases and installations of the NVA would be rolled up, while a usable fraction would be retained after the transitional period.[7]

Germany as a whole would enter into the territory of NATO as stipulated by Article VI of the Washington Treaty, but the forces stationed in the five new states would only become part of the alliance integrated military structure on 1 January 1995, once the Soviet/Russian group of forces had withdrawn from Germany. No foreign NATO forces were to be stationed in the five new states, in contrast to the allied bases in the old-FRG. The Germans and their western allies intended this measure to re-assure the Soviets of their peaceful intent in the enlargement of NATO to include united Germany.

With the advent of unity, echelons of the defunct NVA would be integrated into the *Bundeswehr*, and, in general, they would then be disbanded. This process was to take from three months to two years. Certain troops, however, were to survive in a new form and undergo a radical re-organization. These units would have significant contingents of NVA veterans filled, over time, with draftees from the new states. One-hundred-and-fifty-six "command groups" as well as 175 "training groups" were dispatched from the West to assume command of those former NVA regiments and battalions that would form the cadre for new *Bundeswehr* units. For instance, the ninth armored division of the NVA at Eggesin, Western Pomerania, was to become a territorial mechanized brigade. In the case of former NVA units soon to be disbanded, western advisors aided the former NVA officers, who put on *Bundeswehr* olive for a limited period of service as so-called *Weiterverwender*, that is, soldiers with a circumscribed term of duty. The commanders of senior echelons and defense civilians came exclusively from the West. The *Bundeswehr* Eastern Command was to make its headquarters at Strausberg in the former ministry of national defense. This organization was to become the forward command element of the ministry of defense (MoD) in Bonn and would include some 2,000 soldiers from the old *Bundeswehr* together with 250 defense civilians from the FRG seconded to positions throughout the five new states.[8]

The enormity of what lay ahead for these 2,250 western men and women was breathtaking enough in the variety of tasks that unfolded after 3 October 1990. Never before had West German soldiers confronted anything remotely like this mission. The greatest challenge, as one of the chief figures of military unity, Lieutenant General Jörg Schönbohm observed, lay in the union of differing soldierly mentalities and self-images. As he wrote in 1992, ". . . the central problem after the take-over by the *Bundeswehr* of the NVA has been to promote a change in consciousness and establish ideals of the citizen in uniform."[9] Few people in a position of responsibility in 1990 fully understood the degree of divergence between the two armies. This difference of mentality and world view about the soldier's service lay embedded in a clash of four decades about German military ideals. This struggle had played out within the opposing ranks of the cold-war orders of battle for a very long time.

For anyone who has observed the transformation of state and society in Europe after 1989, one well knows that bureaucratic reform generally rests upon a foundation of hearts and minds. In this particular instance, significant for the soldier's fate in unity was the German-German struggle over what constituted the valid features of the soldier's professional code of command and obedience. These features bulk large in what Americans all too simply call "doctrine"—that is, the idea and practices whereby an army commands its force in peace and war, and in how such a code shows itself in the daily behavior of lieutenants and corporals on the parade ground and in the field.[10]

From the early 1950s, each German army had claimed for itself enlightened principles of command, obedience, discipline, and morale. The altercation resulted in an east-west struggle for control of the lexicon of military reform. Each German army vied for the laurels of "genuine military reform" and recognition for being fully de-nazified. West and East Germans wielded a cudgel-like version of the soldierly past to demolish the other's so-called reformed ideals of military service. The founders of the *Bundeswehr* and *Nationale Volksarmee* strove to separate their customs, practices, and traditions from the principles of command, obedience, and morale in the Wehrmacht in National Socialism, the *Reichswehr*, and pre-1918 armies. In particular, soldiers in National Socialism, who fashioned the principles of command, obedience and morale from 1934 until 1945 (along with their allies in brown uniforms) had laid claim to the ideals of military reform from the Prussian-German past. The cult of Prussia bulked large among the keepers of the Nazi military ethos, who had enlisted Scharnhorst, Gneisenau, and Boyen to serve the armed forces of a racially pure nation, steeled by wars of conquest.[11]

Anti-communist and communist German soldiers alike asserted endlessly after 1950 that only one side could rightfully claim the wholesome German martial past. Conversely, according to this view, the opponent dug in across the inner-German border manifested a reprehensible militarism. In either case, this antagonist wrongly seized the features of this broken heritage of military reform. From the middle-1950s until the 1970s, the hopes, ideals, and practices of German military reform became locked in a manichean struggle between the makers of command and morale in east and west. This phenomenon applied especially to the German-German ideal of the "citizen-in-uniform," which together with the West German phrase *Innere Führung* stood for a style of command and morale to accord with civil-military integration in the face of a profoundly anti-military, almost pacifist, German political culture.[12]

The founders of the *Bundeswehr*, who gave the phrase "citizen-in-uniform" a new and more prominent meaning than ever before in the German military experience, sought to transfer the spirit of the Basic Law of 1949 into the barracks of the new army. The military reformers in the FRG of the first half of the 1950s aspired to an ideal type of soldier, who would reconcile the militarist heritage with modern democracy.[13] The training of the young male conscript was to spare him the cult of the warrior that had long exalted the honor of the battlefield above bourgeois values. The reformers desired that the recruit first be a human being, second, a citizen, and third, a soldier. This soldier would serve in an "army without pathos," that is, a functional, corps of fighting men stripped of braid and ribbons, who would waste no time marching on the parade ground saluting tattered, silken battle flags in an age of mass politics, total war, and high-technology. Rather, this new kind of German soldier must orient himself solely to a sober military efficiency and ideological toughness in its mid-20th century form. The recruit should enjoy as many of his rights as possible when in arms, while nonetheless adjusting himself to the hierarchical requirements of combat. At the same time, the citizen-in-uniform should be a free personality, rather than an armed automaton, who would further act as a responsible citizen conscious of his duties to the whole. The spirit of the new army and its institutions of command and morale were to adjust to this new paradigm of soldierly existence, while striving for high readiness for defense-within-the-alliance. Ideological firmness against communism and psychological preparation for the atomic battlefield, as poorly understood as this was in German military minds of the 1950s and 1960s, imposed heavy demands on the spirit of the future soldier.

Naturally enough, the SED guardians of the NVA institutions of command, obedience and morale made the intellectual demolition of reform ideals in the *Bundeswehr* a major goal of the psychological combat waged by the Main Political Administration of the NVA--the Soviet-style party institution-in-arms that fought the war of words between the two German armies.[14] Such an effort during the SED consolidation reflected the overall attempt of the early communist regime to destabilize the Bonn Republic as the bastard successor of the Hitler Reich.

According to NVA doctrine, such FRG concepts as the "citizen-in-uniform" and *Innere Führung* represented an outstanding feature of the oppressive class character of the *Bundeswehr*. This nazified code of command, obedience and morale enabled Bonn's NATO soldiers to provide the spear's tip of aggression to the imperialist Atlantic alliance. The rank and file of the *Bundeswehr* was held prisoner by a military discipline of brutal drill and moral intimidation achieved with psychological coercion. Central to *Innere Führung* and the West German concept of the "citizen-in-uniform" was an anti-communist creed that filled the senior ranks with a blind fanaticism. The founders of *Innere Führung* sought to create a human fighting machine capable of independent, aggressive action and prepared it to carry out criminal orders without scruples under rising atomic clouds. Revanchism, political arrogance, and a spirit of blissful servitude to his imperialist masters distinguished the West German soldier. The NVA faced in him a brutal, underhanded, sneaky, and bloodthirsty enemy.[15]

In contrast, by its own credo, the NVA was the legitimate guardian of the " citizen-in-uniform." [16] Only with the foundation of the NVA in the early 1950s had East German soldiers restored this broken heritage of reform and made it into a living reality for millions of German soldiers. The founders of the NVA had done so with the addition of enlightened reform ideals from Soviet Russia. The NVA assumed from the Red Army the mission of creating the "citizen in the soldier's tunic." This task had first emerged in Soviet experience amid the revolutionary events from 1917 until the 1920s. This ideal of civil-military integration under the red banner became the center-piece of the Soviet military ethos as a kind of Bolshevik school of the nation. Military service was to make workers and peasants into citizens and soldiers of a revolutionary *avant garde*. Once the Soviets re-organized the armies of their new Central and Eastern European subject-states in the late 1940s, this code became indispensable to newly re-founded military institutions later integrated into the Warsaw Pact. This code had two outstanding facets.

First, the image of the soldier in the NVA was promulgated as part of an ideology of obedience which recognized the leading role of the SED in state and society. The state-party alone could determine the image of a new German army and a socialist German soldier and realize it in turn. Second, the NVA authors of reform asserted that the GDR represented a final resolution of class conflict and social friction in Germany. The NVA soldier embodied a fusion of state, citizen, and army as never before in the national experience. While *Bundeswehr* soldiers were NATO mercenaries led by Nazis, the NVA represented the advance of human progress to a higher level of development: the leaders of communist military institutions would no longer turn their arms against workers and peasants. The theory and practice of the "citizen-in-uniform" in its East German form meant the end of this central conflict of Prussian-German politics and society. Granted that the NVA, and especially its institutions of supreme command, derived from the people and shared its mind and soul, its single mission was to protect the achievements of the East German people. The NVA, with its code of command, obedience and morale, asserted that it had created a true citizen in uniform, unlike the fake in the West. The subjects-in-arms of the Federal Republic, dressed in their un-German, Yankee-style uniforms, remained in military bondage to imperialist strategic interests that had endured from the world before 1945.[17]

One should step back from this summary of NVA ideals to instead suggest that East German military reform served a two-fold purpose: first, to subordinate military power to the SED state and Warsaw Treaty Organization and, secondly, to wage a victorious campaign against the imperialist west under extremely difficult strategic conditions. This image of war and its soldierly ideal stemmed from Soviet strategic and operational experience since June 1941. The reformers added to their work the realities of ideological, nuclear combat, that is, to carry the battle to the enemy homeland and to destroy NATO forces there. As Clausewitz wrote in *On War*, "fighting is the central military act [of war]" (rather than maneuver and siege-craft). This insight applied especially to the NVA, whose leaders claimed Clausewitz as their own.[18] The NVA sought to perfect the total political and human motivation of the soldier within the echelons of the Unified Command of the Warsaw Pact, an enterprise that grew more intense in the final decade of the regime. The SED claimed to have fetched up the blackened standard of military reform in the 1950s and carried it forward alongside the armed forces of the Soviet Union.

By the end of the 1980s, however, the ebb of communist power had brought the resolution of this struggle between the idealized German-German images of soldierly service. From the heights of state-socialist aspirations of the 1950s and 1960s, the communist German "citizen-in-uniform" plunged into the abyss of the regime's strategic failures of the 1980s. The rise of Mikhail Gorbachev's course of reform and the decline of the regime accelerated the rot in the inner structure of the NVA.

As West German officers, non-commissioned officers (NCOs) and civil-servants arrived in the East in August-October 1990, they found soldierly practice and customs that differed markedly from the ideals put forward by the Main Political Administration, not to mention from that of the *Bundeswehr* itself. Above all, what the West Germans discovered about the inner structure of the NVA in October 1990 came as a great surprise. As the cold war had dragged on, the West German soldier had failed to pay sufficient attention to the institutions of NVA command and leadership and neglected to notice the full impact of the evolution of state and society upon the East German armed forces.[19]

The Ethos of the NVA Officer in Reality

As Werner von Scheven has observed, the reality of military life in the NVA had little to do with the Prussian antecedents claimed by the Main Political Administration. In its head and limbs in 1990, the NVA remained a germanized version of the Soviet army.[20] The senior officer corps of the NVA passed through the Moscow halls of Soviet army professional military education. The lexicon of NVA command stemmed from Soviet army practice and doctrine. All features of the East German institutions of leadership, command, morale, and obedience arose from this Soviet-Russian source. In this connection, the NVA was far less national than the armies of some of its neighbors, in particular, the Poles. These Soviet institutions of command, leadership, and morale comprised such features as:

- a divisible, dual form of command
- a highly compartmentalized, multiple-tracked hierarchy of ranks
- the leading role of the party in the ranks
- the intrusion of the secret police into garrison life
- a wide gap between various grades in service, as well as the absence of the NCO corps in command and leadership.

Officers had to quantify every aspect of military service and measure these against absolute norms set down by higher headquarters; further, "socialist competition" for the achievements of the "best" replaced conventional military esprit-de-corps and comradeship. This imperative to fulfill the military version of the "plan" dominated the ideals of command and obedience. Here the labor of the Main Political Administration was paramount.[21]

The 170,000 soldiers of the NVA fell subject to a double form of discipline: those of the SED and the army high command. The Main Political Administration insisted that career soldiers leave the bosom of the church to fetch the SED membership book. The education and training of the career soldier aimed to create military specialists (as opposed to generalists) who mastered a single aspect of the military profession in detail. This education and training allowed little room for initiative and for no dispersal of military authority to lower ranks. The exalted place of the "big picture," that is, how the action of an individual fits within the whole, represents an ideal of Prussian-German soldierly professionalism that endures in the *Bundeswehr*. NVA officers, however, actively prevented such customs of command, obedience, and morale in their troops.

Specialists of armored warfare knew little of what their comrades did in the signals branch, while officers of all arms in company grade had no insight into the operational level of command. This style of leadership and obedience amounted to what the *Bundeswehr* darkly calls *Befehlstaktik*, that is, a style of command and obedience in which the subordinate enjoys little or no latitude in carrying out orders according to varying circumstances.[22]

For all this, the NVA had plenty of officers to be controlled minutely from above and, in turn, to command one another: four times as many general and flag officers as the *Bundeswehr*, with three times as many officers overall. In contrast, the NVA had essentially no NCO corps on the Prussian-German model. The leadership of the NVA regarded these grades as little better than exalted conscripts, devoid of capacity for command in garrison or in the field.

Paramount in Soviet-German command and obedience loomed an ideal battlefield derived from the operational experience of 1941-1945 and the likely use of nuclear weapons. From the late-1970s until 1988, the Warsaw Pact put in hand a "bolt-from-the-blue" nuclear and conventional strategy against U.S. and German forces in NATO's central and northern commands. This doctrine required an extremely high state of combat-effectiveness, essentially unknown and unobtainable in NATO. The NVA had regularly to maintain 85 percent readiness (that is, 85 percent of forces were poised for war at a moment's warning), thus to march out of barracks fully prepared for battle within an hour's time.[23] Constant alerts and readiness inspections belonged to the officer's lot, and, during the 1980s, the conditions under which this high state of mobilization proceeded grew steadily more adverse as the state-party marched its soldiers off to coal mines and grain fields to boost sagging production.

The capacity to withstand such trials under difficult conditions--for instance, repeated yuletide alerts called at the last minute against a phantom NATO assault--became a badge of honor for NVA officers. This ideal of service explains in large part the patient, staid behavior of many such officers in the turbulence of military unification in 1990-1993.[24] Such stoicism contrasted sharply with the growing aversion in West German society to overtime and extra, unexpected burdens of service.

Military professionalism and pride-in-arms in the NVA were based upon this tactical-operational capacity to launch a lightning strike against the West. Only a tiny number of NVA general officers in the National Defense Council and the United Command of the Warsaw Pact had any idea of what such military power meant as an instrument of policy. Certainly, the average NVA draftee or even company grade officer knew nothing of such strategy and its full implications. In the end, this accumulation of combat power in the late-1970s and 1980s had undermined the strength of SED state and society and hastened the demise of the NVA itself as an opposition movement formed in the GDR of the middle and late 1980s.

The Integration of Career NVA Veterans into the *Bundeswehr*, 1990-1995

Shaken in mid-1990 by the collapse of the regime and gutted by shrinking ranks, the officer corps of the NVA (the draftees had generally deserted by the summer of 1990) looked to the *Bundeswehr* as the only hope for professional salvation. In this regard, the career NVA officer expected far too much; sadly they believed Minister Rainer Eppelmann's plan for "two-armies and-one fatherland" long after such a pipedream had become unfeasible in summer 1990. The Eppelmann defense ministry had dismissed the officers of the Main Political Administration *en masse* in the summer of 1990, while the cabinet of Lothar de Maizière had retired all the general officers and colonels above the age of 55 years shortly before unification itself.[25]

The strategic and bureaucratic parameters of military unification were tight indeed; these circumstances did much to limit the number of NVA veterans who could resume a career in the *Bundeswehr*. Such restrictions had been set rather less by the personnel section of the Bonn ministry of defense (whom critics of the soldier-in-unity might all too readily blame) than by the diplomacy of German unification--the "Two-Plus-Four" dictates of 370,000 soldiers by the close of 1994--and by the major cuts imposed by the Conventional Forces, Europe treaty. These requirements of diplomacy meant a vast reduction in force of the 495,000-strong pre-1990 *Bundeswehr*. Further, one must remember that the transformation of NATO strategy from the collision of opposing army groups in the central region toward the so-called crisis-reaction expeditionary forces similarly imposed a radical re-organization and reduction in the size of the *Bundeswehr* in the 1990s.

Thus, fewer positions-at-arms would exist in the future. As a result, only 25,000 career soldiers of the former NVA had hopes for long-term or career positions in the *Bundeswehr*.[26] With its reliance upon a strong non-commissioned officer corps, the new *Bundeswehr* faced a deficit of sergeants in the lower grades in contrast to the surplus of officers produced by the ex-NVA. This problem of a weak NCO corps loomed in the central and eastern European armies of the 1990s in the midst of reform within "Partnership for Peace" and NATO accession.

Twenty-one-thousand potential NCO billets emerged in the table of organization for the *Bundeswehr* Eastern Command, in comparison with some 18,000 former NCOs in the ranks of the new *Bundeswehr* in October 1990.[27] This dis-equilibrium between east and west positions was aggravated, however, by the disparity of military occupation specialties between the two armies. The NCOs of the NVA were generally ill-suited to transfer into the *Bundeswehr* in their old functions. These NCO veterans, of whom 11,500 applied for a position in the *Bundeswehr*, lacked requisite education and training. They tended to be qualified in the combat service support branches rather than in the echelons of the combat arms. In a word, there was an abundance of communications specialists and a scarcity of junior sergeants of armor and mechanized infantry. In practice, the tasks necessary to transform such individuals from "tail to tooth," often proved too difficult, as might well be the case in an army of the NATO model.

In the day-to-day labor after 3 October, the military in unity brought the migration of NVA veterans into the schools of *Bundeswehr* professional military education.[28] The dispatch of new *Bundeswehr*-NVA veterans to courses in such places as the branch schools of the army, air force, and navy (e.g., Infantry, Armor, and Army Officers' School); the *Zentrum Innere Führung*; and the Command and General Staff Academy, as well as improvised instruction in the so-called *Coleurverbände* (partnership units) caused numerous vacancies in units. This syndrome disturbed the daily cycle of troop training and operations, lessened *esprit-de-corps*, and harmed the bearing of units. Only the rise of a de-centralized, well-organized NCO training establishment in the five new states by 1994 improved this situation significantly.[29]

The officers' lot, however, proved to be more problematic. There simply existed fewer billets than applicants, and the force reductions from 495,000 to 370,000 (the so-called Personnel Structure Model 370,000) brought general turmoil into the ranks of all *Bundeswehr* officers new and old in the 1990s. Due to *Bundeswehr* personnel policies of the mid-1960s and 1970s, at the time of unification the West German officer corps was already somewhat uneven in the distribution of ranks and rather overage, especially in comparison to the U.S. armed forces. This so-called *Verwendungsstau* or assignment bottle-neck derived from clogged up middle to senior ranks. This difficulty resulted, in turn, in aged company grade officers facing a cohort of twenty-year-old draftees. Measures to reduce this disproportion of age and rank by voluntary early retirement with a bonus had been only partially successful.[30]

Of the 23,354 officers of the NVA present on 3 October 1990, only 12,700 remained in uniform in March 1991. The others had taken advantage of the transitional period to leave service by the end of 1990 with their NVA pensions in hand. This measure had assured a degree of continuity in daily operations past 3 October, while it avoided the worst ills of a mass dismissal of officers.

Eleven-thousand-five-hundred men applied for a two-year probationary contract for an eventual long term (*Soldat auf Zeit* or SaZ) or career *Bundeswehr* position. Others remained in uniform as so-called *Weiterverwender* to leave service once their particular unit disappeared or their specialist skills ceased to be required. The personnel department of the ministry of defense projected the placement of 4,000 former NVA officers within the so-called regular line service as well as in the specialist warrant service (*Truppendienst* and *Militär-fachlichendienst*) so long as these men were born after 1944. The civilian *Bundeswehr* administration offered further career civil-service positions for specialists in resource management, construction engineering, and military real-estate. Such figures had served in NVA uniform, while the ministry of defense put these functions in civilian hands in the *Bundeswehr*.[31]

As the process of integration moved forward in the first months of 1991, 6,056 former NVA officers received the coveted two-year probationary contract. This figure, higher than foreseen by personnel officials in Bonn, became an object of contention between east and west. This circumstance proved all too typical of the human dimension of military unification, where the specific tasks of an unprecedented situation demanded solutions at odds with bureaucratic custom. General Schönbohm had secured from Defense Minister Gerhard Stoltenberg this higher number of officer billets despite the objections of the ministerial personnel directorate. The leadership of the army, in particular, wished to make such choices upon an assessment of individuals over time. From the outset, because of their role as the senior service and their requirement to grapple with the largest fraction of people and things, the army commands in Strausberg, Leipzig and Neubrandenburg had the clearest conception of the variety and scale of difficulties associated with military unification and the best means to master its problems.[32]

The Process of Selection in Detail

Granted the over-reliance upon officers for command and leadership in all Warsaw Pact forces, the *Bundeswehr* often reduced the ranks of the NVA veterans on two-year contracts by one to two grades, and in some isolated cases, by three grades.[33] This step reflected, in part, the realities of *Bundeswehr* rank structure and command; further, this measure assured an equity between officers of the old and new *Bundeswehr* as to the basis upon which an individual had attained his grade in service. Although such an act might appear as the cruelest discrimination against NVA veterans, as Werner von Scheven properly observes, the command of a company of infantry or armor in the *Bundeswehr* requires a greater degree of initiative and the mastery of complexity than did the command of a battalion in the NVA. The ills of Soviet-style *Befehlstaktik* made the latter tasks more routine than the command of lower echelons in NATO-style forces. Indeed, in certain cases, faced with the transformed institutions of command and leadership, NVA officers were satisfied to carry on as NCOs in the *Bundeswehr*, since such figures enjoy status, pay, respect, and high authority. Indeed, in some instances, once the probationary period passed, certain officers regained grades in service with some speed.[34]

By the beginning of 1991, some 45,000 former NVA regulars and draftees and 1,200 soldiers of the old *Bundeswehr* served in army garrisons and headquarters in the five states. As the two-year contracts expired, the number of soldiers from the old Federal Republic increased to 5,500 officer and NCO grades, as well as 3,000 draftees sent to do their basic training in the East. The mixing of Easterner and Westerner on a mutual geographical basis became routine after 1993.

Daily life for the NVA veterans in the first years of the military in unity meant attendance at so-called "supplementary courses," which took place throughout the educational institutions of the *Bundeswehr*. Such labor formed an additional, unexpected duty for teaching staffs, who soon became expert in the spirit and character of the ex-NVA officers. For example, upon unification, two-week introductory symposia for officers on *Innere Führung* began at the *Zentrum Innere Führung* at Koblenz. Such instruction was based upon already existing offerings in the theory and practice of the "citizen-in-uniform," political education in a democracy, military law, and the duties and rights of a soldier according the soldier's law. On the basis of military-to-military agreements between Germany and its eastern neighbors, the Koblenz school also began similar courses for Polish and Czech officers. These courses continued for non-Germans once the initial education of ex-NVA soldiers ceased in 1992. By the middle of the decade soldiers and civilians from many Central and East European "Partnership for Peace" countries became a regular sight in the seminar rooms at Koblenz and the school's branch at Strausberg.[35] Such seminars set a pattern for the more generalized civil-military education embraced within "Partnership for Peace" from 1994 and 1995.

Further, NVA veterans visited specialist schools and received instruction in weapons and equipment. Some 2,000 officers undertook temporary duty of four to six weeks with partner units in the West. There, these men received hands-on instruction in all aspects of garrison life and service in the field. Such effort demonstrated *Innere Führung* as a guiding force of daily service, in contrast to some doctrine scribbled upon a chalk-board. As an adjunct to instruction in *Innere Führung*, NVA veterans attended seminars in German civil and military law and judicial aspects of NATO offered by the legal staff of the *Bundeswehr* Eastern Command.

The results of this practical and theoretical education and training thus provided the basis for the evaluation process that unfolded in the spring of 1991. Within a few weeks, all the officers and NCO's with a two-year contract were vetted by two of their superiors, with particular attention to qualities of character, achievements since 1990, and potential for service. This effort led to an avalanche of some 8,282 evaluations that piled up in the headquarters of the separate services, where these documents provided a basis for a subsequent categorization in five levels. Eighty percent of the evaluations resulted in three grades of "highly suited," "fully suited," and "well suited," with twenty percent of the evaluations falling into the two categories of "partially suited" or "unsuited."[36]

Surely the most intractable human challenge in this connection arose from the past role of Administration 2000/Ministry for State Security (MfS) operatives in the NVA. [37] The 6,056 applicants furnished as an annex to their application a statement that they had no clandestine contacts with the MfS beyond the normal dictates of service. Based upon the fitness reports of the officer in question, the personnel experts in Bonn and Strausberg further examined the candidates' files. Such scrutiny was made no easier by the fact that the Modrow government had allowed NVA officers to remove from their records all materials connected with SED membership or whatever else might appear unsuitable in the new era.

The military counter-intelligence service (MAD) conducted its own investigation for a security clearance, as is normally the case with prospective officers. Further, the independent committee for the suitability of personnel conducted their own hearings in 1992-1993 upon examination of personnel files and the evaluations of *Bundeswehr* superiors. In 500 cases, this committee, headed by former Under-secretary of Defense Dr. Hildegard Hurland-Büring, summoned the candidate for a hearing. Of these cases, the committee turned down forty men as unsuited.

The Gauck agency, the federal office that administers the state security archives, examined the names of the two-year candidates in search of clandestine contacts amid the MfS dossiers. In the event, one out of five candidates had such secret dealings as "unofficial agents." These men had either knowingly or unwittingly failed to describe such encounters on the forms completed as part of the two-year contract. This grave misdeed led to so-called "red cases" and the requirement to appear before a board. While certain individuals had apparently forgotten their covert agreements, others reckoned wrongly that no one would ever discover this aspect of their past. They miscalculated the energy of Pastor Gauck and the volume of damning files in his care.

If the "red case" officer remained within his two-year contract, he was then allowed to serve it out, while those taken over into career service left immediately once the Gauck researcher uncovered compromising files. The frequency of such "red cases" varied widely from branch to branch and service to service. For reasons not readily apparent, there existed a high incidence of clandestine agents in the ranks of the signals branch, the medical corps, and among jet pilots. The "red cases" proved to be the greatest detriment to the successful integration of NVA veterans in the *Bundeswehr*. The testimony of the secret files carried away several hundred such hopefuls, whose failure to disclose fully all aspects of their past disqualified them from an office of high public trust.

Of the 5,662 ex-NVA officers who applied, during 1992 some 3,575 of these men received career or term military appointments. The average rank among these men was captain. Additionally, some 600 NVA veterans got NCO's stripes, and 1,600 became civil-servants in the senior and lower grades in the eastern *Bundeswehr* administration.

Conclusion

Despite the toll inflicted by the dead hand of the Stasi on new *Bundeswehr* soldiers, their integration into the ranks brought an unexpected victory for the ideals of command and obedience in the *Bundeswehr*. Without *Innere Führung* as the guiding principle of leadership and morale of the West German soldier since the middle-1950s, little of military unity would have unfolded as it did. The events of unification brought an end to the war of words between the *Bundeswehr* and NVA about military reform in contemporary Germany. The doctrine of soldierly command and obedience on the Soviet pattern culminated in piles of discarded red banners and gray uniform caps for sale before the Brandenburg Gate; in derelict, moldering army barracks covered in coal dust; and in seminars about the theory and practice of *Innere Führung* for *Bundeswehr* soldiers of the ex-NVA and for those soldiers and civilians of NATO's "Partnership for Peace."

To be sure, not everything about the soldier in unity was exemplary. One hardly failed to notice that, in certain isolated cases, a western second-rater took advantage of unity to flee a stagnant career and left a disastrous impression on his ex-NVA charges. Further, one found instances of western officers who swaggered into garrison as if they were colonial lords and who made a mockery of *Innere Führung*. Finally, there were numerous cases of disappointed eastern officers who quit in disgust before their terms were up. Such instances were the exceptions rather than the rule.

Above all, however, the outcome of this struggle meant hard work and sacrifice for all concerned from east and west. This common effort and the solidarity between former opponents stands out above everything else one might say about this episode of German military reform. The stoicism of the ex-NVA career candidate repeatedly impressed his new commanders and comrades. The need to re-learn aspects of the military art and craft, while accepting the uncertainties of a cloudy future, were compounded by difficult tasks of command and obedience in units amid great personnel and material turmoil. At the same time, these soldiers in limbo had to assure the well-being of their families and prepare for civilian life if their bid to remain at arms were to fail. The career veterans of the NVA who carried on as soldiers of the new *Bundeswehr* demonstrated an exemplary loyalty and expertise in the challenges of demobilization and reconstruction associated with the military in unification.[38]

As the Article X enlargement of NATO proceeds towards the accession of the first Central European countries in 1999, German soldiers of east and west were the first in the *avant-garde* of what is perhaps the most remarkable maneuver of the present era of policy and strategy in the Euro-Atlantic area. They began the general reorganization of Central and Western European armies according to western command, leadership, morale, and obedience within the overall reform of NATO and its adjoining countries. As the only country that has been *twice* included in the Article VI area of the Washington Treaty (1955 and 1990), Germans naturally took a lead in this critical aspect of extending Euro-Atlantic military institutions into Central and Eastern Europe. As this process gathers momentum in the final years of this century and into the next, the manner in which soldiers of formerly hostile camps have junked the propagandists' images of doom and joined hands to refashion ideals of military service makes one nourish cautious hope about the century to come.

Notes

1. In addition to this writer having observed the *Bundeswehr* in unity during 1989-1997, this account relies upon Jörg Schönbohm, *Zwei Armeen und ein Vaterland: Das Ende der Nationalen Volksarmee* (Berlin: Siedler, 1992); Hans-Peter von Kirchbach, *et al.*, *Abenteuer Einheit: Zum Aufbau der Bundeswehr in den neuen Ländern* (Frankfurt and Bonn: Report, 1992); *Militärgeschichtliches Forschungsamt* (MGFA) (eds.), *Vom Kalten Krieg zur deutschen Einheit: Analysen und Zeitzeugenberichte zur deutschen Militärgeschichte* (Munich: Oldenbourg, 1995); Dieter Farwick, (ed.), *Ein Staat--Eine Armee: von der NVA zur Bundeswehr* (Frankfurt and Bonn: Report, 1992); Detlef Bald (ed.) *Die Nationale Volksarmee: Beiträge zu Selbstverständnis und Geschichte des deutschen Militärs* (Baden-

Baden: Nomos, 1992); Frithjof Knabe, *Unter der Flagge des Gegners* (Opladen: Westdeutscher Verlag, 1994); Udo Baron, *Die Wehrideologie der Nationalen Volksarmee der DDR* (Bochum: Universitätsverlag Dr. Brockmeyer, 1993); Volker Koop, *Abgewickelt: Auf den Spuren der Nationalen Volksarmee*, (Bonn: Bouvier, 1995). Also of note are two works in English: Hans-Peter von Kirchbach, *Reflections on the Growing Together of the German Armed Forces* (Carlisle: U.S. Army War College, 1992); Mark Victorson, *Mission in the East: Building an Army in a Democracy in the New German States* (Newport: Naval War College, 1994). In particular, this writer wishes to thank the German Ministry of Defense in Bonn, and Ms. Diana Blundell, Mr. Warren Olsen, and Mr. Keith Webster of the Defense Security Assistance Agency, Program of Expanded International Military Education and Training, Washington, D.C., for support of this research.

2. See, for instance, Reinhard Bruehl *et al.* (eds.), *Armee für Frieden und Sozialismus: Geschichte der Nationalen Volksarmee der DDR* (Berlin: Militärverlag, 1985), pp. 236-56; Hajo Herbell, *Staatsbürger in Uniform, 1789-1961* (Berlin: Militärverlag, 1969), pp. 443-56; Gerhard Foerster *et al.*, *Der preussisch-deutsche Generalstab, 1640-1965* (Berlin: Militärverlag, 1966).

3. For NATO reforms since 1990, see NATO's Office of Information and Press (eds.), *NATO Handbook* (Brussels: NATO, 1995), pp. 31ff, with pp. 231-34 including the Washington Treaty; Jeffrey Simon, *NATO Enlargement and Central Europe* (Washington DC: National Defense University, 1996), pp. 7ff; Marco Carnovale, "NATO Partners and Allies: Civil-Military Relations and Democratic Control of Armed Forces," in *NATO Review*, Vol. 20, No. 2 (1997) pp. 32-35.

4. See Bundeskanzleramt, "Einleitende Erklärung von Bundeskanzler Dr. Helmut Kohl vor der Bundespressekonferenz am Dienstag, 17. Juli 1990," manuscript; Horst Teltschik, *329 Tage: Innenansichten der Einigung* (Berlin: Siedler, 1991), pp. 313-45.

5. On the term "inner structure" in German military usage, see Bundesministerium der Verteidigung (BMVg), Führungsstab der Streitkräfte (Fue S) I 4, "Definitionen" (Bonn: 3 May 1979), manuscript; Donald Abenheim, *Reforging the Iron Cross: The Search for Tradition in the West German Military* (Princeton: Princeton University Press, 1988) pp. 11ff.

6. BMVg, "Punktation für das Pressegespräch des Ministers am 10.09.1990 zu drei Schwerpunktthemen: Perspektiven der Bundeswehrplanung; Reduzierung der alliierten Streitkräfte in Deutschland; Bildung gesamtdeutscher Streitkräfte; die künftige Bundeswehr" (5 September 1990), manuscript.

7. This account derives from Werner von Scheven, "Die Bundeswehr und der Aufbau Ost," in MGFA (eds.), *Vom Kalten Krieg zur deutschen Einheit*, pp. 473-503 [note 1]; and Edgar Trost, "Probleme der Personalauswahl," in Dieter Farwick, (ed.), *Ein Staat-- eine Armee*, pp. 170-205 [note 1]. This writer wishes to thank Lieutenant General (Retired) Werner von Scheven and Lieutenant General Edgar Trost for their generous support of this research.

8. BMVg, Stellvertreter des Generalinspekteurs der Bundeswehr (Fue S) IV 1, "Organisationsbefehl für die Aufstellung des Bundeswehrkommandos Ost" (Bonn: 25 September 1990), manuscript.

9. Jörg Schönbohm, "Deutsche Kommen zu Deutschen," in Farwick (ed.), *Ein Staat--eine Armee*, p. 43 [note 1].

10. Abenheim, *Reforging the Iron Cross*, pp. 17-22; compare BMVg, Führungsstab der Bundeswehr (Fue B) (eds.), *Handbuch Innere Führung: Hilfen zur Klärung der Begriffe* (Bonn: BMVg, 1957); Politische Hauptverwaltung der NVA (eds.), *Vom Sinn des Soldatenseins* (Berlin: NVA, 1987); Siegfried Bartsch, *Bundeswehr und NVA: die gegenseitige Darstellung zwischen Konfrontation und Vertrauensbildung* (Berlin: Wissenschaft, 1989).

11. On the Nazi cult of Prussia, see Abenheim, *Reforging the Iron Cross*, pp. 33-39; on the German-German battle over military reform, see Herbell, *Staatbürger*, pp. 11ff [note 2]; Edgar Doehler *et al.*, *Militär-historische Traditionen der DDR und der NVA* (Berlin: Militärverlag, 1989); Bernd Proell, *Bundeswehr und Nationale Volksarmee in Staat und Gesellschaft* (Frankfurt am Main: Haag und Herchen, 1983).

12. Ulrich Simon, *Die Integration der Bundeswehr in die Gesellschaft: Das Ringen um die Innere Führung* (Heidelberg: Decker's, 1980); Hans-Jürgen Rautenberg, "Zur Standortbestimmung für künftige deutsche Streitkräfte," in *Anfänge westdeutscher Sicherheitspolitik*, Vol. 1 (Munich: Oldenbourg, 1982); Abenheim, *Reforging the Iron Cross*, pp. 64ff; Ulrich de Maizière, *In der Pflicht Lebensbericht eines deutschen Soldaten im 20. Jahrhundert* (Bonn and Herford: Mittler, 1989); Detlef Bald, *Militär und Gesellschaft, 1945-1990* (Baden-Baden: Nomos, 1994), pp. 53ff; Dieter Walz (ed.), *Drei Jahrzehne Innere Führung* (Baden-Baden: Nomos, 1987).

13. Abenheim, *Reforging the Iron Cross*, pp. 64ff; BMVg (eds.), *Handbuch Innere Führung* [note 10]; BMVg (eds.), *Zentrale Dienstvorschrift, 10/1: Hilfen für die Innere Führung* (Bonn: BMVg, 1972); BMVg (eds.), *Zentrale Dienstvorschrift, 10/1: Innere Führung* (Bonn: BMVg, 1993). The latter are the official regulations on *Innere Führung*, command, obedience, and morale in the Bundeswehr.

14. For an older NVA example of this, see Herbell, *Staatsbürger in Uniform*, pp. 361ff. [note 2]; also valuable are Peter Jungermann, *Die Wehrideologie der SED und das Leitbild der NVA vom sozialistischen deutschen Soldaten* (Stuttgart: Seewald, 1973), pp. 135ff; Baron, *Wehrideologie der NVA*, pp. 38ff. [note 1].

15. Herbell, *Staatsbürger in Uniform*, pp. 420-42; Politische Hauptverwaltung der NVA (eds.), *Die Bundeswehr der BRD--eine imperialistische Aggressionsarmee* (Berlin, 1985), pp. 1-32; Politische Hauptverwaltung der NVA (eds.), *Hinweise für die marxistische-leninistische und pädagogische Qualifizierung der Schulungsgruppenleiter der politischen Schulung, 1989-90* (n.d. circa 1989). Also see citations in note 14.

16. Herbell, *Staatsbürger in Uniform*, pp. 490-504; Jungermann, *Wehrideologie der SED*, pp. 184ff.

17. Jungermann, *Wehrideologie der SED*, pp. 227-56; Politische Hauptverwaltung der NVA (eds.), *Bundeswehr*, pp. 1-32. [note 15].

18. Carl von Clausewitz, *On War*, Michael Howard and Peter Paret, translators (New York: Knopf, 1993), pp. 83-114; Politische Hauptverwaltung der NVA (eds.), *Bewusste militärische Diziplin--Grundlage hoher Kampfkraft--Mutter des Sieges* (Berlin: 1985); Reinhard Bruehl *et al.*, *Armee für Frieden und Sozialismus*, pp. 463-97, 700ff. [note 2].

19. The last official *Bundeswehr* publication on the NVA appeared in 1978: BMVg (eds.), *Die NVA: Schriftenreihe Innere Führung* (Bonn: BMVg, 1978). Of the various post-1990 assessments on the inner structure of the NVA by veterans and Bundeswehr observers, see Wolfgang Markus, "Das Offizierskorps der NVA: ein soziales Porträt," in Detlef Bald (ed.), *Die Nationale Volksarmee* (Baden-Baden: Nomos, 1992), pp. 51-64; Hans-Werner Weber, "Gläubigkeit, Opportunismus und späte Zweifel: Anmerkungen zu den Veränderungen im politisch-moralischen Bewusstsein des Offizierkorps der NVA," in Manfred Backerra (ed.), *NVA: Rückblick für die Zukunft* (Cologne: Markus, 1992), pp. 43-68; Rüdiger Volk *et al.*, "Der Innere Zustand der NVA," in Dieter Farwick (ed.), *Ein Staat--eine Armee*, pp. 235-67.

20. Unless otherwise cited, this account draws from Werner von Scheven, "Bundeswehr, Nationale Volksarmee, und die Vereinigung Deutschlands" (June 1992), manuscript, p.1; Werner von Scheven, "Die Bundeswehr und der Aufbau Ost," in MGFA (eds.), *Vom Kalten Krieg*, pp. 483ff. Also of interest is Klaus-Jürgen Engellien *et al.*, "Wer bist Du Kamerad? Der Versuch einer Beschreibung des ehemaligen NVA Offiziers," *Truppenpraxis*, Vol. 25, No. 3 (1990), pp. 650-53.

21. von Scheven, "Aufbau Ost," pp. 486-87 [note 20]; see also "Politorgane in der NVA," in Militärakademie Friedrich Engels *et al.*, (eds.), *Militärlexikon*, 2d ed. (Berlin: Militärverlag, 1973); Kurt Held *et al.*, "Politische Bildung und Erziehung in der NVA," in Backerra, *NVA*, pp. 205-32 [note 19].

22. von Scheven, "Aufbau Ost," p. 487. On Prussian-German institutions of leadership, command, and obedience as well as Soviet practice, see Karl-Volker Neugebauer (ed.), *Grundzüge der deutschen Militärgeschichte: Historischer Überblick* (Freiburg: Rombach, 1993), pp. 39ff.; Dirk Oetting, *Auftragstaktik: Geschichte und Gegenwart einer Führungskonzeption* (Frankfurt am Main and Bonn: Report, 1993); *Motivation und Gefechtswert: Vom Verhalten des Soldaten im Kriege* (Frankfurt am Main and Bonn: Report, 1988); Erich Sobik, "Truppenführung bei den sowjetischen Landstreitkräften," *Truppenpraxis*, Vol. 25, No. 4 (1980), pp. 640-50; Werner von Scheven, "Die Truppenführung: zur Geschichte ihrer Vorschrift und zur Entwicklung ihrer Struktur von 1933 bis 1962," unpublished thesis (Hamburg: 1969); "Heeresdienstvorschrift 300/1: *Truppenführung*," Wehrmacht/army field service regulation (Berlin: Mittler, 1936).

23. von Scheven, "Aufbau Ost," pp. 487-88; Hans-Georg Loeffler, "Gefechtsbereitschaft--das Ziel der Ausbildung," in Backerra, *NVA*, pp. 91-112; Hans-Werner Deim, "Die NVA in der ersten strategischen Staffel der Streitkräfte des Warschauer Vertrages," in Backerra, *NVA*, pp. 311-32; Horst-Henning Basler,

"Das operative Denken der NVA," in Klaus Naumann (ed.), *NVA: Anspruch und Wirklichkeit* (Berlin, Bonn, and Herford: Mittler, 1993), pp. 179-220.

24. von Scheven "Aufbau Ost," pp. 488-489; Wolfgang Scheler, "Vorlesung: Die geistige Situation der Zeit und die Neubestimmung der Werte--Die Globalisierung der Sicherheit," September, 1990, manuscript; "[Ost-] Deutsche Soldaten im geistigen Umbruch," in *Interdiziplinärer Wissenschaftsbereich Sicherheit: Arbeitspapiere der Nationalen Volksarmee, Militärakademie "Friedrich Engels"* (Dresden: 1990), pp. 7-19; Paul Heider, "'Nicht Freund, nicht Gegner, sondern Partner.' Zum Transformationsprozess der Nationalen Volksarmee auf dem Wege in die deutsche Einheit," in MGFA (eds.), *Vom Kalten Krieg*, pp. 419-42.

25. Jörg Schönbohm, *Zwei Armeen*, pp. 24-41 [note 1]; von Scheven, "Aufbau Ost," pp. 484-86.

26. von Scheven, "Aufbau Ost," p. 489; Trost, "Probleme der Personalauswahl," pp. 170ff [note 7]; BMVg, P II 1, Aktenzeichen 02-06-00/3, "Richtlinien für die Berufung von Angehörigen der ehemaligen NVA in das Dienstverhältnis eines Soldaten auf Zeit für die Dauer von 2 Jahren" (Bonn: 17 September 1990), manuscript. This document contains the question about clandestine intelligence contacts.

27. von Scheven, "Aufbau Ost," p. 490; Trost, "Probleme der Personalauswahl," pp. 184ff.

28. This writer taught in such classes at Koblenz in the Fall of 1990; see "Arbeitspapier, Zentrum Innere Führung: Gesamtdeutsche Streitkräfte, Vorlaufausbildung für Schlüsselpersonal der NVA" (Koblenz: 1990), manuscript.

29. von Scheven, "Aufbau Ost," p. 490; on the support offered by units in the West, see Trost, "Probleme der Personalauswahl," pp. 175-81.

30. von Scheven, "Aufbau Ost," pp. 490-91; Trost, "Probleme der Personalauswahl," pp. 189-202.

31. von Scheven, "Aufbau Ost," p. 491. On the civilian, administrative branch of the *Bundeswehr*, see Hubert Reinfried, *Streitkräfte und Bundeswehrverwaltung* (Regensburg: Walhalla, 1979).

32. von Scheven, "Aufbau Ost," p. 491; Trost, "Probleme der Personalauswahl," pp. 192-95.

33. Trost, "Probleme der Personalauswahl," pp. 187-88.

34. von Scheven, "Aufbau Ost," p. 492.

35. *Zentrum Innere Führung* (eds.), "Co-Referat: Das Menschenbild in der Bundeswehr und in der Inneren Führung," (Strausberg: 19 September 1995), manuscript. This writer has taught in such classes in Strausberg within the U.S. Expanded International Military Education and Training program.

36. von Scheven, "Aufbau Ost," p. 493.

37. von Scheven, "Aufbau Ost," pp. 491, 493-4; interview with Lieutenant Colonel (Ret.) Dieter Sailer, Research and Publications Branch, Gauck Agency (Berlin: September 1995).

38. von Scheven, "Aufbau Ost," pp. 494-503; Trost, "Probleme der Personalauswahl," pp. 195-202; an official retrospective is BMVg. (eds.),

"Informationen zur Sicherheitspolitik: Fünf Jahre Armee der Einheit--eine Bilanz" (Bonn: 3 October 1995); of further interest are Peter Schneider, "Die neuen Kameraden: Eine Meisterleistung der Vereinigung--Wie die NVA aufgelöst würde," in *Der Spiegel*, No. 24 (1994), pp. 74-89; BMVg (eds.), *Weißbuch 1994: zur Sicherheit der Bundesrepublik Deutschland und zur Lage der Bundeswehr* (Bonn: 1994), pp. 11-21; on NATO enlargement, see BMVg, "Reihe Stichworte für die Öffentlichkeitsarbeit und Truppeninformation: NATO Assignierung der Streitkräfte in den neuen Bundesländern" (Bonn: January 1995), manuscript; NATO (eds.), "Study on NATO Enlargement" (Brussels: September 1995), manuscript, especially pp. 23ff. For a more skeptical view of the Bundeswehr in unification, see Knabe, *Unter der Flagge des Gegners* [note 1]; Peter Joachim Lapp, *Ein Staat--eine Armee, von der NVA zur Bundeswehr* (Bonn: Ebert Stiftung, 1992).

13

German Foreign Policy Between Tradition and Innovation: The Geopolitical Imperative of *Scharnierpolitik*[1]

Dirk Verheyen

The unexpected and dramatic events that rocked Europe from Berlin to Moscow between 1989 and 1991 abruptly transformed the structures and patterns of international affairs that had marked the divided continent for more than four decades. The re-emergence of a united Germany in the heart of Europe, along with the spectacular demise of the Soviet Union, constituted the most climactic episodes in this process of breathtaking change. Presumably "solved," or at least dormant, in a context of seemingly definitive national division, the old "German Question" suddenly reappeared on the European diplomatic landscape. Writing about this question, W. R. Smyser has suggested that

[e]ver since the dawn of the European state system, the countries of Europe and the world have faced two German questions. Now that the cold war is over they must begin dealing with a third--and different--German question. The first question was how to treat a weak and divided Germany. . . . The second German question was how to deal with a united and strong Germany. . . . Now there is a third and new German question: How should the world react to a Germany that is united, democratic, and responsible, that is not bent on aggression, but that remains powerfully influential and that has its own interests and pursues them?[2]

How has this "new" Germany defined and developed its foreign and security policies, and what have been the domestic as well as foreign reactions? How has unification changed the policies that had come to enjoy considerable public consensus in the "old" Federal Republic?

In 1993, three years after the re-emergence of a single, united Germany on the European diplomatic stage, Andrei S. Markovits and Simon Reich published an essay with the direct and fairly provocative title: "Should Europe Fear the Germans?" Pointing to the persistent scholarly and journalistic preoccupation with an often elusive "German Question," they noted that the contemporary debate focuses on "the issue of the new Germany's role in a changing European and global environment," adding that the various "commentaries are divisible into two major categories: the majority optimistic, basically viewing Germany's unification as a boon to Germany, Europe, and global peace; and the minority pessimistic, worrying that a strong Germany will repeat the mistakes of its past."[3]

As far as the optimists are concerned, Markovits and Reich suggested that some of them, inspired and reassured by functionalist integration theory, perceive "a Germany tamed by its international ties."[4] In contrast to such external constraints on German international behavior, rooted in both NATO and the European Union, institutionally focused optimists emphasize "internal constraints to [sic] German dominance," pointing to "the acceptance of a system of federalism and democratic values as the new Germany assimilates the political structure of the old Federal Republic."[5] The underlying assumption is that the united Germany is in the end nothing more than a successful enlargement of the formerly West German Federal Republic. A third group of optimists, using a more sociological line of analysis, essentially argues that "the new German political and economic elites represent the postwar triumph of the bourgeoisie with its liberal and democratic values over the traditionally imperialist and aggressive ways of the feudal and aristocratic Junkers before 1945."[6] Much of this echoes the now classic analysis of postwar West Germany by Ralf Dahrendorf.[7] In this view, contemporary

> German economic, intellectual, and political elites have been acutely aware of their responsibility for Germany's terrible past and thus stand vigil, guarding against the reemergence of militarist, antiliberal, xenophobic, and cryptofascist tendencies in the new united Germany.[8]

Turning to the pessimists, Markovits and Reich suggest that their "anguish concerning prospective [German] hegemony, in view of Germany's unification and the vacuum in power and leadership created by American and Soviet withdrawals from Europe, takes two primary forms: one historical, the other cultural. In different ways, both stress evidence that predates 1945."[9] Worried by a German tradition of democratic failure in domestic politics and militarist and economic aggressiveness in foreign policy, the historical pessimists fear a resurgence of destabilizing German assertiveness, in part as the by-product of socioeconomic and political turmoil at home.[10]

Debating the Foundations of Policy

The opposing perspectives of optimists and pessimists sketched by Markovits and Reich and summarized above are not merely a matter of analysis and commentary by foreign observers. They find their reflection, at least in part, in an on-going debate within a Germany searching for a clear sense of role and identity as central power in a post-cold war Europe.[11] As Josef Janning has argued,

> the most controversial notions in the intellectual debate on the country's future policy all have to do with different interpretations of the meanings of the past. In this discourse, traditionalists who perceive themselves as realists stand against modernists educated in a structural analysis of international affairs.[12]

In a deeper sense, this debate among Germans over their country's foreign policy is connected to a more fundamental philosophical and even ideological dispute between those who advocate a greater sense of German "normalcy," expressed in occasionally revisionist histori-ography and a positive attitude regarding "healthy" patriotism,[13] and those who would ultimately argue that post-Auschwitz Germany can never pretend or afford to be "normal." To the latter, the German *Sonderweg* ("special path") that culminated in Nazism and the Holocaust represents a shadow and burden that cannot and may not be pushed aside in favor of a partly revisionist and partly ahistorical sense of post-unification "normalcy." The prominent philosopher Jürgen Habermas, for example, has raised strong questions about the tendency to seek a restoration of "normalcy" in Germany's domestic as well as foreign affairs.[14]

In the contemporary German foreign policy debate, "realists" or "traditionalists" emphasize the importance of underlying continuity in European diplomatic history and suggest the enduring relevance of classical balance of power and *Realpolitik* perspectives. Their views are not without influence in leading German policy-making circles, particularly in the Christian Democratic Union (CDU) and its Bavarian sister-party, the Christian Social Union (CSU). As Janning puts it, in the realist-traditionalist perspective, "states as actors-- their interests and power, their constellations and coalitions--domi- nate and foreign policy is statecraft conducted to maximize nationally accountable benefits in a primarily anarchic environment."[15]

In contrast to the "realist" or "traditionalist" perspective, a considerable number of German scholars and commentators stresses the importance of multilateralist and integrationist aspects of European as well as global affairs. Summarizing their line of analysis, Janning notes that for them

> the integration of Germany in these supra-, multi- and transnational contexts is so fundamental that it transcends the analytical separation of national vs. integration policies. This has been proven in the four decades of West German integration and should remain the focus of the united country as well. Therefore any foreign policy, be it conducted from Bonn or Berlin, should be rooted in the development and nurturing of those institutions which have to steer these interdependencies.[16]

The arguments advanced in this context span across a considerable spec- trum, including those who envisage a post-national Germany as "civilian" power in a transformed international political arena.[17]

And where does the general public in Germany stand? In the course of the 1990s, a series of in-depth opinion surveys have been carried out in order to obtain insight into the evolving state of the German public mind with regard to a variety of foreign and security policy issues.[18] The results show a deeply-rooted pro-western foreign policy culture. Respondents expressed a considerable and to some extent even growing level of support for NATO, but less solid backing for a continued U.S. military presence on German soil. Divergences in opinion between eastern and western Germans on these and other questions have narrowed at least somewhat in recent years, despite continuing contrasts on matters of security policy. Over time, this might suggest the possibility of a relative erosion of mental contrasts that were rooted in the cold war era.

Most Germans support a more active NATO role in "out-of-area" operations, including crisis management in Eastern and Southeastern Europe and security guarantees for future new EU members in Central and Eastern Europe, yet a still deeply engrained "culture of reticence" blocks broader support for active German military participation in both NATO- and UN-sponsored missions. At least half of the German public favors the eastward expansion of NATO membership, with Central and Eastern Europe, along with Russia, increasingly defined as areas of "vital interest."

Overall support for further European integration as well as expanded EU membership remains strong, but worries about the implications for the FRG of a full economic and monetary union (EMU), as envisaged in the Maastricht Treaty of 1991, have clearly grown over the past few years. The German public appears to be increasingly conscious of Germany's enhanced post-cold war influence and responsibility, and of the corresponding importance of the country's national interests, yet support for a non-military, multilateralized exercise of German power continues to be striking.

The argument advanced in this essay is situated between the optimist and pessimist camps, and between the neo-realist and integrationist perspectives, by stressing the extent to which post-unification German foreign policy continues to evolve, thus precluding definitive evaluation, and by suggesting that Germany's post-cold war foreign policy environment is characterized by a partial re-nationalizing "return of history," particularly to the East and South-east, along with a continuing presence of western integrationist constraints and commitments. These commitments, in turn, are the product of a genuine post-1945 re-orientation in German foreign policy culture, although in a united Germany with its peculiar national sensitivities and vulnerabilities vis-à-vis an adjacent zone of post-communist turmoil they must coexist and even compete with more nationally focused inclinations and temptations.

The essence of Germany's foreign policy environment is the country's central, continental location.[19] West German and East German foreign policies were the product of defeated, traumatized, and slowly rehab-ilitated states of a partitioned nation on the front-line of a cold war dominated by superpower patrons and overshadowed by nuclear peril. With prospects for national reunification uncertain at best and wary neighbors eager to tame a restless and aggressive Germany once and for all, foreign policy options were limited. Each state became a loyal member of its respective "camp." The tradition of German *Schaukel-politik*, whereby a united Germany had floated along its *Sonderweg* between East and West, gave way to *Westbindung* for the FRG and *Ostbindung* for the GDR.

The end of the cold war has produced a united Germany once more, yet in a considerably transformed European setting (despite some sug-gestive similarities to an older Europe, especially in the post-communist East).[20] Jochen Thies tries to capture the significance and implications of this mixture of continuity and change when he notes, history starts to matter again. Germany cannot escape from it, nor can the country run away from the new realities of geography. There is no relief from being positioned in the middle of Europe. Germany has to accept the fact and must act in order to overcome the traumatic memories of the past when the middle position after Bismarck led to great European wars, bringing to an end the history of the German Reich, founded in 1871, after just two generations in 1945.[21]

Integrated more decisively into the western world than ever before, constrained by a maze of military, economic, and political commitments and limitations, and guided by a considerably transformed foreign policy culture, today's Germany strives to combine its western links and the imperatives of its Central-European geopolitical location in a new type of policy, which may be called *Scharnierpolitik* ("hinge-policy"). Eager to preserve and strengthen the achievements of postwar integration and reconciliation in the West and to extend these successes and benefits to a struggling and unstable East, Germany has assumed a leading role in the western "outreach" effort to post-communist Central and Eastern Europe (including the Commonwealth of Independent States (CIS) in general and Russia in particular), within the frameworks of the European Union (EU), the North Atlantic Treaty Organization (NATO), and the Conference on Security and Cooperation in Europe (CSCE, with its organizational component known as OSCE). The Federal Republic is in fact reaching out to the post-cold war East in ways that are at times reminiscent of the American approach to Western Europe (and western Germany) after 1945. In the view of W. R. Smyser, "Germany's principal foreign policy objective since unification has been to link East and West."[22] In other words, it is turning from a pair of cold war frontline states into the strategic "hinge" between the continent's two halves.

Placed once more at the center of European affairs, Germany has, as Daniel Hamilton puts it,

> embarked on an active policy of pan-European entente, seeking to build a stable political, economic, and security framework that can make Europe safe from its history. During the cold war, European stability had been organized from the periphery; the premise of European entente is that it must now be facilitated from the center. Germany, united and free, is the nation most able, anxious, and willing to spur its partners to commission the actual construction of a Common European Home and underwrite the accompanying *Hausordnung*.[23]

In pursuit of these objectives, Germany's pivotal role gives it a unique weight vis-à-vis its neighbors on all sides, since its "significance within the European Community and the West increases its influence within the East while its growing sway in the East enhances its ability to shape western institutions and policies."[24] In fact, Smyser argues, "Germany sits at the center of a vast network of contacts and communications across the Northern Hemisphere."[25]

Even prior to the end of the cold war, some of these developments were in a way foreshadowed by the accelerating pace of *Deutschland-politik* between the FRG and the GDR during the 1970s and 1980s. In the words of Arnulf Baring, "[t]he slow return of West Germany to the old central European position started with détente."[26] At that time, such a policy matched the fundamental strategic and political interests of a divided nation benefitting from East-West detente. Today, the pursuit of *Scharnierpolitik* corresponds to a united Germany's fundamental national interest in promoting East-West reconciliation and integration. The alternative of inaction would amount to a more or less benign neglect of a politically turbulent and economically struggling power vacuum that could destabilize and threaten the entire continent. In fact, one might argue that the success of an activist German policy, pursued within multilateralist frameworks, is in the more general European interest as well. In this case, one might say that what is good for Germany is good for Europe. Germany's new *Scharnierpolitik* is still evolving, both in terms of definition and execution, thus rendering most proclamations of optimism or pessimism rather premature. Moreover, the impulses and dynamics underlying this policy reflect both "realist" and "integrationist" tendencies, characteristic of Germany's complex foreign policy environment.

From *Schaukelpolitik* to *Scharnierpolitik*

Factors of power, geography, identity, and developmental timing have historically combined to turn the question of Germany's place in the international arena into a fundamental problem for German foreign policy and a basic feature in the development of German foreign policy culture.[27] In terms of its power, Germany has tended to be either too weak to alleviate the perennial security fears that permeate the country's foreign policy culture, or too strong to leave wary neighbors reassured about their own safety. The country's geopolitical location has often been profoundly associated with a sense of fluidity, vulnerability, and encirclement.

In the definition and conduct of pre-1945 foreign policy, Germany's fluid identity problem mixed cultural-ideological, geographic, and political elements. Highly Germanocentric attitudes promoted a considerable alienation from the West and invidiously anti-Slavic feelings toward the East, combined with a hyper-nationalist imperialism fed by glorified visions of German *Kultur*, particularly during the Wilhelmine era. Explicitly racist elements were added during the National Socialist era. The result was a comprehensive and extremely damaging degree of German international isolation.

Furthermore, the timing of Germany's unification in 1871 and subsequent industrial-military development was highly unfortunate, to say the least. The consolidation of German power in the center of Europe had a profoundly destabilizing effect on the nineteenth century balance of power, and served to enhance the risk of conflict on the continent. Germany's illiberal and increasingly militarist domestic order did little to alleviate these growing dangers. A fragmented Germany had served as a useful buffer zone among various powers, but now that "vacuum" was turned into a new competitor with compensatory ambitions. Carrying this line of analysis to its (revisionist) geopolitical conclusion, David Calleo has argued that "[t]he German Problem ought properly to be seen within the context of [the] broad evolution of the Western national states and the international issues which that evolution inevitably posed." He suggests,

> Germany was the last of the great European states to be formed.... A good part of the Germans' ill fortune came from having failed to consolidate a national state before their neighbors.... [D]ynamic Germany was found to appear an aggressor, challenging the arrangements that had grown up in its absence and that presumed its continuing weakness . . . . To analyze Germany's ambitions and fears as essentially the product of its own unusual political culture subtly distorts history in favor of Germany's victors. For Britain, France, Russia, and the United States were great powers with appetites no less ravenous than Germany's. . . . In short, Germany's "aggressiveness" against international order may be explained as plausibly by the nature of that order as by any peculiar characteristics of the Germans.[28]

From an historical perspective, German foreign policy culture has seen a succession of distinct strategic visions aimed at dealing with this problem of Germany's power, role, and position in international affairs. The first vision, especially associated with Bismarck, had as its point of departure the realization that Germany is first and foremost a Central European state (a *Land in der Mitte*), geopolitically and in many ways geoculturally located between East and West. From this vantage-point, Germany was seen at times as a "bridge" between East and West, an entity with a balancing and mediating role. Close attention was paid to the maintenance of a European balance of power and the legitimate interests of other powers. Insofar as revisionist intentions entered German foreign policy, they were to be pursued with caution and considerable respect for the existing status quo. Germany intended to avoid overly rigid alliances, aimed at keeping diplomatic options open. The notion of *Schaukelpolitik* was enshrined in such doctrines of diplomatic maneuverability. This intricate policy was increasingly neglected and undermined by Bismarck's more careless successors, however, culminating in World War I. Elements of the *Schaukelpolitik* tradition returned during the Weimar era, often summarized by reference to the Rapallo agreement with the Soviet Union.

While much of Bismarck's vision of Germany's position and role in international politics was rendered obsolete in the context of the cold war and the country's division, its influence could still be noted in the newly created Federal Republic. The idea of Germany as "bridge" between East and West, as developed by politicians like Jakob Kaiser (CDU) in the late 1940s, comes to mind. Or the various plans that were floated by the Social Democratic Party (SPD) and the Free Democratic Party (FDP) in the course of the 1950s, aimed at the reunification of Germany based on German military neutrality, European military disengagement zones, and the creation of an all-European collective security system. Some of these ideas were interestingly enough resurrected by GDR communist caretaker prime minister Hans Modrow and Soviet leader Mikhail Gorbachev in early 1990, on the eve of German reunification. Or one might consider the idea of a special German *Sicherheits- und Friedenspartnerschaft* (partnership for security and peace) involving the FRG and the GDR, in the shadow of superpower bipolarity, as it emerged in the context of *Ostpolitik* and *Deutschlandpolitik* during the 1970s and 1980s. Throughout the 1949-1989 period, however, such ideas were very much at odds with the Federal Republic's dominant, western-oriented foreign policy. They were frequently denounced, both inside West Germany and in various western capitals, as a dangerous revival of an obsolete German tradition of *Schaukelpolitik* between East and West, based on the illusion of some positive German *Sonderweg* in international affairs.

A second vision, associated with the militant *Großmachtpolitik* (great power policy) of Kaiser Wilhelm II and his entourage and the much more extreme racial and geopolitical imperialism of Hitler, shared with the first vision an essentially nationalist focus on Germany's position and role in international affairs. But the problems of Germany's international situation were not solved by cautious revisionism, an avoidance of diplomatic isolation, and due regard for the balance of power and the proper interests of others. Instead, there was aggressive revisionism, reckless power politics, and expansionist behavior, all of it aimed at breaking the fetters supposedly imposed on the country by geopolitical encirclement and disadvantage. The German *Sonderweg* led directly to imperialism and war. After 1945, fundamental philosophical rejection and lack of opportunity rendered obsolete all these militant, imperialist perspectives, in spite of repeated charges of "revanchism" leveled at the FRG by its various neighbors to the East during the cold war. A slight revival might have occurred by means of some more extremist "roll-back" and "liberation" rhetoric at the height of East-West confrontation, but these were never a realistic option.

A third vision for German foreign policy developed after World War II, and is particularly associated with the legacy of CDU Chancellor Konrad Adenauer. The emergence of this vision cannot be separated from the international setting in which West German foreign policy had to be pursued. This was a setting characterized by defeat and occupation, national division, integration of the two German states into cold war alliances, West German security dependence on the West (especially the United States), and revisionism regarding Central and Eastern Europe's communist status-quo. The fact that the FRG could only be understood as a product of the cold war and as the rehabilitated opponent of a not-so-distant past served to circumscribe Bonn's foreign policy *Spielraum* (room to maneuver) in many decisive ways, often forestalling choices and imposing particular needs. In addition, defeat, occupation, and subsequent security dependence in the cold war made the FRG into a uniquely "penetrated" political system, susceptible and sensitive to outside influences that deeply affected policy conceptions and directions.

Eager to achieve Germany's rehabilitation and sovereignty, longing for a firm peace with the West and German integration into the western community of nations, and hoping to obtain western allied support for reunification on West German terms, Adenauer single-mindedly pursued the two key facets of his *Westpolitik* the "supranationalization" and the "westernization" (*Verwestlichung*) of German foreign policy.[29] Supranationalization implied a basic abandonment of the almost exclusively nationalist thinking in earlier German foreign policy. The new West German state became a leading champion of schemes for European and Atlantic integration, although domestic political debate was lengthy and intense over the degree to which a pursuit of integration might or might not be compatible with the goal of national reunification.

"Westernization" aimed at a basic reconciliation of the historical alienation between Germany and the West. The *Verwestlichung* of

German foreign policy was aided by a number of important factors, rooted in ideology and environmental compulsion. Among West German political parties, the CDU in particular was animated by what may be called an *Abendland* ("western civilization") ideology, stressing the political, philosophical, and religious beliefs and values that Germany was felt to share with the West. There was a strong Catholic and even Carolingian component in the thinking of Adenauer and many of his supporters. Just as the supranationalism of Adenauer's *Westpolitik* constituted a sharp break with past nationalist traditions in German foreign policy culture, so did the reorientation effected by Germany's westernization imply an abandonment of older Central-European geopolitical perspectives. In the context of the cold war, Germany became the divided heart of Europe, whereby each German state turned into the outer rampart of its respective alliance system. Adenauer's *Westpolitik* was at least in part shaped by a persistent "Potsdam complex," based on the fear of great power agreements at Germany's expense. Only western integration would prevent Germany from becoming or remaining a mere pawn or object in international politics. Hans-Peter Schwarz has concluded that Adenauer's "basic point of departure was simple: the Federal Republic, but also a reunited Germany, is only secure, both for the Germans and their neighbors, if it is irrevocably connected . . . . with the Western democracies." This was nothing less than a "new foreign policy tradition."[30]

Upon Germany's reunification in October of 1990, Volker Rühe (CDU) remarked that the new Germany would undoubtedly be *östlicher und protestantischer* (more eastern and more protestant). Rather than interpreting this observation solely as a commentary about German domestic politics, it can also be considered an interesting speculation about the geopolitical and cultural implications of reunification for the country's foreign policy. The demise of communism and the Iron Curtain has placed the united Germany back in the center of the continent, yet the traditions and benefits of Adenauer's *Westpolitik* as well as the aversion against an exposed, nationalist diplomacy appear to have taken firm root in German foreign policy culture. Moreover, Germany's continued integration into western economic, political, and security structures, combined with the country's inability to address, let alone solve, the challenges to the East independently from broader, multilateralist frameworks of "outreach," entail a series of real constraints that limit its foreign policy choice environment.

A Central European Germany is back, but it is no longer the Germany or the Europe of 1871, 1914, or even 1945. As the old Federal Republic's Bonn gives way to the newly united Germany's Berlin, the fully sovereign country's western ties and interests are now indeed increasingly

complemented by eastern worries and interests.[31] Hence the clearly dis-
cernible emergence of a new, fourth vision or tradition in German foreign
policy: a *Scharnierpolitik* that seeks to blend the geopolitical imperatives (and temptations) that once undergirded the *Schaukelpolitik* of
the post-1871 era with the deeper philosophical orientations and principles developed through "supranationalization" and "westernization"
in the *Westpolitik* of the years between 1949 and 1989. We can grasp
the broad outlines of this new direction in German foreign policy by examining post-1990 developments in the country's European integration
and security policies.

Toward a Grand European Union?

Throughout the postwar period, as we have noted, the Federal
Republic has been a prominent and convinced advocate of ever-closer
European integration. A strong reaction against the excesses of previous
nationalism, combined with a need to achieve international rehabilitation and alleviate the concerns of neighbors regarding the exercise of German power, served to generate a widely shared political
consensus in West Germany in favor of the construction of an
increasingly post-national European unity.   Looking back from the
1990s, it can be argued that the FRG's European policy has in fact been
the product of mixed motivations: philosophical and ideological
conviction has been essential, but so have calculations of (West) German "national interest" and the imperatives imposed by international
(especially cold war) conditions.[32]

The advent of unification quickly raised questions among Germany's
neighbors, however, about the future reliability of the country's commitment to continued, let alone expanded, European integration.[33]
Preoccupation with the massive task of rebuilding the former GDR in a
context of economic recession, in addition to the removal of earlier
constraints on German national sovereignty: might they not give rise to
a Germany less reticent in advancing its national interest and wielding
the instruments of its considerable diplomatic and economic clout?
Simon Bulmer and William E. Paterson admit that "German unification
has certainly placed the question of the country's role in Europe back
under the spotlight," but they argue that "the dramatic changes of 1989
have not yet led to a correspondingly dramatic change in Germany's
role. . . . The principal response has seen the FRG reiterate its European
identity; the Europeanization of Germany became once again a goal of
policy."[34]

For years, the members of the European Community have grappled with two fundamental objectives that have often been presented as in some ways mutually exclusive: further integration among the EC's existing members (known as "deepening") and membership expansion (referred to as "widening" or "broadening"). Great Britain, an outspoken opponent of further surrender of sovereignty to the Brussels "Eurocracy," has tended to emphasize the objective of broadened membership, as part of its vision of a more loosely constructed "intergovernmental" Europe of national states. France, meanwhile, has been more interested in the goal of further integration from time to time, seeking to promote a "supranational" Europe in which France might enhance the exercise of its power by means of the Franco-German axis. Other EC members have been scattered across and between these two "camps." The Federal Republic has always been an advocate of both objectives, reflecting both a sense of policy conviction and a need to maintain amicable relations with two key European allies.[35] Prior to the end of the cold war, West Germany championed the membership causes of Austria and the Scandinavian countries, and also lent crucial support to the creation of the Single European Act of 1986 and the initiation of the Europe 1992 project, which aimed at the comprehensive removal of fiscal, physical, and technical barriers that hindered the completion of a fully integrated internal EC market.

Reflecting both ideological orientation and a calculation of German interests, the Federal Republic continues to encourage the simultaneous pursuit of "deepening" and "widening" today. Hence the country's strong support for the Maastricht Treaty of 1991, which launched the European Union (EU) and envisions a common European currency (the *Euro*) and a common foreign and security policy (CFSP) among EU members. Although, as Hans Schauer has suggested, Germany's postwar political elite has been quite favorable to supranational Europeanist visions and schemes (often in contrast to the more nationally sensitive British and French, for example), current developments and recent polling data nevertheless suggest at least a relative weakening of traditional "Europhoria" in the Federal Republic, among the political elite as well as the general public.[36] Worry about the exchange of a strong *Deutschmark* for a possibly weaker *Euro* is particularly pronounced in this regard.

It should also be noted here, if only in passing, that the urgency felt by many EC states regarding the creation of a more integrated European Union after 1989 was very considerably enhanced by the unexpected advent of German unification and a resultant desire to maintain and deepen supranational restraints on a potentially "renationalized" united Germany. At the same time, as far as the process of "widening" is concerned, it is clear that the Federal Republic has emerged as the leading advocate of EU membership for several post-communist Central and East European countries, most notably Poland, the Czech Republic, Slovakia, and Hungary. More than is the case for other EU member states, Germany's support for eastward enlargement is an unmistakable reflection of its central geopolitical location and its desire to promote socioeconomic prosperity and stability on its eastern frontier. New market opportunities and a concern about the flow of "economic refugees" constitute significant motivating factors here.

The Federal Republic's current interest in the economic trans-formation of Eastern Europe has its roots in a long-standing tradition of German economic involvement in the region, going back centuries. After 1949, as the cold war evolved, the FRG pursued a more active *Ost-handel* (trade in the East) than any other western country. Aside from its obvious geopolitical, economic, and financial significance to the countries to its east, Markovits and Reich have argued that "the newly united Germany's position will in due course become even more formidable by virtue of inheriting the former German Democratic Republic's close 'socialist' ties with Eastern Europe and the [former] Soviet Union." They add that Germany's economic "hegemony" in Central and Eastern Europe will (once again) be matched by an equally important degree of cultural dominance, whereby "German cultural hegemony in the region will assume a commercialized and capitalist character."[37]

The simultaneous pursuit of "deepening" and "widening" does entail a fundamental tension, however, which German policy will not be able to avoid. The result is the likelihood of a "two-speed" Europe, with a more fully integrated core surrounded by those who are primarily interested in or eligible for an intergovernmental European design. Official German policy continues to tread carefully in this area, eager to avoid a harmful split among EU members. However, the circulation of an unofficial but widely noted CDU discussion paper, produced by Wolfgang Schäuble and Karl Lamers (leader and foreign policy spokesman of the party's *Bundestagsfraktion*, respectively) and calling for acceptance of a "two-speed" EU, would suggest that the seeds of policy adjustment may indeed have been planted.[38]

In the pursuit of its European integration policies, the Federal Republic is able to draw upon a considerable reservoir of economic and diplomatic clout. This was already the case before 1990. The advent of unification and the demise of the Iron Curtain and many of the restrictions imposed by the cold war have, however, further enlarged German influence and maneuverability. Although German economic growth rates have slowed markedly in the course of the 1990s, particularly as a result of the high costs associated with eastern German reconstruction, the German economy continues to perform a crucial "locomotive" function within the EU. The *Deutschmark* is clearly Europe's leading currency, playing a central role in the Exchange-Rate Mechanism (ERM) and slated to become the core element in any future common currency. Among European central banks, the *Bundesbank* occupies an often dominant position, which is in turn reflected in the decision to locate Europe's future central bank (dubbed the "Eurofed") in Frankfurt, Germany's financial capital. Qualification criteria for participation in a common currency after 1999 have been heavily shaped by German policy preferences, in particular a desire to preserve such a currency's health by placing restrictions on permissible national budget deficits and other inflation-inducing tendencies.

Germany's economic clout is not without its weak spots, however, such as the continued financial drain of eastern reconstruction, the less-than-optimal competitiveness of the German economy in a larger comparative perspective (sometimes referred to as the *Standort Deutschland* question), and the rather inflexible regulatory structure of the German economy. Nonetheless, as Bulmer and Paterson point out, "Germany is emerging as the core economy of the 'new Europe.'"[39] This considerable economic clout translates itself indirectly (and at times more directly) into EU policy, for example, by means of the FRG's role as economic policy "model," in EU budgetary negotiations, and in the articulation of membership criteria in the areas of a common currency and eastward expansion. In the final analysis, "German economic strength makes an important indirect contribution to the FRG's role in the EU."[40]

Germany's economic prominence, along with a newly gained reputation for political stability and reliability, forms the basis for a considerable degree of *diplomatic* clout in EU matters as well. The FRG's foreign policy choice environment has expanded, and so has the country's opportunity to play a more explicitly leading role, if it chooses to do so. According to Bulmer and Paterson, "[i]n the particular context of the EU, integration is no longer a means whereby Germany seeks to compensate for its semi-sovereignty. Now, with Germany's position in integration approaching 'normality,' integration has a much greater potential to be used to enhance German international power."[41]

Yet this is, in fact, exactly the basis for concern in some quarters in Europe: will the EU increasingly turn into a vehicle for the exercise and projection of German power and the pursuit of national German interests? Will the newly united Germany merely be a "gentle giant," or is it the "emergent leader" of an EU shaped and run according to

German interests and preferences? However, the fact that the explicitly national exercise of German power is even more certain in the absence of an EU and further integration suggests that skeptics and critics may consider themselves caught between a German-dominated EU and a far less predictable non-integrated Europe where German power would be exercised in an at best intergovernmental setting featuring re-nationalized foreign policies. Such wary observers are likely to take note of the emergence in some quarters in Germany of what one might call a "Teutonic Thatcherism," which suggests limits to further integration in favor of the pursuit of more intergovernmental scenarios, accompanied by a more explicit exercise of German power based on calculations of national interest.[42]

Aware of the anxieties felt by many of its neighbors, and convinced about the success and benefits of integration and multilateralism, Germany's foreign policy-making elite continues to stress its collaborative European commitment. In the past, West Germany sought to coordinate key aspects of its policy by means of the European Political Cooperation (EPC) mechanism launched in the 1970s. In the post-Maastricht era, the FRG is eager to see the promise of a Common Foreign and Security Policy fulfilled. When coordinating mechanisms fail, however, Germany is showing less and less hesitation in proceeding in a more unilateralist fashion, as was illustrated in 1991 by the country's assertiveness regarding the recognition of Slovenian and Croatian independence (although domestic public opinion pressures also played a role here).[43] As a result, one might argue that "German power will become more evident where European institutions prove to be too weak."[44]

Summarizing their conclusions regarding the united Germany's status and role in a deepening and widening European Union, Bulmer and Paterson write:

> German unification has certainly had a liberating effect on the *potential* for German diplomacy. German singularities, such as the situation of Berlin or domestic sensitivity to cold war defence strategies, have disappeared; the FRG no longer has to employ European integration as a way of compensating for its diplomatic weaknesses. As a non-nuclear, largely civilian power the FRG is less disadvantaged by the new security circumstances. The 'redefined' Europe post-1989 has Germany at its geographical core, a configuration likely to be reflected in the federal government's policy as entry of the Visegrad countries [Poland, the Czech Republic, Slovakia, and Hungary] into the EU approaches. These circumstances add to the existing character of Bonn's European diplomacy: the priority given to multilateral frameworks; the bilateralization of

policy through the 'inner core' of the Franco-German relationship; and the attempt to project a European identity as intrinsic to that of Germany.[45]

The result is a Germany that so far is more a "gentle giant" than assertive leader, with considerable economic and diplomatic clout, but more likely to exercise this power indirectly than directly. Echoing this conclusion, William Wallace agrees that "Germany is Europe's leading state" and the continent's "natural hegemon," but adds that although this "Germany may be Europe's central power, ... it is also its reluctant leader."[46]

The Federal Republic's great interest in the EU's eastward expansion is not merely the result of calculations of economic interest. Equally important are concerns about instability and conflict in Central, Eastern, and Southeastern Europe, and the resultant flows of refugees, leading to a keen interest in an effective western response. Consequently, German policy on questions of deepening and widening the European Union cannot be considered in isolation from the related and in some ways larger question of European security. It is here that the implications of the cold war's end and German unification, leading to Germany's re-emergence as a Central European power, become most noticeable. It is to this question of European security that we must therefore now turn.

Securing a Post-Cold War Europe

The dramatic events of the years 1989-1991, with the collapse of Eastern European communism, the unification of Germany, and the demise of the USSR as watersheds, have not only transformed the political and economic stage on which the on-going endeavor of European integration is played out. Perhaps more importantly, they have radically altered the general European security environment. In this new setting, the united Germany has an essential role to play. And once again, the impact of geopolitical imperatives on the country's policy is strikingly evident. James Sperling has tried to capture the significance of the transformation:

> The long European peace after the Second World War was the product of political-military bipolarity, the nuclear stalemate between the Soviet Union and the United States, and the division of Germany. German foreign and security policies were constrained by the triple imperative of acquiescing to American superiority in Europe without shattering its fragile political-security partnership with France, of suffering French pretentions to European leadership without jeopardizing the American

protectorate or foreclosing the prospect of Franco-German codetermina-
tion, and of acknowledging Soviet interests in Europe without foregoing
the objective of German unification. Today, the postwar bonds on German
policy are dissolving; the threat of war between the major European states
has receded into the background; political-military bipolarity has evapo-
rated as has the ideological hostility that helped sustain it; Germany is
unified and fully sovereign; and France, the United States, and Russia
acknowledge Germany's leadership role in Europe and seek its partnership.[47]

Yet Sperling's description of contemporary conditions is open to at
least some question. To what extent are those "postwar bonds on German policy" indeed "dissolving?" What is the likelihood of a
continued degree of implicit bipolarity between an expanding NATO
and a wary, turbulent Russia? Insofar as the East-West conflict of the
cold war era was partly rooted in deeper, historical divergence between
the West and Slavic Russia, might not at least some degree of East-
West estrangement continue to complicate the European diplomatic and
security landscape? In view of the many ties, from NATO to the EU,
that link Germany to immediate and more distant neighbors and
partners, what does it mean to declare the country "fully sovereign?"
And finally, is Germany willing and able to play the "leadership role"
that, according to Sperling, its allies and partners expect it to perform?

It is essential to note that post-cold war Europe faces security
threats and dilemmas that are not easily summed up in traditional,
military categories. With the immediate nuclear peril and the possibility of all-out military conflict between major European states receding, other challenges have come to the fore to preoccupy policy-makers
in Germany and elsewhere. These include ethno-political upheaval in
the Balkans and inside the area of the former Soviet Union, large-scale
flows of refugees fleeing conflict and/or seeking a share of the West's
economic prosperity and opportunity, the threats posed by various
forms of terrorism (including militant Islamic fundamentalism), the
infiltration of economically oriented organized crime unleashed by a
breakdown of law and order in the post-communist societies of Central
and Eastern Europe (including Russia), and other matters related to
economic security (industrial espionage, resource and market access,
financial stability, and so forth).

Any analysis of the united Germany's evolving security policy must,
therefore, take account of several factors: the ties that continue to bind
the country into NATO, the persistence of a western-oriented "security
policy culture" developed during the cold war era, the new security
challenges shared with other European/western states, the security-

related potential available through multilateral institutions other than NATO (especially the EU, the Western European Union, and the CSCE/OSCE), and, once again, the impact of the country's Central European geopolitical location. These and other factors characterize the environment in which today's German policy-makers define Germany's interests, conceptualize the country's preferred role in security matters, and conceive of Germany's international identity in a post-cold war world.

Considerations of power, role, and identity have caused German officials and political leaders to place special emphasis on the notion of Germany as a "civilian" power.[48] This entails caution in the use and display of military capability, rooted in an enduring reaction to the legacy of aggressive German militarism and a sensitivity to the perceptions of wary neighbors to the East and West. Upon unification, the country reaffirmed its commitment to the status of being a non-nuclear power and agreed to clear limitations on the overall size of its armed forces. The notion of being a "civilian" power, focused on economic and political aspects of leadership, may be seen by many as a partial continuation of Germany's cold war era "self-containment." However, it is not without an element of convenient German self-interest either, as Sperling has noted.

> Germany remains satisfied to contribute to the economic requirements of security and to accelerate the demilitarization of interstate relations, particularly in Europe--a development that plays to Germany's economic capacity and not coincidentally enhances German influence in the reconstruction and recasting of the European order.[49]

At the time of the Gulf War, a Germany that is still "susceptible to bouts of self-pity and urgent moralizing"[50] was the scene of vigorous debate and controversy regarding the possible use of German military force outside the NATO area.[51] Many argued that the country's Basic Law did not permit such use, and would have to be amended. However, the Federal Republic's Constitutional Court decided in 1994 that deployment of *Bundeswehr* troops in "out-of-area" operations was not at odds with the constitution. The argument was also made, particularly on the German Left, that German military activity ought to be limited to UN-sanctioned "blue helmet" operations at most. By contrast, Chancellor Helmut Kohl, Defense Minister Volker Rühe, and others in the CDU maintained that broader military ventures were both constitutional and in accordance with Germany's international obligations as well as its renewed status as a "normal" power in world affairs. As a result, the 1990s has witnessed German military participation in a variety of settings and situations, although in the immediate case of the Gulf War the country's primary contribution had remained financial ($10.7 billion).[52]   Nonetheless, even the more conservative CDU cannot escape the shadows of Germany's past. As a result, and despite all claims of "normalcy," German policy-makers continue to look favorably upon their country's role and status as a "civilian" power.[53]

A further important component in the Federal Republic's official self-definition and self-conception today continues to be its western orientation and commitment, reiterated and re-emphasized by its leaders and representatives like a religious mantra. These foreign policy cultural orientations are reinforced by tangible links produced by the organizations of which the FRG is a member, particularly NATO and the EU. Although the presence of U.S. and other Allied forces on German soil has been radically reduced, ventures such as the Eurocorps (in which *Bundeswehr* troops serve alongside forces from several other West European states) serve to reflect Germany's western orientation and commitment and evince the modified sovereignty enjoyed by both the FRG and its partners.

A third important component in the Federal Republic's preferred role and identity is its multilateralist orientation. A history of nationalist excesses and disasters, coupled with an awareness of the sensitivity of any unilateralist exercise of its strategic, Central European power, have induced among German policy-makers a considerable appreciation of the substantive as well as cosmetic advantages of multilateralist initiatives and diplomacy. As Sperling puts it, "German policymakers have systematically translated German interests into the interests of the many over the course of the postwar period."[54] Similarly, Christoph Bertram has noted that "[o]f all western countries, post-war Germany has been most conscious of the need to be part of a team in international affairs," although he argues also that "[t]he collective cosiness of German foreign policy exists no longer."[55] In the end, this is also the meaning of the often professed desire to become and remain a "European Germany" and avoid the impression of wanting to create a "German Europe." As a result, despite a growing sense of specific German interests in the geopolitical heart of a dynamically changing continent, Germany's leaders continue to show clear evidence of their preference for the pursuit of policy through multilateral channels, ranging from NATO to the European Union and the OSCE.

"Civilian," western, and multilateralist: it is with these conceptions of its identity and role that the enlarged Federal Republic exercises its power in Europe today. In the realm of security policy, two areas of focus stand out in particular. First, the question of a stronger and clearer European pillar or identity in the western alliance, coupled with the question of America's future role in Europe. Second, the integration of Central and Eastern Europe into western security institutions, tied to the issue of an integrating Europe's relationship with a post-communist but still far from stabilized Russia. If the first area of policy tends to find the FRG caught between the Atlantic connection with the U.S. and the Euro-Gaullist ambitions of France, the second issue-area shows Germany in its quintessentially central continental role, eager to connect a vacuum-prone Eastern Europe with the western security community without alienating or aggravating Russia.[56]

As with the "widening" versus "deepening" debate regarding the European Union, these issues on the German security policy agenda might suggest the necessity of making choices. Yet, once again, choices are exactly what the Federal Republic would very much like to avoid. Thus we notice a clear interest in the development of a stronger European defense identity coupled with a re-emphasized commitment to the transatlantic linkage with the U.S. Similarly, a desire for the effective security integration of Central and Eastern Europe into existing western institutions is accompanied by a willingness to see the OSCE strengthened as a forum that might transcend cold war products like NATO and serve to placate a wary Russia.

One might conclude that in the areas of European integration as well as European security, German diplomacy reveals a tendency to "genscher," in the words of Timothy Garton Ash, referring to former (West) German Foreign Minister Hans-Dietrich Genscher's inclination to avoid unpleasant choices and pursue the reconciliation of seemingly incompatible goals. Garton Ash has described "Genscherism" as an attempt "to maintain and improve Germany's ties with a wide range of states, which were themselves pursuing quite different and contradictory objectives. This complex balancing act involved saying somewhat different things in different places. Fudge was the hard core of Genscherism."[57]

In the context of the analysis presented in this chapter, one might, in fact, argue that this tendency of "genschering" is the behavioral expression of the logic inherent in *Scharnierpolitik*. In the realm of security policy, the Federal Republic thus serves as Europe's "hinge," preserving the gains and successes of Atlantic and West European endeavors rooted in the cold war era while seeking to extend and to some extent transform these by integrating its neighbors to the East and cultivating the goodwill of post-Soviet Russia. This *sowohl-als-auch* (A as well as B) quality of German policy is captured succinctly by Sperling when he writes:

The political objectives of German foreign policy have not been fundamentally changed by the transformation of the European security order:
Germany's foreign policy objectives remain the political and economic
unification of Europe and the creation of a pan-European security system
that preserves the indivisibility of German and American security.[58]

It remains to be seen, however, whether this "genscherist"
inclination will continue to fit the requirements of policy in a post-
unification, post-cold war era. At some point, choices may have to be
made, because, as Elizabeth Pond has noted,

> balancing EU and transatlantic commitments, NATO and the European
> "pillar," France and the United States, western and eastern Europe,
> central Europe and Russia, widening and deepening of the EU, joining
> NATO allies in out-of-area operations and doing the tough political
> spadework to make this step domestically acceptable--will be tricky.[59]

The North Atlantic Treaty Organization faced a serious "identity
crisis" when the cold war passed from the European scene. The newly
unified Germany quickly showed its desire for a reformed alliance by
urging the adjustment of NATO strategy from a cold war reliance on
flexible response in the area of nuclear deterrence and forward defense
in the conventional military field to a post-cold war focus on pan-
European collective security and stability. Many of the policy and
posture adjustments adopted by the alliance at its London summit
meeting in July 1990 in fact corresponded with German preferences. In
the course of the 1990s, German officials appear increasingly attracted
to a subtle but important re-definition of NATO as a political
community with shared values and common security interests, instead
of the more explicitly military character of the alliance's former, cold
war identity. This recasting of the organization's identity would
dovetail with the FRG's interest in the demilitarization of European
affairs, the deepening of the links between NATO and the OSCE, and
the reassurance of a Russia still suspicious of western intentions. All of
these objectives could be pursued in and by an adjusted NATO without
jeopardizing the security link with America, which all German policy-
makers continue to see as indispensable to both the Federal Republic
and all of Europe.[60]

The Organization for Security and Cooperation in Europe (OSCE) is
an outgrowth of the Conference on Security and Cooperation in Europe
(CSCE), which in turn was launched in Helsinki in 1975 as the product
of efforts at detente between East and West. The importance of the
CSCE/OSCE has grown in the post-cold war era, with the demise of
the Warsaw Pact and the Soviet Union, as the western alliance found

itself confronted with the need to reach out to erstwhile opponents and construct a viable pan-European security order. Ever since the 1970s, German governments have been prominent supporters of pan-European security schemes, reflective of Germany's precarious cold war status as a divided front-line nation before 1990 and the united Germany's sensitive Central European position today. The Federal Republic's interest in CSCE/OSCE results from a mixture of economic and military security calculations, since the organization "promises the institutionalization of a pan-European peace order based upon the principle of collective security" and "offers an additional mechanism for overcoming the 'prosperity barrier' (*Wohlstandsgrenze*) between the nations of western and eastern Europe with the establishment of a free-market regime throughout Europe."[61]

For a centrally located state like Germany, CSCE/OSCE constitutes an ideal umbrella organization. It includes all NATO partners, including the United States, a variety of neutrals, and all former Warsaw Pact states. Furthermore, it provides a valuable forum of consul-tation and cooperation alongside the more fully established and integrated western alliance. Along with the North Atlantic Cooperation Council (NACC), launched by NATO in 1991 as a vehicle for post-cold war East-West consultation, CSCE/OSCE is seen as a vital ingredient in the western "security outreach" to Central and Eastern European states, irrespective of which ones might in the end join NATO. There has so far been no indication that the German government seriously considers CSCE/OSCE to be a full alternative to the western alliance. Rather, the two organizations are seen as eminently complementary. As far as the Federal Republic is concerned,

> NATO provides insurance against any military threat to the territorial integrity of Germany, while the CSCE makes a positive contribution to European security by integrating the former Warsaw Pact member states, including the former Soviet Union, into the western economic and political orbit.[62]

In the longer run, German-American tension may result from the fact that for the U.S. government the CSCE/OSCE is likely to remain a useful but subordinate addition to the alliance and a forum to engage potential NATO members as well, while for the Federal Republic NATO may decline in importance, increasingly replaced by a strengthened CSCE/OSCE that corresponds more fully to Germany's Central European security calculations and preferences.

Beyond its military security utility, CSCE/OSCE is also seen as valuable in the area of economic security, where a centrally located

Germany, prosperous but burdened by the costs of eastern reconstruction, finds itself a prime migration and asylum target of those in search of more promising economic opportunities. In this sense, CSCE/OSCE is a complement to the European Union, providing a framework for economic integration and assistance. With the overt threat of military attack receding, it is these issues of economic insecurity and instability that have moved to the top of Germany's list of international concerns. In the post-cold war era, the Federal Republic has been the largest recipient of asylum-seekers and economic refugees on the one hand, and the primary donor of western assistance to the former communist bloc on the other hand. CSCE/OSCE is important for the FRG because it can help ensure that Germany does not face a turbulent East alone.

It is clear, then, that the Federal Republic currently pursues a security policy that reflects the country's specific geopolitical location, focuses on concerns that range from the military and political to the economic, and utilizes (or, as some might say, juggles) a variety of existing institutions. In the words of Sperling:

> The German security strategy has three primary elements: self-containment of German power in order that Germany may use its power to influence its European neighbors to effect German policy objectives; the creation of an independent Europe capable of negotiating on an equal basis with the United States on economic issues; and the continued demilitarization of Europe that depends upon the sustained growth of democracy and the free market in the former member states of the Warsaw Pact.[63]

Insofar as the CSCE/OSCE, EU, and WEU might gain weight in German security policy calculations, the future of NATO will become a significant issue. Yet for the time being, neither CSCE/OSCE nor EU/WEU are in a position to impart the security benefits the FRG continues to derive from membership in the Atlantic Alliance and a special relationship with the United States.

As we approach the dawn of a new century and a new millennium, however, one country may once more stand out as absolutely critical to the future shape of German foreign policy and the overall European political and security order: Russia. Even before the demise of the Soviet Union in 1991, the pivotal role played by Gorbachev in the drama of German unification served to open a new chapter in this crucial bilateral relationship. The basis was laid by the Treaty on Good-Neighborliness, Partnership, and Cooperation between the FRG and the USSR of 1990. As W. R. Smyser has put it, this "German-Soviet tie [created] new confluences within Europe's center even as it [renewed] old ones."[64] A political, military, and economic bargain was struck between the two powers, reflecting the interests and historical as well as geopolitical sensitivities of both sides. Arrangements were made for the withdrawal of Soviet troops from eastern Germany (with the Federal Republic covering the DM 8.4 billion price-tag), the future military status of this GDR territory in a united Germany within NATO, and acceptable force levels and structures in the context of the Treaty on Conventional Forces in Europe (CFE), in addition to formal, mutual non-aggression pledges.

In addition to the military aspects of the new relationship, the Federal Republic became the Soviet Union's (and later Russia's) most significant western economic partner, ranging from trade to investment and financial aid. By 1991, Germany had pledged at least $40 billion in various kinds of financial and economic assistance, to be delivered over a number of years. Furthermore, the FRG has lobbied hard for Soviet-Russian interests at G-7 summits and in meetings of the International Monetary Fund (IMF).

At the same time, Germany is required to balance its special relationship with Russia with the concerns of wary neighbors in Central and Eastern Europe, who would be easily suspicious of undue German-Russian coziness at their expense and who are eager to receive their share of the Federal Republic's financial largesse, economic investment, and advocacy in favor of their membership in western economic and security institutions. Furthermore, in its relations with these neighbors in East Central Europe, Germany has had to settle or at least manage a series of thorny issues, ranging from the recognition of the Oder-Neisse border with Poland and the legacy of the 1938 Munich Agreement and its aftermath vis-à-vis the Czech Republic, to compensation for victims of Germany's wartime policies and actions in eastern neighboring countries and the on-going problem of post-cold war migration and organized crime.[65]

As far as NATO is concerned, the need to balance the simultaneous but not necessarily compatible importance of Russia and East Central Europe on the scales of the Federal Republic's diplomacy represents a particular conundrum for German policy-makers: how to reconcile support for alliance membership of Central and Eastern European states with due consideration for the hostile attitude of its strategic partner Russia regarding such eastward enlargement of an organization rooted in the cold war. There is a further dilemma, of course: at what point do closer relations with Russia not only complicate Germany's role in Central and Eastern Europe, but also burden or even jeopardize the crucial partnerships with major western powers such as France, the United Kingdom, and the U.S.? Under what circumstances might concerns or even fears of a German-Russian "neo-Rapallo" re-emerge?

Yet the dictates of geopolitics and history will render a close German-Russian connection all but inescapable, with as yet unforeseeable consequences for those situated in between. In the words of Smyser:

> The new [German-Russian] tie will unfold in a historical context of hundreds of years of dramatically varying relations between the Russian and German peoples. Russian troops were in Berlin as enemies in 1759, as friends in 1814, and as conquerors in 1945. A Prussian expeditionary force joined in Napoleon's invasion of Russia in 1813, and the two German invasions of Russia during World Wars I and II alternated with periods of friendship. From the eighteenth through the twentieth centuries, the Germans and Russians have maintained a fascination for each other, a mixture of fear and attraction that may be unique in international affairs.[66]

Close relations with both the Soviet Union and various neighbors in Central and Eastern Europe formed an integral part of the former East Germany's communist *Staatsräson*. Yet Germany's preoccupation with and interest in those to its east has deeper roots than the years of cold war division and antagonism. The virtual absence of "Ossis" among the Federal Republic's foreign policy-making elite is therefore not as consequential for the country's diplomatic orientations as one might think. In the end, the geopolitical imperatives are almost certainly far more compelling than the political biographies and ideological proclivities of leaders and diplomats in a Germany that is today "a creature of the West" but has "a foot in the East."[67]

Conclusion

In the course of the 1990s, the foreign policy of the reunited Germany has been subjected to close scrutiny and analysis by numerous German and non-German observers alike. As we saw at the outset, many analysts have approached their task with explicit or implicit assumptions or preconceptions about the outlook for German diplomacy, often rooted in worries about a return of history (the pessimists) or confidence in the country's definitive postwar transformation (the optimists). Different analyses stress different factors, policy objectives, and contextual variables, producing varying descriptions of the nature of contemporary German foreign policy and divergent characterizations of the contours of the country's power, role, and identity in European and world affairs.

Many of these characterizations suggest that, despite unification and the reacquisition of full sovereignty, Germany still cannot be seen as a "normal" country. The legacy and trauma of a turbulent past continue to cast their shadows across the present. Any signs of any independent exercise or flexing of German power and muscle are quickly registered among the country's ever-sensitive neighbors. Domestic policy disputes regularly feature direct or indirect references to the implications of aspects of Germany's disastrous prewar past. In addition, the unique burdens of unification, along with the country's often precarious Central-European location, are also factors that help shape a foreign policy that reflects particular predicaments and must meet some difficult challenges. Or, by contrast, Germany is singled out because it is expected to perform a special set of international tasks and provide a distinct degree of diplomatic leadership.

The assortment of perspectives on and evaluations of German foreign policy, scattered across the 1990s and some of them noted in this essay, reminds us of the subjectivity and contingency of most analysis. Germany and Europe are experiencing rapid and dynamic changes that complicate the identification and projection of stable and durable patterns of policy into an uncertain future. The utility of historical criteria and examples may be limited and even misleading in an environment in which national and post-national frameworks of policy calculation and pre- and post-1989 institutional mechanisms complicate a messy diplomatic, economic, and military setting.

As far as the interpretation of German foreign policy is concerned, this pits realists against post-realists and optimists against pessimists, with each case built on a necessarily selective evaluation of policies, pronouncements, and possibilities. It is frequently a matter of the glass being seen as half-full or half-empty, and (to stay with liquid metaphors) a question of old and new bottles filled with new or old wine. Underlying a clear majority of analyses is an incontrovertible fact, however: the united Germany is once again the principal power in the heart of the continent. Whether this fact will be accompanied by a "return of history," or whether a new Germany will play its central role differently than in the past, cannot be answered definitively at this point, at least not in the first post-unification decade. Yet the resultant geopolitical imperatives for its foreign policy are inescapable, and form the core of the growing *Scharnierpolitik* with which the Federal Republic seeks to blend interest and allegiance as well as tradition and innovation, looking East and West and to the future.

Notes

1. I wish to thank Bridget Carberry and Christoph Hupach for their assistance in the accumulation of much of the source material used in this essay.

2. W.R. Smyser, "Dateline Berlin: Germany's New Vision," *Foreign Policy*, No. 97 (Winter·1994-95), p. 140.

3. Andrei S. Markovits and Simon Reich, "Should Europe Fear the Germans?," in Michael G. Huelshoff, Andrei S. Markovits, and Simon Reich (eds.), *From Bundesrepublik to Deutschland: German Politics after Unification* (Ann Arbor, MI: The University of Michigan Press, 1993), p. 271. The optimist versus pessimist outlook is also considered by Eckart Arnold, "German Foreign Policy and Unification," *International Affairs*, Vol. 67, No. 3 (1991), p. 467ff.

4. Markovits and Reich, "Should Europe Fear the Germans?," p. 273.

5. *Ibid.*, pp. 273, 274.

6. *Ibid.*, p. 274.

7. Ralf Dahrendorf, *Society and Democracy in Germany* (New York: W.W. Norton & Co., [1965] 1979).

8. Markovits and Reich, "Should Europe Fear the Germans?," p. 274.

9. *Ibid.*, p. 275.

10. For some examples of wary or pessimistic analysis, see Lanxin Xiang, "Is Germany in the West or in Central Europe?," *Orbis*, Vol. 36, No. 3 (Summer 1992), pp. 411-22; Moishe Postone, "Germany's Future and Its Unmastered Past," in Huelshoff, Markovits, and Reich (eds.), *From Bundesrepublik to Deutschland*, pp. 291-99; Alan Sked, "Cheap Excuses: Germany and the Gulf Crisis," *The National Interest*, No. 24 (Summer 1991), pp. 51-60.

11. See Philip H. Gordon, "The Normalization of German Foreign Policy," *Orbis*, Vol. 38, No. 2 (Spring 1994), pp. 233-38; Gunther Hellmann, "Jenseits von 'Normalisierung' und 'Militarisierung': Zur Standortdebatte über die neue deutsche Außenpolitik," *Aus Politik und Zeitgeschichte*, No. 1-2 (3 January 1997), pp. 24-33.

12. Josef Janning, "A German Europe--a European Germany? On the debate over Germany's Foreign Policy," *International Affairs*, Vol. 72, No. 1(1996), p. 34.

13. In this context, see Roger Boyes and William Horsley, "The Germans as Victims: a British View," *The World Today* (June 1995), pp. 110-14.

14. See his *Die Normalität einer Berliner Republik. Kleine Politische Schriften VIII* (Frankfurt: Suhrkamp Verlag, 1995). Habermas focuses especially on the question of "lessons of history," and whether and how one might learn from history at all. He also makes an impassioned plea for a post-national perspective on world affairs.

15. "A German Europe--a European Germany?," p. 34. For some representative samples from the literature, see Christoph Bluth, "Germany: Defining the National Interest," *The World Today* (March 1995), pp. 51-55; the essays by Hans-Peter Schwarz, Arnulf Baring, Günther Gillessen, and Gregor Schöllgen in Arnulf Baring (ed.), *Germany's New Position in Europe:. Problems and Prospects* (Oxford/Providence: Berg Publishers, 1994); Hans-Peter Schwarz, *Die Zentralmacht Europas. Deutschlands Rückkehr auf die Weltbühne* (Berlin: Siedler Verlag, 1994); Gregor Schöllgen, *Angst vor der Macht. Die Deutschen und ihre Aussenpolitik* (Berlin and Frankfurt: Verlag Ullstein, 1993); Michael Stürmer,

"Deutsche Interessen," in Karl Kaiser and Hanns W. Maull (eds.), *Deutschlands neue Aussenpolitik. Band I: Grundlagen* (Munich: Oldenbourg Verlag, 1994), pp. 39-61.

16. "A German Europe--A European Germany?," p. 36. See, for example, the writings of such scholars as Ernst-Otto Czempiel, Dieter Senghaas, Hanns W. Maull, and Werner Weidenfeld.

17. See the discussion in Karl Kaiser, "Das vereinigte Deutschland in der internationalen Politik," in Kaiser and Maull (eds.), *Deutschlands neue Außenpolitik. Band I: Grundlagen*, pp. 1-14; Hanns W. Maull, "Zivilmacht Bundesrepublik Deutschland. 14 Thesen für eine neue deutsche Außenpolitik," *Europa-Archiv*, No. 10 (1992), pp. 269-78.

18. In connection with the following discussion of German public opinion, see Ronald D. Asmus, *German Strategy and Opinion After the Wall, 1990-1993* (Santa Monica, CA: RAND Corporation, 1994); Ronald D. Asmus, *Germany's Geopolitical Maturation: Public Opinion and Security Policy in 1994* (Santa Monica, CA: RAND Corporation, 1995); Dieter Wulf, "Deutschland im Wandel. Außenpolitische Vorstellungen der Deutschen in West und Ost seit der Wiedervereinigung: Ergebnisse einer repräsentativen Studie," *Deutschland Archiv*, Vol. 26, No. 12 (December 1993), pp. 1354-60. See also Ludger Kühnhardt, "Wertgrundlagen der deutschen Aussenpolitik," in Kaiser and Maull (eds.), *Deutschlands neue Außenpolitik. Band I: Grundlagen*, pp. 99-127.

19. See Daniel Hamilton, "Germany After Unification," *Problems of Communism*, Vol. 41, No. 3 (May-June 1992), p. 13ff.

20. An attempt at comparing the post-cold war shape of European affairs with conditions prevailing after 1815 and 1918, and their implications for the conduct of German foreign policy, is made by Josef Joffe, "German Grand Strategy after the Cold War," in Baring (ed.), *Germany's New Position in Europe*, pp. 79-89.

21. Thies, "Germany and Eastern Europe between Past and Future," in Baring (ed.), *Germany's New Position in Europe*, p. 72.

22. "Dateline Berlin: Germany's New Vision," p. 145.

23. Hamilton, "Germany After Unification," p. 13.

24. *Ibid.*

25. "Dateline Berlin: Germany's New Vision," p. 156.

26. Baring, "'Germany, What Now?'," in Baring (ed.), *Germany's New Position in Europe*, p. 7.

27. The following discussion draws heavily on Dirk Verheyen, *The German Question: A Cultural, Historical, and Geopolitical Exploration* (Boulder, CO: Westview Press, 1991), chapter 4.

28. David Calleo, *The German Problem Reconsidered* (Cambridge: Cambridge University Press, 1978), pp. 3, 4, 5, 6. For similar arguments, see Karl Deutsch and Lewis Edinger, *Germany Rejoins the Powers* (Stanford: Stanford University Press, 1959), p. 19; Paul Kennedy, *The Rise and Fall of the Great Powers* (New York: Random House, 1987), pp. 209-10.

29. For critical perspectives on Adenauer's *Westpolitik* and the accompanying "Westernization" of the Federal Republic, see the essays in parts 2 and 3 of Rainer Zitelmann, Karlheinz Weißmann, and Michael Großheim (eds.), *Westbindung. Chancen und Risiken für Deutschland* (Frankfurt: Verlag Ullstein/Propyläen Verlag, 1993).

30. Hans-Peter Schwarz, "Die westdeutsche Aussenpolitik--Historische Lektionen und politische Generationen," in Walter Scheel (ed.), *Nach Dreissig Jahren* (Stuttgart: Klett-Cotta Verlag, 1979), p. 155. See also Christian Hacke, "Traditionen und Stationen der Aussenpolitik der Bundesrepublik Deutschland," *Aus Politik und Zeitgeschichte*, No. 3 (15 January 1988), pp. 3-15.

31. See Jochen Thies, "Germany and Eastern Europe between Past and Future."

32. For an analysis of the interplay of philosophical conviction and calculated self-interest behind (West) German EC policy, reaching beyond the traditional neofunctionalist and intergovernmentalist theories in the study of integration to include fuller consideration of German domestic political and economic dynamics, see Michael G. Huelshoff, "Germany and European Integration: Understanding the Relationship," in Huelshoff, Markovits, and Reich (eds.), *From Bundesrepublik to Deutschland*.

33. See Anne-Marie LeGloannec, "The Implications of German Unification for Western Europe," in Paul B. Stares (ed.), *The New Germany and the New Europe* (Washington, DC: The Brookings Institution, 1992).

34. Simon Bulmer and William E. Paterson, "Germany in the European Union: Gentle Giant or Emergent Leader?," *International Affairs*, Vol. 72, No. 1 (1996), p. 13. See also David Marsh, *Germany and Europe: The Crisis of Unity* (London: Heinemann Publishers, 1994), chapter 6.

35. See Janning, "A German Europe--a European Germany?," p. 39ff.

36. See Schauer, "Nationale und europäische Identität. Die unterschiedlichen Auffassungen in Deutschland, Frankreich und Großbritannien," *Aus Politik und Zeitgeschichte*, No. 10 (28 February 1997), pp. 3-13.

37. "Should Europe Fear the Germans?," pp. 283, 284. For a discussion of the issues as seen from the Central and Eastern European perspective, see András Inotai, "Economic Implications of German Unification for Central and Eastern Europe," in Stares (ed.), *The New Germany and the New Europe*.

38. CDU/CSU-Fraktion des Deutschen Bundestages, "Überlegungen zur Europapolitik," Bonn (1 September 1994). In his analysis, Josef Janning refers to this school of thought as that of the "core protagonists," ("A German Europe--a European Germany?," pp. 40-41). See also Christian Deubner, *Deutsche Europapolitik: Von Maastricht nach Kerneuropa?* (Baden-Baden: Nomos Verlagsgesellschaft, 1995), who argues for greater clarity regarding German interests in the context of revision of EU institutions and policies.

39. "Germany in the European Union," p. 16, and p. 14ff.

40. Bulmer and Paterson, "Germany in the European Union," p. 16.

41. "Germany in the European Union," p. 17.

42. See, for example, the writings of Hans Arnold: *Europa am Ende? Die Auflösung von EG und NATO* (Munich and Zürich: Piper Verlag, 1993) and *Deutschlands Größe. Deutsche Außenpolitik zwischen Macht und Mangel* (Munich and Zürich: Piper Verlag, 1995).

43. For further discussion, see Bulmer and Paterson, "Germany in the European Union," pp. 17-18; Beverly Crawford, "German Foreign Policy and European Political Cooperation: the Diplomatic Recognition of Croatia in 1991," *German Politics and Society*, Vol. 13, No. 2 (Summer 1995), pp. 1-34; Wolfgang Krieger, "Toward a Gaullist Germany? Some Lessons from the Yugoslav Crisis," *World Policy Journal*, Vol. 11, No. 1 (Spring 1994), pp. 26-38; Hans-Dietrich Genscher, *Erinnerungen* (Berlin: Siedler Verlag, 1995), chapter 19.

44. Bulmer and Paterson, "Germany in the European Union," p. 18.

45. "Germany in the European Union," p. 30. Emphasis in original.

46. William Wallace, "Germany as Europe's Leading Power," *The World Today*, (August-September 1995), pp. 162, 164. See also Jochen Thies, "Germany: Europe's Reluctant Great Power," *The World Today* (October 1995), pp. 186-90. Harald Müller sees Germany somewhere between "new assertiveness" and "self-contained leadership" ("German Foreign Policy after Unification," in Stares, ed., *The New Germany and the New Europe*, p. 161ff.).

47. James Sperling, "German Security Policy and the Future European Security Order," in Huelshoff, Markovits, and Reich (eds.), *From Bundesrepublik to Deutschland*, p. 321. See also James Sperling, "German Security Policy in Post-Yalta Europe," in M. Donald Hancock and Helga A. We lsh (eds.), *German Unification: Process & Outcomes* (Boulder, CO: Westview Press, 1994).

48. See the discussion by Hanns W. Maull, "Germany and Japan: The New Civilian Powers," *Foreign Affairs*, Vol. 69, No. 5 (Winter 1990-91), pp. 91-106. Maull argues that "international relations are undergoing a profound transformation that offers an opportunity to take history beyond the world of the nation-state, with its inherent security dilemmas and its tendency to adjust to change through war. As a result of their own hubris, the farsightedness of the American victors in World War II, and a series of historical accidents, Germany and Japan now in some ways find themselves representing this new world of international relations" (p. 93). See also Maull, "Zivilmacht Bundesrepublik Deutschland. 14 Thesen für eine neue deutsche Außenpolitik."

49. "German Security Policy and the Future European Security Order," p. 323. On Germany's role as international economic power, see Norbert Kloten, "Die Bundesrepublik als Weltwirtschaftsmacht," in Kaiser and Maull (eds.), *Deutschlands neue Außenpolitik. Band I: Grundlagen*, pp. 63-80.

50. Daniel Hamilton and James Clad, "Germany, Japan, and the False Glare of War," *The Washington Quarterly* (Autumn 1991), p. 41.

51. See the discussion in Franz H. U. Borkenhagen, "Militarisierung deutscher Außenpolitik?," *Aus Politik und Zeitgeschichte*, No. 33-34 (9 August 1996), pp. 3-9.

52. For further discussion of German policy during the Gulf War, see Genscher, *Erinnerungen*, chapter 18.

53. For further discussion regarding the broader question of Germany's role and power in world affairs generally, see Hamilton and Clad, "Germany, Japan, and the False Glare of War." A fairly critical evaluation of German policy at the time of the Gulf War is presented by Sked, "Cheap Excuses." See also Jochen Thies, "Germany: Tests of Credibility," *The World Today* (June 1991), pp. 89-90.

54. "German Security Policy and the Future European Security Order," p. 324.

55. Christoph Bertram, "The Power and the Past: Germany's New International Loneliness," in Baring (ed.), *Germany's New Position in Europe*, pp. 92, 94.

56. For Central/Eastern European and Russian perspectives on the future European security order and Germany's policy on this question, see Slawomir A. Dabrowa, "Security Problems Facing Central and Eastern Europe after German Unification" and Sergei A. Karaganov, "Implications of German Unification for the Former Soviet Union," both in Stares (ed.), *The New Germany and the New Europe*.

57. Timothy Garton Ash, "Germany's Choice," *Foreign Affairs*, Vol. 73, No. 4 (July-August 1994), p. 72. See also Lothar Gutjahr, *German Foreign and Defence Policy after Unification* (London and New York: Pinter Publishers, 1994), chapter 5.

58. Sperling, "German Security Policy and the Future European Security Order," p. 325.

59. Elizabeth Pond, "Germany Finds Its Niche as a Regional Power," *The Washington Quarterly*, Vol. 19, No. 1 (Winter 1996), p. 38. For his part, Garton Ash outlines four basic options facing German foreign policy: "Carolingian Completion" (further deepening of the existing European Union around a Franco-German core), "Wider Europe" (widening the EU and NATO to include Germany's eastern neighbors), "Moscow First" (the development of a new-old special relationship with Russia, which Garton Ash describes as "the classic eastern option of German foreign policy"), and "World Power" (seeking the rights and duties of being a world power, such as a permanent seat on the UN Security Council), "Germany's Choice," p. 73ff. Garton Ash concludes that Germany will "choose not to choose," but adds that "to choose not to choose does not mean you make no choices" (p. 79).

60. The role of the U.S. in European affairs since World War II and the importance of the German-American connection are a key area of focus in Gregory F. Treverton, *America, Germany, and the Future of Europe* (Princeton, NJ: Princeton University Press, 1992). See also Dana H. Allin, "German-American Relations After the Cold War," in Gale A. Mattox and A. Bradley Shingleton (eds.), *Germany at the Crossroads. Foreign and Domestic Policy Issues* (Boulder, CO: Westview Press, 1992); Alice Ackermann and Catherine McArdle Kelleher, "The United States and the German Question: Building a New European Order," in Dirk Verheyen and Christian Søe (eds.), *The Germans and Their Neighbors*

(Boulder, CO: Westview Press, 1993); and W. R. Smyser, *Germany and America: New Identities, Fateful Rift?* (Boulder, CO: Westview Press, 1993).

61. Sperling, "German Security Policy and the Future European Security Order," p. 329. Italics added.

62. *Ibid.*, p. 330.

63. *Ibid.*, p. 338.

64. Smyser, "U.S.S.R.-Germany: A Link Restored," *Foreign Policy*, No. 84 (Fall 1991), p. 126.

65. For further discussion of the united Germany's relations with its immediate East-Central European neighbors, see the essays on Polish-German, Czech-German, and Hungarian-German relations by Arthur R. Rachwald, Milan Hauner, and Ivan Volgyes, respectively, in Verheyen and Søe (eds.), *The Germans and Their Neighbors*. See also Stuart Drummond, "Germany: Moving Towards a New Ostpolitik?," *The World Today*, Vol. 49, No. 7 (July 1993), pp. 132-35; Kazimierz Wóycicki, "Zur Besonderheit der deutsch-polnischen Beziehungen," *Aus Politik und Zeitgeschichte*, No. 28 (5 July 1996), pp. 14-20; Jan Kren, "Tschechisch-deutsche Beziehungen in der Geschichte: Von Böhmen aus betrachtet," *Aus Politik und Zeitgeschichte*, No. 28 (5 July 1996), pp. 21-27; Otto Kimminich, "Völkerrecht und Geschichte im Disput über die Beziehungen Deutschlands zu seinen östlichen Nachbarn," *Aus Politik und Zeitgeschichte*, No. 28 (5 July 1996), pp. 28-38.

66. Smyser, "U.S.S.R.-Germany: A Link Restored," p. 136.

67. *Ibid.*, p. 127.

14

Epilogue

David Childs

Should Christian Democrats and Not the D-Mark Go?

On 21 June 1998 Germans celebrated the fiftieth anniversary of the introduction of the D-Mark, the German Mark. By any standards they have made an incredible journey with that currency. It was to be expected that many would have misgivings about its abolition and replacement on 1 January 1999 by the single European currency, the *Euro*. According to a January 1998 poll published in *Der Spiegel*, 56 percent of Germans were against the *Euro* and only 39 percent were in favor.[1] It is hardly surprising that the poll found that in the former GDR, D-Mark supporters accounted for 67 percent of those questioned. The fact is, despite all the problems, despite some disappointments, and despite the foreign media concentrating on German difficulties and divisions, many East Germans believe the introduction of the D-Mark on 1 July 1990 represented for them a dramatic turning point for the better. The poll also revealed that the Germans were rather pessimistic about 1998. About one-third believed there would be no change in the situation regarding pensions, unemployment, and internal security, but 50 percent, 42 percent, and 50 percent respectively felt the situation would get worse. Even more Germans expected worse to come with regard to taxes (65 percent), health care (57 percent), and federal debt (73 percent). On the other hand, 44 percent thought there would be progress towards achieving equality of living conditions in both parts of Germany, 40 percent expected an improvement in economic growth, and 40 percent expected greater European unity. Asked about the election of September 1998, only 30 percent believed that the Christian Democratic-Free Democratic coalition would survive. To 30 percent a Social Democrat-Green coalition seemed likely, while 33 percent expected a grand coalition of Social Democrats and Christian Democrats. An astonishing 69 percent said they wanted a change of government.

"Collaborators" Preferred?

One remarkable fact about the former GDR is the success of the Christian Democrats. I always believed that the party in Bonn which presided over reunification would win the election that followed, but I never imagined that such a party would be as successful as the Christian Democratic Union has been. It must not be forgotten that the CDU in the former GDR emerged from the despised satellite party, which had done the Socialist Unity Party's (SED's) bidding for at least forty years. Other surprises have been the relative failure of the New Forum rebels of 1989-90, the dull performance of the Social Democratic Party (SPD), and the relative success of the Party of Democratic Socialism (PDS).[2]

Taking the last party first, it was to be expected that the party which emerged from the ruling SED would retain a strong following in East Berlin where so many former full-time SED officials, former members of the state apparatus, former professional soldiers and Stasi officers, former officials of trade unions and other mass organizations, and the cultural elite of the GDR still live. Add to them their families and youthful protest voters, and the PDS's ability to win three seats directly in the 1994 federal elections becomes understandable. One cannot but admire the PDS's ability both to remain a club for the dissatisfied old-timers of the SED and to articulate the concerns of left-inclined youth. Both the PDS and the CDU enjoyed the advantage of excellent organization compared to the relatively new SPD and the Greens-Alliance 90. Of course, the PDS also has its share among the large number of unemployed voters in the former GDR. (See chapter 3 by Roesler for more about PDS voters.)

In the case of the old CDU-east, one might have expected it to have been replaced by the German Social Union (DSU), the right of center party built up with the help of the Bavarian Christian Social Union (CSU.) The fact is, the time was too short for this to have been a realistic option,[3] and the Christian Democrats in the western *Länder* therefore backed the reformed CDU-east. Many East German voters associated the CDU-east with the Christian Democrats in West Germany, especially when they saw Helmut Kohl endorsing it at mass rallies in Leipzig and elsewhere. Since reunification, the CDU has lost voters, but even more, it has lost members. This is true of its membership in all the new *Länder*. In 1991 it had over 111,000 members; by 1997 it could claim only 64,000. Some losses must be due to death taking its toll of old members. More important is the fact that in the GDR many people felt it necessary to be a member of one or another of the "bloc" parties, which followed the SED's lead, just to gain or keep a decent job.

Membership in a party is no longer necessary in most spheres, and there is less inclination for younger east Germans to join political parties. In the PDS case, membership still has its advantages as party experts can help members with their complicated pension and social security problems, protect them against attacks because of their SED pasts, and provide social occasions for members attempting to come to terms with, for them, a hostile society. With around 100,000 members the PDS remains the strongest membership party in the former GDR. Its main weakness however is that more than 67 percent of its members are over 60, and only 10 percent are under 40.[4] By contrast, 38 percent of SPD members are under 40. However, PDS voters are younger than party members as indeed are its parliamentary representatives. The PDS hopes that by giving women a prominent place on its platform, pushing women's issues, and taking up a left-libertarian position generally, it can gain new support.

Between 1991 and 1997 the SPD in the five new *Länder* maintained its membership at around 27,300.[5] The SPD suffered because of the mistakes of the West German SPD in 1989-90 over the reunification issue. It also suffered because of its image as a rather austere "preachers' party" due to the prominence of several clergymen like Wolfgang Thierse and Manfred Stolpe in its leadership. Probably many ordinary East Germans feel more at home with parties whose leaders are not so snow-white. Many East Germans feel they compromised with the ruling SED at various stages of their lives in the GDR, and the "martyrs" of the SPD and the Greens-Alliance 90 are a reminder of their own lack of courage. This should not be understood as a criticism of the vast majority of East German "collaborators." It is interesting that the SPD has been most successful where a "collaborator," Manfred Stolpe of Brandenburg, has headed it. A high proportion of the SPD's membership in the five eastern *Länder* hold public office, unlike for the SPD in the West. (Here Stahnke's discussion in chapter 2 is relevant.) The East German SPD is more like an American party in its structure than like the old SPD. It also suffers from the fact that, unlike the PDS, it cannot present itself as a party of total opposition--to "reform" of the welfare state, privatization, mass unemployment in the East, NATO, and the introduction of the *Euro*.[6] In fact, without wishing to exaggerate, the East German SPD is more like New Labor in Britain than is the West German SPD. The composition of the governments of the new *Länder* on 1 April 1997 is given below.

Table 14.1 Composition of New Länder Governments as of 1 April 1997

Land	Date of Last Election	Head of Government	Parties in Government
Berlin	22 Oct. 1995	CDU	SPD-CDU-none party
Brandenburg	11 Sept. 1994	SPD	SPD
Mecklenburg-West Pomerania	16 Oct. 1994	CDU	CDU-SPD
Saxony	11 Sept. 1994	CDU	CDU
Saxony-Anhalt	26 Aug. 1994	SPD	SPD-Greens
Thuringia	16 Oct. 1994	CDU	CDU-SPD

Second Class Citizens?

In July 1997 Chancellor Kohl's government produced a report on the "State of German Unity." It expressed pleasure with its success in promoting growing unity between the two parts of Germany after official unification in October 1990, but it admitted problems in achieving "inner unity." According to polls conducted at the end of 1990, between 85 and 90 percent of East Germans regarded themselves as "second class citizens."[7] This subject was discussed by Baylis (in chapter 1), Stahnke (chapter 2), Roesler (chapter 3), Smith (chapter 6), and McFalls (chapter 7). The number thinking thus dropped steadily to autumn 1995 when only 69 percent thought of themselves as "second class citizens." It then rose from over 74 percent in March 1996 to 80 percent in May 1997. It is not surprising that many East Germans felt this way in 1990 or even in 1997. What is disturbing is that more thought so in 1997 than in 1995.

Most East Germans were glad to get new passports which enabled them to travel freely, but they were less happy that in so many ways they were stripped of everything familiar. The shops became more appealing to visit, the papers more interesting to read, façades received a lick of paint, there were new trams and trains, everyone seemed to be driving new cars, and the police were issued new uniforms, but everything East Germans had spent their lives creating seemed to be found wanting. GDR products were very often regarded as substandard. GDR ways of doing things were at best old-fashioned, and even GDR qualifications came under suspicion. There were new complicated laws to understand; the maze of vehicle, property and health insurance to be mastered; and new authorities to deal with.

After the initial euphoria of feeling free, it was only natural that more skeptical reflection would follow. In 1990, the Allensbach polling organization found that 47 percent of the east German population rated freedom higher than equality; in 1996 the same organization found the figure had fallen to 35 percent. At the same time, the proportion rating equality more highly had risen from 41 percent to 47 percent. In 1996 Allensbach also found only 19 percent of east Germans believed that the social system of the Federal Republic was just, with 23 percent feeling it was unjust. In western Germany the figures were 48 percent and 28 percent respectively.[8] In response to a question as to whether Germany's social order in its present form was worth defending, 50 percent of east Germans expressed doubt, compared with 22 percent of west Germans questioned. The loss of the GDR's "social achievements," such as the right to work and the right to kindergarten places, was regarded with a mixture of nostalgia and regret by 65 percent of those questioned in the former GDR. However, two EMNID researchers[9] believe their opinion polling reveals that East German feelings of being second class citizens is rooted in the poor employment situation of the former GDR, rather than in any feeling that west Germans are arrogant towards their "brothers and sisters."

It is worth reminding ourselves of the employment situation in the former GDR. On average, unemployment between 1991 and 1996 ran at about 1,100,000 in an area which had not known unemployment before 1990. To this must be added about 570,000 who took early retirement, 380,000 who were employed through federal work-creation schemes, 270,000 engaged in retraining schemes, and 210,000 on short-time work.[10] Without such measures, unemployment in the former GDR would have reached an average of 30 to 40 percent. The figures cannot reveal all the pain, stress, and demoralization caused by these conditions. It would be remarkable if many of those affected did not regard themselves as second class citizens.

Youth: "Rock Against Communism"

How have east German youth responded to the changes of the last eight years? Much has been written about youth and political extremism in the former GDR, especially about the "skinhead scene." Most writers find it incomprehensible that there should be sympathy with any aspect of the Third Reich in the former GDR. To the extent that sympathy exists, it is not as strange as it first appears. Curiosity alone would lead some to study in private the Third Reich, a system which had captured the loyalties of millions of ordinary Germans. Some parents or grandparents would defend themselves with the one-liner, "Not everything was bad in pre-war Germany." Many East Germans came to hate the SED regime (or always hated it!); it is only natural that some of them would turn to the other political extreme.

Consider, too, that Germany's past could not be discussed objectively in the GDR, and everything was presented in black and white terms. The communists' and the Soviet Union's responsibility for some of the tragedies which occurred between 1933 and 1945 was ignored. Under Gorbachev the Soviet Union had admitted crimes it had always denied, crimes which it attributed to the Nazis. The Katyn Woods massacre of Polish officers is the outstanding example of this. Once that had been admitted, it was easy for some to rush to the conclusion that many other crimes attributed to the Nazis were either Soviet crimes or myths invented to keep the Germans down.

Another factor is that so many German ex-servicemen who had seen the Soviet system first-hand had little time for it. Were East German young people to believe their fathers and grandfathers (and East German tourists who came back disillusioned from holidays in the Soviet Union) or their school teachers, SED officials, and the like? The SED had always vilified the Americans and the British for the mass bombing of Germany, something the Allies and West Germans did not deny had taken place. The Americans and the British were not, therefore, seen as "the good guys."

One other aspect of the development of far right views among East German youth is their hostility to foreigners. Before the *Wende* foreigners in the GDR were there very largely at the invitation of the SED, and they were from countries whose regimes were allied to the GDR. Whatever the views of individual foreigners, they were very often regarded as SED "stooges." At the very time the SED was engaged in electoral fraud in the local government elections of 1989, party leaders had decided to make foreign residents in the GDR eligible for election to the rubber stamp parliaments.

After reunification, efforts were made to repatriate one high visibility foreign group, the Vietnamese. Numbers of them managed to remain in Germany. In many cases they became part of a Mafia smuggling and selling goods, especially cigarettes. The bitter fights within the Vietnamese Mafia resulted in 28 deaths in 1995 and 1996.[11] As Laster and Ramet observed (in chapter 4), in December 1996 there were 92,291 Vietnamese in Germany, and they constituted 1.3 percent of the over 7.3 million foreigners in the country.[12]

According to the latest official figures, the new *Länder*, with one exception, had the lowest ratio of foreigners to Germans in their total populations. With 1.5 percent, Mecklenburg-West Pomerania had the lowest percentage of foreigners of any *Länd*, East or West. Saxony, Saxony-Anhalt, and Brandenburg had slightly higher percentages, 1.7, 1.7, and 2.5 respectively. Of the eastern *Länder* only Thuringia (8.8 percent) was among the *Länder* with relatively high concentrations of foreigners. United Berlin recorded 13 percent of its population as for-eigners. By comparison, Hamburg, with 16 percent, headed the list.[13] After having put up with the SED all their lives, young East Germans found themselves and their parents made redundant with West Germans and foreigners coming in to take over newly denationalized property and usurp positions of authority. East Germans began to view themselves second class citizens and sought ideological weapons with which to reassert themselves. Having suffered first at the hands of "socialism" and then Western democracy, they fell back on old German nationalism. If we look at the number of crimes committed per 10,000 of population which appear to have a far right motivation, we find that the new *Länder* top the list. For whatever reason, the Catholic *Länder* fall at the bottom of the list. (See Table 14.2.)

A word of caution must be expressed to the extent that some police forces are less willing than others to classify crimes as political. However, even allowing for this, the new *Länder* appear more prone to rightwing extremist activities than do the old western *Länder*. On average, there were 26.4 rightwing crimes per 10,000 inhabitants in the new *Länder* compared with only 8.4 per 10,000 in the old *Länder*.[14] Taking Germany as a whole, membership in rightwing extremist groups fell year by year from 1993, but the number of rightwing extremists prepared to use force increased. German security authorities estimated the number of rightwing group members at 6,400 in 1996 as compared with 6,200 in 1995.[15] The skinheads were the biggest group, and they were "over-represented" in the new *Länder*.[16] (More details may be found in chapter 4.) Many of the skinheads are influenced by the American Hammer Skins and by the more Nazi-orientated British Blood and Honour group. The latter have held successful music concerts in the former GDR in Brandenburg, Meklenburg-West Pomerania, and Saxony. They claim to be "The Independent Voice of Rock Against Communism."[17]

TABLE 14.2 Crimes with Suspected Rightwing Background in 1996 Per 10,000 Inhabitants

Land	Total Crimes	Crimes in Which Force Was Used
Thuringia	34.91	2.22
Mecklenburg-Western Pomerania	31.27	2.95
Saxony-Anhalt	30.77	1.70
Brandenburg	19.28	3.35
Saxony	15.92	1.94
Hamburg	14.77	1.99
Schleswig-Holstein	11.30	2.70
Bremen	11.03	0.74
Lower Saxony	10.55	0.95
Berlin	8.61	1.09
North Rhine-Westphalia	7.30	0.73
Hesse	6.96	0.35
Bavaria	6.94	0.25
Rhineland-Palatinate	0.40	6.35
Baden-Wurttemberg	6.31	0.49
Saar	2.03	0.37

Source: *Verfassungsschutzbericht 1996* (Bonn: 1997), p. 99.

One example of rightwing extremist violence was that of a 19-year-old in Flecken-Zechlin, Brandenburg, who on 15 January 1996 attempted to run over a 16-year-old Turkish girl with his car. He claimed that his ideology was *deutsch-national* and he believed foreigners had no right to be in Germany. He was sentenced to three years and six months for attempted murder. Also in Brandenburg, on 12 October 1996 at Sternhagen, several rightwingers aged between 16 and 22, armed with baseball bats, attacked a youth club and severely injured the director. They regarded the club as a haunt for left-wingers.[18] Of the 751 individuals involved in such politically motivated violence (throughout Germany), only 30 were women.[19] Of the total, 66 percent were aged between 16 and 20.[20] The percentage of rightwing incidents has gone up steadily since the early 1990s, but no separate figures were available for the new *Länder*. The police regularly take active measures against far right bodies and individuals and groups suspected of attempting to form terrorist organizations. On 30 October 1996, the police in Berlin, Brandenburg, and Thuringia raided the homes of nine people between the ages of 15 and 29 whom they suspected of forming a criminal body. Authorities seized explosive materials, several weapons, uniforms, T-shirts of the banned *Wiking-Jugend*, computers, and rightwing extremist propaganda material. The group, which called itself the *Werwolf-Jagd und Sturmkommado* (Werewolf Hunt and Storm Commando), was said to have carried out military sport exercises and was planning a number of crimes.[21]

A 1997 survey of the federal ministry for families, pensioners, and youth found nearly 29 percent of east Germans between ages 15 and 30 would be prepared to "hit back" to defend their own group. Among their peers in west Germany only 16 percent expressed their readiness to take such action.[22] Despite such evidence, it should be remembered (from chapter 4) that most young people in the former GDR are not violent or involved in rightwing groups and do not sympathize with them. Another survey found young east Germans independent, achievement-orientated, disciplined and flexible.[23]

Easterners Under-Represented in German Elite

Another reason why some east Germans feel they are second class citizens is that many elite positions in the former GDR--in politics, the administration, the universities, industry, and the armed forces--are occupied by west Germans. The two outstanding examples of this are the Christian Democratic heads of governments in Saxony and Thuringia, Professor Kurt Biedenkopf and Bernhard Vogel, who were brought in from West Germany. Behind them stands an army of similar, lesser figures. To make matters worse, east Germans are under-represented in Germany's national elite. According to the *Potsdammer Elitestudie* of 1995, 88.4 percent of the elite were from the old Federal Republic and only 11.6 percent from the former GDR.[24] Proportionate to population, the east German share should have been about 20 percent. Investigators from the University of Potsdam selected 2,341 individuals who had held the highest leadership positions in politics, the economy, the trade unions, science, the administration, the media, culture, the legal system, the armed services, and the churches. They found that the German elite had become somewhat more diverse, but only 11 percent of those questioned from the old Federal Republic and only 14 percent of those from the former GDR had working-class fathers. Among the east Germans, nearly one-third claimed to have been in opposition to the SED before 1989, roughly one-third had no political involvement, and the final third had been in the SED. (Chapter 3 by Roesler also discusses the composition of the PDS.)

The lack of east German representation among the elite is explained by the lack of qualified individuals able to cope with the new structures and ways of doing things, and by the fact that many of the old communist elite would not be considered suitable. Although most east Germans understand this, it can be demoralizing to be confronted at every turn by west Germans in positions of authority. One statistic helps to confirm the high visibility of Westerners in positions of authority in the former GDR. The federal authorities and the *Länder* delegated 35,000 officials to go from the West to the East after 1990.[25] A PDS publication claimed, "A mere 12 percent of managerial staff are east Germans in east Germany: 0 percent in industry, 0 percent in the military, 3 percent in science, 30 percent in politics."[26] In 1994, 14 of the 50 ministers in the governments of the new *Länder* were from the old Federal Republic.[27] Of the 21 top radio and television bosses in the former GDR in 1994, only four were east Germans.[28]

According to *Das Parlament*,[29] 12 percent of all households in Germany owned more than half the wealth, and 37 percent of households owned over 90 percent of the wealth. No details were given about the differences between the new *Länder* and the old *Länder* in this respect, but it says something that the top ten towns favored by millionaires, and headed by Baden-Baden, did not include any in the former GDR.

European Investment Bank Help

Although many East Germans are skeptical about the European Union (EU) and the *Euro*, they overlook the fact that their part of Germany has received massive help from the European Investment Bank (EIB) and from other EU funds.[30] The EIB was on the scene immediately after reunification, which brought about the admission of the former GDR into the EU. Since then the Bank has granted loans worth around European Currency Units (ECU) 7 billion, thereby co-financing investment totaling some ECU 20 billion and helping to safeguard and create jobs. In the 1990s Germany became the EIB's second largest borrower, just behind Italy. About half of the EIB's total volume of financing in Germany goes to the new *Länder*. Their rundown and depressed state resulted in their classification as Objective 1 areas for German and European regional development purposes. They therefore became eligible for the maximum authorized investment aid involving long-term financing on favorable terms, while at the same time qualifying for technical and organizational expertise. (See chapter 6 for more discussion of this issue.)

According to the Bank's criteria, aid is restricted to developing infrastructure, energy, and environmental protection as well as to enhancing the competitiveness of industry and parts of the service sector. The first projects to be financed were industrial projects that already involved western investors. Among these were Volkswagen's new assembly and engine plants in Saxony. Others assisted included Opel's vehicle factory in Thuringia, Haindl Papier's paper plant in Brandenburg, and Lafarge Coppee's cement-making works in Saxony-Anhalt. In the commercial sector EIB financed modern warehouses for the mail-order companies Quelle and Otto Verstand.

With the economic downturn in Germany in 1993-94 the EIB took a more cautious view of the prospects in the new *Länder* and shied away from further large-scale investment in the industrial and commercial sectors. Instead it orientated itself toward helping small and medium-scale ventures. The funds were steered into German financial institutions that in turn lent the money according to EIB guidelines, but at their own risk. Meanwhile the EIB also assisted infrastructure improvements, with help going to the Rostock tramway system, the Leipzig-Halle airport, and the Bundespost and DBP Telekom to fund development of high-performance communications networks. The Bundespost also received financial assistance for equipping modern mail distribution centers. In the energy sector the EIB financed regional urban natural gas grids for the purpose of converting energy supplies to environmentally friendly natural gas. Loans financed the construction of modern heat and power plants and the extension and modernization of district heating networks in Potsdam, Dresden, Berlin, Halle, and Neubrandenburg. The brown coal power stations *Schwarze Pumpe* and *Schkopau*, notorious for their pollution, have been replaced by modern, efficient plants, which still use lignite but do not pollute. The EIB also helped improve water quality by financing wastewater treatment facilities in Bitterfeld, Wittenberg, Saalfeld, Eisenach, and Dresden.

In some respects it was lucky that the EIB could not, under its rules, finance property development. The former GDR has been something of a paradise for property speculators, who often have built their fortunes at public expense. Finance Minister Theo Waigel has encouraged property investment in the former GDR by allowing massive tax reductions for those making such investments. The result is empty office buildings and apartment blocks in Leipzig, Dresden, and elsewhere. As *Der Spiegel* commented, "Countless office palaces and housing parks, that in this number no one needs, stand there like Potemkin villages in the blossoming landscape." In Leipzig an estimated 35 percent of office accommodation, old as well as new, stand empty.[31] In Dresden and Madgeburg something like 20 percent are unused. In western cities like Hamburg and Munich only around 3 to 5 percent are empty.

Scarred Landscape

During the last decade of the GDR more than 130,000 miners excavated 300 million metric tons of lignite annually.[32] Brown coal contributed nearly 79 percent of the fuel needed for the GDR's electricity supply. Sometimes the GDR would boast that it was only second to the Soviet Union in world production of brown coal, and mining it took up nearly one percent of the GDR's land.[33] Reunification brought about the speedy demise of the industry and exposed the hollow claims of the SED that the mined areas were restored step by step. In 1996 production of lignite was down to 80 million tons, and only 13,000 persons work in the nine mines still operational. Another 12,000 men and women, many of them ex-miners, are employed in the great clean-up operation.

In what is considered Europe's biggest environmental restoration project, the Lausitz region south of Cottbus and around Leipzig is being changed beyond recognition. This scarred landscape covers some 70,000 hectares of land and is an area similar in size to Berlin. In the GDR era the region and the surrounding towns and villages were perpetually covered in dust from the mines, and the atmosphere was badly polluted. The area contained what was often considered the dirtiest village in Europe, Möblis, south of Leipzig, and those who could left the area. Since reunification some 48 million trees have been planted and the reforestation of broad expanses of land embarked upon. Lakes are being created and on their shores yachting marinas, camp sites, and golf and other recreational facilities are being provided. Bonn and the *Länder* have been spending DM 1.5 billion annually on reclamation, and spending will remain at DM 1.2 billion until the year 2002. The restoration of the lignite mining areas is just one of a number of massive environmental problems facing the inheritors of the GDR. One must not forget the ravaged frontier zones and the former training areas of the Soviet armed forces full of mines, unexploded ammunition, oil, and other pollutants.

Germany still faces an enormous task of rehabilitating the former GDR. At the same time the Federal Republic is committed to providing aid to the Third World and to Eastern Europe. It is worth recording that Germany devotes a higher share (0.32 percent) of its gross domestic product to supporting developing or transitioning countries than do Britain (0.27), Canada (0.31), Italy (0.20), Japan (0.20), or the USA (0.12). Of the major economies, France (0.48) alone provides more. In absolute terms, only Japan and the USA provide higher sums.[34] At the same time, Germany provides sanctuary for far more refugees than any other European state. According to the German Ministry of Interior, at the end of 1996 there were around 1.6 million refugees and asylum seekers living legally in Germany,[35] and no one knows how many were living illegally. Germany is also attempting to integrate ethnic Germans from Eastern Europe. From 1968 to reunification, well over one million came, and since 1992 more than one million more have arrived.

When Will True Unity be Achieved?

When Germany was formally reunited there were any number of estimates about the time it would take the former GDR to catch up with West Germany in economic terms. The most optimistic predicted a time span of between three and ten years; the more pessimistic thought 20 years; and the most pessimistic ran to 70 years. (See chapter 6 for further information.) By 1997 a great deal of progress had been made, but much still needed to be achieved. By 1995 the catching up process had slowed, and by 1997 the economies of the west German *Länder* were once more growing faster than those of the East. It is hardly surprising in these circumstances that the new *Länder* suffered a net loss of population between 1990 and 1996. The population of the former GDR fell year by year from 16,614,000 in 1989 to 15,451,000 in 1996. During the same period Germany's population increased from 78,677,000 to 81,896,000.

Nevertheless, highlighting the continuing discrepancies ignores the fact that most countries contain areas which appear to be doomed to permanently lag behind other regions, with southern Italy and the North East of England just two cases in point. In any case, Germany as a whole has, to a degree, been ravaged by the changes in the world economy in the 1990s. As elsewhere, there have been winners and losers. Inequality has grown. The old West Germany was certainly one of the least divided societies among the modern industrial nations, and today's Germany still appears less divided than many other states. However, statistics reveal the growth of inequality. Between 1991 and the first half of 1997, net wages and salaries increased by 8.4 percent, but the value of companies listed on the DAX stock index increased by

188.2 percent over the same period.[36]   Overall, unemployment in Germany stands at 11.9 percent. It rose every month last year, and it is not much comfort to those out of work that the percentage of unemployed remains lower in Germany than in France, Italy, or Spain.

In virtually every West European state there are big differences within countries, and it seems entirely possible that different regions of the former GDR will develop at different rates rather than all going forward at the same speed. Would such a development help to break down the division between the former GDR and the western *Länder?* In any case, in other countries there are regions whose inhabitants see themselves in some ways as "second class citizens" and different from those in the more prosperous parts of the country. This is certainly true of England where there is a North-South divide, in addition to the differences between England and Scotland, let alone between England and Northern Ireland. The differences within Britain could eventually lead to the break up of the United Kingdom, but not the differences within England.

It seems plausible to argue that differences within Germany based on the GDR-old Federal Republic cleavage will gradually fade. To many young east Germans today the GDR and its protagonists must seem parochial, out of date, down right ancient. Growing instability outside Western Europe, increasing integration within it, the growing power of Asia, the changes to our way of life brought on by the explosion of electronic technology and medical research, the rapidly changing relations between the sexes, environmental problems, crime, and terrorism--all of these seem destined to reduce the GDR to a sad little footnote in history, as the next generation struggles to cope with the challenges of the twenty-first century.

Notes

1. *Der Spiegel*, No. 2 (19 January 1998), p. 24.

2. Among a number of useful contributions on the PDS is Heinrich Bortfeldt, *Von der SED zur PDS. Wandlung zur Demokratie* (Bonn and Berlin: Bouvier Verlag, 1992). See also Hans-Georg Betz and Helga A. Welsh, "The PDS in the New German Party System," *German Politics*, Vol. 4 (December 1995), pp. 92-111.

3. Ute Schmidt, "Sieben Jahre nach der Einheit. Die ostdeutsche Parteien-landschaft im Vorfeld der Bundestagswahl 1998," in *Aus Politik und Zeitge-schichte. Beilage zur Wochenzeitung Das Parlament*, No. 2 (2 January 1998), p. 45.

4. *Der Spiegel*, No. 19 (5 May 1997).

5. Elmar Wiesendahl, "Wie geht es weiter mit den Großparteien in Deutsch-land?" in *Aus Politik und Zeitgeschichte*, No. 2 (2 January 1998), p. 19.

6. *PDS Newsletter* (English edition), September 1997, p. 5.

7. Dieter Waltz and Wolfram Brunner, "Das Sein bestimmt das Bewußtsein. Oder: Warum sich die Ostdeutschen als Bürger 2. Klasse fühlen," in *Aus Politik und Zeitgeschichte,* No. 52 (December 1997), p. 13.

8. Michael Krapp, "Six Years of Growing Together," *German Comments* (October 1996), p. 55.

9. Waltz and Brunner, "Das Sein," p. 13.

10. Ulrich Heilemann and Hermann Rappen, "Sieben Jahre deutsche Einheit: Rückblick und Perspektiven in fiskalischer Sicht," in *Aus Politik und Zeitgeschichte,* No. 40-41 (26 September 1997), p. 42.

11. Klaus Severin, "Illegale Einreise und internationale Schleuserkriminalität" in *Aus Politik und Zeitgeschichte,* No. 46 (7 November 1997), p. 25. Foreigners are *over-represented* among those convicted of certain crimes which promotes fear and suspicion of foreigners. Of 746 individuals convicted of murder or manslaughter in 1995, 257 were foreigners. Of the 31,334 convicted for theft in aggravated circumstances, 8,870 were foreigners. Of the 31,393 convicted for drug-related offenses, 9,596 were foreigners. Of the 5,469 (5,128 men) convicted of depriving others of "sexual self-determination," 1,114 were foreigners. Finally, of the 23,461 convicted for falsifying documents, 11,196 were foreigners. See *Statistisches Jahrbuch der Bundesrepublik Deutschland für 1997* (Weisbaden: 1997), p. 374. Foreigners also bring with them the old hatreds from their homelands. According to the *Verfassungsschutzbericht 1996,* in 1996 there were 63 foreign political extremist organizations in Germany. The largest, a Turkish Moslem extremist group, had an estimated 28,300 members. Foreign extremists were responsible for two bomb attacks, 120 arson attacks, and many other crimes in 1996.

12. *Woche im bundestag,* 21 January 1998, p. 16.

13. *Ibid.*

14. Bundesministerium des Innern, *Verfassungsschutzbericht 1996* (Bonn: 1997), p. 97. For the far right in post-war Germany see David Childs, "The Nationalist and Neo-Nazi Scene since 1945," in Klaus Larres and Panikos Panayi (eds.), *The Federal Republic of Germany Since 1949* (London and New York: Longman, 1996). Thomas Assheuer and Hans Sarkowicz, *Rechtsradikale in Deutschland* (Munich: Verlag C. H. Beck, 1992). For the new *Länder* see Landeszentrale für politische Bildung Thüringen, *Rechtsextremismus in den neuen Bundesländern* (Erfurt: 1992). To put the German far right in European perspective, see Luciano Cheles, Ronnie Ferguson, and Michalina Vaughan (eds.), *The Far Right In Western and Eastern Europe* (London and New York: Longman, 1995).

15. Bundesministerium des Innern, *Verfassungsschutzbericht 1996,* p. 88.

16. *Ibid,* p. 102.

17. *Ibid,* p. 103.

18. *Ibid,* p. 95.

19. *Ibid,* p. 97.

20. *Ibid,* p. 97.

21. *Ibid,* p. 102.

22. *Der Spiegel,* No. 48 (24 November 1997), p. 71. For a useful study of the attitude of East German school children to violence see Thomas Claus and Detlef Herter, "Jugend und Gewalt Ergebnisse einer empirischen Untersuchung an

Magdeburger Schulen," in *Aus Politik und Zeitgeschichte*, No. 38 (23 September 1994).

23. *Der Spiegel*, No. 48 (24 November 1997), p. 71.

24. Wilhelm Bürklin, "Durchlässigkeit der Elite" in *Das Parlament*, No. 8 (15 August 1997), p. 15.

25. Heilemann and Rappen, "Sieben Jahre deutsche Einheit," p. 39.

26. *PDS Newsletter* (English edition), April 1997, p. 7.

27. Hans-Ulrich Derlien, "Elitezirkulation in Ostdeutschland 1989-1995" in *Aus Politik und Zeitgeschichte*, No. 5 (23 January 1998), p. 12.

28. *Ibid.*, p. 14.

29. Wilhelm Bürklin, "Durchlässigkeit der Elite," p. 15.

30. "Six Years of EIB Financing in the New German *Länder*," in *EIB Information*, No. 93 (March 1997).

31. *Der Spiegel*, No. 46 (10 November 1997), p. 44.

32. The figures in this paragraph are taken from *Deutschland*, No. 1 (February 1998), pp. 40-43.

33. *Handbuch Deutsche Demokratische Republik* (Leipzig: Verlag Enzyklopädie, 1984), p. 325.

34. *Deutschland*, No. 1 (February 1998), p. 39.

35. Severin, "Illegale Einreise," p. 15.

36. *Der Spiegel*, No. 40 (29 September 1997), p. 89.

37. Imanuel Geiss, Fred Bridgham, translator, *The Question of German Unification 1806-1996* (London and New York: Routledge, 1997), p. 119.

Acronyms
and Abbreviations

ABM	Arbeitsmarktpolitische Maßnahme (public job creation measures)
ARD	Arbeitsgemeinschaft der öffentlichrechtlichen Rundfunkanstalten der Bundesrepublik Deutschland (Joint Association of Public Broadcasting Corporations of the Federal Republic of Germany)
CDU	Christian Democratic Union
CFSP	Common Foreign and Security Policy
CIS	Commonwealth of Independent States
CMEA	Council for Mutual Economic Aid or COMECON
CSCE	Conference on Security and Cooperation in Europe
CSU	Christian Social Union
DFF	Deutscher Fernsehfunk (GDR State Television)
DGB	Deutsche Gewerkschaftsbund (Federation of German Trade Unions)
DM	Deutsche Mark (currency of the Federal Republic of Germany)
DSU	German Social Union
EIB	European Investment Bank
EPC	European Political Cooperation
ERM	Exchange Rate Mechanism
EU	European Union
Euro	Currency of the European Union as of 1999
FDP	Free Democratic Party
FRG	Federal Republic of Germany (West Germany)
GDR	German Democratic Republic (East Germany)
IMF	International Monetary Fund
KPD	Communist Party of Germany
LDPD	Liberal Democratic Party of Germany

MDR   Mitteldeutscher Rundfunk (central German
                radio)
MfS   Ministerium für Staatssicherheit (Ministry for
                State Security), East Germany
MoD   Ministry of Defense
NACC   North Atlantic Cooperation Council
NATO   North Atlantic Treaty Organization
NCO   Non-commissioned officer
NDR   Norddeutscher Rundfunk (north German radio)
NORA   Nordostdeutsche Rundfunkanstalt (north-east
                German radio)
NDPD   National Democratic Party (GDR)
NVA   Nationale Volksarmee (National People's
                Army), East Germany
ORB   Ostdeutscher Rundfunk Brandenburg (east
                German radio Brandenburg), Rotfunk ("Red
                Radio")
OSCE   Organization for Security and Cooperation in
                Europe
OWUS   Offener Wirtschaftsverband der klein und
                mittelständischen Unternehmer, Freiberufler,
                und Selbständigen (employers' organization in
                eastern Germany)
PDS   Party of Democratic Socialism (formerly SED)
RIAS   Radio in the American Sector (Berlin radio
                station)
SAT 1   Germany's first privately-owned television
                station
SaZ   Soldat auf Zeit (career soldier)
SED   Sozialistische Einheitspartei Deutschlands
                (Socialist Unity Party of [East] Germany)
SFB   Sender Freies Berlin (Berlin radio station)
SPD   Social Democratic Party
Stasi   East German state security police
UN   United Nations
WTO   Warsaw Treaty Organization, Warsaw Pact
ZDF   Zweites Deutsches Fernsehen (Second German
                Television)

Glossary of Terms

Abwicklung	Liquidation of East German firms and agencies
Angestelle	Mid and lower level employees
Aufschwung Ost	Upswing East
Ausländerfrei	Free of foreigners
Autonoms	Leftwing anarchist group
Beamte	Upper level civil servants and office holders
Bezirk	Administrative region in the GDR
Bundesrat	Upper house in legislature of Federal Republic of Germany
Bundesrepublik Deutschland	Federal Republic of Germany
Bundestag	Lower house in legislature of Federal Republic of Germany
Bundeswehr	Military of the Federal Republic
Bündnis '90	Alliance '90, citizens' movement group
Doppelgänger	Double
Democratischer Aufbruch	Democratic Awakening, a citizens group originating in the GDR in 1989
Eigensinn	Sources of strength for east German women developed in the GDR
Einrichtung	Agency responsible for privatizing East German media
Erwerbsarbeit	Professional work
Gebeit Reform	Consolidation of counties, towns, and villages into larger units
Geschlechtervertrag	Gender contract
Grundgesetz	Basic Law, the constitution of the Federal Republic
Grufti	Rightwing group also known as Goths
Informeller Mitarbeiter	"Informal collaborator;" East Germans used by Stasi to spy on family, friends, co-workers

Innere Führung	"Inner direction," a tenet of West German military, which sought to create soldiers capable of independent, aggressive action
Jugendweihe	Secular youth dedication ceremonies replacing confirmation in the GDR
Kreis	County or district
Land (Pl. Länder)	State in Federal Republic of Germany
Lebenszusammenhang	Life context
Marxistisches Forum	Marxist faction within Party of Democratic Socialism
Mitteleuropa	Central Europe
Mittelstand	Middle class
Nationale Alternative	Rightwing political organization
Neues Forum	New Forum, citizens group in GDR
New Länder	East German states, after unification
Old Länder	West German states, after unification
Ossis	East Germans
Ostbindung	Ties to the East
Osthandel	Trade with the East
Ostpolitik	Policy towards the East
Rathaus	Town hall
Realpolitik	Realist (power) politics
Rechtsstaat	State based on the rule of law
Rundfunk der DDR	GDR state radio
Selbstverwaltung	Local government self-administration
Stasi, Staatssicherheit	State security police
Treuhand	Trust agency responsible for privatizing East German firms
Verwestlichung	Westernization
Volksarmee	East German army
Volkskammer	East German legislature
Vorstand	Party governing board
Wende	Fundamental change; refers generally the changes occurring during and after November 1989 in East Germany
Wessis	West Germans
Westbindung	Ties to the West
Westpolitik	Policy towards the West
Wohlstandsgrenze	"Prosperity barrier"

Index

The German Democratic Republic, *or* GDR, *refers to pre-unification East Germany. The* Federal Republic of Germany, *or* FRG, *refers to pre-unification West Germany. By itself,* Germany *refers to post-unification Germany. Capitalized* East *or* West German(y) *refers to the period before unification, while lower case* east *or* west German(y) *refers to the period after unification.*